Prentice Hall Multimedia Series in Automotive Technology

Automotive Brake Systems

Second Edition

Prentice Hall Multimedia Series in Automotive Technology

Other books by James D. Halderman and Chase D. Mitchell, Jr. in the
Prentice Hall Multimedia Series in Automotive Technology include:

Automotive Technology: Principles, Diagnosis, and Service, 0-13-359969-8.

Advanced Engine Performance Diagnosis, 0-13-576570-6.

Automotive Steering, Suspension, and Alignment, Second Edition, 0-13-799719-1.

Automotive Chassis Systems, Second Edition, 0-13-079970-X.

Prentice Hall Multimedia Series in Automotive Technology

Automotive Brake Systems

Second Edition

James D. Halderman   Sinclair Community College
Chase D. Mitchell, Jr.   Utah Valley State College

Prentice Hall
Upper Saddle River, New Jersey   *Columbus, Ohio*

Library of Congress Cataloging-in-Publication Data

Halderman, James D.
    Automotive brake systems / James D. Halderman, Chase D. Mitchell,
Jr. -- 2nd ed.
      p.   cm. -- (Prentice Hall multimedia series in automotive
technology)
    Includes index.
    ISBN: 0-13-090616-6
    1. Automobiles--Brakes.   I. Mitchell, Chase D.   II. Title.
III. Series.
TL269.H35   2000   99-38254
6629999.2'46--dc21   CIP

Editor: Ed Francis
Production Editor: Stephen C. Robb
Design Coordinator: Karrie M. Converse-Jones
Cover Designer: Jason Moore
Cover Photo: James D. Halderman
Production Manager: Patricia A. Tonneman
Illustrations: Carlisle Communications, Ltd.
Production Supervision: Kelli Jauron, Carlisle Publishers Services
Marketing Manager: Chris Bracken

This book was set in Century Book and Gill Sans by Carlisle
Communications, Ltd., and was printed and bound by The
Banta Company. The cover was printed by Phoenix Color Corp.

Printed in the United States of America

10 9 8 7 6 5 4

ISBN: 0-13-090616-6

Prentice-Hall International (UK) Limited, *London*
Prentice-Hall of Australia Pty. Limited, *Sydney*
Prentice-Hall Canada, Inc., *Toronto*
Prentice-Hall Hispanoamericana, S. A., *Mexico*
Prentice-Hall of India Private Limited, *New Delhi*
Prentice-Hall of Japan, Inc., *Tokyo*
Prentice-Hall (Singapore) Pte. Ltd., *Singapore*
Editora Prentice-Hall do Brasil, Ltda., *Rio de Janeiro*

Contents

4

Wheel Bearings and Service   90

5

Drum Brake Operation, Diagnosis, and Service   110

6

Disc Brake Operation, Diagnosis, and Service   137

APPENDIXES

Tech Tips, Frequently Asked Questions, Diagnostic Stories, and High-Performance Tips

Photo Sequences

Preface

Diagnostic Approach

The primary focus of this textbook is to satisfy the need for problem diagnosis. Time after time, the authors have heard that automotive technicians need more training in diagnostic procedures and skill development. To meet this need, diagnostic stories are included throughout the text to help illustrate how real problems are solved. Each new topic covers the parts involved, their purpose, function, and operation, as well as how to test and diagnose each system.

Other important features in the second edition are photo sequences, tech tips, and answers to frequently asked questions (FAQs).

ASE Content Approach

This comprehensive textbook covers the material necessary for the Brake System (A5) area of certification as specified by the National Institute for Automotive Service Excellence (ASE) and the National Automotive Technicians Education Foundation (NATEF). The book also includes two chapters devoted to antilock brake systems.

Multimedia System Approach

Thirteen photo sequences are included in the text. These photo sequences are included on a videotape for instructors available upon adoption of the textbook. A multi-media CD-ROM that accompanies the textbook makes learning more fun for the student. The CD includes sound, animation, color photo sequences with narration, a glossary of automotive terms, sample ASE test questions, sample worksheets, and the ASE (NATEF) task list for the Automotive Brake Systems ASE area.

Internet (World Wide Web) Approach

Included with the book is a coupon that entitles the owner to free access to an ASE test preparation Web site for an extended time period. Students can practice and take the ASE certification tests with confidence. Included at this Web site are ASE-type questions for brake systems. The questions are presented 20 at a time, then graded (marked). The correct answer is then given as the students scroll back through the questions. This feature allows students to study at their own pace.

Worktext Approach

A worktext is also included with the book. The worksheets help the instructor and students apply the material presented to everyday-type activities and typical service and testing procedures. Also included are typical results and a listing of what could be defective if the test results are not within the acceptable range. These sheets help build diagnostic and testing skills.

Acknowledgments

Many people and organizations have cooperated in providing the reference material and technical information used in this text. The authors express sincere thanks to the following organizations for their special contributions:

Allied Signal Automotive Aftermarket

Arrow Automotive

ASE

Automotion, Inc.

Automotive Parts Rebuilders Association (APRA)

Bear Automotive

Bendix

British Petroleum (BP)

Cooper Automotive Company

CR Services

DaimlerChrysler

Dana Corporation

Fluke Corporation

Ford Motor Company

FMC Corporation

General Motors Corporation Service Technology Group

Hennessy Industries

Lee Manufacturing Company

John Bean Company

Monroe Shock Absorbers

Oldsmobile Division, GMC

Perfect Hofmann—USA

Reynolds and Reynolds Company

SKF USA, Inc.

Society of Automotive Engineers (SAE)

Specialty Products Company

Toyota Motor Sales, USA, Inc.

TRW Inc.

Wurth USA, Inc.

Portions of materials contained herein have been reprinted with the permission of General Motors Corporation, Service Operations.

Technical and Content Reviewers

The authors gratefully acknowledge the following people who reviewed the manuscript before production and checked it for technical accuracy and clarity of presentation. Their suggestions and recommendations were included in the final draft of the manuscript.

Victor Bridges
Umpqua Community College

Dr. Roger Donovan
Illinois Central College

A. C. Durdin
Moraine Park Technical College

Herbert Ellinger
Western Michigan University

Al Engledahl
College of Dupage

Oldrick Hajzler
Red River Community College

Betsy Hoffman
Vermont Technical College

Carlton H. Mabe, Sr.
Virginia Western Community College

Kerry Meier
San Juan College

Fritz Peacock
Indiana Vocational Technical College

Dennis Peter
NAIT (Canada)

Mitchell Walker
St. Louis Community College at Forest Park

Photo Sequences

The authors thank Rick Henry, who photographed all of the photo sequences. Some of the sequences were taken in automotive service facilities while live work was being performed. Special thanks to all who helped, including:

B P ProCare
Dayton, Ohio
   Tom Brummitt
   Jeff Stueve
   John Daily
   Bob Babal
   Brian Addock
   Jason Brown
   Don Patton
   Dan Kanapp

Rodney Cobb Chevrolet
Eaton, Ohio
   Clint Brubacker

Dare Automotive Specialists
Centerville, Ohio
   David Schneider
   Eric Archdeacon
   Jim Anderson

Foreign Car Service
Huber Heights, Ohio
   Mike McCarthy
   George Thielen
   Ellen Finke
   Greg Hawk
   Bob Massie

Genuine Auto Parts Machine Shop
Dayton, Ohio
   Freddy Cochran
   Tom Berger

Import Engine and Transmission
Dayton, Ohio
   Elias Daoud
   James Brown
   Robert Riddle
   Felipe Delemos
   Mike Pence

J and B Transmission Service
Dayton, Ohio
   Robert E. Smith
   Ray L. Smith
   Jerry Morgan
   Scott Smith
   Daryl Williams
   George Timitirou

Saturn of Orem
Orem, Utah

We also thank the faculty and students at Sinclair Community College in Dayton, Ohio, and Utah Valley State College in Orem, Utah, for their ideas and suggestions. Most of all, we thank Michelle Halderman for her assistance in all phases of manuscript preparation.

James D. Halderman
Chase D. Mitchell, Jr.

Vehicle Construction, Fasteners, and Safety

Objectives: After studying Chapter 1, the reader should be able to:

1. Describe the various types of frames and construction used on vehicles.
2. Explain how the body is constructed and how to locate the lift points under a vehicle.
3. Explain the safe use of tools, automotive chemicals, and hoisting methods.
4. Discuss hazardous materials and how to handle them.

The chassis is the framework of any vehicle. The suspension, steering, braking components, and drivetrain components are mounted to the chassis. The chassis has to be a rigid and strong platform to support the suspension components. The suspension system allows the wheels and tires to follow the contour of the road. The connections between the chassis, the suspension, and the drivetrain must be made of rubber to dampen noise, vibration, and harshness (NVH). The construction of today's vehicles requires the use of many different materials.

■ FRAME CONSTRUCTION

Frame construction usually consists of channel-shaped steel beams welded and/or fastened together.

There are many terms used to label or describe the frame of a vehicle, including:

Ladder Frame Ladder frame is a common name for a type of perimeter frame where the transverse connecting members are straight across, as in Figure 1–1.

Perimeter Frame A perimeter frame consists of welded or riveted frame members around the entire perimeter of the body (see Figure 1–2).

X-Type Frame An X-type frame uses frame members crossing the center of the perimeter members, forming an "X" shape (see Figure 1–3).

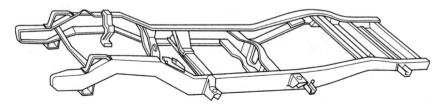

Figure 1–1 Typical frame of a vehicle.

Figure 1–2 Perimeter frame.

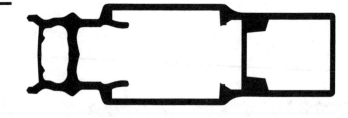

Figure 1–3 X-type frame.

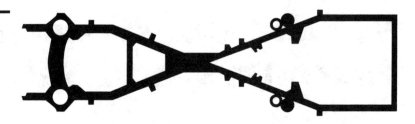

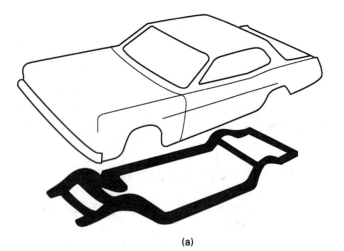

(a)

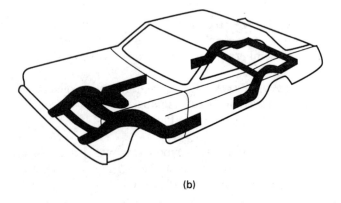

(b)

Figure 1–4 (a) Separate body and frame construction. (b) Unitized construction—the small frame members are for support of the engine and suspension components. On many vehicles the suspension components are attached directly to the reinforced sections of the body and do not require the rear frame section.

Stub-Type Frame   A stub frame is a partial frame often used on unit-body vehicles to support the power train and suspension components (see Figure 1–4). It is also called a "cradle" on many front-wheel-drive vehicles.

■ UNIT-BODY CONSTRUCTION

Unit-body construction (sometimes called *unibody*) is a design that combines the body with the structure of the frame. The body is composed of many individual stamped steel panels welded together (see Figures 1–5 and 1–6). The strength of this type of construction lies in the *shape* of the assembly. The typical vehicle uses 300 separate stamped steel panels that are spot-welded together to form the vehicle's body.

NOTE: A typical vehicle contains about 10,000 individual parts.

Figure 1–5 Camaro body without its plastic molded compound panels. All of these models are designed structurally for a T-top roof with removable roof panels.

■ SPACE FRAME CONSTRUCTION

Space frame construction consists of formed sheet steel used to construct a framework for the entire vehicle. The vehicle is driveable without the body, which consists of plastic or steel panels covering the steel framework (see Figure 1–7 on page 5).

■ THREADED FASTENERS

Most of the threaded fasteners used on engines are **cap screws.** They are called cap screws when they are threaded into a casting. Automotive service technicians usually refer to these fasteners as *bolts*, regardless of how they are used. In this chapter, they are called bolts.

Sometimes, studs are used for threaded fasteners. A **stud** is a short rod with threads on both ends. Often, a stud will have coarse threads on one end and fine threads on the other end. The end of the stud with coarse threads is screwed into the casting. A nut is used

---

TECH TIP ✔

Use the Hollander Interchange Manual to Save Time and Money

Most salvage businesses that deal with wrecked vehicles use a reference book entitled the *Hollander Interchange Manual* (see Figure 1–8 on page 5). In this yearly publication, every vehicle part is given a number. If a part from another vehicle has the same Hollander number, the parts are interchangeable.

---

on the opposite end to hold the engine parts together (see Figure 1–9 on page 5).

The fastener threads *must* match the threads in the casting or nut. The threads may be either measured in fractions of an inch (called fractional) or metric. The size is measured across the outside of the threads. This is called the **crest** of the thread.

Fractional threads are either coarse or fine. Coarse threads are called UNC (Unified National Coarse) and

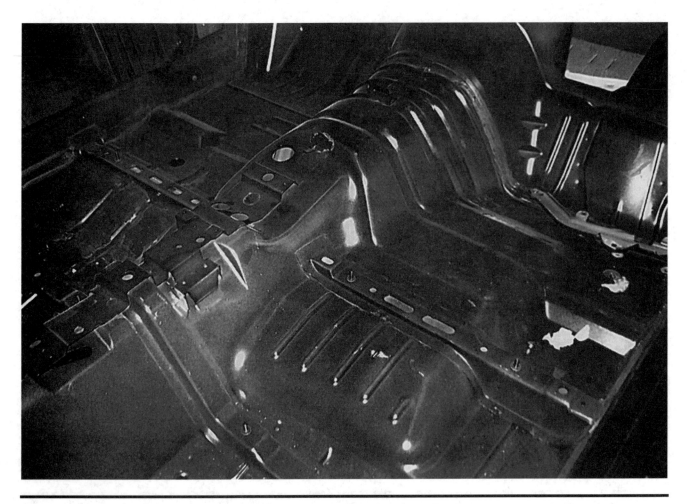

Figure 1–6 Note the ribbing and the many different pieces of sheet metal used in the construction of this body.

fine threads are called UNF (Unified National Fine). Standard combinations of sizes and number of threads per inch (called **pitch**) are used. Pitch can be measured with a thread gauge (see Figure 1–10 on page 6). Fractional threads are specified by giving the diameter in fractions of an inch and the number of threads per inch. Typical UNC thread sizes would be 5/16-18 and 1/2-13. Similar UNF thread sizes would be 5/16-24 and 1/2-20.

Metric threads used in automotive engines are coarse threads. The size of a metric bolt is specified by the letter M followed by the diameter in millimeters across the outside (crest) of the threads. Typical metric sizes would be M8 and M12. Fine metric threads are specified by the thread diameter followed by 2 and the distance between the threads measured in millimeters (M8 × 1.5). Both fractional and metric threads have tolerance. A loose-fitting thread has a lot of tolerance. A very close-fitting thread has very little tolerance. Bolts are identified by their diameter and length as measured from below the head, as shown in Figure 1–11 on page 6.

Bolts are made from many different types of steel. For this reason, some are stronger than others. The strength or classification of a bolt is called the **grade.** The bolt heads are marked to indicate their grade

strength. Fractional bolts have lines on the head to indicate the grade.

The actual grade of these bolts is two more than the number of lines on the bolt head. Metric bolts have a decimal number to indicate the grade. More lines or a higher grade number indicate a stronger bolt (see Figures 1–12 and 1–13 on pages 6–7).

When installing or replacing threaded fasteners, technicians should check all of the following:

1. Proper tightening torque
2. Correct fractional or metric threads
   a. diameter
   b. thread pitch
3. Bolt length
4. Length of the threads on the bolt
5. Grade of the bolt

CAUTION: *Never* use hardware store (nongraded) bolts, studs, or nuts on any vehicle steering, suspension, or brake component. Always use the exact size and grade of hardware that is specified and used by the vehicle manufacturer.

Figure 1–7 Space frame for a GM van, showing it without exterior body panels. The framework surrounding the vehicle is a three-dimensional measuring system capable of accurate measurement of the vehicle.

Figure 1–8 A *Hollander Interchange Manual* is available for both domestic and imported vehicles.

Nuts

Most nuts used on cap screws have the same hex size as the cap screw head. In some specialized cases when clearance is a problem, the next smaller hex size is used. Some inexpensive nuts use a hex size larger than the cap screw head. Metric nuts are often marked with dimples to show their strength. More dimples indicate stronger nuts. Some nuts and cap screws use interference-fit threads to keep them from loosening accidentally. This is done by slightly distorting the shape of the nut or by deforming part of the

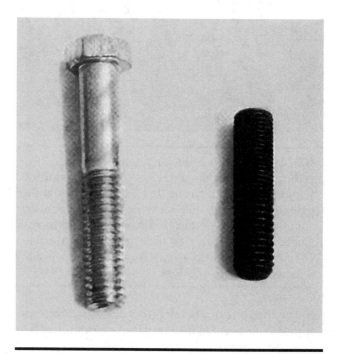

Figure 1–9 Typical bolt on the left and stud on the right. Note the different thread pitch on the top and bottom portions of the stud.

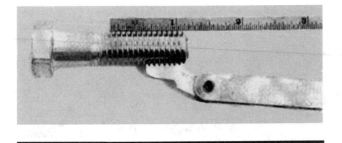

Figure 1–10 Thread pitch gauge used to measure the pitch of the thread. This is a 1/2"-diameter bolt with 13 threads to the inch (1/2 × 13).

Figure 1–12 Typical bolt (cap screw) grade markings and approximate strength.

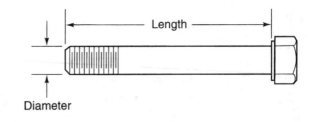
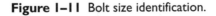

Figure 1–11 Bolt size identification.

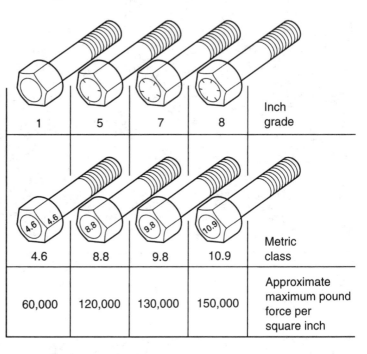

Inch grade	1	5	7	8
Metric class	4.6	8.8	9.8	10.9
Approximate maximum pound force per square inch	60,000	120,000	130,000	150,000

NOTE: Most of these locking nuts are grouped together and are commonly referred to as **prevailing torque nuts.** This means that the nut will hold its tightness or torque and not loosen with movement or vibration. Most prevailing torque nuts should be replaced whenever removed to be assured that the nut will not loosen during service. Always follow manufacturer's recommendations.

threads. Nuts can also be kept from loosening with a nylon washer fastened in the nut, or with a nylon patch or strip on the threads (see Figure 1–15).

Anaerobic sealers, such as Loctite, are used on the threads where the nut or cap screw must be both locked or sealed.

Figure 1–14 Synthetic wintergreen oil can be used as a penetrating oil to loosen rusted bolts or nuts.

Figure 1–15 Types of locknuts: on the left, a nylon ring; in the center, a distorted shape; and on the right, a castle for use with a cotter key.

Figure 1–13 Every shop should have an assortment of high–quality bolts and nuts to replace those damaged during vehicle service procedures.

Figure 1–16 Combination wrench. The openings are the same size at both ends. Notice the angle of the open end to permit use in close spaces.

Washers

Washers are often used under cap screw heads and under nuts. Plain flat washers are used to provide an even clamping load around the fastener. Lock washers are added to prevent accidental loosening. In some accessories, the washers are locked onto the nut to provide easy assembly.

■ BASIC TOOL LIST

Hand tools are used to turn fasteners (bolts, nuts, and screws). The following is a list of hand tools every automotive technician should possess. Specialty tools are not included. See Figures 1–16 through 1–40 on pages 7–15.

Tool chest

1/4″ drive socket set

1/4″ drive ratchet

1/4″ drive 2″ extension

1/4″ drive 6″ extension

1/4″ drive handle

3/8″ drive socket set

3/8″ drive Torx set

3/8″ drive 13/16″ plug socket

3/8″ drive 5/8″ plug socket

3/8″ drive ratchet

3/8″ drive 1 1/2″ extension

3/8″ drive 3″ extension

3/8″ drive 6″ extension

3/8″ drive 1″ extension

3/8″ drive universal

1/2″ drive socket set

1/2″ drive ratchet

1/2″ drive breaker bar

1/2″ drive 5″ extension

1/2″ drive 10″ extension

3/8″ to 1/4″ adapter

1/2″ to 3/8″ adapter

3/8″ to 1/2″ adapter

3/8″ through 1″ combo wrench set

10 mm through 19 mm combo wrench set

1/16″ through 1/4″ hex wrench set

2 mm through 12 mm hex wrench set

3/8″ hex socket

13 mm to 14 mm flare nut wrench

15 mm to 17 mm flare nut wrench

5/16″ to 3/8″ flare nut wrench

7/16″ to 1/2″ flare nut wrench

1/2″ to 9/16″ flare nut wrench

Diagonal pliers

Needle pliers

Adjustable-jaw pliers

Locking pliers

Snap-ring pliers

Stripping or crimping pliers

Ball-peen hammer

Rubber hammer

Dead-blow hammer

Five-piece standard screwdriver set

Four-piece Phillips screwdriver set

#15 Torx screwdriver

#20 Torx screwdriver

Crowfoot set (fractional inch)

Crowfoot set (metric)

Awl

Mill file

Center punch

Pin punches (assorted sizes)

Chisel

Utility knife

Valve core tool

Coolant tester

Filter wrench (large filters)

Filter wrench (smaller filters)

Safety glasses

Circuit tester

Feeler gauge

Scraper

Pinch bar

Sticker knife

Magnet

■ SAFETY TIPS FOR USING HAND TOOLS

1. Always *pull* a wrench toward you for best control and safety. Never push a wrench.
2. Keep all wrenches and hand tools clean to help prevent rust and for a better, firmer grip.
3. Always use a six-point socket or a box-end wrench to break loose a tight bolt or nut.
4. Use a box-end wrench for torque and an open-end wrench for speed.
5. Never use a pipe extension or other types of "cheater bars" on a wrench or ratchet handle. If more force is required, use a larger tool or use penetrating oil and/or heat on the frozen fastener. (If heat is used on a bolt or nut to remove it, always replace it with a new part.)
6. Always use the proper tool for the job. If a specialized tool is required, use the proper tool—do not try to use another tool improperly.
7. Never expose any tool to excessive heat. High temperatures can reduce the strength ("draw the temper") of metal tools.
8. Never use a hammer on any wrench or socket handle unless you are using a special "staking-face" wrench designed to be used with a hammer.
9. Replace any tools that are damaged or worn.

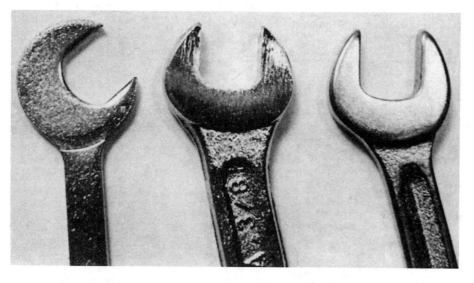

Figure 1-17 Three different qualities of open-end wrenches. The cheap wrench on the left is made from weaker steel and is thicker and less accurately machined than the standard in the center. The wrench on the right is of professional quality (and price).

Figure 1-18 Flare-nut wrench. Also known as a *line wrench, fitting wrench,* or *tube-nut wrench.* This style of wrench is designed to grasp most of the flats of a six-sided (hex) tubing fitting to provide the most grip without damage to the fitting.

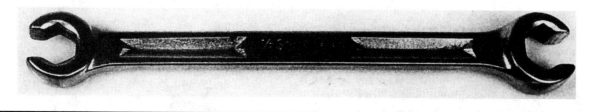

Figure 1-19 Box-end wrench. Recommended to loosen or tighten a bolt or nut where a socket will not fit. A box-end wrench has a different size at each end and is better to use than an open-end wrench because it touches the bolt or nut around the entire head instead of at just two places.

Figure 1-20 Open-end wrench. Each end has a different-sized opening and is recommended for general usage. Do not attempt to loosen or tighten bolts or nuts from or to full torque with an open-end wrench because it could round the flats of the fastener.

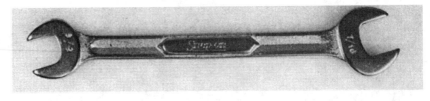

Figure 1-21 Adjustable wrench. The size (12″) is the *length* of the wrench, not how far the jaws open!

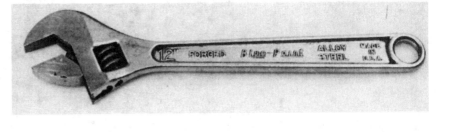

Figure 1-22 A flat-blade (or straight-blade) screwdriver (on the left) is specified by the length of the screwdriver and width of the blade. The width of the blade should match the width of the screw slot of the fastener. A Phillips-head screwdriver (in the middle) is specified by the length of the handle and the size of the point at the tip. A #1 is a sharp point, #2 is most common (as shown), and a #3 Phillips is blunt and is only used for larger sizes of Phillips-head fasteners.

Figure 1-23 Assortment of pliers. Slip-joint pliers (far left) are often confused with water pump pliers (second from left).

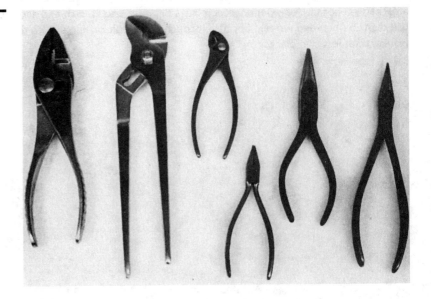

TECH TIP ☑

Wearing Rubber Gloves Saves Your Hands

Many technicians wear rubber gloves not only to help keep their hands clean but also to help protect their skin from the effects of dirty engine oil and other possibly hazardous materials. Several types of gloves and their characteristics include:

- **Latex surgical gloves**—These gloves are relatively inexpensive, but tend to stretch, swell, and weaken when exposed to gas, oil, or solvents.
- **Vinyl gloves**—These gloves are also inexpensive and are not affected by gas, oil, or solvents.
- **Polyurethane gloves**—These gloves are more expensive, yet very strong. Even though these gloves are also not affected by gas, oil, or solvents, they do tend to be slippery.

- **Nitrile gloves**—These gloves are exactly like latex gloves but are not affected by gas, oil, or solvents, yet they tend to be expensive.

Many service technicians prefer to use the vinyl-type gloves, but with an additional pair of nylon gloves worn under the vinyl. Nylon gloves look like white cotton gloves and when worn under the others help keep moisture under control. (Plastic gloves on a hot summer day can soon become wet with perspiration.) The nylon gloves provide additional protection and are washable.

Figure I–24 A ball-peen hammer (top) is purchased according to weight (usually in ounces) of the head of the hammer. At bottom is a soft-faced (plastic) hammer. Always use a hammer that is softer than the material being driven. Use a block of wood or similar material between a steel hammer and steel or iron parts to prevent damage to the parts.

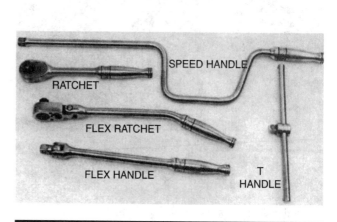

Figure I–25 Typical drive handles for sockets.

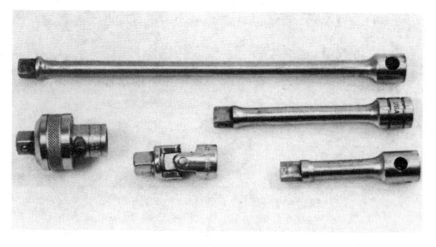

Figure I–26 Various socket extensions. The universal joint (U-joint) in the center (bottom) is useful for gaining access in tight areas.

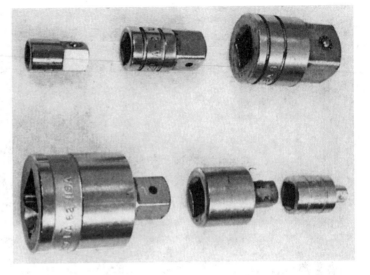

Figure I–27 Socket drive adapters. These adapters permit the use of a 3/8″ drive ratchet with 1/2″ drive sockets, or other combinations as the various adapters permit. Adapters should *not* be used where a larger tool used with excessive force could break or damage a smaller-sized socket.

Figure I–28 Twelve-point, six-point, and eight-point sockets. Six-point sockets are recommended because they contact all six sides of a typical bolt or nut and can exert more force without rounding the head.

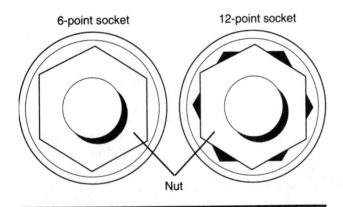

Figure I–29 A six-point socket fits the head of the bolt or nut on all sides. A twelve-point socket can round off the head of a bolt or nut if a lot of force is applied.

Figure I–30 Standard twelve-point short socket (left), universal joint socket (center), and deep-well socket (right). Both the universal and deep well are six-point sockets.

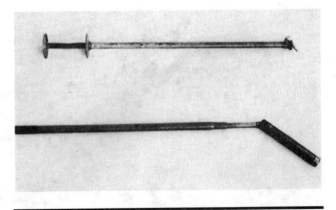

Figure I–31 Mechanical pickup finger (top) and extendable magnet (bottom) are excellent tools to have when a nut drops down into a small area where fingers can never reach.

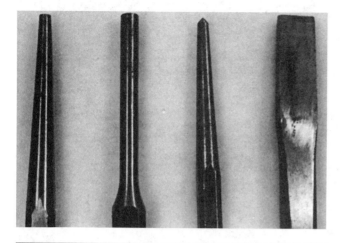

Figure 1–33 Using a die to cut threads on a rod.

Figure 1–32 Various punches on the left and a chisel on the right.

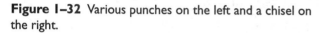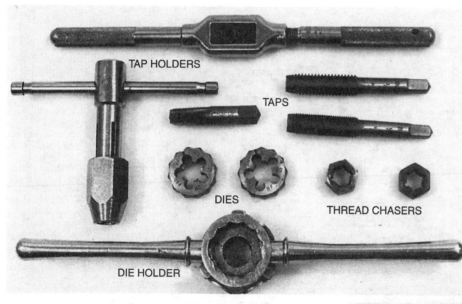

Figure 1–34 Dies are used to make threads on the outside of round stock. Taps are used to make threads inside holes.

TAP HOLDERS

TAPS

DIES

THREAD CHASERS

DIE HOLDER

TECH TIP ✔

It Just Takes a Second

Whenever removing any automotive component, it is wise to put the bolts back into the holes a couple of threads with your hand. This ensures that the right bolt will be used in its original location when the component or part is put back on the vehicle. Often, a same-diameter fastener is used on a component, but the length of the bolt may vary. Spending just a couple of seconds to put the bolts and nuts back where they belong when the part is removed can save a lot of time when the part is being installed. Besides making certain that the right fastener is being installed in the right place, this method helps prevent bolts and nuts from being lost or kicked away. How much time have you wasted looking for that lost bolt or nut?

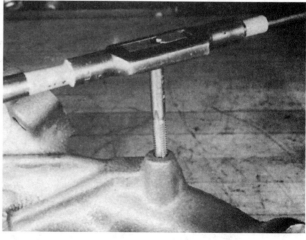

Figure 1–35 Starting a tap in a drilled hole. The hole diameter should be matched exactly to the tap size for proper thread clearance. The proper drill size to use is called the **tap drill** size.

Figure 1–36 Typical micrometers used for dimensional inspection.

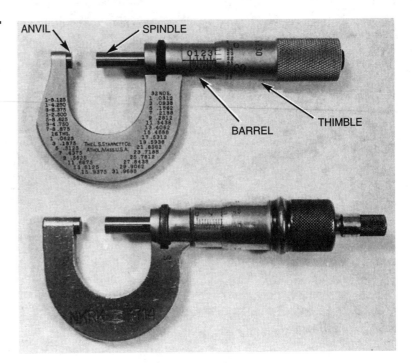

Figure 1–37 Sample micrometer readings. Each larger line on the barrel between the numbers represents 0.025″. The number on the thimble is then added to the number showing and the number of lines times 0.025″.

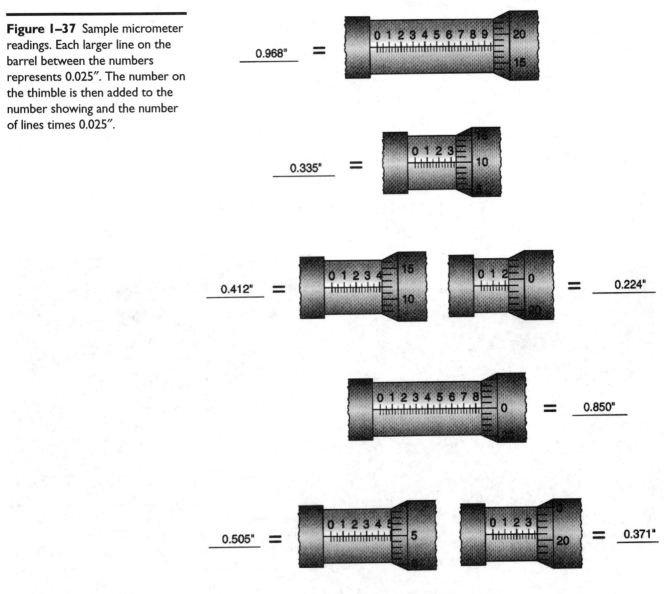

Figure 1-38 An inexpensive muffin tin can be used to keep small parts separated.

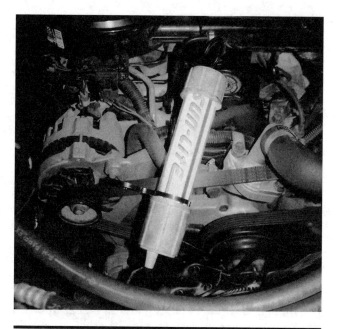

Figure 1-39 A good fluorescent trouble light is essential. A fluorescent light operates cooler than an incandescent light and does not pose a fire hazard if gasoline were accidentally dropped on an unprotected bulb.

(a)

(b)

Figure 1-40 (a) A beginning technician can start with some simple basic hand tools. (b) An experienced serious technician often spends several thousand dollars a year for tools such as found in this large (and expensive) toolbox.

■ SAFETY TIPS FOR TECHNICIANS

Safety is not just a buzzword on a poster in the work area. Safe work habits can reduce accidents and injuries, ease the workload, and keep employees pain-free. Suggested safety tips include:

1. *Safety glasses should be worn at all times while servicing any vehicle.*
2. Watch your toes—always keep your toes protected with steel-toed safety shoes. If safety shoes are not available, leather-topped shoes offer more protection than canvas or cloth.
3. Wear gloves to protect your hands from rough or sharp surfaces. The use of thin rubber gloves is recommended when working around automotive liquids such as engine oil, antifreeze, transmission fluid, or any other liquids that may be hazardous.
4. Service technicians working under a vehicle should wear a **bump cap** to protect their head against under-vehicle objects and the pads of the lift.
5. Remove jewelry, which can get caught on something or act as a conductor to an exposed electrical circuit.
6. Avoid loose or dangling clothing.
7. When lifting any object, get a secure grip with solid footing. Keep the load close to your body to minimize the strain. Lift with your legs and arms, not your back.
8. Do not twist your body when carrying a load. Instead, pivot your feet to help prevent strain on the spine.
9. Ask for help when moving or lifting heavy objects.
10. Push a heavy object rather than pulling it. (This is opposite to the way you should work with tools—never push a wrench! If a bolt or nut loosens, your entire weight is used to propel your hand(s) forward. This usually results in cuts, bruises, or other painful injury.)
11. Always connect an exhaust hose to the tailpipe of any running vehicle to help prevent the buildup of carbon monoxide inside a closed garage space (see Figure 1–41).
12. Store all flammable liquids in an approved fire safety cabinet as shown in Figure 1–42.
13. Always be sure the hood is securely held open (see Figures 1–43 and 1–44).

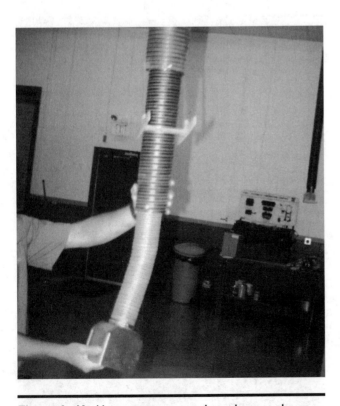

Figure 1–41 Always connect an exhaust hose to the tailpipe of the engine of a vehicle to be run inside a building.

Figure 1–42 Typical fireproof flammable storage cabinet.

Figure 1–43 To properly secure a hood in the open position, be certain that the prop rod is inserted into the designated opening in the hood.

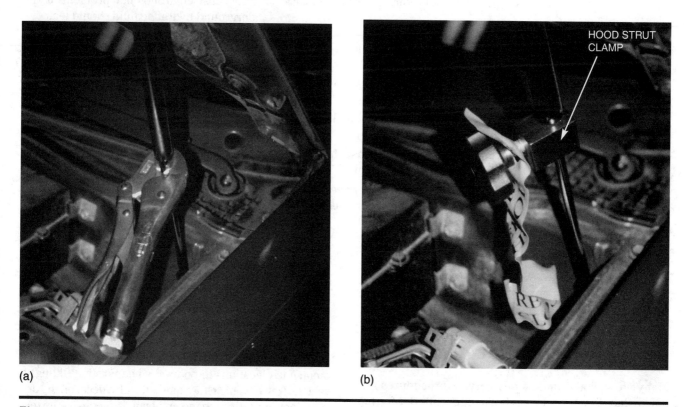

(a)

(b)

HOOD STRUT CLAMP

Figure 1–44 (a) A crude but effective method is to use locking pliers on the chrome-plated shaft of a hood strut. Locking pliers should only be used on defective struts because the jaws of the pliers can damage the strut shaft. (b) A commercially available hood clamp. This tool uses a bright orange tag to help remind the technician to remove the clamp before attempting to close the hood. The hood could be bent if force is used to close the hood with the clamp in place.

Table 1–1 Vehicle Lifting Methods

	Advantages	Disadvantages
Drive-on ramps: Always use high-quality reinforced ramps with a long, low-angle approach (see Figure 1–45).	1. Inexpensive 2. Easy to store—can be hung on the wall 3. Portable—can be easily moved	1. Can "kick out" when driving the vehicle onto ramps 2. Can only be used for under-vehicle service, cannot service wheels, brakes, or suspension components, except shock absorbers 3. Height distance fixed to ramp height
Jack and safety stands: Always use a high-quality hydraulic jack with large wheels and a wide stance. Safety stands should be rated higher than the weight they support (see Figure 1–46).	1. Relatively inexpensive 2. Portable 3. Easily stored 4. Allow for work on brakes and other components when the wheels must be removed	1. Can slip, especially during lifting operation 2. Opposite end of vehicle must be chocked. 3. Could be dangerous—care must be taken to place safety stands at vehicle manufacturer's recommended jacking and support points under the vehicle. 4. Under-body service is limited.
In-ground pneumatic hydraulic lifts: See Figure 1–47.	1. Can be driven over, then set under the vehicle 2. Allow doors of the vehicle to be opened fully 3. Deep yoke or twin post side-by-side models permit lots of room under the vehicle.	1. Expensive to install 2. Technician has to kneel down (and sometimes under the vehicle) to set the pads. 3. Some in-ground lifts do not permit clearance under the center of the vehicle. 4. May cause environmental problems if underground hydraulic fluid should leak. (Biodegradable fluids are available.) 5. Require at least 6 cubic feet per minute (CFM) of compressed air at 150 psi (1000 kPa) for a single post lift and 8 CFM at 150 psi for a twin post lift.
Surface-mounted (electromechanical) lifts: See Figure 1–48 on page 20.	1. Lower cost to install than for hydraulic in-ground units 2. Environmentally safer because there is no hydraulic fluid underground 3. Require electrical hookup service only (usually 220 to 230 v); compressed air not needed for lifts	1. Require more service dollars and have more moving parts 2. Require additional overhead clearance space beyond that needed for an in-ground unit 3. Vertical posts often make it difficult to get in or out of the vehicle unless an asymmetrical type of lift is used 4. Must have an adequate concrete floor because surface-mounted lifts are lag bolted to the floor.

■ SAFETY IN LIFTING (HOISTING) A VEHICLE

Many chassis and under-body service procedures require that the vehicle be hoisted or lifted off the ground. The simplest methods involve the use of drive-on ramps or a floor jack and safety (jack) stands, while in-ground or surface-mounted lifts provide greater access. Each method of raising a vehicle has both advantages and disadvantages, as shown in Table 1–1.

Setting the Pads

All automobile and light truck service manuals include recommended locations to be used when hoisting (lifting) a vehicle. Newer vehicles are marked with a decal on the driver's door indicating the recommended lift points. The recommended standard for the lift points is in SAE Standard JRP-2184. These locations typically include the following:

1. The vehicle should be centered on the lift or hoist so as not to overload one side or put too much force either too far forward or too far rearward.

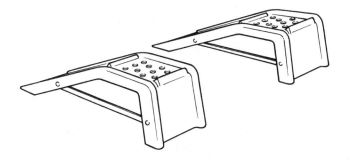

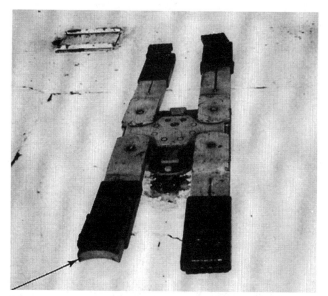

(a)

Figure 1–45 Drive-on type ramps. The wheels on the ground level *must* be chocked (blocked) to prevent accidental movement down the ramp.

(a)

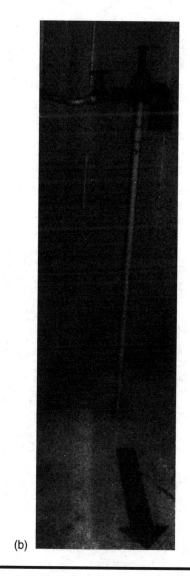

(b)

(b)

Figure 1–46 (a) Portable hydraulic jack and safety (jack) stands. The wheels opposite those being raised off the ground *must* be chocked (blocked) to prevent accidental movement that could cause the vehicle to slip off the safety stands. (b) Safety stands should be placed on a hard, flat surface such as this race shop floor.

Figure 1–47 (a) In-ground lifts must be driven over and may cause damage to a tire or wheel if the vehicle operator is not careful to avoid the ends of the lift arms. (b) In-ground hydraulic lift that uses compressed air over hydraulic fluid to raise the lifting pads. Note the arrow painted on the floor. This helps prevent using the controls for the wrong lift.

(a)

(b)

Figure 1–48 (a) Surface-mounted electromechanical lift. (b) Warning labels should always be observed.

2. The pads of the lift should be spread as far apart as possible to provide a stable platform.
3. The pad should be placed under a portion of the vehicle that is strong and capable of supporting the weight of the vehicle, including:
   a. Pinch welds at the bottom edge of the body are generally considered to be strong.

> **CAUTION:** Even though pinch weld seams are the recommended location for hoisting many vehicles with unitized bodies, care should be taken not to place the pad(s) too far forward or rearward. Incorrect placement of the vehicle on the lift could cause imbalance of the vehicle on the lift and the vehicle could fall. This is exactly what happened to the vehicle in Figure 1–49.

   b. Boxed areas of the body are the best places to place the pads on a vehicle without a frame. Be careful to note whether the arms of the lift may come in contact with other parts of the vehicle before the pad touches the intended location. Commonly damaged areas include:
      (1) Rocker panel moldings
      (2) Exhaust system (including catalytic converter)
      (3) Tires, especially if the edges of the pads or arms are sharp
   c. Frame or boxed perimeter frame members of the body are always good places to put the pads. (see Figures 1–50 through 1–52 on pages 21–22).
4. Before using a hoist for the first time, always check with an instructor or other responsible person for directions and/or suggestions.
5. The vehicle should be raised about 1 ft (30 cm) off the floor, then stopped. The vehicle should be shaken to check for stability. If the vehicle seems to be stable when checked a short distance from the floor, continue raising the vehicle and continue to view the vehicle until it has reached the desired height.
6. Before lowering the hoist, the safety latch(es) must be released and the direction of the controls reversed to lower the hoist. The downward speed is often adjusted to the slowest possible, for additional safety.

> **CAUTION:** Do not look away from the vehicle while it is being raised (or lowered) on a hoist. Often, one side or one end of the hoist can stop or fail, resulting in the vehicle being slanted enough to slip or fall, creating physical damage not only to the vehicle and/or hoist but also to the technician or others who may be near.

Figure 1–49 This car fell from the lift because the pads were not set correctly. A technician had just removed the left front strut assembly when the car fell. No one was hurt, but the car was a total loss.

SAFETY ARM CLIP

Figure 1–50 The safety arm clip should be engaged to prevent the possibility that the hoist support arms can move.

(a)

Figure 1–51 (a) An assortment of hoist pad adapters that are often necessary to use to safely hoist many pickup trucks, vans, and sport utility vehicles. (b) A view from underneath a Chevrolet pickup truck showing how the pad extensions are used to attach the hoist lifting pad to contact the frame.

(b)

(a)

(b)

Figure 1–52 (a) In this photo the pad arm is just contacting the rocker panel of the vehicle. (b) This photo shows what can occur if the technician places the pad too far inward underneath the vehicle. The arm of the hoist has dented in the rocker panel.

Figure 1–53 All solvents and other hazardous waste should be disposed of properly.

HINT: Most hoists can be placed safely at any desired height. For ease while working, the area that you are working on should be at chest level. When working on brakes or suspension components, it is not necessary to work on them down near the floor or over your head; raise the hoist so that the components are at chest level.

■ HAZARDOUS MATERIALS

The Environmental Protection Agency (EPA) regulates and controls the handling of hazardous materials in the United States. A material is considered hazardous if it meets one or more of the following conditions:

1. It contains over 1000 parts per million (PPM) of halogenated compounds (halogenated compounds are chemicals containing chlorine, fluorine, bromine, or iodine). Common items that contain these solvents include:
   • Carburetor cleaner
   • Silicone spray
   • Aerosols
   • Adhesives
   • Stoddard solvent
   • Trichloromethane
   • Gear oils
   • Brake cleaner
   • A/C compressor oils

• Floor cleaners
• Anything else that contains "chlor" or "fluor" in its ingredient name
2. It has a flash point below 140°F (60°C).
3. It is corrosive (a pH of 2 or less, or 12.5 or higher).
4. It contains toxic metals or organic compounds. Volatile organic compounds (VOCs) must also be limited and controlled. This classification greatly affects the painting and finishing aspects of the automobile industry.

Always follow recommended procedures for handling of any chemicals and dispose of all used engine oil and other possible waste products according to local, provincial, state, or federal laws.

To help safeguard workers and the environment, the following are recommended:

1. A technician's hands should always be washed thoroughly after touching used engine oils, transmission fluids, and greases. Dispose of all waste oil according to established standards and laws in your area.

NOTE: The Environmental Protection Agency (EPA) current standards mandate that for used engine oil to be recyclable, it must contain less than 1000 parts per million (PPM) of total halogens (chlorinated solvents). Oil containing greater amounts of halogens must be considered hazardous waste (see Figure 1–53).

---

2. Asbestos and products that contain asbestos are known cancer-causing agents. Even though most brake linings and clutch facing materials being manufactured today do not contain asbestos, millions of vehicles are serviced every day that *may* contain asbestos. The general procedure for handling asbestos is to put the used parts into a sealed plastic bag and return the parts as cores for rebuilding, or to be disposed of according to current laws and regulations.
3. Eyewash stations should be readily accessible near the work area and near areas where solvents or other contaminants could get into the eyes (see Figure 1–54).

■ MATERIAL SAFETY DATA SHEETS

Businesses and schools in the United States are required to provide a detailed data sheet on each of the chemicals or materials that a person may be exposed to in an area. These sheets of information on each of the materials that may be harmful are called material safety data sheets or MSDS. Figure 1–55 shows a notebook containing these sheets for the various materials and chemicals used at an automotive training center.

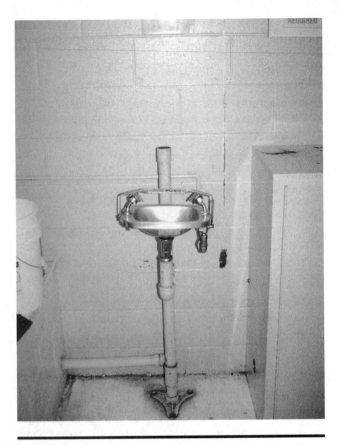

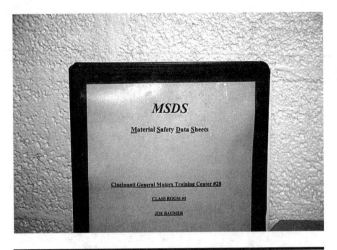

Figure 1–55 A notebook containing the MSDS for the various materials and chemicals used at an automotive training center.

Figure 1–54 An eye washer station should be centrally located in the shop and near where solvent may be splashed.

PHOTO SEQUENCE   How to Set the Pads and Safely Hoist a Vehicle

PS1–1 The first step in hoisting a vehicle is to properly align the vehicle in the center of the stall.

PS1–2 Most vehicles will be correctly positioned when the left front tire is centered on the tire pad.

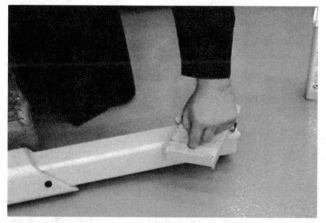

PS1–3 Most pads at the end of the hoist arms can be rotated to allow for many different types of vehicle construction.

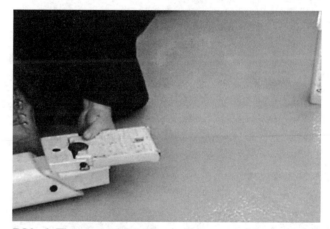

PS1–4 The arms of the lifts can be retracted or extended to accommodate vehicles of many different lengths.

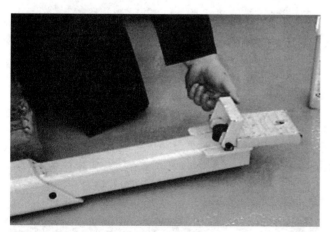

PS1–5 Most lifts are equipped with short pad extensions that are often necessary to use to allow the pad to contact the frame of a vehicle without causing the arm of the lift to hit and damage parts of the body.

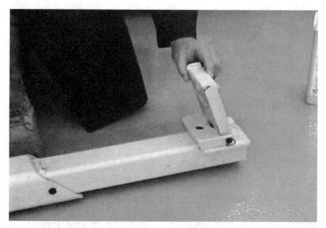

PS1–6 Tall pad extensions can also be used to gain access to the frame of a vehicle. This position is needed to safely hoist many pickup trucks, vans, and sport utility vehicles (SUVs).

How to Set the Pads and Safely Hoist a Vehicle—continued

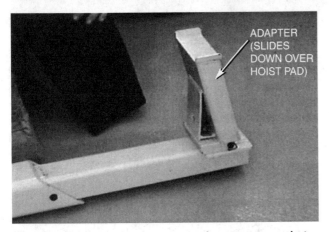

ADAPTER (SLIDES DOWN OVER HOIST PAD)

PS1–7 An additional extension may be necessary to hoist a truck or van equipped with running boards to give the necessary clearance.

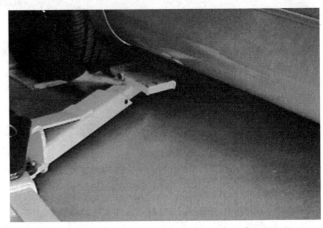

PS1–8 Position the front hoist pads under the recommended locations as specified in the owner's manual and/or service information for the vehicle being serviced.

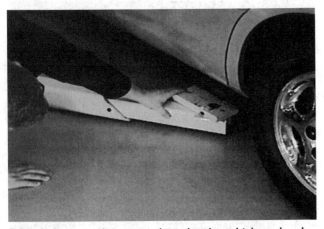

PS1–9 Position the rear pads under the vehicle under the recommended locations.

PS1–10 This photo shows an asymmetrical lift where the front arms are shorter than the rear arms. This design is best used for passenger cars and allows the driver to exit the vehicle easier because the door can be opened wide without it hitting the vertical support column.

PS1–11 After being sure all pads are correctly positioned, use the electromechanical controls to raise the vehicle.

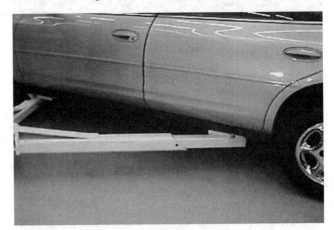

PS1–12 Raise the vehicle about 1 ft (30 cm) and stop to double-check that all pads contact the body or frame in the correct positions.

PS1–13 With the vehicle raised about 1 ft off the ground, push down on the vehicle to check to see if it is stable on the pads. If the vehicle rocks, lower the vehicle and reset the pads. If the vehicle is stable, the vehicle can be raised to any desired working level. Be sure the safety is engaged before working on or under the vehicle.

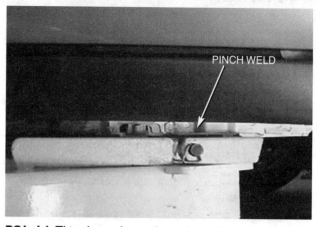

PS1–14 This photo shows the pads set flat and contacting the vertical pinch welds of the body. This method spreads the load over the entire length of the pad and is less likely to dent or damage the pinch weld area.

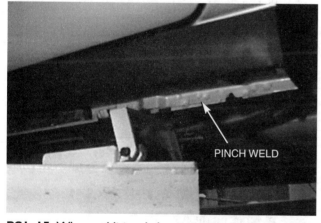

PS1–15 Where additional clearance is necessary for the arms to clear the rest of the body, the pads can be raised and placed under the pinch weld area as shown.

PS1–16 When the service work is completed, the hoist should be raised slightly and the safety released before using the hydraulic lever to lower the vehicle.

PS1–17 After lowering the vehicle, be sure all arms of the lift are moved out of the way before driving the vehicle out of the work stall.

PS1–18 Carefully back the vehicle out of the stall. Notice that all of the lift arms have been neatly moved out of the way to provide clearance so that the tires will not contact the arms when the vehicle is driven out of the stall.

■ SUMMARY

1. Vehicle chassis designs include frame, unit-body, and space frame construction. A full-frame vehicle is often stronger and quieter and permits the towing of heavier loads. Unit-body and space frame construction is often lighter and more fuel efficient.

2. Lifting a vehicle above the ground can be accomplished with drive-on ramps, jack and safety stands, or hydraulic or electric-powered lifts.

3. Whenever a vehicle is raised above the ground, it must be supported at a substantial section of the body or frame.

4. Hazardous materials include common automotive chemicals, liquids, and lubricants, especially those whose ingredients contain "chlor" or "fluor" in the name. Asbestos fibers should be avoided and removed according to current laws and regulations.

5. Bolts, studs, and nuts are commonly used as fasteners in the chassis. The sizes for fractional and metric threads are different and are not interchangeable. Grade is the rating of the strength of a fastener.

■ REVIEW QUESTIONS

1. List two advantages and two disadvantages of frame and unit-body chassis construction.

2. List three necessary precautions to be followed when hoisting (lifting) a vehicle.

3. List five common automotive chemicals or products that may be considered hazardous materials.

4. List five precautions every technician should take when working with automotive products and chemicals.

■ ASE CERTIFICATION-TYPE QUESTIONS

1. Two technicians are discussing the hoisting of a vehicle. Technician A says to put the pads of a lift under a notch at the pinch weld of a unit-body vehicle. Technician B says to place the pads on four corners of the frame of a full-frame vehicle. Which technician is correct?
   a. Technician A only
   b. Technician B only
   c. Both Technician A and B
   d. Neither Technician A nor B

2. The correct location for hoisting or jacking the vehicle can often be found in
   a. The service manual
   b. The shop manual
   c. The owner's manual
   d. All of the above

3. Hazardous materials include all *except*
   a. Engine oil
   b. Asbestos
   c. Water
   d. Brake cleaner

4. To check if a product or substance being used is hazardous, consult
   a. A dictionary
   b. The MSDS
   c. The SAE
   d. The EPA

5. For best heavy-duty towing, the tow vehicle should have what type of construction?
   a. Space frame
   b. Unit-body
   c. Frame
   d. Body

6. For the best working position, the work should be at
   a. Neck or head level
   b. Knee or ankle level
   c. Overhead about 1 ft
   d. Chest or elbow level

7. When working with hand tools, always
   a. Push the wrench—don't pull toward you
   b. Pull the wrench—don't push away from you

8. A high-strength bolt is identified by the
   a. UNC symbol
   b. Lines on the head
   c. Strength letter codes
   d. Coarse threads

9. Extensions may be needed on the hoist pads when lifting a
   a. Truck
   b. Sport utility vehicle
   c. Van
   d. All of the above

10. A flare-nut wrench can also be called a
    a. Line wrench
    b. Fitting wrench
    c. Tube-nut wrench
    d. All of the above

Braking System Principles, Components, and Operation

Objectives: After studying Chapter 2, the reader should be able to:

1. State the operating principles of the braking system.
2. List the parts and terms for disc and drum brakes.
3. Describe how the hydraulic brake system can be used to transfer pressure to each wheel.
4. Discuss the coefficient of friction and describe how the friction between the lining material and the drum or rotor stops wheels.
5. List the types of brake fluids and their application.
6. Discuss how ABS units help in braking and vehicle stability when stopping on slippery surfaces.

Brakes are by far the most important mechanism on any vehicle because the safety and lives of those riding in the vehicle depend on proper operation of the braking system. It has been estimated that the brakes on the average vehicle are applied 50,000 times a year!

"Brakes stop wheels—not vehicles." This basic fact means that the best brakes in the world only stop rotation of the tire/wheel assembly. It is the friction between the tire and the pavement that accomplishes the stopping or slowing of the vehicle. A vehicle being driven on an icy street will take an extremely long time to stop. Even with a vehicle equipped with an antilock braking system (ABS), there still has to be **friction** (traction) between the tire and the road for the vehicle to stop.

■ HOW BRAKES STOP VEHICLES

Brakes are an energy-absorbing mechanism that converts vehicle movement into heat while stopping the rotation of the wheels. All braking systems are designed to reduce the speed and stop a moving vehicle and to keep it from moving if the vehicle is stationary. **Service brakes** are the main driver-operated brakes of the vehicle (see Figure 2–1). Service brakes are also called **base brakes** or **foundation brakes.**

Most vehicles built since the late 1920s use a brake on each wheel. To stop a wheel, the driver exerts a force on a brake pedal. The force on the brake pedal pressurizes brake fluid in a master cylinder. This hydraulic force (liquid under pressure) is transferred through steel lines to a wheel cylinder or caliper at each wheel. Hydraulic pressure to each wheel cylinder or caliper is used to force friction materials against the brake drum or rotor. The friction between the stationary friction material and the rotating drum or rotor (disc) causes the rotating part to slow and eventually stop. Since the wheels are attached to the drums or rotors, the wheels of the vehicles also stop.

The heavier the vehicle and the higher the speed, the more heat the brakes have to be able to absorb. Long, steep hills can cause the brakes to overheat, reducing the friction necessary to slow and stop a vehicle (see Figures 2–2 and 2–3).

■ DRUM BRAKES

Drum brakes are used on the rear of many rear-wheel-drive, front-wheel-drive, and four-wheel-drive vehicles.

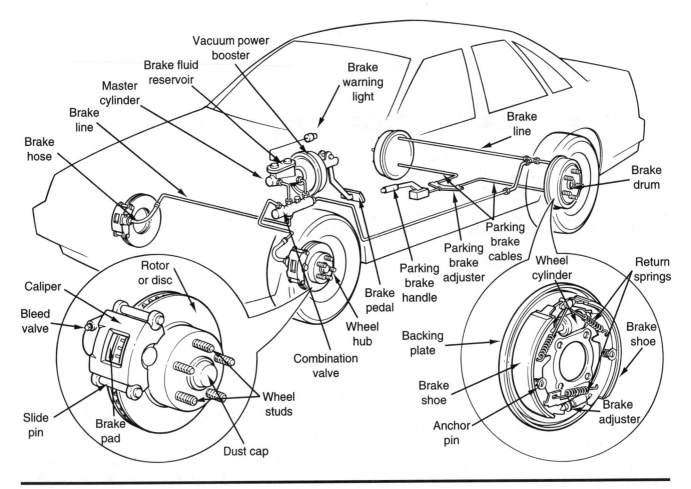

Figure 2–1 Typical vehicle brake system showing all typical components.

Figure 2–2 Brakes change the energy of the moving vehicle into heat. Too much heat and brakes fail, as indicated on this sign coming down from Pike's Peak in Colorado at 14,000 ft (4300 m).

Figure 2–3 When driving down long, steep grades, select a lower transmission gear to allow the engine compression to help maintain vehicle speed.

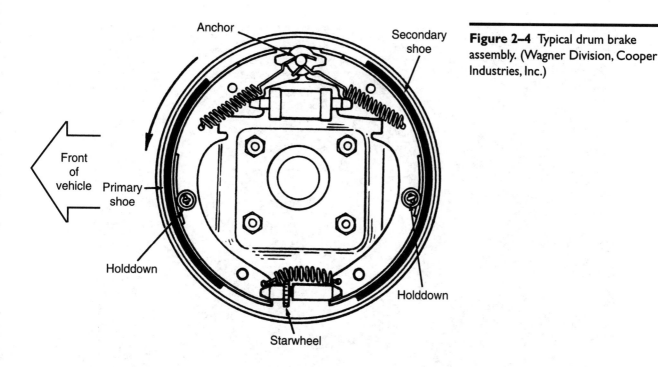

Figure 2–4 Typical drum brake assembly. (Wagner Division, Cooper Industries, Inc.)

Labels on figure:
- Anchor
- Secondary shoe
- Front of vehicle
- Primary shoe
- Holddown
- Holddown
- Starwheel

Since the early 1970s, few vehicles have been manufactured with drum brakes on the front wheels. When drum brakes are applied, brake shoes are moved outward against a rotating brake drum. The wheel studs for the wheels are attached to the drum. When the drum slows and stops, the wheels also slow and stop.

Drum brakes are economical to manufacture, service, and repair. Parts for drum brakes are generally readily available and reasonably priced. On some vehicles, an additional drum brake is used as a parking brake on vehicles equipped with rear disc brakes (see Figures 2–4 and 2–5).

■ DISC BRAKES

Disc brakes are used on the front of most vehicles built since the early 1970s and on the rear wheels of many vehicles. A disc brake operates by squeezing brake pads on both sides of a rotor or disc that is attached to the wheel (see Figure 2–6).

Type of Brake	Rotating Part	Friction Part
Drum brakes	Brake drum	Brake shoes
Disc brakes	Rotor or disc	Brake pads

Due to the friction between the road surface and the tires, the vehicle stops. To summarize, the events necessary to stop a vehicle include:

1. The driver presses on the brake pedal.
2. The brake pedal pressure is transferred hydraulically to a wheel cylinder or caliper at each wheel.
3. Hydraulic pressure inside the wheel cylinder or caliper presses friction materials (brake shoes or pads) against rotating brake drums or rotors.

4. The friction slows and stops the drum or rotor. Since the drum or rotor is bolted to the wheel of the vehicle, the wheel also stops.
5. When the wheels of the vehicle slow and stop, the tires must have friction (traction) with the road surface to stop the vehicle.

■ WEIGHT TRANSFER DURING BRAKING

Whenever the brakes are applied on a vehicle in motion, the weight of the vehicle is transferred forward while driving forward. Most vehicles can be observed "nosing downward" whenever the brakes are applied. Greater braking power is required for the front brakes because of this weight transfer (see Figure 2–7).

It is estimated that the front brakes handle about 60 to 70 percent of the braking power on rear-wheel-drive vehicles and 80 percent on front-wheel-drive vehicles (see Figure 2-8). This is why many vehicles have disc brakes only on the front. Rear drum brakes handle less heat, are less expensive, and are easier to use as a parking brake.

■ DECELERATION RATES

Deceleration rates are measured in units of "feet per second per second." (No, this is not a misprint.) What it means is that the vehicle will change in velocity during a certain time interval divided by the time interval. Deceleration is abbreviated "ft/sec^2" (pronounced "feet per second per second" or "feet per second squared") or meters per sec^2 (m/s^2) in the metric system. Typical deceleration rates include:

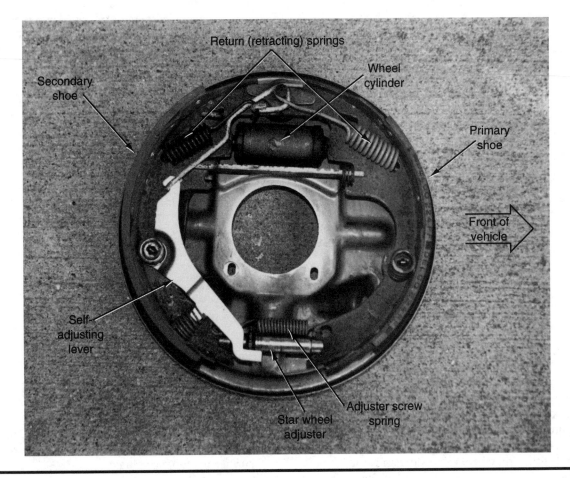

Figure 2–5 Drum brake assembly as used on the right rear wheel.

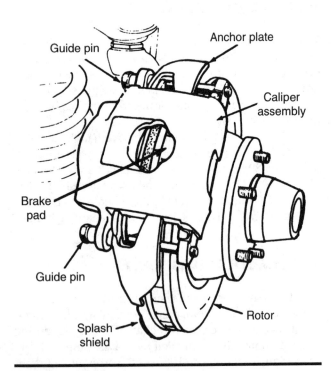

Figure 2–6 Typical disc brake assembly. (Wagner Division, Cooper Industries, Inc.)

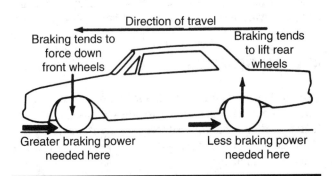

Figure 2–7 When brakes are applied, vehicle weight is transferred toward the front. This weight transfer requires that more braking power be available on the front wheels and less on the rear wheels to avoid rear-wheel lockup. (Courtesy of EIS Brake Parts)

Comfortable deceleration is about 8.5 ft/sec^2 (3m/s^2).

Loose items in the vehicle will "fly" above 11 ft/sec^2 (3.5 m/s^2).

Maximum deceleration rates for most cars and light trucks range from 16 to 32 ft/sec^2 (5 to 10 m/s^2).

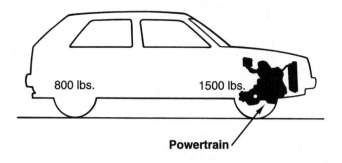

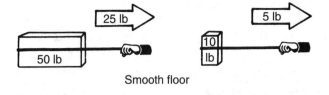

Smooth floor

Figure 2–10 Friction varies with the load applied between the sliding surfaces. The greater the weight, the greater the friction. (Wagner Division, Cooper Industries, Inc.)

Figure 2–8 Front-wheel-drive vehicles have much of their vehicle weight over the front wheels. This means that most of the braking power occurs with the front brakes. (Courtesy of Hunter Engineering Company)

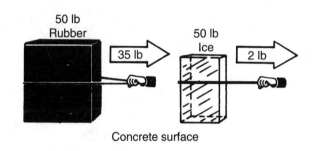

Concrete surface

Figure 2–11 Friction varies with the type of material. A slippery surface has less friction (traction) than other surfaces. (Wagner Division, Cooper Industries, Inc.)

Figure 2–9 A brick being pushed against the floor creates heat from the friction between the two surfaces. (Courtesy of EIS Brake Parts)

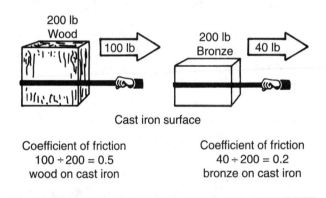

Cast iron surface

Coefficient of friction
100 ÷ 200 = 0.5
wood on cast iron

Coefficient of friction
40 ÷ 200 = 0.2
bronze on cast iron

An average deceleration rate of 15 ft per second per second (FPSPS) (3 m/s^2) can stop a vehicle traveling at 55 mph (88 km/h) in about 200 ft (61 m) in less than 4 seconds. During a standard brake system test, a vehicle is braked at this rate fifteen times. Temperatures at the front brake pads can reach 1300°F (700°C) or higher, sometimes reaching as high as 1800°F (980°C). Brake fluid and rubber components may reach 300°F (150°C) or higher.

Figure 2–12 The coefficient of friction is the ratio of the force required to move an object divided by the weight of the object. (Wagner Division, Cooper Industries, Inc.)

■ FRICTION

Friction is the force that resists the motion between two objects that are in contact (see Figures 2–9 and 2–10). The amount of friction between two surfaces is called the **coefficient of friction** and is represented by a number from zero to one. The Greek lowercase letter **mu (μ)** is used to represent this factor.

μ = 0 (no friction between surfaces)

μ = 1 (maximum friction between surfaces)

To stop a vehicle there must be friction between the brake lining material and the rotating brake part, such as

the brake drum or rotor. The coefficient of friction depends on the friction material, temperature, and surface finish of the drum or rotor. For example, friction material with a μ value of 0.5 has a higher friction than friction material with a μ of 0.4 (see Figures 2–11 and 2–12).

Road surfaces also provide varying amounts of traction (friction) for the tires. On ice, tires cannot "grip the road" because, even if the brakes are working perfectly, the vehicle will not stop quickly because of the lack of friction between the tires and the ice. Braking is especially dangerous when one side of the vehicle is traveling over normal high-friction road surfaces while the other wheel on the other side of the vehicle is running on gravel or ice. Brake engineers call these **split-mu** conditions. Antilock braking systems are especially important during braking under these conditions. Without ABS, one side would have greater stopping power than the other side, which could cause the vehicle to skid.

■ BRAKES AS ENERGY CONVERTERS

The energy of a moving vehicle must be converted to heat by the braking system during a stop. Brakes have to be able to absorb or dissipate this heat. Stopping in half the time will generate heat twice as fast. The energy of a moving vehicle increases with the square of the speed. This energy, called **kinetic energy,** represents the energy in any moving object. The formula for kinetic energy is

$$KE = 1/2\ MV^2$$

KE = kinetic energy
M = mass (weight of the vehicle)
V = velocity (speed)

If the vehicle speed doubles, such as from 25 mph to 50 mph, the amount of energy that has to be converted to heat is increased four times. Since it is not always possible for the brakes to dissipate heat as fast as it is generated, the storage capacity of the brakes is important to keep the temperatures from getting too hot. This means that the brake rotors or drums must be able to absorb heat. See Chapter 8 for details on rotor and drum design and service procedures to follow to ensure proper braking.

■ FEDERAL MOTOR VEHICLE SAFETY STANDARD

The U.S. federal government's Motor Vehicle Safety Standard (FMVSS) Number 105 specifies requirements for hydraulic service brake and parking brake systems. The current standard for passenger vehicles with a gross vehicle weight rating of less than 8000 lb (3630 kg) includes:

Service brakes	Stop from a speed of 60 mph (100 km/h) in less than 216 ft (65.8 m). [The vehicle must stay within a 12-ft (3.7-m) wide lane.]
Service brakes with an inoperative power assist unit	Stop from a speed of 60 mph in less than 456 ft (139 m).
Parking brake	Must be capable of holding the vehicle stationary for 5 minutes in both forward and reverse directions on a 30 percent grade. See Chapter 7 for details on parking brake operation and service.

NOTE: Most vehicles can stop in a much shorter distance than required by law. For example, many high-performance vehicles can stop from 60 mph in about 100 ft (33 m) or about half of the distance specified in the federal standard.

■ BRAKE DESIGN REQUIREMENTS

All braking forces must provide for the following:

1. Equal forces must be applied to both the left and right sides of the vehicle to ensure straight stops.
2. Hydraulic systems must be properly engineered and serviced to provide for changes as vehicle weight shifts forward during braking. Hydraulic valves must be incorporated into the hydraulic system to permit the maximum possible braking forces but still prevent undesirable wheel lockup. Antilock braking systems (ABS) are specifically designed to prevent wheel lockup under all driving conditions, including wet or icy road conditions.
3. The hydraulic system must use a fluid that will not evaporate or freeze. The fluid has to withstand extreme temperatures without boiling and must not damage rubber or metal parts of the braking system.
4. The friction material (braking lining or brake pads) must be designed to provide adequate friction between the stationary axles and the rotating drum or rotor. The friction material should be environmentally safe. Nonasbestos lining is generally considered to be safe for the environment and the technician.
5. The design of the braking system should secure the brake lining solidly to prevent the movement of the friction material during braking.

NOTE: It is this movement of the friction material that causes brake noise (squeal). Various movement dampers are used by the vehicle manufacturers to help control any movement that does occur. It is important that every technician restore the operation of all aspects of the braking system whenever they are serviced, even the noise dampers.

6. Most braking systems incorporate a power assist unit that reduces the driver's effort. The most commonly used brake booster is vacuum operated. The vacuum from the intake manifold is the most commonly used source of vacuum for power brake boosters. Therefore, the engine itself must be functioning correctly for proper operation of the power vacuum booster.

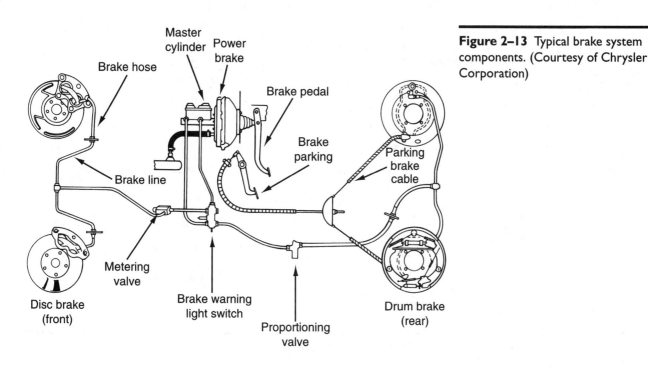

■ BRAKE SYSTEM CATEGORIES

Brake system components can be classified and placed into six subsystem categories, depending on their function (see Figure 2–13).

Apply System

The driver starts the operation of the braking system by pressing on the **brake pedal** or applying the **parking brake.** The apply system includes all the levers, pedals, or linkage needed to activate a braking force.

Boost System

The boost system is used on most vehicles to increase the brake pedal force. (See Chapter 9 for details on power brake assist units.)

Hydraulic System

The brake pedal force is transferred to the hydraulic system, where the force is directed through pipes and hoses to the wheel brakes.

Wheel Brakes

Hydraulic pressure from the hydraulic system moves a piston, in either a disc or drum brake system, that uses friction to press material against a rotating drum or rotor. The resulting friction slows the rotation of the wheels.

Brake Balance Control System

Mechanical, electrical, and hydraulic components are used to ensure that brakes are applied quickly and with balanced pressure for safe operation. Components in this category include metering valves, proportioning valves, and antilock braking system components.

Instrument Panel Warning Lights

The red brake warning lamp lights whenever a hydraulic system failure occurs. The amber ABS warning lamp or dim red brake light indicates an ABS self-test and/or a possible problem in the ABS system.

■ ANTILOCK BRAKE SYSTEM OPERATION

The purpose of an antilock braking system (ABS) is to prevent the wheels from locking during braking, especially on low-friction surfaces such as wet, icy, or snowy roads. Remember, it is the friction between the tire tread and the road that does the actual stopping of the vehicle. Therefore, ABS does not mean that a vehicle can stop quickly on all road surfaces. ABS uses sensors at the wheels to measure the wheel speed. If a wheel is rotating slower than the others, indicating possible lockup (for example, on an icy spot), the ABS computer will control the brake fluid pressure to that wheel for a fraction of a second. *A locked wheel has less traction to the road surface than a rotating wheel.*

The ABS computer can reapply the pressure from the master cylinder to the wheel a fraction of a second later. Therefore, if a wheel starts to lock up, the purpose of the ABS system is to pulse the brakes on and off to maintain directional stability with maximum braking force. Many ABS units will cause the brake pedal to pulse if the unit is working in the ABS mode. The pulsating brake pedal is a cause for concern for

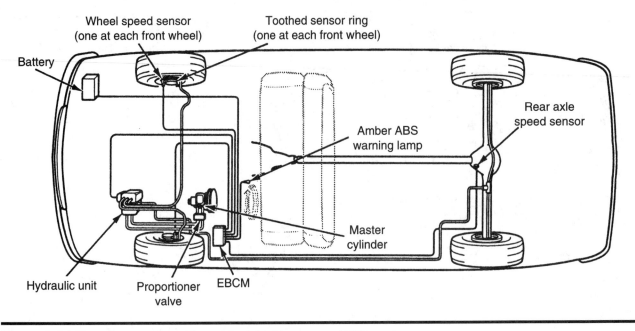

Figure 2–14 Typical components of an antilock braking system (ABS) used on a rear-wheel-drive vehicle. (Courtesy of General Motors)

some drivers; however, the pulsing brake pedal informs the driver that the ABS is being activated. Some ABS units use an isolator valve in the ABS unit to prevent brake pedal pulsations during ABS operation. With these types of systems, it is often difficult for the driver to know if and when the ABS unit is working to control a locking wheel. See Figure 2–14 for an overview of a typical ABS on a rear-wheel-drive vehicle.

Another symptom of normal ABS unit operation is the activation of the hydraulic pressure pump used by many ABS units. In some ABS units, the hydraulic pump is run every time the vehicle is started and moved. Other types of units operate randomly or whenever the pressure in the system calls for the pump to operate. See Chapters 10 and 11 for additional details on antilock braking systems.

■ BRAKE FLUID

Brake fluid boiling point is one of the most critical aspects and ratings for brake fluid. As brake fluid ages, it absorbs moisture, which lowers its boiling point and causes increased corrosion of the brake system components.

> **NOTE:** Because brake fluid absorbs moisture over time, many vehicle manufacturers recommend "changing the brake fluid" as part of the standard services to be performed routinely. The typical recommended brake fluid change interval is every two years or every 30,000 miles (48,000 km), whichever comes first. This is particularly important for vehicles equipped with an antilock braking system (ABS) because of the problem of expensive brake component wear or corrosion caused by contaminated brake fluid.

All automotive experts agree that brake fluid should be changed regularly as part of normal routine service. Even through the driver may not notice an immediate improvement, the reduced corrosion will eventually result in less money being spent for brake system component replacement in the future. Getting the old low-boiling-point brake fluid out of the system could prevent a total loss of brakes due to brake fluid boiling!

All brake fluids must be able to pass tests for:

1. Fluidity at low temperatures
2. Controlled percentage loss due to evaporation at high temperatures [tested at 212°F (100°C)]
3. Compatibility with other brake fluids
4. Resistance to oxidation
5. Specific effects on rubber, including:
   a. No disintegration
   b. No increase in hardness of the rubber tested
   c. Limited amount of decrease in hardness of the rubber

■ BRAKE FLUID TYPES

Brake fluid is made from a combination of various types of glycol, a non-petroleum-based fluid. Brake fluid is a polyalkylene-glycol-ether mixture called **polyglycol** for short. *All polyglycol brake fluid is clear to amber in color.* Brake fluid has to have the following characteristics:

1. A high boiling point
2. A low freezing point
3. Will not damage rubber parts in the brake system

Table 2–1 Automotive Brake Fluid Temperature Values

	DOT 3	DOT 4	DOT 5
Dry boiling point			
°F	401	446	500
°C	205	230	260
Wet boiling point			
°F	284	311	356
°C	140	155	180

> **CAUTION:** DOT 3 brake fluid is a very strong solvent and can remove paint! Care is required when working with DOT 3 brake fluid to avoid contact with the vehicle's painted surfaces. It also takes the color out of leather shoes.

■ BRAKE FLUID SPECIFICATIONS

All automotive brake fluid must meet federal Motor Vehicle Safety Standard 116. The Society of Automotive Engineers (SAE) and the Department of Transportation (DOT) have established brake fluid specification standards (see Table 2–1).

The wet boiling point is often referred to as ERBP, or equilibrium reflux boiling point. ERBP refers to the method in the specification (SAE J1703) by which the fluid is exposed to moisture and tested.

■ DOT 3

This brake fluid is the type most often used. There are, however, certain important characteristics.

1. DOT 3 absorbs moisture. According to SAE, DOT 3 can absorb 2 percent of its volume in water per year. Moisture is absorbed by the brake fluid through microscopic seams in the brake system and around seals. Over time, the water will corrode the system and thicken the brake fluid. The moisture can also cause a spongy brake pedal, due to reduced vapor-lock temperature (see Figure 2–15).
2. DOT 3 must be used from a sealed (capped) container. If allowed to remain open for any length of time, DOT 3 will absorb moisture from the surrounding air.
3. Always check the brake fluid recommendations on the top of the master cylinders of imported vehicles before adding DOT 3.

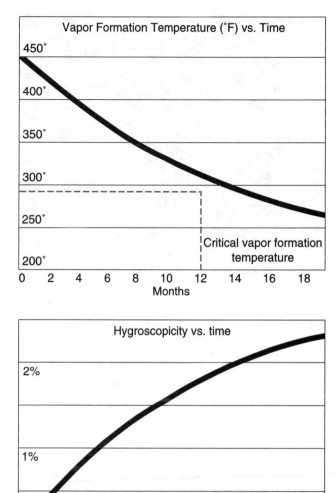

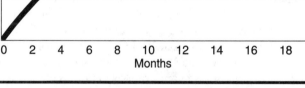

Figure 2–15 Brake fluid absorbs moisture from the air at the rate of about 2 percent per year. As the brake fluid absorbs water, its boiling temperature decreases.

■ DOT 4

This brake fluid is formulated for use by all vehicles, imported or domestic. It is commonly called LMA (low moisture absorption). DOT 4 does not absorb water as fast as DOT 3, but is still affected by moisture and should be used only from a sealed container. DOT 4 is approximately double the cost of DOT 3. *DOT 4 can be used wherever DOT 3 is specified* (see Figure 2–16).

■ DOT 5

This brake fluid is commonly called **silicone brake fluid** and is made from polydimethylsiloxanes. It does not absorb any water. This is called **nonhygroscopic.**

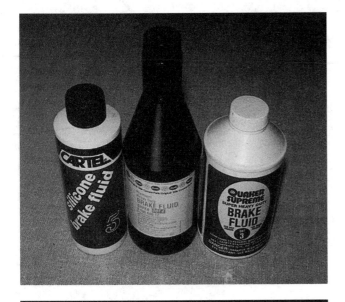

Figure 2–16 Brake fluid should be purchased in small containers to help prevent contamination and the possibility of moisture absorption after the container has been opened. On the left is silicone (DOT 5) brake fluid, with DOT 4 in the center and DOT 3 on the right.

Diagnostic Story 📖

The Sinking Brake Pedal

This author has experienced what happens when brake fluid is not changed regularly. Just as many technicians will tell you, we do not always do what we know should be done to our own vehicles.

While driving a four-year-old vehicle on vacation in very hot weather in mountainous country, the brake pedal sank to the floor. When the vehicle was cold, the brakes were fine. But after several brake applications, the pedal became soft and spongy and sank slowly to the floor if pressure was maintained on the brake pedal. Because the brakes were okay when cold, I knew it had to be boiling brake fluid. Old brake fluid (four years old) often has a boiling point under 300°F (150°C). With the air temperature near 100°F (38°C), it does not take much more heat to start boiling the brake fluid. After bleeding over a quart (1 liter) of new brake fluid through the system, the brakes worked normally. I'll never again forget to replace the brake fluid as recommended by the vehicle manufacturer. See Figure 2–17 for a tester that can be used to measure the boiling point of brake fluid.

NOTE: Even though DOT 5 does not normally absorb water, it is still tested using standardized SAE procedures in a humidity chamber. After a fixed amount of time, the brake fluid is measured for boiling point. Since it has had a chance to absorb moisture, the boiling point after this sequence is called the minimum wet boiling point.

NOTE: The characteristics of DOT 5 silicone brake fluid to absorb air is one of the major reasons why it is not recommended for use with an antilock braking system (ABS). In ABS, valves and pumps are used which can aerate the brake fluid. Brake fluid filled with air bubbles cannot properly lubricate the ABS components and will cause a low, soft brake pedal.

DOT 5 brake fluid is purple (violet) in color to distinguish it from DOT 3 or DOT 4 brake fluid. Silicones have about three times the amount of dissolved air as glycol fluids (about 15 percent of dissolved air versus only about 5 percent for standard glycol brake fluid). It is this characteristic of silicone brake fluid that causes the most concern about its use.

1. Silicone brake fluid has an affinity for air; therefore, it is more difficult to bleed the hydraulic system of trapped air.
2. The trapped air expands with increasing temperature. This causes the brake pedal to feel "mushy" because the pressure exerted on the hydraulic system simply compresses the air in the system and does not transfer the force to the wheel cylinders and calipers as it should.

3. The air trapped in the silicone brake fluid can also "off-gas" at high altitudes, causing a mushy brake pedal and reduced braking performance. DOT 5 brake fluid has been known to create a braking problem during high-altitude [over 5000 ft (1500 m)] and high-temperature driving. The high altitude tends to vaporize (off-gassing) some parts of the liquid, creating bubbles in the brake system, similar to having air in the brake system.
4. DOT 5 brake fluid should not be mixed with any other type of brake fluid. Therefore, the entire braking system must be completely flushed and refilled with DOT 5.
5. DOT 5 does not affect rubber parts and will not cause corrosion.
6. DOT 5 is expensive. It is approximately four times the cost of DOT 3 brake fluid.

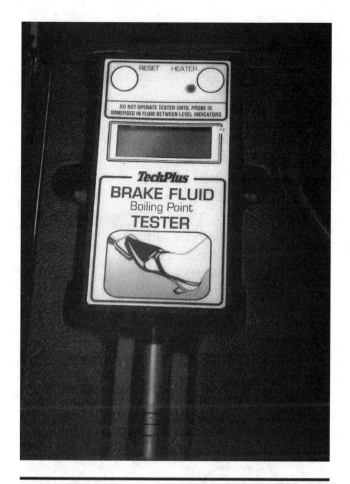

Figure 2–17 A brake fluid tester can test brake fluid for boiling point.

Figure 2–18 Both rubber sealing cups were exactly the same size. The cup on the left was exposed to mineral oil. Notice how the seal greatly expanded.

To help prevent hydraulic system mineral oil from being mixed with glycol brake fluid, *hydraulic mineral oils are green.*

■ BRAKE FLUID CONTAMINATION TEST

If brake fluid is mixed with any mineral oil, such as engine oil, power steering fluid, or automatic transmission fluid, rubber components will swell and cause brake system failure. To check for possible contamination, remove the reservoir cover from the master cylinder. If the rubber diaphragm is swelled or distorted, brake fluid contamination is likely. To check the brake fluid, use a Styrofoam cup filled with water. Place a teaspoon (1 ml) of brake fluid from the master cylinder into the water. Pure brake fluid will completely dissolve in the water. Petroleum or mineral oil fluids will float on the surface of the water and retain their color. Petroleum fluids will also dissolve the Styrofoam cup at the waterline. If the brake fluid is contaminated, the entire braking system must be drained and flushed and all rubber components replaced (see Figure 2–19).

■ HYDRAULIC SYSTEM MINERAL OIL

Some French-built Citroen and British-designed Rolls-Royce vehicles use hydraulic system mineral oil (HSMO) as part of their hydraulic control systems. The systems in these vehicles use a hydraulic pump to pressurize hydraulic oil for use in the suspension leveling and braking systems.

> **CAUTION:** Mineral hydraulic oil should never be used in a braking system that requires DOT 3 or DOT 4 polyglycol-based brake fluid. If any mineral oil, such as engine oil, transmission oil, or automatic transmission fluid (ATF), gets into a braking system that requires glycol brake fluid, every rubber part in the entire braking system must be replaced. Mineral oil causes the rubber compounds that are used in glycol brake fluid systems to swell (see Figure 2–18).

■ BRAKE FLUID SERVICE PROCEDURES AND PRECAUTIONS

1. Store brake fluid only in its original container.

> **HINT:** To help prevent possible contamination with moisture, air, or other products, purchase brake fluid in small containers. Keep all brake fluid containers tightly closed to prevent air (containing moisture) from being absorbed.

2. Before opening a brake fluid container, remove any dirt, moisture, or other contamination from the top and outside of the container.

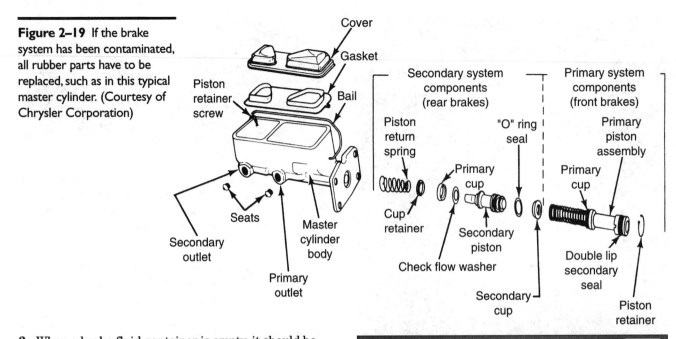

Figure 2–19 If the brake system has been contaminated, all rubber parts have to be replaced, such as in this typical master cylinder. (Courtesy of Chrysler Corporation)

3. When a brake fluid container is empty, it should be discarded—the container should never be used for anything except brake fluid.
4. Do not transfer brake fluid to any other container that may have contained oil, kerosene, gasoline, antifreeze, water, cleaners, or any other liquids or chemicals.
5. Do not reuse brake fluid that has been siphoned from another vehicle or drawn out during a brake bleeding operation. (Brake bleeding means to open special bleeder valves in the hydraulic system to rid the system of any trapped air.)
6. Use only fresh new brake fluid for flushing the hydraulic brake system.

> **CAUTION:** Alcohol or flushing fluids should not be used because they cannot be totally removed and will contaminate the system. Disassembled parts, however, can and should be cleaned with denatured alcohol or spray brake cleaner where the parts can be visually inspected to be free of cleaning solutions.

■ BRAKE FLUID HANDLING CONSIDERATIONS

Polyglycol brake fluid presents little toxicity hazard, but for some individuals, brake fluid may produce moderate eye and skin irritation. For good safety practice, protective clothing and safety glasses or goggles should be worn.

■ BRAKE FLUID DISPOSAL

Current EPA laws permit used brake fluid to be disposed of with used engine oil. Brake fluid spilled on the floor should be cleaned up using absorbent material

Diagnostic Story

The Pike's Peak Brake Inspection

All vehicles must stop about halfway down Pike's Peak mountain in Colorado [14,110 ft (4300 m)] for a "brake inspection." When this author stopped at the inspection station, a uniformed inspector simply looked at the right front wheel and waved us on. I pulled over and asked the inspector what he was checking. He said that when linings and drums/rotors get hot, the vehicle loses brake effectiveness. But if the brake fluid boils, the vehicle loses its brakes entirely. The inspector was listening for boiling brake fluid at the front wheel and feeling for heat about 1 ft (30 cm) from the wheel. If the inspector felt heat 1 ft away from the brakes, the brakes were definitely too hot to continue, and you would be instructed to pull over and wait for the brakes to cool. The inspector recommended placing the transmission into a lower gear, which uses the engine to slow the vehicle during the descent without having to rely entirely on the brakes.

and the material disposed of in the regular trash. Brake fluid becomes a hazardous waste if spilled onto open ground, where it can seep into groundwater. The disposal requirements for brake fluid spilled onto open ground varies with the exact amount spilled and other factors. Refer to local EPA guidelines and requirements for the exact rules and regulations in your area.

■ RUBBER TYPES

Vehicles use a wide variety of rubber in the braking system, suspension system, steering system, and engine.

Table 2–2 Rubber Compatibility Chart

Name	Abbreviations	OK	Not OK	Uses
Ethylene propylene diene (developed in 1963)	EPM, EPDM, EPR	Brake fluid, silicone fluids	Petroleum fluids	Most brake system seals and parts
Styrene, butadiene (developed in 1920s)	SBR, BUNA S, GRS	Brake fluid, silicone fluids, alcohols	Petroleum fluids	Some drum brake seals, O-rings
Nitrile (nitrile butadiene rubber)	NBR, BUNA N	Petroleum fluids, ethylene glycol (antifreeze)	Brake fluid	Engine seals, O-rings
Neoprene (polychloroprene)	CR	Refrigerants (Freons: R-12 and R-134a), petroleum fluids	Brake fluids	Refrigerant, O-rings
Polyacrylate	ACM	Petroleum fluids, automatic transmission fluids	Brake fluids	Automatic transmission and engine seals
Viton (fluorocarbon)	FKM	Petroleum fluids	Brake fluid, 134a refrigerant	Engine seals, fuel system parts
Natural rubber	NR	Water, brake fluid	Petroleum fluids	Tires

Rubber products are called **elastomers.** Some are oil- and grease-resistant elastomers and can be harmed by brake fluid, while others are brake fluid resistant and can swell or expand if they come in contact with oil or grease. See Table 2–2 for types and compatible fluids.

See Figures 2-20 through 2-22 for examples of where rubber is used in the braking system. Brake fluid (DOT 3 or DOT 4 glycol brake fluid) affects all elastomers and causes a slight swelling effect (about 5 percent). This swelling action is necessary for the seals to withstand high hydraulic pressures. Silicone (DOT 5) brake fluid does not cause rubber to swell; therefore, a rubber swell additive is used in silicone brake fluid.

While these additives work well for EPDM rubber, it can cause SBR rubber to swell too much. Although most seals today use EPDM, many drum brakes still use SBR seals. This is a major reason that DOT 5 brake fluid is not recommended by many vehicle manufacturers.

■ BRAKE LINING COMPOSITION

Friction materials such as disc brake pads or drum brake shoes contain a mixture of ingredients. These materials include a binder such as a thermosetting resin, fibers for reinforcement, and friction modifiers to obtain a desired

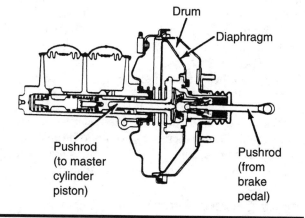

Figure 2–20 The master cylinder piston seals are usually constructed from EPDM rubber and the diaphragm of the vacuum power brake booster is usually made from SBR.

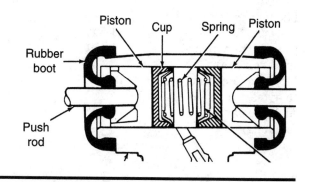

Figure 2–21 Cross-sectional view of a typical drum brake wheel cylinder. Most wheel cylinder boots and cups are either SBR or EPDM rubber.

Figure 2–22 Exploded view of a typical disc brake caliper. Both the caliper seal and dust boot are constructed of EPDM rubber.

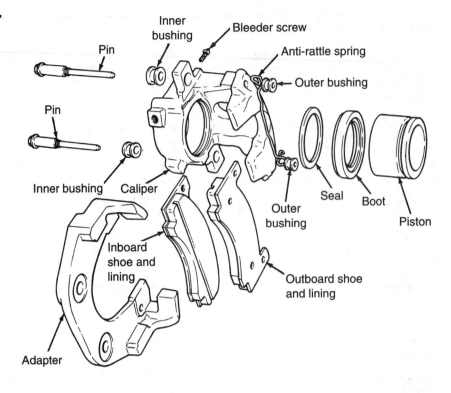

Figure 2–23 An integrally molded disc brake pad that has been worn down to the steel backing plate. Note that the lining was molded into holes in the backing plate and even though the lining was worn beyond normal replacement thickness, the lining remained attached to the steel backing.

HOLES IN BACKING PLATE OF DISC BRAKE PAD

coefficient of friction (m). The various ingredients in brake lining are mixed and molded into the shape of the finished product. The fibers in the material are the only thing holding this mixture together. A large press is used to force the ingredients together to form a **brake block,** which eventually becomes the brake lining. Many disc brake pads are **integrally molded** (see Figure 2–23).

Typical Compositions for Asbestos (Organic) Lining

Ingredient	Typical Formula Range
Phenolic resin (binder)	9–15%
Asbestos fiber	30–50%
Organic friction modifiers (rubber scrap)	8–19%
Inorganic friction modifiers (barytes, talc, whiting)	12–26%
Abrasive particles (alumina)	4–20%
Carbon	4–20%

Semimetallic Friction Material

The term *semimetallic* refers to brake lining material that uses metal rather than asbestos in its formulation. It still uses resins and binders and is, therefore, not 100 percent metal, but rather, semimetallic. Semimetallics are commonly called **semi-mets.** The metal in most metallic linings is made from metal particles that have been fused together without melting. This process is called **sintering** and the result is called **sintered metal** linings (see Figure 2–24).

Ingredient	Formula range
Phenolic resin	15–40%
Graphite or carbon particles	15–40%
Steel fibers	0–25%
Ceramic powders	2–10%
Steel, copper, brass metal powders	15–40%
Other modifiers (rubber scrap)	0–20%

Most semimetallic linings do not contain asbestos. Semimetallic linings require a very smooth finish on the rotor because the metal in the lining does not conform to the surface of the rotor, as does asbestos lining.

Nonasbestos Friction Material

Brake pads and linings that use synthetic material such as aramid fibers instead of steel are usually referred to as **nonasbestos, nonasbestos organic (NAO),** or

Figure 2–24 Poor-quality semimetallic disc brake pad. The screwdriver is pointing to large chunks of steel embedded in the lining.

Figure 2–25 Typical drum brake lining edge code.

nonasbestos synthetic (NAS). Linings are called **synthetic** because synthetic (man-made) fibers are used. These linings use **aramid fiber** instead of metal as the base material. Aramid is the generic name for aromatic polyamide fibers. **Kevlar** is the Dupont brand name of aramid and a registered trademark of E.I. Dupont de Nemours and Company. Nonasbestos linings are often quieter than semimetallics and do not cause as much wear to brake rotors as do semimetallic pads.

Carbon Fiber Friction Material

Carbon fiber brake lining is the newest and most expensive of the lining materials. Carbon fiber material is often called **carbon fiber–reinforced carbon (CFRC).** It is composed of a carbon mix into which reinforcing carbon fibers are embedded. CFRC is commonly used in the brakes of jet aircraft and racing cars. CFRC brakes provide constant friction coefficient whether cold or hot, low wear rates, and low noise development.

■ LINING EDGE CODES

The edge coding contains three groups of letters and numbers:

- The first group is a series of letters that identify the manufacturer of the lining.
- The second group is a series of numbers, letters, or both that identify the lining compound or formula. This code is usually known to the manufacturer of the lining material and helps them identify the lining after manufacture.
- The third group is two letters that identify the coefficient of friction (see Figures 2–25 and 2–26).

The coefficient of friction is a pure number that indicates the amount of friction between two surfaces. A coefficient of friction will always be less than 1 and the higher the number, the greater the amount of friction between two surfaces. (For example, a material with 0.55 coefficient of friction has more friction than a material with a coefficient of friction of 0.39.)

These codes were established by the Society of Automotive Engineers (SAE):

Code C	0.00 to 0.15
Code D	0.15 to 0.25
Code E	0.25 to 0.35
Code F	0.35 to 0.45
Code G	0.45 to 0.55
Code H	0.55 and above
Code Z	ungraded

The first letter, which is printed on the side of most linings, indicates its coefficient of friction when brakes are cold, and the second letter indicates the coefficient of friction of the brake lining when the brakes are hot. (For example, FF indicates that the brake lining material has a coefficient of friction between 0.35 and 0.45 when both cold and hot.)

These letters should not be interpreted to mean the relative quality of the lining material. Lining wear, fade resistance, tensile strength, heat recovery rate, wet friction, noise, and coefficient of friction must be considered when purchasing high-quality linings. Unfortunately, there are no standards that a purchaser can check regarding all of these other considerations. For best brake performance, always purchase the best-quality name-brand linings that you can afford.

> **HINT:** While many brands of replacement brake lining provide acceptable stopping power and long life, purchasing factory brake lining from a dealer is usually the best opportunity to get lining material that meets all vehicle requirements. Aftermarket linings are not required by federal law to meet performance or wear standards that are required of original factory brake linings.

Figure 2–26 Even the lining that cannot be seen is labeled. This drum brake lining has been formed and drilled and is ready to be assembled (riveted) to steel brake shoes. This photo was taken at the Delphi (Delco) Chassis Brake Division Plant in Dayton, Ohio.

■ REPLACEMENT LINING RECIPE

The actual amount of each ingredient in typical brake lining is varied for each application. Each vehicle has its own "recipe" based on vehicle weight and options. For example, a Chevrolet with a light four-cylinder engine and no air conditioning may use a different brake lining recipe than the same vehicle, but with the heavier V-6 engine, air conditioning, and other options that increase the vehicle weight. Both of these brake linings (shoes or pads) may physically fit other similar vehicles, yet their brake lining recipe is different.

Replacement linings are usually a compromise "generic" recipe that will give acceptable service. The brake lining recipe is just one of many factors that results in the fact that new brakes always seem to last longer than any replacement lining. Replacement lining should have the same friction code as the original. Although this will not guarantee the same braking performance, this edge code rating does help assure the service technician that the replacement brakes will give "as new" performance.

■ THE DANGERS OF EXPOSURE TO ASBESTOS

Friction materials such as brake and clutch linings often contain asbestos. Although asbestos has been eliminated from most original equipment friction materials, the automotive service technician cannot know whether the vehicle being serviced is equipped with friction materials con-

TECH TIP ✔

Competitively Priced Brakes

The term "competitively priced" means lower cost. Most brake manufacturers offer "premium" as well as lower-price linings, to remain competitive with other manufacturers or with importers of brake lining material produced overseas by U.S. or foreign companies. Organic asbestos brake lining is inexpensive to manufacture. In fact, according to warehouse distributors and importers, the box often costs more than the brake lining inside!

Professional brake service technicians should only install brake linings and pads that will give braking performance equal to that of the original factory brakes. "Competitive" asbestos linings should never be substituted for semimetallic or NAO original linings or pads. For best results, always purchase high-quality brake parts from a known brand-name manufacturer.

taining asbestos. It is important that all friction materials be handled as if they do contain asbestos.

Asbestos exposure can cause scar tissue to form in the lungs. This condition is called **asbestosis.** It causes gradually increasing shortness of breath and permanent scarring to the lungs.

Even low exposures to asbestos can cause **mesothelioma,** a type of fatal cancer of the lining of the chest or abdominal cavity. Asbestos exposure can also increase the risk of **lung cancer** as well as cancer of the voice box, stomach, and large intestine. It usually takes fifteen to thirty years or more for cancer or asbestos lung scarring to show up after exposure. (Scientists call this the **latency period.**)

Government agencies recommend that asbestos exposure should be eliminated or controlled to the lowest level possible. These agencies have developed recommendations and standards that the automotive service technician and equipment manufacturer should follow. These U.S. federal agencies include the National Institute for Occupational Safety and Health (NIOSH), Occupational Safety and Health Administration (OSHA), and Environmental Protection Agency (EPA).

■ OSHA STANDARDS

The Occupational Safety and Health Administration (OSHA) has established three levels of asbestos exposure. Any vehicle service establishment that does either brake or clutch work must limit employee exposure to asbestos to less than 0.2 fibers per cubic centimeter (cc) as determined by an air sample.

If the level of exposure to employees is greater than specified, corrective measures must be performed and a large fine may be imposed.

> **NOTE:** Research has found that worn asbestos fibers such as from automotive brakes or clutches may not be as hazardous as first believed. Worn asbestos fibers do not have sharp flared ends that can latch onto tissue, but rather are worn down to a dust form that resembles talc. Grinding or sawing operations on unworn brake shoes or clutch discs *will* contain *harmful* asbestos fibers. To limit health damage, always use proper handling procedures while working around any component that may contain asbestos.

■ EPA REGULATIONS OF ASBESTOS

The federal Environmental Protection Agency (EPA) has established procedures for the removal and disposal of asbestos. The EPA procedures require that products containing asbestos be "wetted" to prevent the asbestos fibers from becoming airborne. According to the EPA, asbestos-containing materials can be disposed of as regular waste—only when asbestos becomes airborne is it considered to be hazardous.

■ ASBESTOS HANDLING GUIDELINES

The air in the shop area can be tested by a testing laboratory, but this can be expensive. Tests have determined that asbestos levels can easily be kept below the recommended levels by using a solvent or a special vacuum.

> **NOTE:** Even though asbestos is being removed from brake lining materials, the service technician cannot tell whether the old brake pads or shoes contain asbestos. Therefore, to be safe, the technician should assume that all brake pads or shoes contain asbestos.

HEPA Vacuum A special high-efficiency particulate air (HEPA) vacuum system has been proven to be effective in keeping asbestos exposure levels below 0.1 fibers per cubic centimeter.

Solvent Spray Many technicians use an aerosol can of brake cleaning solvent to wet the brake dust and prevent it from becoming airborne. Commercial brake cleaners are available that use a concentrated cleaner that is mixed with water (see Figure 2–27).

The waste liquid is filtered, and when dry, the filter can be disposed of as solid waste.

Figure 2–27 Portable brake wash units are popular because the brakes can be wetted down before removal of the brake drum or caliper, reducing the chances of airborne brake dust. (Courtesy of Clayton)

Frequently Asked Question ???

What Does "D³EA" Mean?

Original equipment brake pads and shoes are required to comply with the Federal Motor Vehicle Safety Standard (FMVSS) 105 which specifies maximum stopping distances. There is also a requirement for fade resistance, but no standard for noise or wear. Aftermarket (replacement) brake pads and shoes are not required to meet the FMVSS standard. However, several manufacturers of replacement brake pads and shoes are using a standardized test that closely matches the FMVSS standard and is called the "Dual Dynamometer Differential Effectiveness Analysis" or D³EA. This test is currently voluntary and linings that pass the test can have a "D³EA certified" seal placed on the product package.

CAUTION: Never use compressed air to blow brake dust. The fine talclike brake dust can create a health hazard even if asbestos is not present or is present in dust rather than fiber form.

Disposal of Brake Dust and Brake Shoes

The hazard of asbestos occurs when asbestos fibers are airborne. Once the asbestos has been wetted down, it is currently considered to be solid waste, and not hazardous waste. Old brake shoes and pads should be enclosed, preferably in a plastic bag, to help prevent any of the brake material from becoming airborne. *Always follow current federal and local laws considering disposal of all waste.*

■ SUMMARY

1. Brakes stop wheels—not vehicles.
2. The amount of friction between two surfaces is called the coefficient of friction and is represented by a number 0 to 1 where 0 means no friction and 1 represents maximum friction between the surfaces.
3. The six brake subsystems include: apply system, boost system, hydraulic system, wheel brakes, brake balance control system, which includes ABS, and instrument panel warning lights.
4. All brake fluid is specified by DOT and SAE. DOT 3 brake fluid is the most commonly recommended brake fluid for all types of vehicles.
5. An antilock braking system (ABS) pulses the hydraulic force to the wheels to prevent the tires from locking up. A locked tire has lower friction than a rolling tire.

■ REVIEW QUESTIONS

1. Explain how hydraulic pressure is used to stop the rotation of the wheels.
2. Explain the coefficient of friction.
3. List the coefficient of friction edge codes.
4. Describe brake fluid and how it should be used and handled.
5. Explain how ABS units prevent wheel lockup.

■ ASE CERTIFICATION-TYPE QUESTIONS

1. Disc brakes use replaceable friction material called
   a. Linings
   b. Pads
2. A wheel that locks up during braking
   a. Has less friction than a rolling tire
   b. Results in straighter stops
   c. Results in shorter stops
   d. Has more friction to the road than a rolling tire
3. The front brakes handle about what percentage of braking on a front-wheel-drive vehicle?
   a. 50 percent
   b. 60 percent
   c. 70 percent
   d. 80 percent
4. Deceleration rate is measured in what units?
   a. Miles per hour
   b. Feet per second
   c. Feet per second per second
   d. Square feet per mile per hour
5. What kind of rubber is used mostly in the hydraulic braking system?
   a. EPM
   b. Nitrile
   c. Neoprene
   d. Polyacrylate
6. The letters "EF" on the edge of brake lining mean
   a. Wear resistance codes
   b. Relative noise level codes
   c. Coefficient of friction codes
   d. Brake lining recipes
7. What type of brake fluid is recommended by almost every vehicle manufacturer?
   a. DOT 2
   b. DOT 3
   c. DOT 4
   d. DOT 5

8. Brake fluid should be kept in a closed container because
   a. Dirt can get into brake fluid if the top is off of the container
   b. Brake fluid can turn to acid if exposed to air
   c. Brake fluid absorbs moisture from the air and lowers its boiling point
   d. Brake fluid evaporates rapidly

9. If automatic transmission fluid or power steering fluid gets into a master cylinder, all of the rubber parts must be replaced because
   a. The rubber seals will shrink in size and cause internal leaks
   b. The rubber seals will stretch in size and cause external leaks
   c. The rubber seals will swell and cause brake failure
   d. The rubber seals will melt and cause brake failure

10. An owner of a vehicle equipped with ABS brakes complained that whenever he tried to stop on icy or slippery roads, the brake pedal would pulse up and down rapidly. Technician A says that this is normal for many ABS units. Technician B says that the ABS unit is malfunctioning. Which technician is correct?
    a. Technician A only
    b. Technician B only
    c. Both Technician A and B
    d. Neither Technician A nor B

Master Cylinders and Hydraulic System Diagnosis and Service

Objectives: After studying Chapter 3, the reader should be able to:

1. Describe the function, purpose, and operation of the master cylinder.
2. Explain how hydraulic force can be used to supply high pressures to each individual wheel brake.
3. Describe the process of troubleshooting master cylinders and related brake hydraulic components.
4. List the purposes and functions of the metering valve and proportional valve.
5. Discuss the methods that can be used to bleed the hydraulic braking system.

The master cylinder is the heart of the entire braking system. No braking occurs until the driver depresses the brake pedal. The brake pedal linkage is used to apply the force of the driver's foot into a closed hydraulic system.

■ BRAKE PEDAL MECHANICAL ADVANTAGE

The first thing that happens when the driver steps on the brake pedal is that the force measured in pounds (lb.) or Newtons (N) is transmitted through linkage to the master cylinder. The normal stroke distance of a brake pedal is about 1.5″ (3.8 cm), yet the total pedal travel should not exceed 4″ (10 cm). Because of the off-set relationship of the pivot point (called the **fulcrum**) of the brake pedal mechanism, the force exerted into the master cylinder is increased by almost three times (the average for all vehicles being 2.7:1). See Figure 3–1.

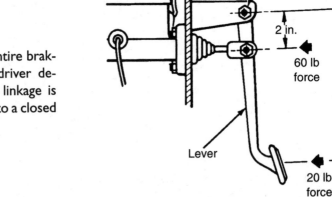

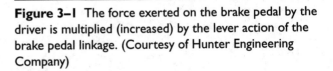

Figure 3–1 The force exerted on the brake pedal by the driver is multiplied (increased) by the lever action of the brake pedal linkage. (Courtesy of Hunter Engineering Company)

Figure 3–2 Hydraulic brake lines transfer the brake effort to each brake assembly attached to all four wheels. (Courtesy of General Motors)

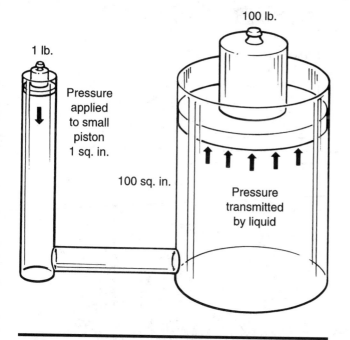

100 lb.

1 lb.

Pressure applied to small piston 1 sq. in.

100 sq. in.

Pressure transmitted by liquid

Figure 3–3 A 1-lb. force exerted on a small piston in a sealed system transfers the pressure to each square inch throughout the system. In this example, the 1-lb. force is able to lift a 100-lb. weight because it is supported by a piston that is 100 times larger in area then the small piston.

■ THE HYDRAULIC BRAKING SYSTEM

All braking systems require that a driver's force is transmitted to the drum or rotor attached to each wheel (see Figure 3–2). The force that can be exerted on the brake pedal varies due to the strength and size of the driver. Engineers design braking systems to require less than 150 lb. of force (660 N) from the driver, yet provide the force necessary to stop a heavy vehicle from high speed.

■ PASCAL'S LAW

The hydraulic principles that permit a brake system to function were discovered by a French physicist, Blaise Pascal (1632–1662). He discovered that "when a force is applied to a liquid confined in a container or an enclosure, the pressure is transmitted equal and undiminished in every direction." To help understand this principle, assume that a force of 10 pounds (lb.) is exerted on a piston with a surface area of 1 square inch (sq. in.). Since this *force* measured in pounds (lb.) or Newtons (N) is applied to a piston with an area measured in square inches, the *pressure* is the force times the area or "10 pounds per square inch" (psi). It is this "pressure" that is transmitted, without loss, throughout the entire hydraulic system (see Figure 3–3).

Pascal's Law can be stated mathematically:

$F = P \times A$ or $P = F/A$ or $A = F/P$
F = force (lb.) (Newtons)
P = pressure in lb. per sq. in. kilo Pascals (kPa)
A = area in sq. in. (cm^2)

A practical example involves a master cylinder with a piston area of 1 sq. in. and one wheel cylinder also with an area of 1 sq. in. and one wheel cylinder with a piston area of 2 sq. in. (see Figure 3–4).

What is nice about hydraulics is that the applied force can be sent to more than one wheel cylinder.

The real "magic" of a hydraulic brake system is the fact that different forces can be created at different wheel cylinders. More force is necessary for front brakes than for rear brakes because as the brakes are applied, the weight of the vehicle moves forward.

Larger (area) pistons are used in wheel cylinders (calipers, if disc brakes) on the front wheels to increase the force used to apply the front brakes.

Not only can hydraulics act as a "force machine" (by varying piston size), but the hydraulic system also can be varied to change piston stroke distances.

Figure 3–4 The amount of force on the piston is the result of pressure multiplied by the surface area. (Courtesy of General Motors)

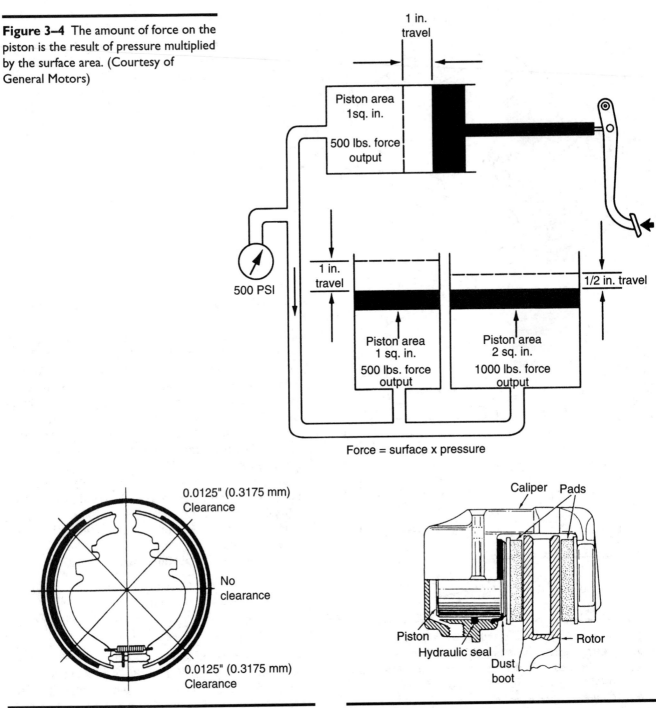

Force = surface x pressure

Figure 3–5 Drum brake illustrating the typical clearance between the brake shoes (friction material) and the rotating brake drum represented as the outermost black circle. (Courtesy of Cooper Industries)

Figure 3–6 The brake pad (friction material) is pressed on both sides of the rotating rotor by the hydraulic pressure of the caliper. (Courtesy of EIS Brake Parts)

On a typical vehicle, a driver-input force of 150 lb. (660 N) is boosted both mechanically (through the brake pedal linkage) and by the power booster to a fluid pressure of about 1700 psi (11,700 kPa). During a typical brake application only about *1 teaspoon (5 ml or cc) of brake fluid* actually is moved from the master cylinder and into the hydraulic system to cause the pressure build-up to occur. With a drum brake, the

wheel cylinder expands and pushes the brake shoes against a brake drum. *The distance the shoes move is only about 0.005–0.012" (5 to 12 thousandths of an inch) (0.015–0.30 mm).* See Figure 3–5.

With a disc brake, brake fluid pressure pushes on the piston in the caliper a small amount and causes a clamping of the disc brake pads against both sides of a rotor (disc). See Figure 3–6. **The typical distance the**

Is Bigger Better?

A vehicle owner wanted better braking performance from his off-road race vehicle. Thinking that a larger master cylinder would help, a technician replaced the original 1″-bore-diameter master cylinder with a larger master cylinder with a 1 1/8″ bore diameter.

After bleeding the system, the technician was anxious to test-drive the "new" brake system. During the test drive the technician noticed that the brake pedal "grabbed" much higher than with the original master cylinder. This delighted the technician. The owner of the vehicle was also delighted until he tried to stop from highway speed. *The driver had to use both feet to stop!*

The technician realized, after the complaint, that the larger master cylinder was able to move more brake fluid, but with *less* pressure to the wheel cylinders. The new master cylinder gave the impression of better brakes because the fluid was moved into the wheel cylinders (and calipers) quickly, and the pads and shoes contacted the rotor and drums sooner because of the greater volume of brake fluid moved by the larger pistons in the master cylinder.

To calculate the difference in pressure between the original (stock) master cylinder and the larger replacement, the technician used Pascal's Law with the following results:

Original master cylinder (1″ bore)

$$\text{pressure} = \frac{\text{force}}{\text{area}}$$

$$\text{psi} = \frac{450 \text{ lb.}}{\text{area}} \text{ (typical)}$$

$$\text{area} = \pi r^2 = 3.14 \times .5^2$$
$$(\tfrac{1}{2} \text{ of } 1″)$$

$$\text{area} = 3.14 \times 0.25$$

$$\text{area} = 0.785 \text{ sq in.}$$

$$\text{pressure} = \frac{450}{0.785} = 573 \text{ psi}$$

Replacement master cylinder (1 1/8″ bore)

$$\text{pressure} = \frac{\text{force}}{\text{area}}$$

$$\text{psi} = \frac{450 \text{ lb.}}{\text{area}} \text{ (typical)}$$

$$\text{area} = \pi r^2 = 3.14 \times 0.5625^2$$
$$(\tfrac{1}{2} \text{ of } 1\tfrac{1}{8}″)$$

$$\text{area} = 3.14 \times 0.316$$

$$\text{area} = 0.992 \text{ sq. in.}$$

$$\text{pressure} = \frac{450}{0.992} = 454 \text{ psi}$$

The difference in pressure is 119 psi less with the larger master cylinder (573 − 454 = 119).

The stopping power of the brakes was reduced because the larger diameter master cylinder piston produced lower pressure (the same force was spread over a larger area and this means that the pressure [psi] is less).

All master cylinders are sized correctly from the factory for the correct braking effort, pressure, pedal travel, and stopping ability. *A technician should never change the sizing of any hydraulic brake component on any vehicle!*

---

pads move is only about 0.001–0.003″ (1 to 3 thousandths of an inch) (0.025–0.076 mm).

■ MASTER CYLINDER RESERVOIRS

Most vehicles built since the early 1980s are equipped with see-through master cylinder reservoirs, which permit owners and service technicians to check the brake fluid level without having to remove the top of the reservoir. Some countries have laws that require this type of reservoir (see Figure 3–7).

The reservoir capacity is great enough to allow for the brakes to become completely worn out and still have enough reserve for safe operation. The typical capacity of the entire braking system is usually 2 to 3 pints (1 to 1.5 liters). Vehicles equipped with four-wheel disc brakes usually hold 4 pints (2 liters) or more.

■ MASTER CYLINDER RESERVOIR DIAPHRAGM

The entire brake system is filled with brake fluid up to the "full" level of the master cylinder reservoir.

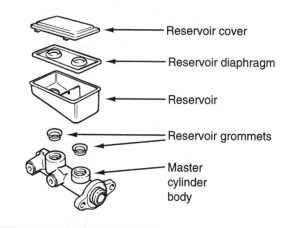

Reservoir cover
Reservoir diaphragm
Reservoir
Reservoir grommets
Master cylinder body

Figure 3–7 Typical master cylinder showing the reservoir and associated parts. The reservoir diaphragm lays directly on top of the brake fluid which helps keep air from the surface of the brake fluid because brake fluid easily absorbs moisture from the air. (Courtesy of Allied Signal Automotive Aftermarket)

CAUTION: The master cylinder should never be filled higher than the recommended full mark to allow for brake fluid expansion that occurs normally when the brake fluid gets hot due to the heat generated by the brakes.

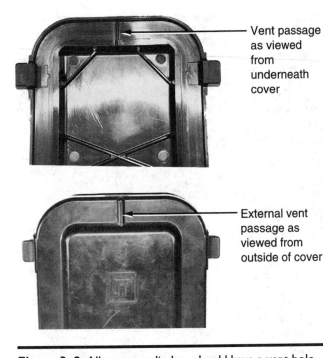

Vent passage as viewed from underneath cover

External vent passage as viewed from outside of cover

Figure 3–8 All master cylinders should have a vent hole on the outside cover that allows air between the cover and the rubber diaphragm.

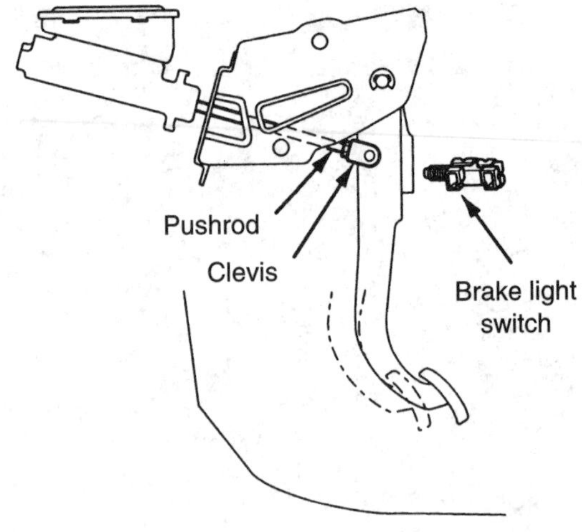

The reservoir is vented to the atmosphere so the fluid can expand and contract without difficulty as would be the case if the reservoir were sealed.

Being open to the atmosphere, however, allows the possibility of moisture-laden air coming in contact with the brake fluid! This moisture in the air is readily and rapidly absorbed into the brake fluid because brake fluid has an affinity (attraction) to moisture (water).

Master cylinders use a rubber diaphragm or floating disc to help seal outside air from direct contact with brake fluid and still allow the brake fluid to expand and contract as the fluid heats up and cools down during normal brake system operation. This rubber diaphragm is vented between the steel cap and diaphragm. As the

Pushrod

Clevis

Brake light switch

Figure 3–9 The typical brake pedal is supported by a mount and attached to the pushrod by a U-shaped bracket. The pin used to retain the clevis to the brake pedal is usually called a clevis pin. (Courtesy of General Motors)

brake fluid level drops due to normal disc brake pad wear, the rubber diaphragm also lowers to remain like a second skin on top of the brake fluid.

Whenever adding brake fluid, push the rubber diaphragm back up into the cover. Normal atmospheric pressure will allow the diaphragm to return to its normal position on top of the brake fluid. Whenever servicing a brake system, be sure to check that the vent hole is clear on the cover to allow air to get between the cover and the diaphragm (see Figure 3–8).

■ MASTER CYLINDER OPERATION

The master cylinder is the heart of any hydraulic braking system. Brake pedal movement and force are trans-

Figure 3–10 This cast iron master cylinder is equipped with bleeder valves for both the primary and secondary pressure-building chambers.

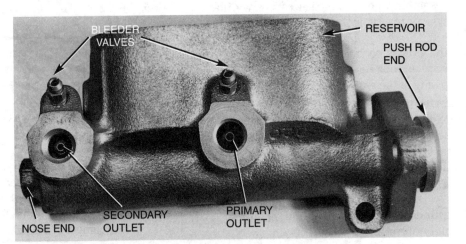

BLEEDER VALVES

RESERVOIR

PUSH ROD END

NOSE END

SECONDARY OUTLET

PRIMARY OUTLET

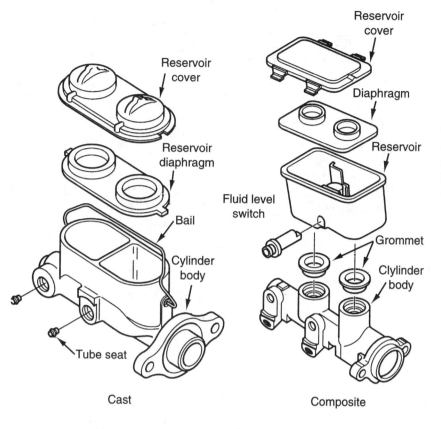

Reservoir cover

Reservoir diaphragm

Bail

Cylinder body

Tube seat

Cast

Reservoir cover

Diaphragm

Reservoir

Fluid level switch

Grommet

Clylinder body

Composite

Figure 3–11 Note the cast iron master cylinder (left) uses a wire reservoir cover clamp called a **bail.** The composite master cylinder is made from two different materials—aluminum for the body and plastic materials for the reservoir and reservoir cover. This type of reservoir feeds both primary and secondary chambers, and therefore uses a fluid level switch that activates the red dash warning lamp if the brake fluid level drops.

TECH TIP ✔

Too Much Is Bad

Some vehicle owners or inexperienced service people may fill the master cylinder to the top. Master cylinders should only be filled to the "MAXIMUM" level line or about 1/4" (6 mm) from the top to allow room for expansion when the brake fluid gets hot during normal operation. If the master cylinder is filled to the top, the expanding brake fluid has no place to expand and the pressure increases. This increased pressure can cause the brakes to "self-apply," shortening brake friction material life and increasing fuel consumption. Overheated brakes can result and the brake fluid may boil, causing a total loss of braking.

---

ferred to the brake fluid and directed to wheel cylinders or calipers (see Figure 3–9). The master cylinder is also separated into two pressure-building chambers (or circuit) to provide braking force to one-half of the brake in the event of a leak or damage to one circuit (see Figures 3–10 and 3–11).

Both pressure-building sections of the master cylinder contain two holes from the reservoir. The Society of Automotive Engineers (SAE) term for the for-

ward (tapered) hole is the **vent port,** and the rearward straight drilled hole is called the **replenishing port** (see Figure 3–12).

Various vehicle and brake component manufacturers call these ports by various names. For example, the **vent port** is the high-pressure port. This tapered forward hole is also called the **compensating port** or **bypass** (a GM term).

The **replenishing port** is the low-pressure rearward, larger diameter hole. The inlet port is also called the **bypass port, filler port, breather port,** or **compensating port** (a GM term).

The function of the master cylinder can be explained from the at-rest, applied, and released positions.

At-Rest Position The primary sealing cups are between the compensating port hole and the inlet port hole. In this position, the brake fluid is free to expand and move from the calipers, wheel cylinders, and brake lines up into the reservoir through the vent port (compensation port) if the temperature rises and the fluid expands. If the fluid was trapped, the pressure of the brake fluid would increase with temperature causing the brakes to **self-apply** (see Figure 3–13). The pistons (primary and secondary) are retained by a clip at the pushrod end and held in position by return springs.

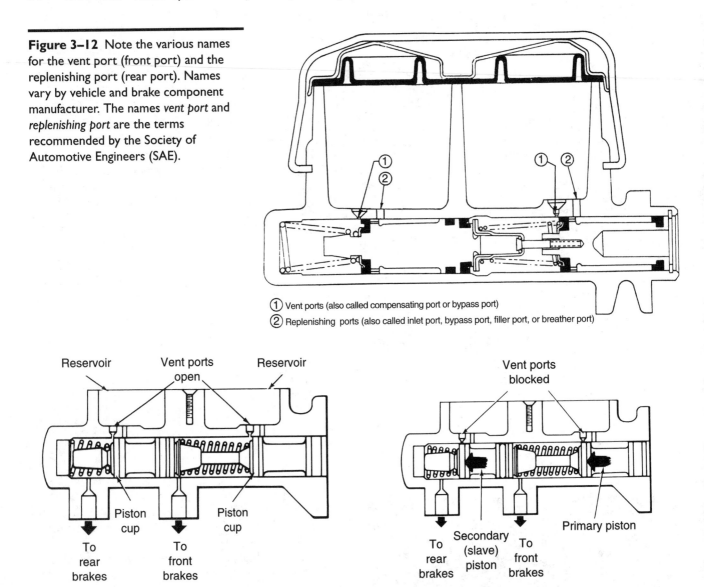

Figure 3–12 Note the various names for the vent port (front port) and the replenishing port (rear port). Names vary by vehicle and brake component manufacturer. The names *vent port* and *replenishing port* are the terms recommended by the Society of Automotive Engineers (SAE).

① Vent ports (also called compensating port or bypass port)
② Replenishing ports (also called inlet port, bypass port, filler port, or breather port)

MASTER CYLINDER UNAPPLIED

MASTER CYLINDER APPLIED

Figure 3–13 The vent ports must remain open to allow brake fluid to expand when heated by the friction material and transferred to the caliper and/or wheel cylinder. As the brake fluid increases in temperature, it expands. The heated brake fluid can expand and flow back into the reservoir through the vent ports. (Courtesy of Chrysler Corporation)

Figure 3–14 As the brake pedal is depressed, the pushrod moves the primary piston forward, closing off the vent port. As soon as the port is blocked, pressure builds in front of the primary sealing cup which pushes on the secondary piston. The secondary piston also moves forward, blocking the secondary vent port and building pressure in front of the sealing cup. (Courtesy of Chrysler Corporation)

Applied Position When the brake pedal is depressed, the pedal linkage forces the pushrod and primary piston down the bore of the master cylinder (see Figure 3–14). As the piston moves forward, the primary sealing cup covers and blocks off the vent port (compensating port). Hydraulic pressure builds in front of the primary seal as the pushrod moves forward. The back of the piston is kept filled through the replenishing port (see Figure 3–15). This stops any suction (vacuum) from forming behind the piston. The secondary piston is moved forward as pressure is

exerted by the primary piston. If, for any reason such as a leak, the primary piston cannot build pressure, a mechanical link on the front of the primary piston will touch the secondary piston and move it forward, as the primary piston is pushed forward by the pushrod and brake pedal.

Released Position Releasing the brake pedal removes the pressure on the pushrod and master cylinder pistons. A spring on the brake pedal linkage returns the brake pedal to its normal at-rest (up) position. The

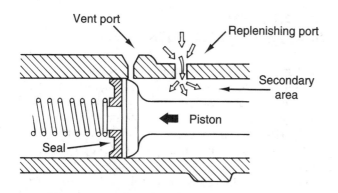

Figure 3–15 The purpose of the replenishing port is to keep the volume behind the primary piston filled with brake fluid from the reservoir as the piston moves forward during a brake application.

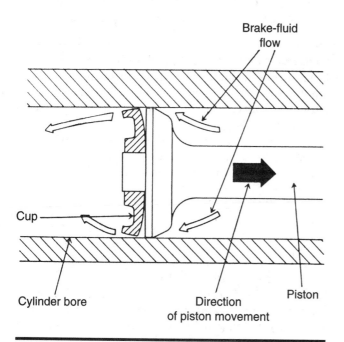

Figure 3–16 When the brake pedal is released, the master cylinder piston moves rearward. Some of the brake fluid is pushed back up through the replenishing port, but most of the fluid flows past the sealing cup. Therefore, when the driver pumps the brake pedal, the additional fluid in front of the pressure-building sealing cup is available quickly.

spring in front of the master cylinder piston expands, pushing the pistons rearward. At the same time, pressure is released from the entire braking system and the released brake fluid pressure is exerted on the master cylinder pistons forcing them rearward. As the piston is pushed back, the lips of the seal fold forward allowing fluid to quickly move past the piston, as shown in Figure 3–16. Some pistons have small holes that allow the fluid to move more quickly. Once the primary seal passes the vent port, the remaining hydraulic pressure forces any excess fluid into the reservoir.

■ RESIDUAL CHECK VALVE

A residual check valve has been used on some drum brake systems to keep a slight amount of pressure on the entire hydraulic system for drum brakes (5–12 psi). This residual check valve is located in the master cylinder at the outlet for the drum brakes. The check ball and spring in the residual check valve permit all the brake fluid to return to the master cylinder until the designated pressure is reached.

This slight pressure prevents air leaks into the hydraulic system in the event of a small hole or leak. With a low pressure kept on the hydraulic system any small hole will cause fluid to leak out rather than permit air to enter the system. This slight pressure also keeps the wheel cylinder sealing cups tight against the inside wall of the wheel cylinder.

Residual check valves are often *not* used on late model vehicles equipped with front disc/rear drum brakes. The residual check valve has been eliminated by equipping the wheel cylinder internal spring with a sealing cup **expander** to prevent sealing cup lip collapse.

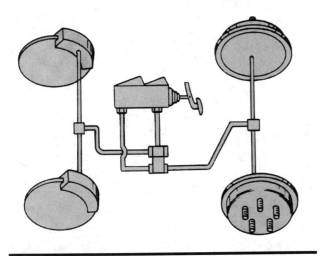

Figure 3–17 Rear-wheel-drive vehicles use a dual split master cylinder where one portion of the master cylinder applies the front brakes and the other section applies the rear brakes. The front brakes are not always activated by the front section of the master cylinder. The rear section of this master cylinder is used for the front brake. (Courtesy of Ford Motor Company)

Figure 3–18 The primary outlet is the outlet closest to the pushrod end of the master cylinder and the secondary outlet is closest to the nose end of the master cylinder.

■ DUAL SPLIT MASTER CYLINDERS

Dual split master cylinders use two separate pressure-building sections. One section operates the front brakes and the other section operates the rear brakes on vehicles equipped with a front/rear-split system (see Figure 3–17). The *nose end* of the master cylinder is the closed end toward the front of the vehicle. The open end is often called the *pushrod end* of the master cylinder (see Figure 3–18). Some manufacturers operate the front brakes (which do the most braking) from the "nose end" section (secondary piston end) of the master cylinder. The secondary piston has only one pressure-building seal. The primary piston (pushrod end) requires two seals to build pressure. Therefore, the nose end of the master cylinder is considered the more reliable of the two master cylinder pressure-building sections.

> **NOTE:** On vehicles equipped with front and rear split master cylinders, the front brakes may or may *not* be operated from the front chamber. General Motors typically uses the front (nose end) chamber for the front brakes and the rear (pushrod end) for the rear brakes. Many other makes and models of vehicles use the rear chamber for the front brakes. If in doubt, consult the factory service manual for the exact vehicle being serviced.

If the rear section of the hydraulic system fails, the primary piston will not build pressure to operate the secondary piston. To permit the operation of the secondary piston (nose end piston) in the event of a hydraulic failure of the rear section, the primary piston extension will mechanically contact and push on the secondary piston (see Figure 3–19). If there is a failure

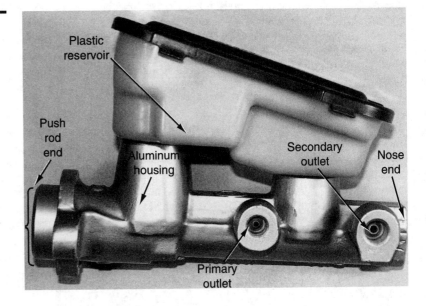

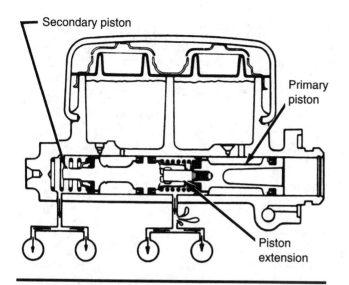

Figure 3–19 label: Secondary piston

Figure 3–19 label: Primary piston

Figure 3–19 label: Piston extension

Figure 3–19 In the event of a primary system failure, no hydraulic pressure is available to push the secondary piston forward. As a result, the primary piston extension contacts the secondary piston and pushes on the secondary piston mechanically rather than hydraulically. The loss of pressure in the primary system is usually noticed by the driver by a lower-than-normal brake pedal and the lighting of the red brake warning lamp. (Wagner Division, Cooper Industries Inc.)

of the front section hydraulic system, the primary piston (pushrod end) operates normally and exerts pressure on the secondary piston. The secondary piston, however, will not be able to build pressure because of the leak in the system.

■ DIAGONAL SPLIT MASTER CYLINDERS

With front-wheel-drive vehicles, the weight of the entire power train is on the front wheels and 80 to 90 percent of the braking force is achieved by the front brakes. This means that only 10 to 20 percent of the braking force is being handled by the rear brakes. If the front brakes fail, the rear brakes alone would not provide adequate braking force. The solution was the diagonal split system (see Figures 3–20 and 3–21).

In a diagonal split braking system, the left front brake and the right rear brake are on one circuit, and the right front with the left rear is another circuit of the master cylinder. If one circuit fails, the remaining circuit can still stop the vehicle in a reasonable fashion because each circuit has one front brake. To prevent this one front brake from causing the vehicle to pull toward one side during braking, the front suspension is designed with negative scrub radius geometry. This effectively eliminates any handling problem in the event of a brake circuit failure.

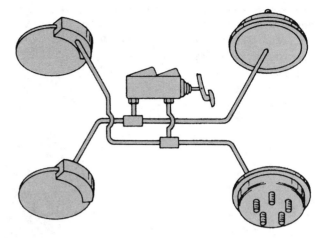

Figure 3–20 Front-wheel-drive vehicles use a diagonal split master cylinder. In this design, one section of the master cylinder operates the right front and the left rear brake and the other section operates the left front and right rear. In the event of a failure in one section, at least one front brake will still function. (Courtesy of Ford Motor Company)

■ COMPOSITE MASTER CYLINDERS

Composite master cylinders are constructed using an aluminum valve area with plastic reservoirs (see Figure 3–22). In older vehicles the master cylinders were constructed of cast iron. These heavier units usually were one piece with the reservoir cast together with the mounting and pressure-building valve area (see Figure 3–23).

■ QUICK TAKE-UP MASTER CYLINDERS

Many newer vehicles use low drag disc brake calipers to increase fuel economy. However, due to the larger distance between the rotor and the friction pads, excessive brake pedal travel would be required before the pads touched the rotor. The solution to this problem is a master cylinder design that can take up this extra clearance.

The design of a "quick take-up master cylinder" includes a larger diameter primary piston (low-pressure chamber) and a quick take-up valve. This type of master cylinder is also called **dual-diameter bore, step-bore, or fast-fill** master cylinders.

A spring-loaded check ball valve holds pressure on the brake fluid in the large diameter rear chamber of the primary piston. When the brakes are first applied, the movement of the rear larger piston forces this larger volume of brake fluid forward past the primary piston seal and into the primary high-pressure chamber. This extra volume of brake fluid "takes up" the extra

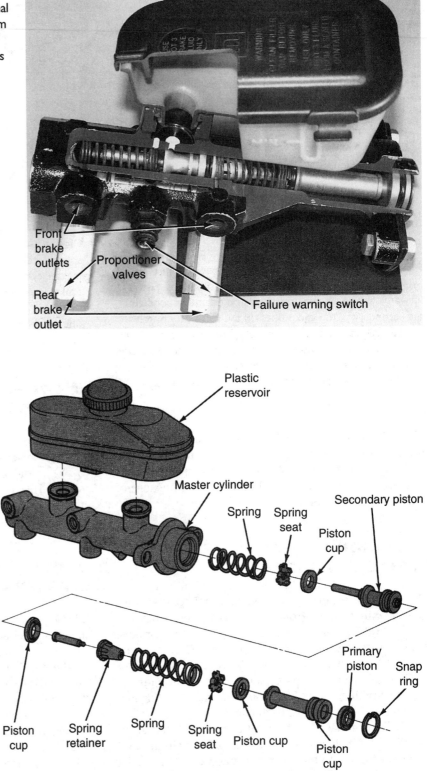

Figure 3–21 Typical General Motors diagonal split master cylinder. Notice the two aluminum proportioner valves. These valves limit and control brake fluid pressure to the rear brakes to help eliminate rear-wheel lockup during a rapid stop.

Figure 3–22 Exploded view of a composite master cylinder, showing all internal parts and their relationship. (Courtesy of Ford Motor Company)

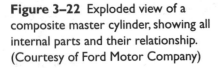

clearance of the front disc brake calipers without increasing the brake pedal travel distance (see Figure 3–24).

At 70–100 psi, the check ball valve in the quick take-up valve allows fluid to return to the brake fluid reservoir. Because the quick take-up "works" until 100 psi is reached, a metering valve is not required to hold back the fluid pressure to the front brakes.

■ DIAGNOSING AND TROUBLESHOOTING MASTER CYLINDERS

A thorough visual inspection is important when inspecting any master cylinder. The visual inspection should include a check of the following items:

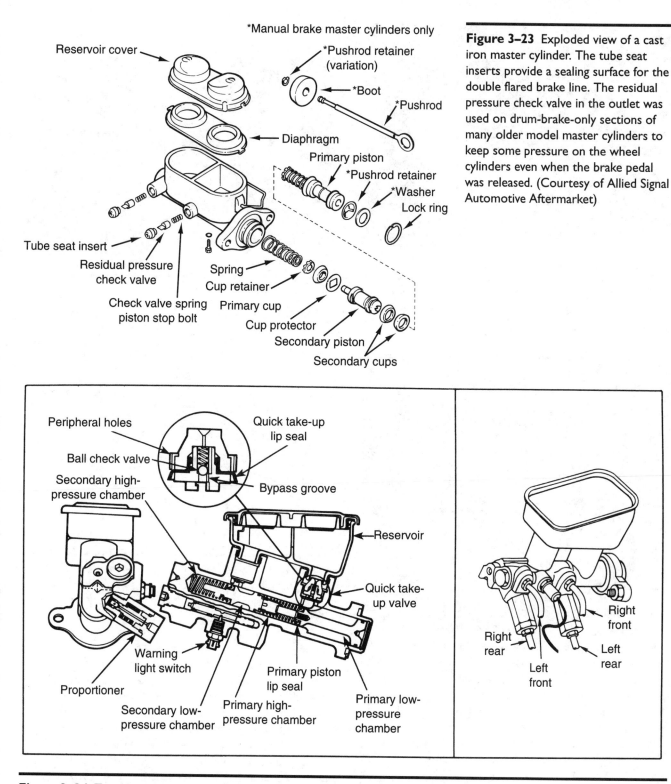

Figure 3–23 Exploded view of a cast iron master cylinder. The tube seat inserts provide a sealing surface for the double flared brake line. The residual pressure check valve in the outlet was used on drum-brake-only sections of many older model master cylinders to keep some pressure on the wheel cylinders even when the brake pedal was released. (Courtesy of Allied Signal Automotive Aftermarket)

Figure 3–24 Typical quick-take-up master cylinder, showing the ball check valve and spring. (Courtesy of Allied Signal Automotive Aftermarket)

1. Check the brake fluid for proper level and condition. (Brake fluid should not be rusty, thick, or contaminated.)
2. Check that the vent holes in the reservoir cover are open and clean.
3. Check that the reversion cover diaphragm is not torn or enlarged.

NOTE: If the cover diaphragm is enlarged, this is an indication that a mineral oil, such as automatic transmission fluid or engine oil, has been used in or near the brake system, because rubber that is brake fluid resistant expands when exposed to mineral oil.

(a)

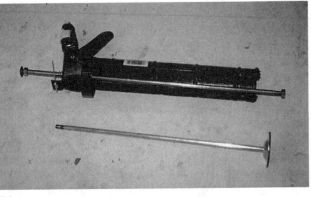
(b)

Figure 3–25 (a) A homemade brake pedal depressor. (b) A caulking gun with a removable extension rod is used. The removable extension rod allows the tool to be disassembled so that it can fit into a drawer of a toolbox.

TECH TIP ✔

The Brake Pedal Depressor Trick

The master cylinder can be used to *block* the flow of brake fluid. Whenever any hydraulic brake component is removed, brake fluid tends to leak out because the master cylinder is usually higher than most other hydraulic components such as wheel cylinders and calipers.

To prevent brake fluid loss that can easily empty the master cylinder reservoir, simply *depress* the brake pedal slightly or prop a stick or other pedal depressor to keep the brake pedal down. When the brake pedal is depressed, the piston sealing cups move forward blocking off the reservoir from the rest of the braking system. The master cylinder stays full and the brake fluid stops dripping out of brake lines that have been disconnected. See Figure 3–25.

HINT: Try this—put a straw into a glass of water. Use a finger to seal the top of the straw and then remove the straw from the glass of water. The water remains in the straw because air cannot get into the top of the straw. This is why the brake pedal depressor trick works to prevent the loss of brake fluid from the system even if the brake line is totally disconnected.

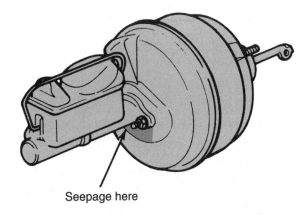
Seepage here

Figure 3–26 Some seepage is normal when a trace of fluid appears on the vacuum booster shell. Excessive leakage, however, indicates a leaking secondary (end) seal. (Courtesy of Ford Motor Company)

4. Check for any external leaks at the lines or at the pushrod area (see Figure 3–26).

After a thorough visual inspection, check for proper operation of **pedal height, pedal free play,** and **pedal reserve distance** (see Figures 3–27 and 3–28).

Proper brake pedal height is important for the proper operation of the stop (brake) light switch. If the pedal is not correct, the pushrod may be in too far forward preventing the master cylinder cups from uncovering the compensation port. If the pedal is too high, the free play will be excessive. Pedal reserve height is easily checked by depressing the brake pedal with the right foot and attempting to slide your left foot under the brake pedal (see Figure 3–29). Free play is the distance the brake pedal travels before the primary piston in the master cylinder moves. *Most vehicles require brake pedal free play between 1/8" to 1 1/2" (3 to 38 mm).* Too little or too much free play can cause braking problems that can be mistakenly contributed to a defective master cylinder.

Spongy Brake Pedal A spongy pedal with a larger than normal travel indicates air in the lines. Check for leaks and bleed the air from the system as discussed later in this chapter.

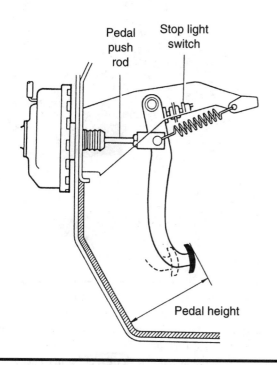

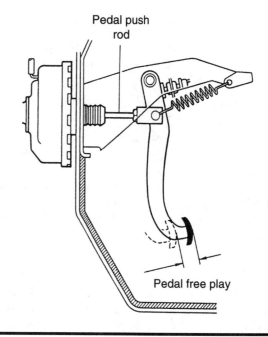

Figure 3–27 Pedal height is usually measured from the floor to the top of the brake pedal. Some vehicle manufacturers recommend removing the carpet and measuring from the asphalt matting on the floor for an accurate measurement. Always follow the manufacturer's recommended procedures and measurements. (Courtesy of Toyota Motor Sales, U.S.A., Inc.)

Figure 3–28 Brake pedal free play is the distance between the brake pedal fully released and the position of the brake pedal when braking resistance is felt. (Courtesy of Toyota Motor Sales, U.S.A., Inc.)

Lower Than Normal Brake Pedal A brake pedal that travels downward more than normal and then gets firm is an indication that one circuit of the dual-circuit hydraulic system is probably not working. Check for leaks in the system and repair as necessary. Another possible reason is an out-of-adjustment drum brake allowing too much pedal travel before the shoes touch the brake drum.

> **NOTE:** A lower than normal brake pedal may also be an indication of air in the hydraulic system.

See Chapter 5 for additional information on drum brakes.

Sinking Brake Pedal If the brake pedal sinks all the way to the floor, suspect a defective master cylinder that is leaking internally. This internal leakage is often called **bypassing** because the brake fluid is leaking past the sealing cup. See the Tech Tip, "Check for Bypassing."

■ DISASSEMBLY OF THE MASTER CYLINDER

Many master cylinders can be disassembled, cleaned, and restored to service.

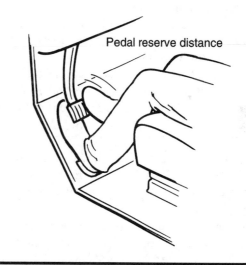

Figure 3–29 Brake pedal reserve is usually specified as the measurement from the floor to the top of the brake pedal with the brakes applied. A quick-and-easy test of pedal reserve is to try to place your left toe underneath the brake pedal while the brake pedal is depressed with your right foot. If your toe will *not* fit, then pedal reserve *may* not be sufficient.

> **NOTE:** Check vehicle manufacturer's recommendation before attempting to overhaul or service a master cylinder. Many manufacturers recommend replacing the master cylinder as an assembly.

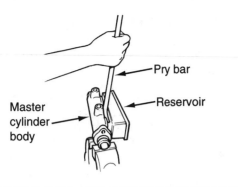

Figure 3–30 Use a pry bar to remove the reservoir from the master cylinder. (Courtesy of Allied Signal Automotive Aftermarket)

Step 1 Remove the master cylinder from the vehicle being careful to avoid dripping or spilling brake fluid onto painted surfaces of the vehicle. Dispose of all old brake fluid and clean the outside of the master cylinder.

Step 2 Remove the reservoir, if possible, as shown in Figure 3–30.

Step 3 Remove the retaining bolt that holds the secondary piston assembly in the bore.

Step 4 Depress the primary piston with a *blunt* tool such as a Phillips screwdriver, a rounded wooden dowel, or an engine pushrod. Use of a straight blade screwdriver or other non-rounded tool can damage and distort the aluminum piston.

> **CAUTION:** If holding the master cylinder in a vise, use the flange area; never clamp the body of the master cylinder.

Remove the snap ring and slowly release the pressure on the depressing tool. Spring pressure should push the primary piston out of the cylinder bore (see Figure 3–31).

Step 5 Remove the master cylinder from the vise and tap the open end of the bore against the top of a workbench to force the secondary piston out of the bore. If necessary, use compressed air in the outlet to force the piston out.

> **CAUTION:** Use extreme care when using compressed air. The piston can be shot out of the master cylinder with a great force.

■ INSPECTION AND REASSEMBLY OF THE MASTER CYLINDER

Inspect the master cylinder bore for pitting, corrosion, or wear. Most cast iron master cylinders cannot be honed because of the special bearingized surface fin-

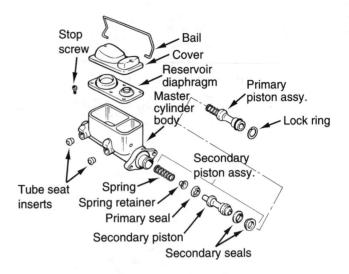

Figure 3–31 Whenever disassembling a master cylinder, note the exact order of parts as they are removed. Master cylinder overhaul kits (when available) often include entire piston assemblies rather than the individual seals. (Courtesy of Allied Signal Automotive Aftermarket)

Figure 3–32 Nylon brush used to clean the bore of aluminum master cylinders by a national remanufacturer. The soft nylon will not harm the anodized surface coating.

ish that is applied to the bore during manufacturing. Slight corrosion or surface flaws can usually be removed with a hone or crocus cloth; otherwise, the master cylinder should be replaced as an assembly. Always follow the recommended procedures for the vehicle being serviced.

Aluminum master cylinders cannot be honed. Aluminum master cylinders have an **anodized** surface coating applied that is hard and wear resistant. Honing would remove this protective coating (see Figure 3–32).

Thoroughly clean the master cylinder and any other parts to be reused (except for rubber components) in clean denatured alcohol. If the bore is okay, replacement **piston assemblies** can be installed into the master cylinder after dipping them into clean brake fluid.

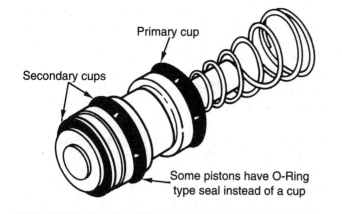

Figure 3–33 Piston assembly. (Courtesy of Allied Signal Automotive Aftermarket)

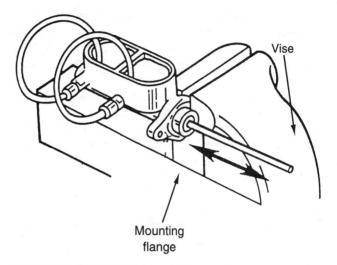

Figure 3–35 Bleeding a master cylinder before installing it on the vehicle. The master cylinder is clamped into a bench vise while using the rounded end of a breaker bar to push on the pushrod end with bleeder tubes down into the brake fluid. Master cylinders should be clamped on the mounting flange as shown to prevent distorting the master cylinder bore.

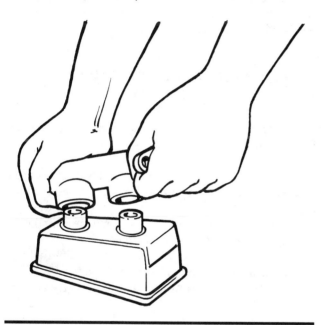

Figure 3–34 To reinstall the reservoir onto a master cylinder, place the reservoir on a clean flat surface and push the housing down onto the reservoir after coating the rubber seals with brake fluid. (Courtesy of Allied Signal Automotive Aftermarket)

> **TECH TIP** ✔️
>
> **Check for Bypassing**
>
> If a master cylinder is leaking internally, brake fluid can be pumped from the rear chamber into the front chamber of the master cylinder. This internal leakage is called **bypassing**. When the fluid bypasses, the front chamber can overflow while emptying the rear chamber. Therefore, whenever checking the level of brake fluid, do not think that a low rear reservoir is always due to an external leak. Also, a master cylinder that is bypassing (leaking internally) will usually cause a lower than normal brake pedal.

Step 4 Install the stop bolt.

Step 5 Reinstall the plastic reservoir, if equipped, as shown in Figure 3–34.

Step 6 Bench bleed the master cylinder. This step is very important (see Figure 3–35).

NOTE: While most master cylinder overhaul kits include the entire piston assemblies, some kits only contain the sealing cups and/or O-rings. Always follow the installation instructions that accompany the kit and always use the installation tool that is included to prevent damage to the replacement seals.

Step 1 Install the secondary (smaller) piston assembly into the bore, spring end first (see Figure 3–33).

Step 2 Install the primary piston assembly, spring end first.

Step 3 Depress the primary piston and install the snap ring.

■ PRESSURE-DIFFERENTIAL SWITCH (BRAKE WARNING SWITCH)

A pressure-differential switch is used on all vehicles built after 1967 with dual master cylinders to warn the driver of a loss of pressure in one of the two separate systems by lighting the dashboard red brake warning indicator lamp (see Figures 3–36 and 3–37).

The brake lines from both the front and the rear sections of the master cylinder are sent to this switch which lights the brake warning indicator lamp in the event of a "difference in pressure" between the two sections (see Figure 3–38).

A failure in one part of the brake system does not result in a failure of the entire hydraulic system. After the hydraulic system has been repaired and bled, moderate pressure on the brake pedal will center the piston in the switch and turn off the warning lamp.

If the lamp remains on, it may be necessary to:

1. Apply light pressure to the brake pedal.
2. Momentarily open the bleeder valve on the side that did not have the failure.

Figure 3–36 Red brake warning lamp.

Figure 3–37 Most red brake warning lamps indicate only hydraulic or brake fluid level. However, some such as General Motors light trucks can indicate ABS, parking, or hydraulic failure depending on its brightness. This can be confusing to vehicle owners as well as technicians especially if the brightness level is not noticed.

This procedure should center the pressure differential switch valve in those vehicles that are not equipped with self-centering springs.

■ BRAKE FLUID LEVEL SENSOR SWITCH

Many master cylinders, especially systems that are a diagonal split, usually use a brake fluid level sensor switch in the master cylinder reservoir. This sensor will light the red "BRAKE" warning lamp on the dash if low brake fluid level is detected. A float-type sensor or a magnetic reed switch are commonly used and provide a complete electrical circuit when the brake fluid level is low. After refilling the master cylinder reservoir to the correct level, the red "BRAKE" warning lamp should go out (see Figures 3–39 and 3–40).

■ DIAGNOSING A RED "BRAKE" DASH WARNING LAMP

Activation of the red brake dash warning lamp can be for any one of several reasons:

1. Parking brake "on"—The same dash warning lamp is used to warn the driver that the parking brake is on.
2. Low brake fluid—This lights the red dash warning lamp on vehicles equipped with a master cylinder reservoir brake fluid level switch.
3. Unequal brake pressure—The pressure differential switch is used on most vehicles with a front/rear brake split system to warn the driver whenever

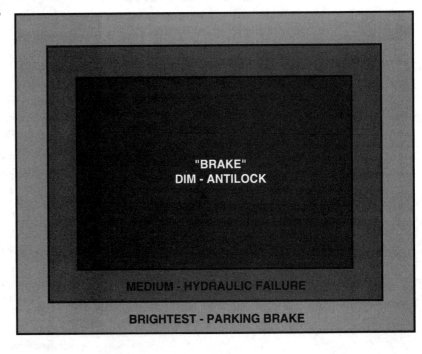

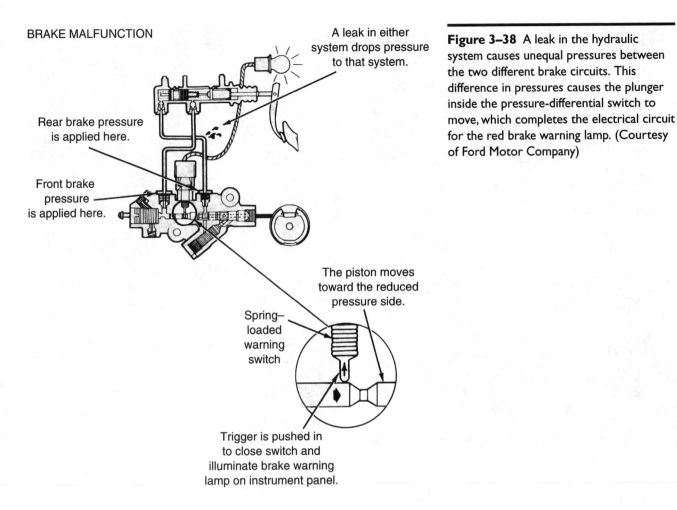

BRAKE MALFUNCTION

A leak in either system drops pressure to that system.

Rear brake pressure is applied here.

Front brake pressure is applied here.

The piston moves toward the reduced pressure side.

Spring-loaded warning switch

Trigger is pushed in to close switch and illuminate brake warning lamp on instrument panel.

Figure 3–38 A leak in the hydraulic system causes unequal pressures between the two different brake circuits. This difference in pressures causes the plunger inside the pressure-differential switch to move, which completes the electrical circuit for the red brake warning lamp. (Courtesy of Ford Motor Company)

there is low brake pressure to either the front or rear brakes.

> **NOTE:** Brake systems use *either* a pressure-differential switch *or* a low brake fluid switch to light the dash red "BRAKE" lamp, but not both.

The most likely cause of the red "BRAKE" warning lamp being on is low brake fluid caused by a leaking brake line, wheel cylinder or caliper. Therefore, the first step in diagnosis is to determine the cause of the lamp being on, then to repair the problem.

Step 1 *Check the level of the brake fluid*—If low, carefully inspect the entire hydraulic brake system for leaks and repair as necessary.

Step 2 *Disconnect the wire from the pressure-differential switch*—If the lamp is still "on," the problem is due to the parking brake lever switch "on" or grounded, or the wire going to the switch is shorted to ground. If the red brake warning lamp is "off" after being disconnected from the pressure-differential switch, then the problem is due to a hydraulic failure (a low pressure in either the front or the rear system that creates a difference in pressure of at least 150 psi).

> **NOTE:** Many Japanese vehicles energize the relay that turns off the red "BRAKE" warning lamp from the output terminal of the alternator. If a quick inspection of the brake system seems to indicate that everything is okay, check for correct charging voltage before continuing a more detailed brake system inspection.

■ PROPORTIONING VALVE OPERATION

A proportioning valve may or may not be used on all types of braking systems. When used, it prevents rear wheel lockup by limiting the amount of pressure sent to the rear wheels. A proportioning valve **reduces the pressure increase** to the rear brakes. A proportioning valve is also called a **pressure control valve** by some vehicle manufacturers.

A proportioning valve permits full master cylinder pressure to be sent to the rear brakes up to a certain point, called the **split point** or **changeover pressure.** Above the split point, the pressure is reduced to a certain ratio, called the **slope,** of the front brake pressure. The split point is usually 200–300 psi and the ratio (slope) could vary from 0.25 to 0.50 (see Figure 3–41).

Figure 3–39 Many vehicles are equipped with brake fluid level floats that can light the red brake warning lamp if the brake fluid level drops below a certain level. Note that the brake fluid to the secondary section (nose end) is supplied from the reservoir by a hose.

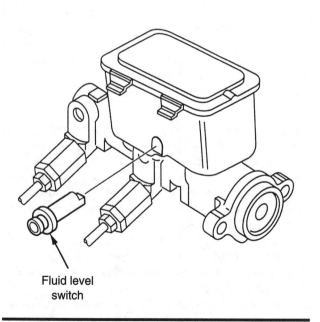

Figure 3–40 A brake fluid level switch (sensor) used on a General Motors vehicle. (Courtesy of General Motors)

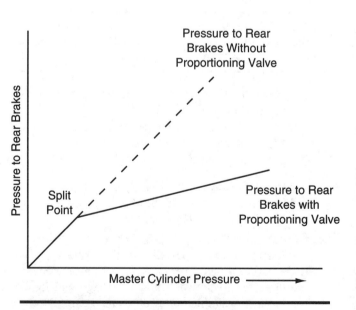

Figure 3–41 Typical proportioner valve pressure relationship. Note that at low pressures, the pressure is the same to the rear brakes as is applied to the front brakes. After the split point, only a percentage (called the slope) of the master cylinder pressure is applied to the rear brakes.

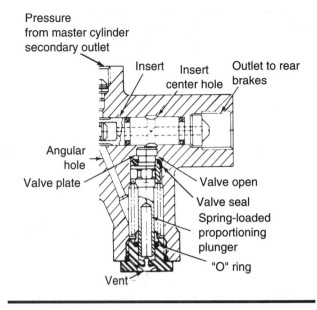

Figure 3–43 Cutaway view of a proportioning (proportioner) valve. Notice the small passages. These areas can trap air and make bleeding the hydraulic system more difficult especially if the brake fluid is allowed to drain out of the system during a brake service. (Courtesy of Chrysler Corporation)

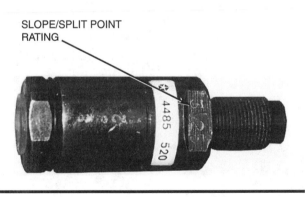

Figure 3–42 A Chrysler proportioning valve. Note that slope and split point are stamped on the housing.

With light brake pedal applications, approximately the same brake pressure is sent to both front and rear brakes. However, when higher pressures are required to stop the vehicle, the pressure is controlled by this proportioning valve to limit the pressure sent to the rear brakes to less than half of the pressure being applied to the front brakes beyond the split point. This prevents rear wheel lockup due to weight transfer forward reducing the weight off the rear tires, plus allowing for the self-energizing forces of some rear drum brakes (see Figure 3–42).

In the event of a front brake system failure, a bypass opens allowing full rear brake hydraulic pressure (see Figure 3–43).

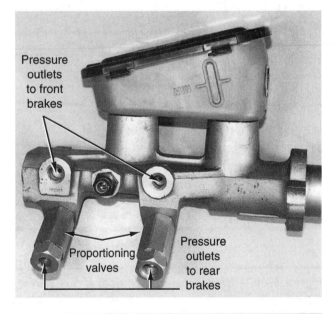

Figure 3–44 Diagonal split braking system used on a front-wheel-drive vehicle uses two proportioning valves, one for each rear wheel.

■ DIAGONAL SPLIT PROPORTIONING VALVES

Vehicles that are diagonal split use a proportioning valve for each rear brake. This can be two separate units as shown in Figures 3–44 and 3–45 or one component part.

Figure 3–45 Portion of the proportioning valve (a) during light braking and (b) during heavy braking.

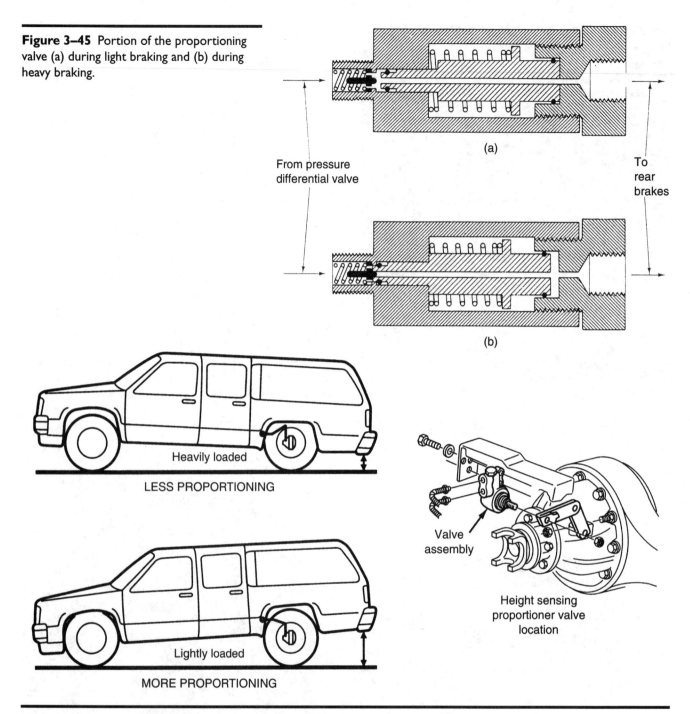

From pressure differential valve

(a)

To rear brakes

(b)

Heavily loaded

LESS PROPORTIONING

Lightly loaded

MORE PROPORTIONING

Valve assembly

Height sensing proportioner valve location

Figure 3–46 A height-sensing proportioning valve allows a higher pressure to be applied to the rear brakes when the vehicle is heavily loaded and less pressure when the vehicle is lightly loaded. (Courtesy of General Motors)

■ HEIGHT-SENSING PROPORTIONING VALVES

Many vehicles use a proportioning valve that varies the amount of pressure that can be sent to the rear brakes depending on the height of the rear suspension. If the vehicle is lightly loaded, the rear suspension is high, especially during braking. In this case, the amount of pressure allowed to the rear brakes is reduced. This *helps* prevent rear wheel lockup and possible skidding. Be-

sides, a lightly loaded vehicle requires less braking force to stop than a heavily loaded vehicle.

When the vehicle is loaded, the rear suspension is forced downward. The lever on the proportioning valve moves and allows a greater pressure to be sent to the rear brakes (see Figure 3–46). This greater pressure allows the rear brakes to achieve more braking force, helping to slow a heavier vehicle. When a vehicle is heavily loaded in the rear, the chances of rear wheel lockup are reduced.

CAUTION: Some vehicle manufacturers warn that service technicians should never install replacement air lift shock absorbers or springs that may result in a vehicle height difference than specified by the vehicle manufacturer.

■ PROPORTIONING VALVE ADJUSTMENT

Height-sensing proportioning valves should be adjusted when replaced. The proper adjustment ensures that the proper pressure is applied to the rear brakes in relation to the loading of the vehicle.

Procedures vary from one vehicle to another. Always consult the factory service manual for the exact procedure. Some trucks require the use of special plastic gauges available from the dealer.

■ PROPORTIONING VALVE DIAGNOSIS AND TESTING

A defective proportioning valve usually allows rear brake pressure to increase too rapidly, causing the rear wheels to lock up during hard braking. When the rear brakes become locked, the traction with the road surface decreases and the vehicle often skids. Whenever rear brakes tend to lock during braking, the proportion-

ing valve should be checked for proper operation. If the proportioning valve is height sensing, verify proper vehicle ride (trim) height and adjustment of the operating lever (see Figure 3–47).

Pressure gauges can also be used to check for proper operation. Install one gauge into the brake line from the master cylinder and the second gauge to the rear brake outlet of the proportioning valve. While an assistant depresses the brake pedal, observe the two gauges. Both gauges should register an increasing pressure as the brake pedal is depressed until the split point. After the split point, the gauge connected to the proportioning valve (rear brakes) should increase at a slower rate than the reading on the gauge connected to the master cylinder.

If the pressures do not react as described, the proportioning valve should be *replaced*. The same procedure can be performed on a diagonal split-type system as used on most front-wheel-drive vehicles.

■ METERING VALVE (HOLD-OFF) OPERATION

The metering valve is used on all front-disc, rear-drum-brake-equipped vehicles. The metering valve prevents the full operation of (holds-off) the disc brakes until between 75–125 psi is sent to the rear drum brakes to overcome rear-brake return spring pressure. This allows the

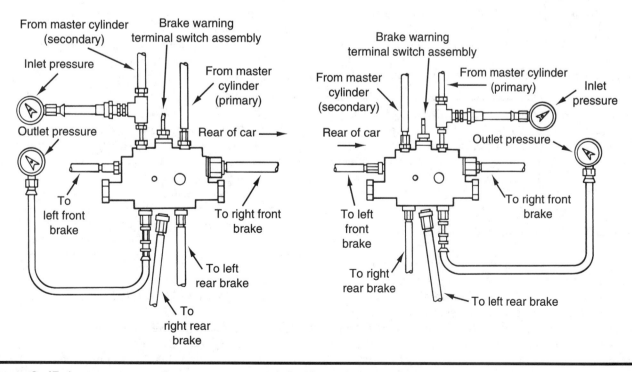

Figure 3–47 A proportioning valve pressure test can be performed using two pressure gauges—one to register the pressure from the master cylinder and the other gauge to read the pressure being applied to the rear brakes. This test has to be repeated in order to read the pressure to each rear wheel. (Courtesy of Chrysler Corporation)

METERING (HOLD-OFF)

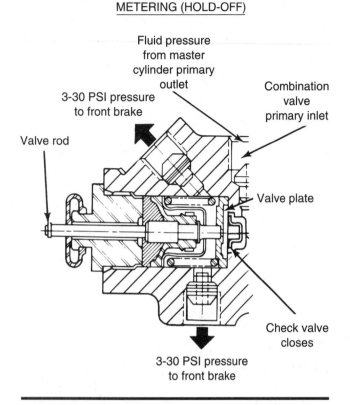

Figure 3–48 Cutaway view of a metering (hold-off) valve. (Courtesy of Chrysler Corporation)

front and rear brakes to apply at the same time for even stopping. Most metering valves also allow for the pressure to the front brakes to be gradually blended up to the metering valve pressure to prevent front brake locking under light pedal pressures on icy surfaces.

The metering valve remains open at pressures below 3 to 30 psi (20 to 200 kPa) to allow the pressure to be equalized when the brakes are not applied (see Figure 3–48).

> **NOTE:** Braking systems that are diagonal split, such as found on most front-wheel-drive vehicles, do *not* use a metering valve. A metering valve is only used on front/rear split braking systems such as those found on most rear-wheel-drive vehicles.

■ METERING VALVE DIAGNOSIS AND TESTING

A defective metering valve can leak brake fluid and/or cause the front brakes to apply before the rear brakes. This is most commonly noticed on slippery surfaces such as on snow or ice or on rain-slick roads. If the front brakes lock up during these conditions, the front wheels cannot be steered. Inspect the metering for these two conditions:

1. Leakage—Look around the bottom on the metering valve for brake fluid leakage. (Ignore slight

dampness.) Replace the metering valve assembly if leaking.

2. As the pressure builds to the front brakes, the metering valve stem should move. If it does not, replace the valve.

More accurate testing of the metering valve can be accomplished using pressure gauges. Install two gauges, one in the pressure line coming from the master cylinder and the other in the outlet line leading to the front brakes. When depressing the brake pedal, both gauges should read the same until about 3 to 30 psi (20 to 200 kPa) when the metering valve shuts thereby delaying the operation of the front brakes. The master cylinder outlet gauge should show an increase in pressure as the brake pedal is depressed further.

Once 75 to 300 psi is reached, the gauge showing pressure to the front brakes should match the pressure from the master cylinder. If the pressures do not match these ranges, the metering valve assembly should be replaced.

> **HINT:** Neither the metering valve nor the proportioning valve can cause a pull to one side if defective. The metering valve controls *both* front brakes, and the proportioning valve controls *both* rear brakes. A defective master cylinder cannot cause a pull either. Therefore, if a vehicle pulls to one side during a stop, look for problems in the individual wheel brakes, hoses, or suspension.

■ COMBINATION VALVE

Most vehicle manufacturers combine the function of a proportioning valve with one or more other valves into one unit called a **combination valve** (see Figure 3–49). On a typical rear-wheel-drive vehicle, a typical combination valve consists of the following components all in one replaceable unit:

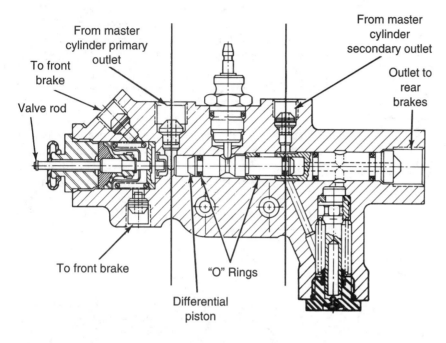

METERING (HOLD-OFF)   WARNING SWITCH   PROPORTIONING

From master cylinder primary outlet

To front brake

Valve rod

To front brake

"O" Rings

Differential piston

From master cylinder secondary outlet

Outlet to rear brakes

Figure 3–49 Combination valve containing metering, pressure-differential (warning switch), and proportioning valves all in one unit. This style is often called a "pistol grip" design because the proportioning valve section resembles the grip section of a hand gun. (Courtesy of Chrysler Corporation)

TECH TIP ✔

Push-In or Pull-Out Metering Valve?

Whenever bleeding the air out of the hydraulic brake system, the metering valve should be bypassed. The metering valve stops the passage of brake fluid to the front wheels until pressure exceeds about 125 psi (860 kPa). It is important not to push the brake pedal down with a great force so as to keep from dispersing any trapped air into small and hard to bleed bubbles. To bypass the metering valve, the service technician has to push or pull a small button located on the metering valve. An easy way to remember whether to push in or to pull out is to inspect the button itself. *If the button is rubber coated, then you push in. If the button is steel, then pull out.*

Special tools allow the metering valve to be held in the bypass position. Failure to remove the tool after bleeding the brakes can result in premature application of the front brakes before the rear drum brakes have enough pressure to operate.

- Metering valve
- Proportioning valve
- Pressure-differential switch

Some combination valves are only two functions and contain the pressure differential and the metering valve while others combine the pressure differential with the proportioning valve.

■ BRAKE LINES

High-pressure double-walled steel brake lines or high-strength flexible lines are used to connect the master cylinder to each wheel. The steel **brake lines** are also called **brake pipes** or **brake tubing** and are coated to help prevent corrosion. The steel brake lines leaving the master cylinder are usually coiled to allow for movement between the master cylinder and the mounting of the brake line to the frame, which could cause fatigue and brake line failure.

CAUTION: Copper tubing should *never* be used for brake lines. Copper tends to burst at a lower pressure than steel.

The ends of all steel brake lines should have a **double flare** or **ISO flare** at each end to ensure the connection will have the necessary strength. **ISO** means **International Standards Organization.** ISO flare may also be called a **ball flare** or **bubble flare** (see Figure 3–50). Whenever replacing steel brake line, new steel tubing can be used and a double lap flare or an ISO flare completed at each end using a special flaring tool. Brake line can also be purchased in selected lengths already correctly flared. They are available in different diameters, the most commonly used being 3/16" (4.8 mm), 1/4" (6.4 mm), and 5/16" (7.9 mm) outside diameter (O.D.).

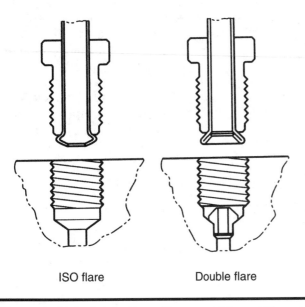

ISO flare   Double flare

Figure 3–50 Brake pipe flares. (Courtesy of General Motors)

Figure 3–51 Note that the replacement line was reinstalled into the factory clips to keep it in the same location as the original factory brake line.

CAUTION: According to vehicle manufacturers' recommended procedures, compression fittings should never be used to join two pieces of steel brake line. Only use double flare ends and connections, if necessary, when replacing damaged steel brake lines (see Figures 3–51, 3–52, and 3–53). See Figures 3–54 and 3–55 for brake line flaring procedures.

Brake line diameter is also very important and replacement lines should be the same as the original. Many vehicle manufacturers use larger diameter brake lines for the rear brakes because the larger line decreases brake response time. *Response time is the amount of time between the pressure increase at the master cylinder and the pressure increase at the brakes.* On most vehicles, the brake lines to the

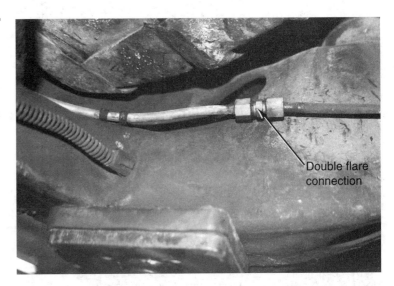

Double flare connection

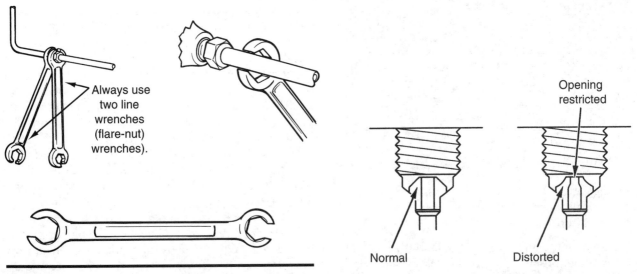

Always use two line wrenches (flare-nut) wrenches).

Opening restricted

Normal   Distorted

Figure 3–52 Whenever disconnecting or tightening a brake line, always use the correct size flare nut wrench. A flare nut wrench is also called a **tube nut wrench** or a **line wrench.**

Figure 3–53 Overtightening can distort and restrict the fitting opening. (Courtesy of General Motors)

(a)

(b)

(c)

(d)

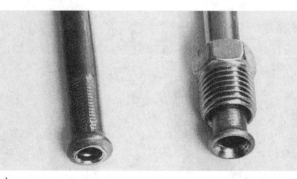

(e)

Figure 3–54 Double flaring the end of a brake line. (a) Clamp the line at the correct height above the surface of the clamping tool using the shoulder of the insert as a gauge. (b) The insert is pressed into the end of the tubing. This creates the first bend. (c) Remove the insert and use the pointed tool to complete the overlap double flare. (d) The completed operation as it appears while still in the clamp. (e) The end of the line as it appears after the first operation on the left and the completed double flare on the right.

front wheels are shorter. To help ensure that the rear brakes apply at the same time as the front brakes, the diameter of the brake lines is increased to the rear brakes. Brake engineers size each line to keep the time lag to less than 0.2 second (200 milliseconds). Fast response time is critical for the proper operation of the antilock braking system. Also as brake fluid ages, its viscosity (resistance to flow) increases, resulting in longer response time.

CAUTION: The exhaust system near brake lines should be carefully inspected for leaks when diagnosing a "lack of brakes" complaint. Exhaust gases can hit the brake line going to the rear brakes causing the brake fluid to boil. Since brake fluid vapors are no longer liquid, they can be compressed, resulting in a total loss of brakes. After the vehicle is stopped and allowed to cool, the brakes often return to normal.

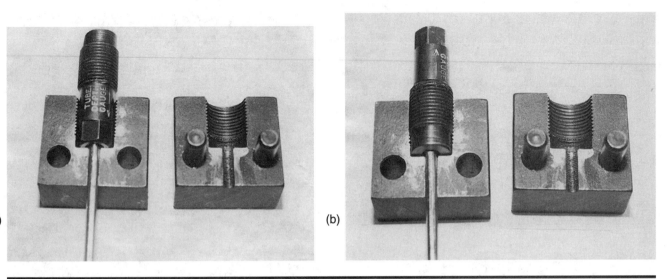

(a)

(b)

Figure 3–55 Making an ISO flare required this special tool. (a) Position the brake line into the two-part tool at the correct height using the gauge end of the tool. (b) Assemble the two blocks of the tool together and clamp in a vise. Turn the tool around and thread it into the tool block. The end of the threaded part of the tool forms the "bubble" or ISO flare.

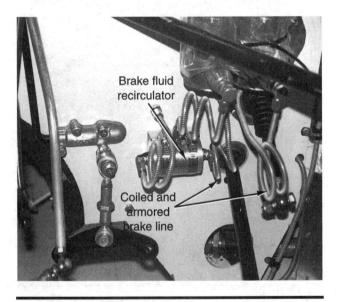

Figure 3–56 Brake lines on a race car showing the coiled brake line to allow for movement (vibration) without braking and armored to help protect the lines from damage. The brake fluid recirculator is used in racing to circulate brake fluid from the calipers back to the master cylinder, then back to the calipers. The system uses the bleeder valve openings in the caliper to circulate brake fluid to keep it cooler to help prevent it from boiling. Boiling brake fluid causes bubbles in the hydraulic system and a total loss of braking.

■ COILED BRAKE LINE

Steel brake line is often coiled as shown on a race car in Figure 3–56. The purpose of the coils is to allow movement between the brake components without stress that could lead to metal fatigue and brake line breakage.

The typical master cylinder attaches to the bulkhead of the vehicle and the combination valve is often attached to the frame. Because the body and frame are usually insulated from each other using rubber isolators, some movement occurs while driving.

■ ARMORED BRAKE LINE

In many areas of the brake system, the steel brake line is covered with a wire coil wrap as shown in Figure 3–57. This armor is designed to prevent damage from stones and other debris that could dent or damage the

TECH TIP ✔

Bend It Right the First Time

Replacing rusted or damaged brake line can be a difficult job. It is important that the replacement brake line be located in the same location as the original to prevent possible damage from road debris or heat from the exhaust. Often this means bending the brake line with many angles and turns. To make the job a lot easier, use a stiff length of wire and bend the wire into the exact shape necessary. Then use the wire as a pattern to bend the brake line. Always use a tubing bender to avoid kinking the brake line. A kink not only restricts the flow of brake fluid, but also weakens the line. To bend brake line without a tubing bender tool, use an old V-belt pulley. Clamp the pulley in a vise and lay the tubing in the groove and smoothly bend the tubing. Different diameter pulleys will create various radius bends. See Figure 3–59.

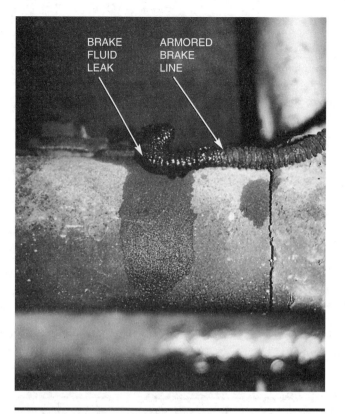

Figure 3–57 Armored brake line is usually used in the location where the line may be exposed to rock or road debris damage. Even armored brake line can leak and a visual inspection is an important part of any brake service.

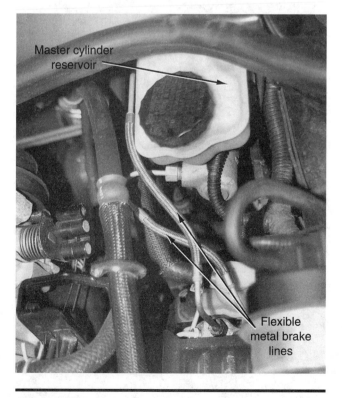

Figure 3–58 Some vehicles such as this front-wheel-drive Chrysler vehicle use flexible braided metal brake line from the master cylinder.

brake line. If a section of armored brake line is to be replaced, armored replacement line should be installed. Braided flexible brake line is also used on some vehicles to allow flexibility and protection against stone damage as shown in Figure 3–58.

> **NOTE:** Always use a tubing cutter instead of a hack saw when cutting brake line. A hacksaw will leave a rough and uneven end that will not flare properly.

■ FLEXIBLE BRAKE HOSE

Flexible brake hoses are used on each front wheel to allow for steering and suspension movement and at the rear to allow for rear suspension travel. See Figure 3–60. These rubber high-strength hoses can crack, blister, or leak, and should be inspected at least every six months. Typical flexible brake hose is constructed of rubber hose surrounded by layers of woven fabric as shown in Figure 3–61. An outside jacket is made from rubber and protects the reinforcement fabric from moisture and abrasion. The outside covering is also ribbed so that a technician can see if the hose is twisted. It is not unusual for flexible brake lines to become turned around and twisted when the disc brake caliper is removed and then replaced during a brake pad change (see Figures 3–62, 3–63, and 3–64 on page 75).

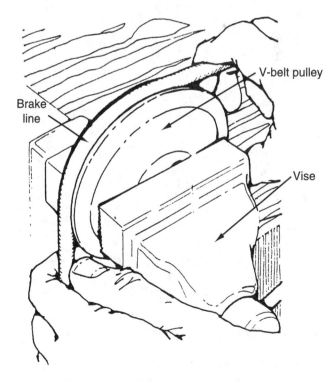

Figure 3–59 Using a V-belt pulley in a vise to bend brake line.

TECH TIP ✓

Don't Fill the Master Cylinder Without Seeing Me!

The boss explained to the beginning technician that there are two reasons why the customer should be told not to fill the master cylinder reservoir when the brake fluid is down to the "minimum" mark as shown in Figure 3–65.

1. If the master cylinder reservoir is low, there may be a leak that should be repaired.
2. As the brakes wear, the disc brake piston moves outward to maintain the same distance between friction materials and the rotor. Therefore, as the disc brake pads wear, the brake fluid level goes down to compensate.

If the customer notices that the brake fluid is low in the master cylinder reservoir, the vehicle should be serviced—either for new brakes or to repair a leak as shown in Figure 3–66.

■ BRAKE BLEEDING

Brake bleeding is removing any trapped air from the hydraulic system. Air can get into the hydraulic system whenever any hydraulic brake line or unit is opened. Air can also be drawn into the hydraulic system through small holes or loose brake line connections during the release of the brake pedal. A common source of air in the brake system of this type can occur through very small holes in rubber flexible brake lines. Another source of air in the braking system is through the absorption of moisture by the brake fluid. When moisture is absorbed, the boiling point of the brake fluid is reduced. During severe braking, the heat generated can cause the brake fluid to boil and create air bubbles in the hydraulic brake system. Air eventually travels to the highest part of the brake system, if not restricted by pressure control valves.

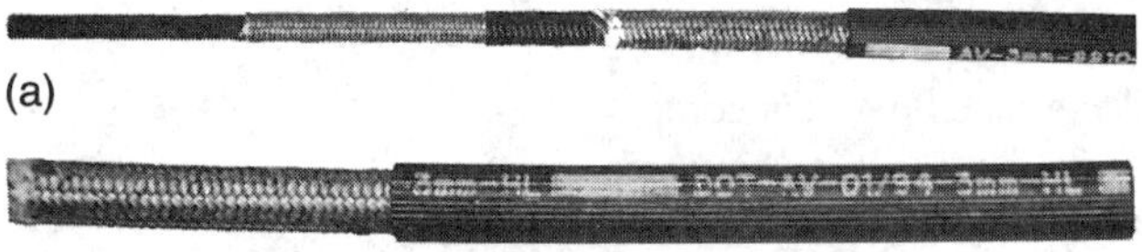

(a)

(b)

Figure 3–61 (a) Typical flexible brake hose showing the multiple layers of rubber and fabric. (b) The inside diameter (I.D.) is printed on the hose (3 mm) and the date it was manufactured (01/94).

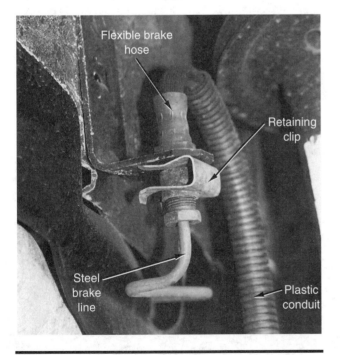

Figure 3–60 Flexible brake hoses are used between the frame or body of the vehicle and the wheel brakes. Because of suspension and/or steering movement, these flexible brake lines must be strong enough to handle high brake fluid pressures, yet remain flexible. Note that this flexible brake hose is further protected against road debris with a plastic conduit covering.

Figure 3–62 Brake hose fabric being woven at the Delco Chassis plant in Dayton, Ohio, USA.

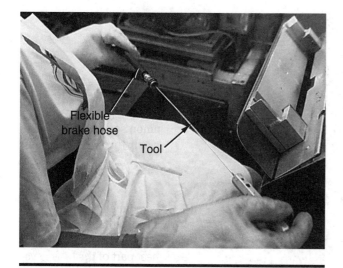

Figure 3–63 All brake hose is carefully inspected and a 3-mm-diameter gauging tool is inserted through the hose to make sure the hose is not restricted. Notice the small diameter of the tool compared with the outside diameter of the hose. Seeing how small the inside diameter of the hose actually is makes it easier to visualize how easy it would be to have a restricted or blocked flexible hose.

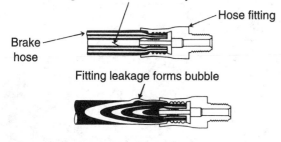

Figure 3–64 Typical flexible brake hose faults. Many faults cannot be seen, yet can cause the brakes to remain applied after the brake pedal is released.

■ BLEEDING THE MASTER CYLINDER

Whenever the master cylinder is replaced or the hydraulic system has been left opened for several hours, the air may have to be bled from the master cylinder. Bleed the master cylinder "on the bench" before installing it on the vehicle. If bleeding the master cylinder after working on the hydraulic system, follow these steps:

Step 1 Fill the master cylinder with clean brake fluid from a sealed container up to the recommended "full" level.

Step 2 Have an assistant slowly depress the brake pedal as you "crack open" the master cylinder bleed screw starting with the section closest to the bulkhead. It is very important that the primary section of the master cylinder be bled before attempting to bleed the air out of the secondary section of the

Figure 3–65 Master cylinder with brake fluid level at the "min" (minimum) line.

Figure 3–66 A caliper was found to be leaking at the rear of this Buick Regal when the master cylinder brake fluid level was first observed to be low.

master cylinder. Before the brake pedal reaches the floor, close the bleeder valve.

> **HINT:** A proper manual bleeding of the hydraulic system requires that accurate communications occur between the person depressing the brake pedal and the person opening and closing the bleeder valve(s). The bleeder valve (also called a **bleed valve**) should be open only when the brake pedal is being depressed. The valve *must* be closed when the brake pedal is released to prevent air from being drawn into the system.

TECH TIP ✔

Bleeder Valve Loosening Tips

Attempting to loosen a bleeder valve often results in breaking (shearing off) of the bleeder valve. Several of these service procedures can be tried that help prevent the *possibility* of breaking a bleeder valve. Bleeder valves are tapered and become wedged in the caliper on the wheel cylinder housing. See Figures 3–67 and 3–68. All of these methods use shock to "break the taper" and to loosen the stuck valve.

Air Impact Method

Use a six-point socket for the bleeder valve and use the necessary adapters to fit an air impact wrench to the socket. Apply some penetrating oil to the bleeder valve and allow to flow around the threads. Turn the pressure down on the impact wrench to limit the force. The hammering effect of the impact wrench loosens the bleeder valve without breaking it off.

Hit and Tap Method

Step 1 Tap on the end of the bleeder valve with a steel hammer. This shock often "breaks the taper" at the base of the bleeder valve. The shock also breaks loose any rust or corrosion on the threads.

Step 2 Using a six-point wrench or socket, *tap* the bleeder valve in the clockwise direction (tighten).

Step 3 Using the same six-point socket or wrench, *tap* the bleeder valve counterclockwise to loosen and remove the bleeder valve.

> **NOTE:** It is the *shock* of the tap on the wrench that breaks loose the bleeder valve. Simply pulling on the wrench often results in breaking off the bleeder.

If the valve is still stuck (frozen), repeat Step 1 through Step 3.

Air Punch Method

Use an air punch near the bleeder valve while attempting to loosen the bleeder valve at the same time. See Figure 3–69.

The air punch creates a shock motion that often loosens the taper and threads of the bleeder valve from the caliper or wheel cylinder. It is also helpful to first attempt to turn the bleeder valve in the clockwise (tightening) direction, then turn the bleeder in counterclockwise direction to loosen and remove the bleeder valve.

Heat and Tap Method

Heat the area around the bleeder valve with a torch. The heat expands the size of the hole and usually allows the bleeder to be loosened and removed.

> **CAUTION:** The heat from a torch will damage the rubber seals inside the caliper or wheel cylinder. Using heat to free a stuck bleeder valve will *require* that all internal rubber parts be replaced.

Wax Method

Step 1 Heat the bleeder valve itself with a torch. The heat causes the valve itself to expand.

Step 2 Remove the heat from the bleeder valve. As the valve is cooling, touch paraffin wax or candle wax to the hot valve. The wax will melt and run down around the threads of the bleeder valve.

Step 3 Allow the bleeder valve to cool until it can be safely touched with your hand. This ensures that the temperature is low enough for the wax to return to a solid and provide the lubricating properties necessary for the easy removal of the bleeder valve. Again, turn the bleeder valve clockwise before turning the valve counterclockwise to remove.

Step 3 Repeat the procedure several times until a solid flow of brake fluid is observed leaving the bleeder valve. If the master cylinder is not equipped with bleeder valves, the outlet tube nuts can be loosened instead.

■ BLEEDING SEQUENCE

After bleeding the master cylinder, the combination valve should be bled if equipped. Follow the same procedure as when bleeding the master cylinder, being careful not to allow the master cylinder to run dry.

> **NOTE:** The master cylinder is located in the highest section of the hydraulic braking system. Some master cylinders are equipped with bleeder valves. All master cylinders can be bled using the same procedure as that used for bleeding calipers and wheel cylinders. If the master cylinder is not equipped with bleeder valves, it can be bled by loosening the brake line fittings at the master cylinder.

Check the level in the master cylinder frequently and keep it filled with clean brake fluid throughout the brake bleeding procedure.

Figure 3–67 Typical bleeder valve from a disc brake caliper. The arrows point to the taper section that does the actual sealing. It is this taper that requires a shock to loosen. If the bleeder is simply turned with a wrench, the bleeder usually breaks off because the tapered part at the bottom remains adhered to the caliper or wheel cylinder. Once loosened, brake fluid flows around the taper and out through the hole in the side of the bleeder valve.

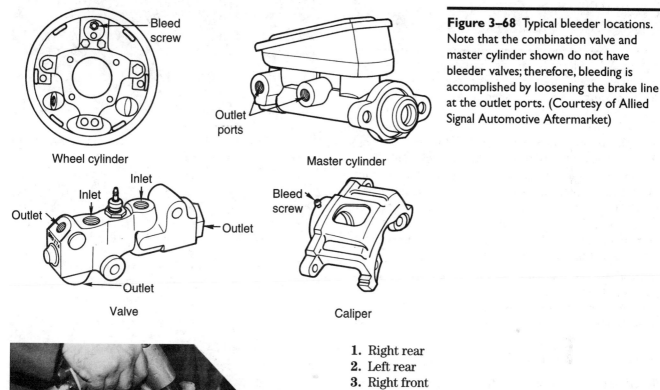

Figure 3–68 Typical bleeder locations. Note that the combination valve and master cylinder shown do not have bleeder valves; therefore, bleeding is accomplished by loosening the brake line at the outlet ports. (Courtesy of Allied Signal Automotive Aftermarket)

Figure 3–69 Using an air punch next to the bleeder valve to help "break the taper" on the bleeder valve.

1. Right rear
2. Left rear
3. Right front
4. Left front

NOTE: Before bleeding the front brakes, attach a holding tool to the stem or the metering valve to allow the brake fluid to flow through the valve unrestricted. See Figure 3–71.

NOTE: If the vehicle has two wheel cylinders on one brake, bleed the upper cylinder first.

For vehicles equipped with a diagonal split section, follow the brake bleeding procedure recommended in the service manual or service information for the vehicle you are servicing.

■ MANUAL BLEEDING

Manual bleeding is the process of applying force (with the help from an assistant) to the brake pedal (service brakes) while the bleeder valve is opened slightly. The brake master

For most rear-wheel-drive vehicles equipped with a front/rear split system, start the bleeding with the wheel farthest from the master cylinder and work toward the closest (see Figure 3–70).

For most vehicles, this sequence is:

Figure 3–70 Most vehicle manufacturers recommend starting the brake bleeding process at the rear wheel farthest from the master cylinder.

cylinder applies pressure on the fluid that is forced out through the bleeder valve along with any trapped air.

In most cases, if only the one wheel cylinder or hydraulic line has been opened, only that wheel cylinder needs to be bled. If the brake system has been opened for an extended period of time or all four wheels have been opened, bleed the system in the sequence recommended by the vehicle manufacturer.

> **NOTE:** See service manual for the exact brake bleeding procedure for the vehicle you are servicing.

Manual Bleeding Procedure

To bleed the brakes, attach a hose to the bleeder screw. Place the other end of the hose into a glass jar, partially filled with fresh brake fluid. Be sure to keep the hose submerged in the brake fluid because it shows air bubbles as it comes out of the system and prevents air from accidentally being drawn into the system through the bleeder valve (see Figure 3–72).

Do It Right—Replace the Brake Fluid

Often, used brake fluid looks like black coffee or coffee with cream. Both conditions indicate contaminated or moisture-laden brake fluid that should be replaced. The following steps will help ensure a complete brake fluid change:

Step 1 Remove the old brake fluid from the master cylinder using a suction bulb. (Dispose of this old brake fluid properly.)

Step 2 Fill the master cylinder with new clean brake fluid from a sealed container.

Step 3 Bleed each wheel brake until the brake fluid is clean.

> **CAUTION:** Do not allow the master cylinder to run out of brake fluid. Recheck and refill as necessary during the bleeding process.

This brake fluid replacement will fully restore the brake hydraulic system to as-new condition and help protect the system from rust and corrosion. Only replacing the friction pads and/or linings is not a complete and thorough brake system service. Customers should be educated as to the importance of this service procedure.

Have an assistant depress the brake pedal several times with the engine *off* to remove the power brake assist reserve. Press the brake pedal slowly and hold. Open the bleeder valve to purge the air from the system. Trapped air will hiss or spurt from the bleeder when the valve is opened. The bleeding sequence should be repeated as necessary until a solid stream of the brake fluid without air bubbles is observed flowing from the opened bleeder valve.

Figure 3–71 Special tool being used to hold out the valve stem on the metering valve. This allows brake fluid to flow unrestricted to the front brakes. If this valve was not released, a lot of brake pedal pressure would have to be used to overcome the metering valve.

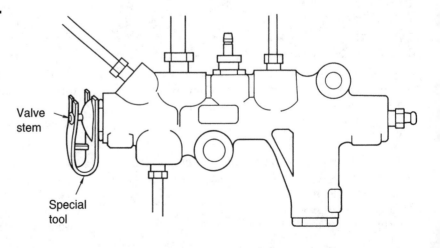

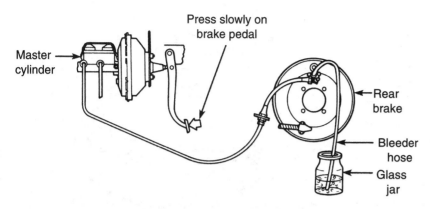

Master cylinder

Press slowly on brake pedal

Rear brake

Bleeder hose

Glass jar

Figure 3–72 Manual brake bleeding is best accomplished using a hose slipped over the outlet of the bleeder valve and submerged in a jar of clean brake fluid. (Courtesy of Allied Signal Automotive Aftermarket)

TECH TIP ✔

Tiny Bubbles

Do not use excessive brake pedal force while bleeding and never normally bleed the brake with the engine running! The extra assist from the power brake unit greatly increases the force exerted on the brake fluid in the master cylinder. The trapped air bubbles may be dispersed into tiny bubbles that often cling to the inside surface of the brake lines. These tiny air bubbles may not be able to be bled from the hydraulic system until enough time has allowed the bubbles to reform. To help prevent excessive force, do *not* start the engine. Without power assistance, the brake pedal force can be kept from becoming excessive. If the dispersal of the air into tiny bubbles is suspected, try tapping the calipers or wheel cylinders with a plastic hammer. After this tapping, simply waiting for a period of time will cause the bubbles to reform into larger and easier-to-bleed air pockets. Most brake experts recommend waiting **fifteen seconds or longer** between attempts to bleed each wheel. This waiting period is critical and allows time for the air bubbles to form.

HINT: To help prevent depressing the brake pedal down too far, some experts recommend placing a wooden 2″ × 4″ under the brake pedal. This helps prevent the seals inside the master cylinder from traveling over unused sections inside the bore that may be corroded or rusty.

Frequently Asked Question ???

What Is Reverse Fluid Injection?

Reverse fluid injection is a procedure that uses an air- or hand-operated injection gun that pushes brake fluid from the bleeder valve into the hydraulic system. See Figure 3–73. By forcing brake fluid into the bleeder valve, any trapped air is forced upward into the master cylinder.

CAUTION: This procedure should only be done after a thorough flushing of the hydraulic system. Many experts warn that debris and sediment in the hydraulic system can be back-flushed into the ABS hydraulic unit and/or master cylinder. Many brake and ABS failures have been caused by forcing old brake fluid back into the system.

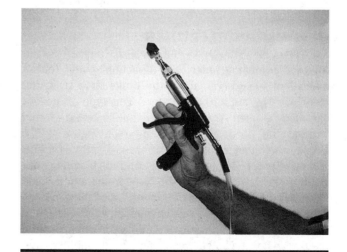

Figure 3–73 A reverse fluid injection gun used to inject brake fluid into the hydraulic system through the open bleeder valve. This method should only be performed after the hydraulic system has been flushed with new brake fluid to avoid the possibility of old contaminated fluid damaging the ABS hydraulic unit and/or the master cylinder.

For best results do not allow the brake pedal to go to the floor. Some vehicle manufacturers recommend placing a block of wood about 1″ (25 mm) thick under the brake pedal to keep it from bottoming. If the brake pedal is allowed to travel down to the floor, the sealing cups inside the master cylinder will be forced to travel further down the bore of the master cylinder than normal. Because rust and dirt can accumulate in this area beyond the working range, the seals can be damaged.

All vehicle manufacturers and brake experts agree that the technician should wait at least fifteen seconds before repeating the bleeding procedure. This wait time is important to allow time for any air bubbles present to reform into larger bubbles that can be more easily bled out of the system. See the Tech Tip, "Tiny Bubbles" for details.

> **NOTE:** Make certain all the brake components such as calipers and wheel cylinders are correctly installed with the bleeder valve located on the highest section of the part. Some wheel cylinders and calipers (such as many Ford calipers) can be installed upside down! This usually occurs whenever both front calipers are off the vehicle and they accidentally get reversed left to right. If this occurs, the air will never be completely bled from the caliper.

■ PRESSURE BLEEDING

Pressure bleeding is a term used to describe the use of pressure on top of the master cylinder to rid the hydraulic brake system of trapped air. Pressure bleeders must use the correct master cylinder adapter (see Figures 3–74, 3–75, and 3–76).

Whenever using a power bleeder, do not exceed 20 psi of pressure (140 kPa). Since the pressure is low, the button on the metering valve (if equipped) must be either pushed in or pulled out depending on the design and manufacturer. If the metering valve is not released, no fluid pressure will be applied to the front disc brakes. A major disadvantage to using the pressure bleeding method is the use of the correct master cylinder reservoir adapter fitting. Using the wrong adapter or not installing it correctly can cause brake fluid to leak out under pressure causing damage to the vehicle.

■ VACUUM BLEEDING

Another popular bleeder uses a vacuum pump (either manual or electric) to draw the brake fluid from the bleeder valve and into a container. This type of bleeder can also be used to bleed the hydraulic brake system without the need of an assistant (see Figure 3–77). Loosen the bleeder valve at least three-fourths of a turn and operate the vacuum bleeder. Continue bleeding until clean brake fluid flows into the bleeder container. Some air bubbles may be seen in the clear plastic tubing leading from the bleeder valve to the vacuum bleeder unit. Often these bubbles are the result of air being drawn in around the threads of the bleeder valve and do not indicate that there is air in the brake system (see Figure 3–78).

■ GRAVITY BLEEDING

Gravity bleeding is a slow, but effective, method that will work on many vehicles to rid the hydraulic system

Figure 3–74 Typical pressure bleeder. The brake fluid inside is pressurized with air pressure in the air chamber. This air pressure is applied to the brake fluid in the upper section. A rubber diaphragm separates the air from the brake fluid. (Courtesy of EIS Brake Parts)

of air. The procedure involves simply opening the bleeder valve and waiting until brake fluid flows from the open valve. Any air trapped in the port being bled will rise and escape from the port when the valve is opened. It may take several minutes before brake fluid escapes. If no brake fluid comes out, remove the bleeder valve entirely—it may be clogged. Remember, nothing but air and brake fluid will be *slowly* coming out of the wheel cylinder or caliper when the bleeder valve is removed. *Do not press on the brake pedal with the bleeder valve out while gravity bleeding.*

Gravity bleeding works because any liquid tends to seek its own level. This means that the brake fluid in the master cylinder tends to flow downward toward the wheel cylinders or calipers. As long as the brake fluid level in the master cylinder is higher than the bleeder valve, the brake fluid will flow downward and out the open bleeder as shown in Figure 3–79.

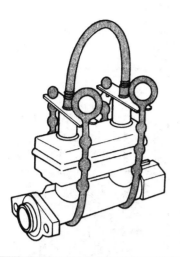

Figure 3–75 Brake fluid under pressure from the power bleeder is applied to the top of the master cylinder. It is very important that the proper adapter be used for the master cylinder. Failure to use the correct adapter or failure to release the pressure on the brake fluid before removing the adapter can cause brake fluid to escape under pressure. (Courtesy of Allied Signal Automotive Aftermarket)

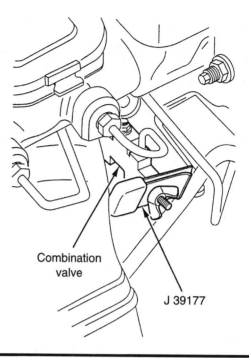

Figure 3–76 Pressure bleeding also requires that the metering valve be released because the pressure from the bleeder is not high enough to overcome the metering valve operation. This special tool holding the metering valve stem works on many General Motors vehicles. (Courtesy of General Motors)

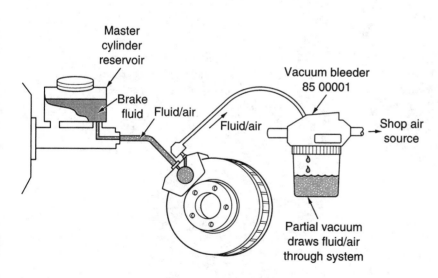

Figure 3–77 Vacuum bleeding is an easy method to use and does not require special adapters or an assistant. The vacuum bleeder shown uses compressed air flowing through a restriction to create a vacuum. A hand-operated vacuum pump is also available and does an excellent job at a moderate cost. (Courtesy of General Motors)

This flow of brake fluid can even get past the metering valve and proportioning valve. The proportioning valve is normally open to the rear brakes until the pressure reaches a predetermined level when it starts to limit increasing pressure to the rear brakes. The metering valve used to control or delay the operation of the front brakes is open to the front wheels until the pressure exceeds 10 to 15 psi (70 to 100 kPa). Therefore, as long as no one is pushing on the brake pedal, the metering valve remains open to the front wheels and the brake fluid from the master cylinder can easily flow downward through the valve and out the open bleeder valve.

Since no pressure is exerted on the brake fluid, the large air bubbles remain large air bubbles and are not separated into smaller, harder-to-bleed air bubbles that can occur with manual bleeding.

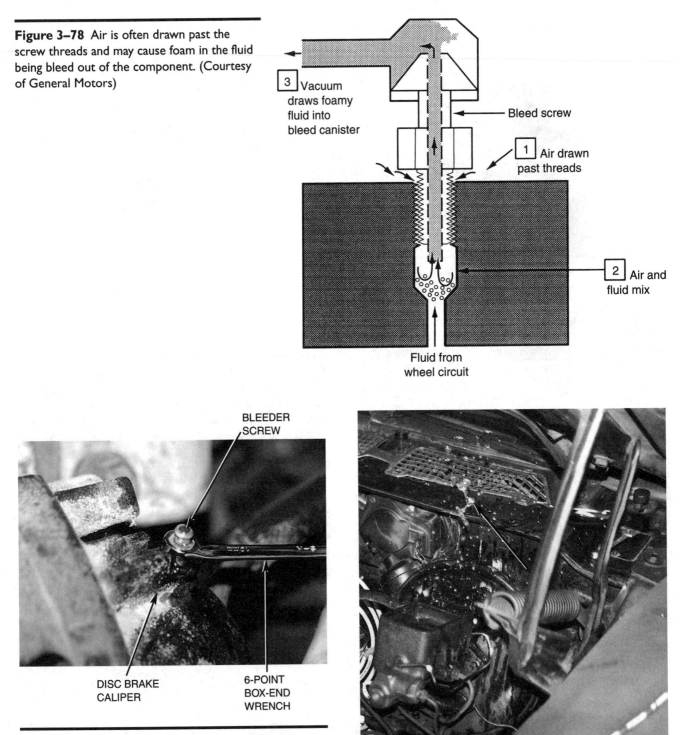

Figure 3–78 Air is often drawn past the screw threads and may cause foam in the fluid being bleed out of the component. (Courtesy of General Motors)

3 Vacuum draws foamy fluid into bleed canister

Bleed screw

1 Air drawn past threads

2 Air and fluid mix

Fluid from wheel circuit

BLEEDER SCREW

DISC BRAKE CALIPER

6-POINT BOX-END WRENCH

Figure 3–79 Gravity bleeding a disc brake caliper. Simply open the bleeder valve and wait until the brake fluid is observed flowing out of the valve. Gravity alone is what forces out all of the air between the master cylinder and the caliper bleeder valve.

Figure 3–80 Note the large drops being squirted from the top of the master cylinder due to trapped air when the brakes were released.

TECH TIP ✔

Quick-and-Easy Test for Air in the Lines

If air is in the brake lines, the brake pedal will be low and will usually feel "spongy" or "mushy." To confirm that trapped air in the hydraulic system is the cause, perform this simple and fast test:

Step 1. Remove the cover from the master cylinder. Have an assistant pump the brake pedal several times and then hold the pedal down.

Step 2. Observe the squirts of brake fluid from the master cylinder when the brake pedal is quickly released. (This is best performed by allowing the foot to slip off the end of the brake pedal.)

Results

If the brake fluid squirts higher than 3″ (8 cm) from the surface, then air is trapped in the hydraulic system. See Figure 3–80.

> *CAUTION:* Always use a fender cover whenever performing this test. Brake fluid will remove paint if it gets onto the unprotected fender. See Figure 3–81 for an example of how to keep fender covers from slipping off.

Explanation

Air can be compressed, liquid cannot be compressed. When pumping the brake pedal, the assistant is compressing any trapped air. When the pedal is released quickly, the compressed air expands and takes up more volume forcing the brake fluid upward through the compensation ports into the reservoir. Some upward movement is normal because of the return spring pressure on the valves in the master cylinder and springs in the wheel cylinders. If, however, the spurt is higher than normal, this is a sure sign of air being trapped in the system. This test is also called "the air entrapment test."

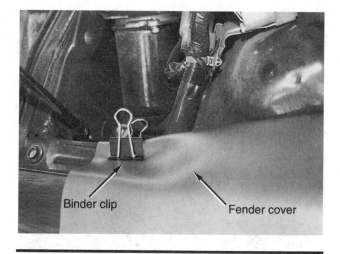

Binder clip   Fender cover

Figure 3–81 It is very important to use fender covers to protect the paint of the vehicle from being splashed with brake fluid. Use a binder clip available at local office supply stores to clip the fender cover to the lip of the fender preventing the fender cover from slipping.

PHOTO SEQUENCE   Brake Bleeding

PS3–1 The first step is to remove the protective rubber cap that covers the bleeder valve.

PS3–2 To help loosen the bleeder valve, use a hammer to tap on the it. The shock of the hammer blow helps free the bleeder valve.

PS3–3 Place a six-point box-end wrench onto the bleeder valve and use a hammer to lightly tap the wrench clockwise as if to tighten the bleeder valve. The shock of the hammer blow again helps loosen the bleeder valve.

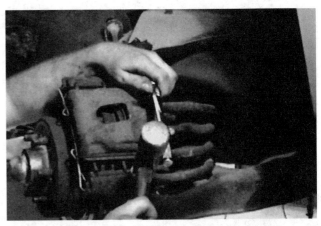

PS3–4 Now use a hammer to tap the wrench in the counterclockwise position. This should loosen the bleeder valve.

PS3–5 The tapered portion of the bleeder valve is what seals the brake fluid in the caliper as shown. The repeated shock blows help break this taper. If the taper is not broken, the bleeder valve is often broken, requiring that the old bleeder valve be drilled and the caliper be tapped for an oversize bleeder valve.

PS3–6 A vacuum-type bleeder being used to draw brake fluid from the open bleeder valve into the handheld unit. Shop air is used to create the vacuum to draw the fluid from the caliper.

Brake Bleeding—continued

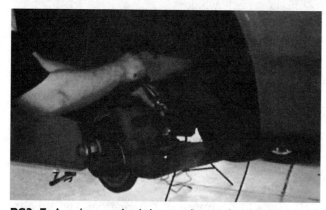

PS3–7 Another method that can be used to bleed a caliper is called a manual method. To manually bleed a caliper, loosen the bleeder valve about one full turn.

PS3–9 Tighten the bleeder valve.

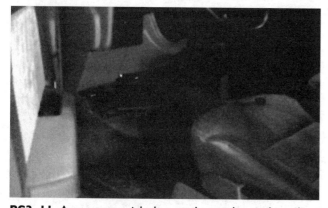

PS3–11 A common trick that can be used to reduce the need to bleed the system after a component has been replaced is to use a brake pedal depressor to depress the brake pedal about 1″ (25 mm).

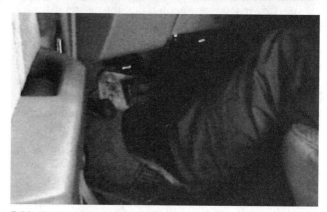

PS3–8 To prevent the possibility of harming the master cylinder, place a block of wood under the brake pedal. This block limits the brake pedal to normal travel. Depress the brake pedal and air and some fluid should flow from the bleeder valve.

PS3–10 After tightening the bleeder valve, release the brake pedal. Failure to tighten the bleeder before releasing the brake pedal will cause air to be drawn back into the caliper. Repeat the procedure as needed until only fluid is observed flowing from the bleeder valve.

PS3–12 With the brake pedal depressed, the primary seals inside the master cylinder block the fluid in the reservoir from dripping out of an open line. Note in this picture, the bleeder valve has been completely removed from the caliper and the brake fluid is not running out.

■ SUMMARY

1. The brake pedal mechanism increases the force of the driver's foot and applies it to the master cylinder.

2. During a typical brake application only about 1 teaspoon (5 ml or cc) of brake fluid actually is moved from the master cylinder and into the hydraulic system.

3. Pascal's Law states: "When a force is applied to a liquid confined in a container or enclosure, the pressure is transmitted equally and undiminished in every direction."

4. Master cylinder reservoirs are large enough for the brakes to be worn completely down and still have a small reserve.

5. The front port of the master cylinder is called the compensating port and the rear port is called the inlet port.

6. A residual check valve was used on some older model vehicles with drum brakes. The purpose of the valve was to keep a slight positive pressure on the brake fluid in the wheel cylinder to keep the lip of the sealing cup from collapsing when the brakes were released.

7. Brake system diagnosis should always start with checking for compensation.

8. Dual split master cylinders that separate the front brakes from the rear brakes are used on rear-wheel-drive vehicles.

9. Diagonal split master cylinders that separate right front and left rear from the left front and right rear brakes are used on front-wheel-drive vehicles.

10. Some master cylinders can be rebuilt, but the cylinder bore should not be honed unless recommended by the manufacturer.

11. A pressure differential or a brake fluid level sensor will light the red brake warning lamp if there is a leak in the hydraulic system.

12. A proportioning valve is used in braking systems to limit and control the pressure sent to the rear brakes to help prevent rear wheel lockup during heavy braking.

13. A metering valve (hold-off valve) delays the operation of the front disc brakes until enough pressure has been sent to the rear drum brakes to overcome return spring pressure. This valve helps prevent front-wheel lockup during light braking on slippery surfaces.

14. Metal brake line should be double-wall steel tubing for strength and use either a double flare or an ISO flare at the ends.

15. Flexible brake line is made from many layers of fabric and rubber.

16. Air trapped in the hydraulic system is removed by bleeding the brakes. Bleeder valves are used to bleed the air from disc brake calipers and drum brake wheel cylinders.

■ REVIEW QUESTIONS

1. Explain Pascal's Law.

2. Describe how a master cylinder works.

3. Discuss the difference between a dual split and a diagonal split master cylinder.

4. Explain the operation of the pressure-differential switch.

5. Describe the purpose of the metering and proportioning valves.

6. List the procedure for bleeding air from the hydraulic brake system.

■ ASE CERTIFICATION-TYPE QUESTIONS

1. Two technicians are discussing master cylinders. Technician A says that it is normal to see fluid movement in the reservoir when the brake pedal is depressed. Technician B says a defective master cylinder can cause the brake pedal to slowly sink to the floor when depressed. Which technician is correct?
   a. Technician A only
   b. Technician B only
   c. Both Technician A and B
   d. Neither Technician A nor B

2. Technician A says a pull to the right during braking could be caused by a defective metering valve. Technician B says a pull to the left could be caused by a defective proportioning valve. Which technician is correct?
   a. Technician A only
   b. Technician B only
   c. Both Technician A and B
   d. Neither Technician A nor B

3. If the brake pedal linkage is not adjusted correctly, brake fluid may not be able to expand back into the reservoir through the _____ port of the master cylinder when the brakes get hot.
   a. Vent port (forward hole)
   b. Replenishing port (rearward hole)

4. The primary brake circuit fails due to a leak in the lines leaving the rear section of a dual split master cylinder. Technician A says that the driver will

notice a lower-than-normal brake pedal and some reduced braking power. Technician B says that the brake pedal will "grab" higher than normal. Which technician is correct?

   a. Technician A only
   b. Technician B only
   c. Both Technician A and B
   d. Neither Technician A nor B

5. Two technicians are discussing a problem where the brake pedal travels too far before the vehicle starts to slow. Technician A says that the brakes may be out of adjustment. Technician B says that one circuit from the master cylinder may be leaking or defective. Which technician is correct?

   a. Technician A only
   b. Technician B only
   c. Both Technician A and B
   d. Neither Technician A nor B

6. The rear brakes lock up during a regular brake application. Technician A says the metering valve could be the cause. Technician B says that stuck front disc brake calipers could be the cause. Which technician is correct?

   a. Technician A only
   b. Technician B only
   c. Both Technician A and B
   d. Neither Technician A nor B

7. A spongy brake pedal is being diagnosed. Technician A says that air in the hydraulic system could be the cause. Technician B says a defective pressure-differential switch could be the cause. Which technician is correct?

   a. Technician A only
   b. Technician B only
   c. Both Technician A and B
   d. Neither Technician A nor B

8. The button on the _____ valve should be held when bleeding the brakes.

   a. Metering
   b. Proportioning
   c. Pressure-differential
   d. Residual check

9. A double lap flare and an ISO flare are interchangeable.

   a. True
   b. False

10. The brake bleeding procedure usually specified for a rear-wheel vehicle with a dual split master cylinder is:

   a. RR, LR, RF, LF
   b. LF, RF, LR, RR
   c. RF, LR, LF, RR
   d. LR, RR, LF, RF

Wheel Bearings and Service

Bearings allow the wheels of a vehicle to rotate and still support the weight of the entire vehicle.

■ ANTIFRICTION BEARINGS

Antifriction bearings use rolling parts inside the bearing to reduce friction. Four styles of rolling contact bearings include ball, roller, needle, and tapered roller bearings as shown in Figure 4–1. All four styles convert sliding friction into rolling motion. All of the weight of a vehicle or load on the bearing is transferred through the rolling part. In a ball bearing, all of the load is concentrated into small spots where the ball contacts the **inner** and **outer race (rings).** See Figure 4–2.

While ball bearings cannot support the same weight as roller bearings, there is less friction in ball bearings and they generally operate at higher speeds. A roller bearing having a greater (longer) contact area can support heavier loads than a ball bearing (see Figure 4–3).

A needle bearing is a type of roller bearing that uses smaller rollers called **needle rollers.** The clearance between the diameter of the ball or straight roller is manufactured into the bearing to provide the proper **radial clearance** and is *not adjustable.*

■ TAPERED ROLLER BEARINGS

The most commonly used automotive wheel bearing is the tapered roller bearing. Not only is the bearing itself tapered, but the rollers are also tapered. By design, this type of bearing can withstand **radial** (up and down) as well as **axial** (thrust) loads in one direction (see Figure 4–4).

Most non-drive-wheel bearings use tapered roller bearings. The taper allows more weight to be handled by the friction-reducing bearings, because the weight is directed over the entire length of each roller rather than concentrated on a small spot as with ball bearings. Because of the taper, these bearings are called tapered roller bearings. The rollers are held in place by a **cage**

Figure 4–1 Rolling contact bearings include (left to right) ball, roller, needle, and tapered roller.

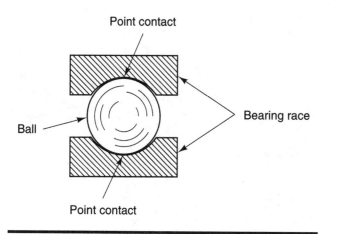

Figure 4–2 Ball bearing point contact.

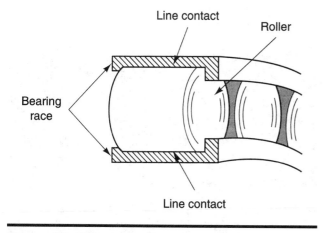

Figure 4–3 Roller bearing line contact.

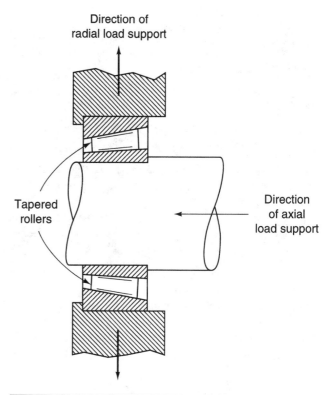

Figure 4–4 A tapered roller bearing will support a radial load and an axial load in only one direction.

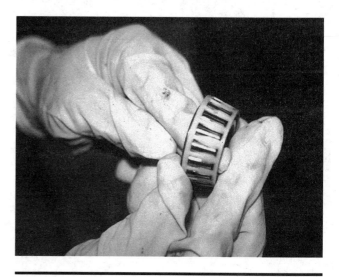

Figure 4–5 Many tapered roller bearings use a plastic cage to retain the rollers.

between the inner race (also called the **inner ring** or **cone**) and the outer race (also called the **outer ring** or **cup**). Tapered roller bearings must be loose in the cage to allow for heat expansion. Tapered roller bearings should always be adjusted for a certain amount of free play to allow for heat expansion. On non-drive-axle vehicle wheels, the cup is tightly fitted to the wheel hub and the cone is loosely fitted to the wheel spindle. New bearings come packaged with rollers, cage, and inner race assembled together with the outer race wrapped with moisture-resistant paper (see Figure 4–5).

■ INNER AND OUTER WHEEL BEARINGS

Most rear-wheel-drive vehicles use an inner and an outer wheel bearing on the front wheels. The inner wheel bearing is always the larger bearing because it is designed to carry most of the vehicle weight and transmit the weight to the suspension through to the spindle (see Figure 4–6). Between the inner wheel bearing and the spindle, there is a grease seal which prevents grease

from getting onto the braking surface and prevents dirt and moisture from entering the bearing.

■ STANDARD BEARING SIZES

Bearings use standard dimensions for inside diameter, width, and outside diameter. The standardization of bearing sizes helps interchangeability. The dimensions

Figure 4–6 Non-drive-wheel hub with inner and outer tapered roller bearings. By angling the inner and outer in opposite directions, axial (thrust) loads are supported in both directions.

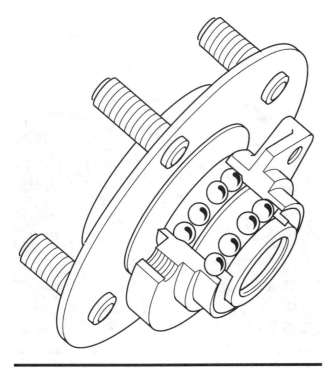

Figure 4–7 This front-wheel bearing assembly is a double row ball bearing design. It is a prelubricated sealed bearing. The bearing assembly is a loose fit in the steering knuckle. The drive axle shaft is a splined fit through the bearing.

that are standardized include bearing bore size (inside diameter), bearing series (light to heavy usage), and external dimensions. When replacing a wheel bearing, note the original bearing brand name and number. Replacement bearing catalogs usually have cross-over charts from one brand to another. The bearing number is usually the same because of the interchangeability and standardization within the wheel bearing industry.

Figure 4–8 Hub and bearing assembly pulled from the knuckle and drive axle shaft.

Figure 4–9 Many sealed wheel bearings incorporate the tone wheel for the antilock brake system (ABS) wheel-speed sensor.

■ SEALED FRONT-WHEEL-DRIVE BEARINGS

Most front-wheel-drive (FWD) vehicles use a sealed nonadjustable front wheel bearing. This type of bearing can include either two preloaded tapered roller bearings or a double row ball bearing. This type of sealed bearing is also used on the rear of many front-wheel-drive vehicles (see Figures 4–7, 4–8, and 4–9).

Double row ball bearings are often used because of their reduced friction and greater seize resistance.

■ BEARING GREASES

Vehicle manufacturers specify the type and consistency of grease for each application. The technician should know what these specifications mean. Grease is an oil with a thickening agent to allow it to be installed in places where a liquid lubricant would not stay. Greases

Figure 4–10 Typical lip seal with a garter spring.

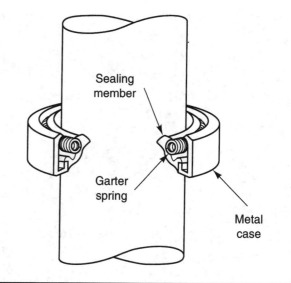

Figure 4–11 A garter spring helps hold the sharp lip edge of the seal tight against the shaft. (Courtesy of Dana Corporation)

are named for their thickening agent such as aluminum, barium, calcium, lithium, or sodium.

The **American Society for Testing Materials (ASTM)** specifies the consistency using a **penetration** test. The **National Lubricating Grease Institute (NLGI)** uses the penetration test as a guide to assign the grease a number. Low numbers are very fluid and higher numbers are more firm or hard. See the following chart.

National Lubricating Grease Institute (NLGI) Numbers

NLGI Number	Relative Consistency
000	Very fluid
00	Fluid
0	Semifluid
1	Very soft
2	Soft (typically used for wheel bearings)
3	Semi-firm
4	Firm
5	Very firm
6	Hard

"Timken OK Load" is from a test that determines the maximum load the lubricant will carry. The "OK Load" is the maximum weight that can be applied without scoring on the test block.

More rolling bearings are destroyed by over-lubrication than by under-lubrication because the heat generated in the bearings cannot be transferred easily to the air through the excessive grease. Bearings should never be filled beyond one-third to one-half of their grease capacity by volume. Molybdenum disulfide is added to grease in amounts up to 10 percent for use as a multipurpose lubrication on automotive equipment parts such as chassis joints, steering joints, U-joints, and kingpins.

■ SEALS

Seals are used in all vehicles to keep lubricant, such as grease, from leaking out and to prevent dirt, dust, or water from getting into the bearing or lubricant. Two general applications of seals include static and dynamic. **Static seals** are used between two surfaces that do not move. **Dynamic seals** are used to seal between two surfaces that move. Wheel bearing seals are dynamic-type seals that must seal between rotating axle hubs and the stationary spindles or axle housing. Most dynamic seals use a synthetic rubber lip seal encased in metal. The lip is often held in contact with the moving part with the aid of a **garter spring** as seen in Figure 4–10.

The sealing lip should be installed toward the grease or fluid being contained (see Figure 4–11).

■ SYMPTOMS AND DIAGNOSIS OF DEFECTIVE BEARINGS

Wheel bearings control the positioning and reduce the rolling resistance of vehicle wheels. Whenever a bearing fails, the wheel may not be kept in position and noise is usually heard. Symptoms of defective wheel bearings include:

1. A hum, rumbling, or growling noise which increases with vehicle speed
2. Roughness felt in the steering wheel which changes with the vehicle speed or cornering
3. Looseness or excessive play in the steering wheel especially while driving over rough road surfaces
4. In severe cases of a defective front wheel bearing, a loud grinding noise

TECH TIP ✔

Bearing Overload

It is not uncommon for vehicles to be overloaded. This is particularly common with pickup trucks and vans. Whenever there is a heavy load, the axle bearings must support the entire weight of the vehicle including its cargo. If a bump is hit while driving with a heavy load, the balls of a ball bearing or the rollers of a roller bearing can make an indent in the race of the bearing. This dent or imprint is called **brinelling**, named after Johann A. Brinell, a Swedish engineer, who developed a process of testing for surface hardness by pressing a hard ball with a standard force into a sample material to be tested.

Once this imprint is made, the bearing will make noise whenever the roller or ball rolls over the indent. Continued use causes wear to occur on all of the balls or rollers and eventual failure. While this may take months to fail, the *cause* of the bearing failure is often overloading of the vehicle. Avoid shock loads and overloading for safety and for longer vehicle life.

5. Pulling during braking
6. With the vehicle off the ground, rotate the wheel by hand listening and feeling carefully for bearing roughness.
7. Grasp the wheel at the top and bottom and wiggle it back and forth checking for bearing looseness.

NOTE: Excessive looseness in the wheel bearings can cause a low brake pedal. If any of the above symptoms are present, carefully clean and inspect the bearings.

■ NON-DRIVE-WHEEL BEARING INSPECTION AND SERVICE

1. Hoist the vehicle safely.
2. Remove the wheel.
3. Remove the brake caliper assembly and support it with a coat hanger or other suitable hook to avoid allowing the caliper to hang by the brake hose.
4. Remove the grease cap (dust cap). See Figure 4–12.
5. Remove the old cotter key and discard.

NOTE: The term *cotter* as in cotter key or cotter pin is derived from the old English verb meaning "to close or fasten."

6. Remove the spindle nut (castle nut).
7. Remove the washer and the outer wheel bearing (see Figure 4–13).

Figure 4–12 Removing the grease cap with grease cap pliers.

Figure 4–13 After wiggling the brake rotor slightly, the washer and outer bearing can be easily lifted out of the wheel hub.

8. Remove the bearing hub from the spindle. The inner bearing will remain in the hub and may be removed (simply lifted out) after the grease seal is pried out (see Figure 4–14).
9. Most vehicle and bearing manufacturers recommend cleaning the bearing thoroughly in solvent or acetone. If there is no acetone, clean the solvent off the bearings with denatured alcohol to make certain that the thin solvent layer is completely washed off and dry. *All solvent must be removed or allowed to dry from the bearing because the new grease will not stick to a layer of solvent.*
10. Carefully inspect the bearings and the races for the following:
    a. the outer race for lines, scratches, or pits
    b. the cage should be round; if the round cage has straight sections, this is an indication of an over-

Figure 4–14 Some technicians remove the inner wheel bearing and the grease seal at the same time by jerking the rotor off the spindle after reinstalling the spindle nut. While this is an quick-and-easy method, sometimes the bearing is damaged (deformed) from being jerked out of the hub using this procedure.

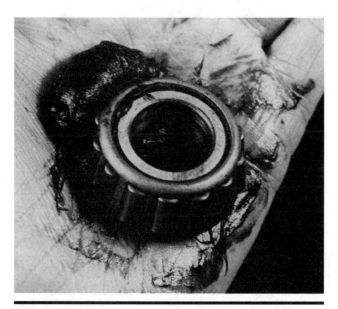

Figure 4–15 When packing grease into a cleaned bearing, force grease around each roller as shown.

Figure 4–16 Installing a grease seal with a special tool after installing the inner bearing.

    tightened adjustment or the cage has been dropped.

    If any of the above are observed, then the bearing, including the outer race, must be replaced. Failure to replace the outer race (which is included when purchasing a bearing) could lead to rapid failure of the new bearing.

11. Pack the cleaned or new bearing thoroughly with clean, new, approved wheel bearing grease using hand packing or a wheel bearing packer. Always clean out all of the old grease before applying the recommended type of new grease. *Because of compatibility problems, it is not recommended that greases be mixed.* See Figure 4–15.

> **NOTE:** Some vehicle manufacturers do *not* recommend that "stringy-type" wheel bearing grease be used. Centrifugal force can cause the grease to be thrown outward from the bearing. Because of the stringy texture, the grease may not flow back into the bearing after it has been thrown outward. The final result is lack of lubrication and eventual bearing failure.

12. Place a thin layer of grease on the outer race.
13. Apply a thin layer of grease to the spindle being sure to cover the outer bearing seat, inner bearing seat, and shoulder at the grease seal seat.
14. Install a new **grease seal** (also called a **grease retainer**) flush with the hub (see Figure 4–16).

Figure 4–17 The wheel bearing adjustment procedure as specified for rear-wheel-drive General Motor's vehicles. (Courtesy of Oldsmobile Division)

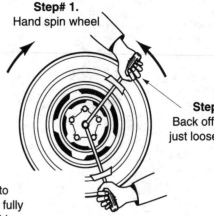

Step# 1.
Hand spin wheel

Step# 3.
Back off nut until just loose position

Step# 2.
Tighten the nut to 12 ft. lbs. (16 N•m) fully seat bearings – this overcomes any burrs on threads.

Step# 4.
Hand "snug up" the nut

Step# 5.
Loosen nut until either hole in the spindle lines up with a slot in the nut – then insert cotter pin.

NOTE: When the bearing is properly adjusted there will be from .001-.005 inches (.03-.13mm) end-play (looseness).

15. Place approximately 3 tablespoons of grease into the grease cavity of the wheel hub. Excessive grease could cause the inner grease seal to fail with the possibility of grease getting on the brakes. Place the rotor with the inner bearing and seal in place over the spindle until the grease seal rests on the grease seal shoulder.
16. Install the outer bearing and the bearing washer.
17. Install the spindle nut and, while rotating the tire assembly, tighten to about 12–30 lb. ft. with a wrench to "seat" the bearing correctly in the race (cup) and on the spindle. See Figure 4–17.
18. While still rotating the tire assembly, loosen the nut approximately 1/2 turn and then *hand tighten only* (about 5 in. lb.).

NOTE: If the wheel bearing is properly adjusted, the wheel will still have about 0.001″ to 0.005″ (0.03 to 0.13 mm) end play. This looseness is necessary to allow the tapered roller bearing to expand when hot and not bind or cause the wheel to lock up.

19. Install a new cotter key. (An old cotter key could break a part off where it was bent and lodge in the bearing causing major damage.)

HINT: Most vehicles use a cotter key that is 1/8″ in diameter by 1 1/2″ long.

20. If the cotter key does not line up with the hole in the spindle, loosen slightly (no more than 1/16″) of a turn until the hole lines up. Never tighten more than hand tight.
21. Bend the cotter key ends up and around the nut, not over the end of the spindle where the end of the cotter key could rub on the grease cap causing noise (see Figure 4–18).
22. Install the grease cap (dust cap) and the wheel cover.

CAUTION: Clean grease off disc brake rotors or drums after servicing the wheel bearings. Use a brake cleaner and a shop cloth. Even a slight amount of grease on the friction surfaces of the brakes can harm the friction lining and/or cause brake noise.

TECH TIP ✔

Wheel Bearing Looseness Test

Looseness in a front wheel bearing can allow the rotor to move whenever the front wheel hits a bump, forcing the caliper piston in, causing the brake pedal to kick back, and causing the feeling that the brakes were locking up.

Loose wheel bearings are easily diagnosed by removing the cover of the master cylinder reservoir and watching the brake fluid as the front wheels are turned left and right with the steering wheel. If the brake fluid moves while the front wheels are being turned, caliper piston(s) are moving in and out caused by loose wheel bearing(s). If everything is okay, the brake fluid should not move.

HINT: Loose wheel bearings can also cause the brake pedal to sink due to movement of the rotor causing the caliper piston to move. This sinking brake pedal is usually caused by a defective master cylinder. Before replacing a master cylinder, check the wheel bearings.

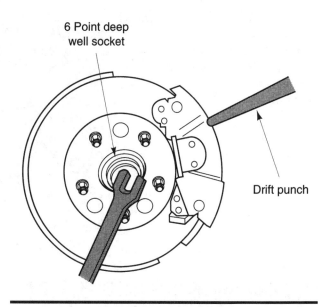

Figure 4–19 Removing the drive axle shaft hub nut. This nut is usually very tight and the drift (tapered) punch wedged into the cooling fins of the brake rotor keeps the hub from revolving when the nut is loosened. (Courtesy of Oldsmobile Division)

Figure 4–18 Properly installed cotter key.

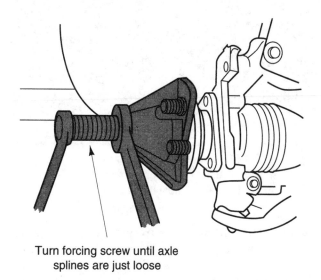

Figure 4–20 A special puller makes the job of removing the hub bearing from the knuckle easy without damaging any component. (Courtesy of Oldsmobile Division)

■ FRONT-WHEEL-DRIVE SEALED BEARING REPLACEMENT

Most front-wheel-drive vehicles use a sealed bearing assembly that is bolted to the steering knuckle and sup-

ports the drive axle. This design incorporates a splined drive hub that transfers power from the drive axle to the wheels that are bolted to the hub (see Figures 4–19, 4–20, and 4–21).

Many front-wheel-drive vehicles use a bearing that must be pressed off the steering knuckle. Special aftermarket tools are also available to remove many of the bearings without removing the knuckle from the vehicle. Check the factory service manual and tool manufacturers for exact procedures for the vehicle being serviced.

Figure 4–21 Be careful not to nick or damage the wheel speed sensor used for input information for traction control and antilock braking functions.

Figure 4–22 Retainer plate-type rear axles can be removed by first removing the brake drum. The fasteners can be reached through a hole in the axle flange.

Figure 4–23 A slide-hammer-type axle puller can also be used.

Diagnosing a defective front bearing on a front-wheel-drive vehicle is sometimes confusing. A defective wheel bearing is usually noisy while driving straight and the noise increases with vehicle speed (wheel speed). A drive axle shaft U-joint (CV joint) can also be the cause of noise on a front-wheel-drive vehicle, but usually makes *more noise* while turning and accelerating.

■ REAR AXLE BEARING AND SEAL REPLACEMENT

The rear bearings used on rear-wheel-drive vehicles are constructed and serviced differently from other types of wheel bearings. Rear axle bearings are either sealed or lubricated by the rear-end lubricant. The rear axle must be removed from the vehicle to replace the rear axle bearing. There are two basic types

of axle retaining methods, **retainer plate type** and the **C-lock.**

Retainer Plate-Type Axles

The retainer plate-type rear axle uses four fasteners that retain the axle in the axle housing. To remove the axle shaft and the rear axle bearing and seal, the retainer bolts or nuts must be removed.

HINT: If the axle flange has an access hole, then a retainer plate-type axle is used. See Figure 4–22.

The hole or holes in the wheel flange permit a socket wrench access to the fasteners. After the fasteners have been removed, the axle shaft must be removed from the rear axle housing. With the retainer plate-type rear axle, the bearing and the retaining ring are press-fit onto the axle and the bearing cup (outer race) is also a tight fit into the axle housing tube. See Figures 4–23, 4–24, and 4–25 for ways to remove the axle shaft.

Figure 4–24 The brake backing plate came off with the rear axle and bearing on this vehicle. The backing plate made it more difficult to press off the old bearing.

Figure 4–25 The ball bearings fell out onto the ground when this axle was pulled out of the axle housing. Diagnosing the cause of the noise and vibration was easy on this vehicle.

T E C H   T I P ✔

The Brake Drum Slide-Hammer Trick

To remove the axle from a vehicle equipped with a retainer-plate-type rear axle, simply use the brake drum as a slide hammer to remove the axle from the axle housing. See Figure 4–26. If the brake drum does not provide enough force, a slide hammer can also be used to remove the axle shaft.

> **NOTE:** When removing the differential cover, rear axle lubricant will flow from between the housing and the cover. Be sure to dispose of the old rear axle lubricant in the environmentally approved way, and refill with the proper type and viscosity (thickness) of rear-end lubricant. Check the vehicle specifications for the recommended grade.

C-Clip-Type Axles

Vehicles that use C-clips use a straight roller bearing supporting a semi-floating axle shaft inside the axle housing. The straight rollers do not have an inner race. The rollers ride on the axle itself. If a bearing fails, both the axle and the bearing usually need to be replaced. The outer bearing race holding the rollers is pressed into the rear axle housing. The axle bearing is usually lubricated by the rear-end lubricant and a grease seal is located on the outside of the bearing.

> **NOTE:** Some replacement bearings are available that are designed to ride on a fresh, unworn section of the old axle. These bearings allow the use of the original axle saving the cost of a replacement axle.

The C-clip-type rear axle retaining method requires that the differential cover plate be removed (see Figure 4–27).

After removal of the cover, the differential pinion shaft has to be removed before the C–clip that retains the axle can be removed (see Figure 4–28 on page 101).

Once the C-clip has been removed, the axle simply is pulled out of the axle tube. Axle bearings with inner races are pressed onto the axle shaft and must be pressed off using a hydraulic press. A bearing retaining collar should be chiseled or drilled into to expand the collar to allow it to be removed (see Figure 4–29 on page 101).

Always follow the manufacturer's recommended bearing removal and replacement procedures. Always replace the rear axle seal whenever replacing a rear axle bearing. See Figure 4–30 on page 101 for an example of seal removal.

See Figure 4–31 on page 102 for an example of a rear axle bearing with a broken outer race.

When refilling the differential, check for a tag or lettering as to the correct lubricant as shown in Figure 4–32 on page 102.

Always check the differential vent to make sure it is clear (see Figure 4–33 on page 102).

A clogged vent can cause excessive pressure to build up inside the differential and cause the rear axle seals to leak. If rear-end lubricant gets on the brake linings, the brakes will not have the proper friction and the linings themselves are ruined and must be replaced.

Figure 4–26 (a) To remove the axle from this vehicle equipped with a retainer-plate rear axle, the brake drum was placed back onto the axle studs backward so that the drum itself can be used as a slide hammer to pull the axle out of the axle housing. (b) A couple of pulls and the rear axle is pulled out of the axle housing.

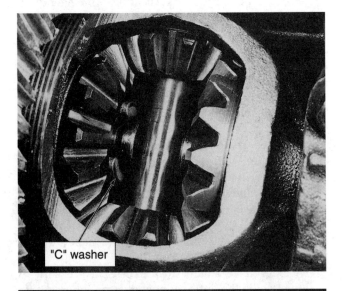

"C" washer

Figure 4–27 The C-clip (C washer) can be seen after removing the differential cover plate. The C-clip fits into a groove in the axle.

■ BEARING FAILURE ANALYSIS

Whenever a bearing is replaced, the old bearing must be inspected and the cause of the failure eliminated. See Figures 4–34 through 4–40 on pages 102–104 for examples of normal and abnormal bearing wear.

For example, a wheel bearing may fail for several reasons including:

Metal Fatigue—Long vehicle usage, even under normal driving conditions, causes metal to fatigue. Cracks often appear and eventually these cracks expand downward into the metal from the surface. The metal between the cracks can break out into small chips, slabs, or scales of metal. This process of breaking up is called **spalling** (see Figure 4–41 on page 104).

Shock Loading—Dents can be formed in the race of a bearing which eventually leads to bearing failure. See the Tech Tip, "Bearing Overload" and Figure 4–42 on page 105.

(a)

(b)

(c)

Figure 4–28 (a) Removing the pinion shaft lock bolt. (b) After the lock bolt has been removed, the pinion shaft can be removed. (c) The axle can be pushed inward slightly to allow the C-clip to be removed. After the C-clip has been removed, the axle can be easily pulled out of the axle housing.

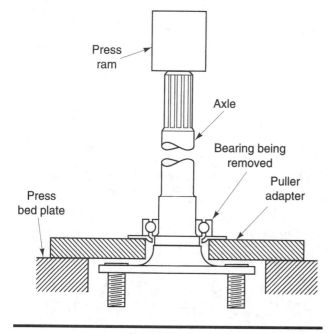

Figure 4–29 Using a hydraulic press to press an axle bearing from the axle. When pressing a new bearing back onto the axle, pressure should only be on the inner bearing race to prevent damaging the bearing.

Figure 4–30 Removing an axle seal using the axle shaft as the tool.

Figure 4–31 This axle bearing came from a high-mileage vehicle. The noise was first noticed when turning because weight transfer increased the load on the bearing. Later, the rumbling sound occurred all the time increasing in noise level as the vehicle speed increased.

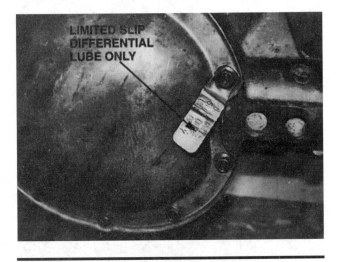

Figure 4–32 Always fill the differential with the correct lubricant as specified by the vehicle manufacturer. Many limited-slip-type differentials have a tag attached indicating that a special friction-reducing additive should be added to ensure proper operation.

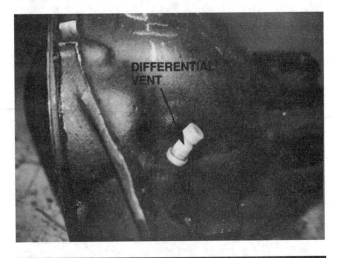

Figure 4–33 All differentials are vented. Some differentials, especially those used on pickup trucks and sport utility vehicles, connect a rubber hose to the differential housing and route the hose upward on the body of the vehicle to prevent water from getting into the differential if the vehicle is driven in high water. (Courtesy of SKF USA Inc.)

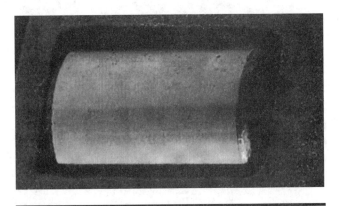

Figure 4–34 This is a normally worn bearing. If it does not have too much play, it can be reused. (Courtesy of SKF USA Inc.)

(a)

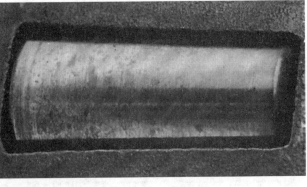

(b)

Figure 4–35 (a) When corrosion etches into the surface of a roller or race, the bearing should be discarded. (b) If light corrosion stains can be removed with an oil-soaked cloth, the bearing can be reused. (Courtesy of SKF USA Inc.)

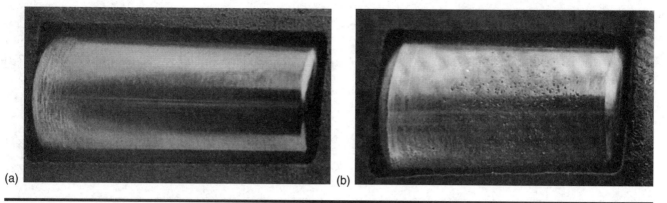

Figure 4–36 (a) When just the end of a roller is scored, it is because of excessive preload. Discard the bearing. (b) This is a more advanced case of pitting. Under load, it will rapidly lead to spalling. (Courtesy of SKF USA Inc.)

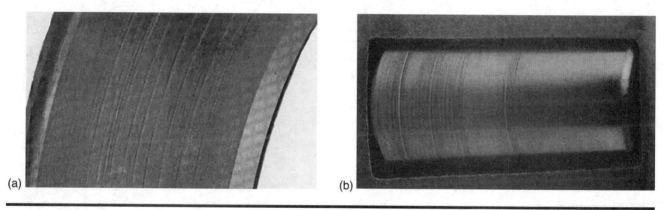

Figure 4–37 (a) Always check for faint grooves in the race. This bearing should not be reused. (b) Grooves like this are often matched by grooves in the race (above). Discard the bearing. (Courtesy of SKF USA Inc.)

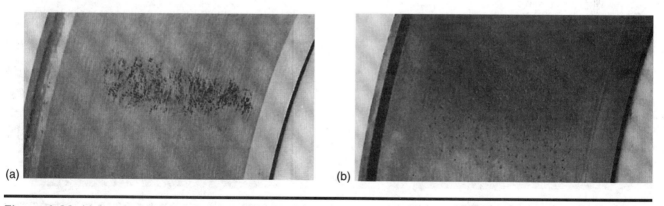

Figure 4–38 (a) Regular patterns of etching in the race are from corrosion. This bearing should be replaced. (b) Light pitting comes from contaminants being pressed into the race. Discard the bearing. (Courtesy of SKF USA Inc.)

Electrical Arcing—Electrical current flowing through a bearing can cause arcing and damage to the bearing, as shown in Figure 4–43 on page 105.

Electrical current can result from electrical welding on the vehicle without a proper ground connection. Without a proper return path, the electrical flow often travels throughout the vehicle attempting to find a ground path. Always place the ground cable as close as possible to the area being welded.

Another very common cause of bearing failure due to electrical arcing is a poor body ground wire connection between the body of the vehicle and the engine. All electrical current for accessories, lights, sound systems,

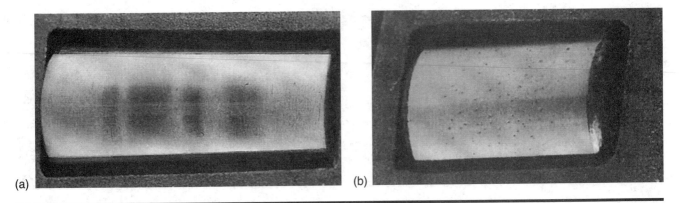

Figure 4–39 (a) This bearing is worn unevenly. Notice the stripes. It should not be reused. (b) Any damage that causes low spots in the metal renders the bearing useless. (Courtesy of SKF USA Inc.)

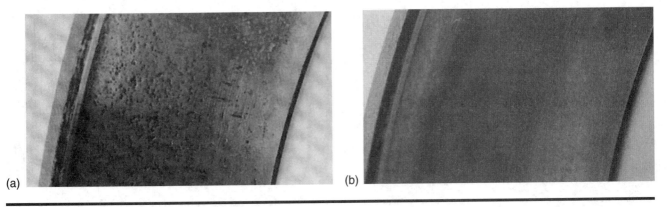

Figure 4–40 (a) In this more advanced case of pitting, you can see how the race has been damaged. (b) Discoloration is a result of overheating. Even a lightly burned bearing should be replaced. (Courtesy of SKF USA Inc.)

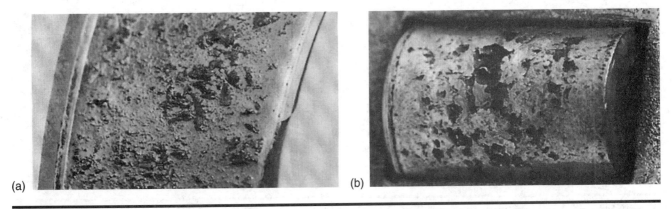

Figure 4–41 (a) Pitting eventually leads to spalling, a condition where the metal falls away in large chunks. (b) In this spalled roller, the metal has actually begun to flake away from the surface. (Courtesy of SKF USA Inc.)

etc., must return to the negative (−) terminal of the battery. If this ground wire connection becomes loose or corroded, the electrical current takes alternative paths to ground. The engine and entire drivetrain are electrically insulated by rubber mounts. Even the exhaust system is electrically insulated from the body or from the vehicle with rubber insulating **hangers.**

Suspension and wheel bearings are also insulated electrically by rubber control arm and shock absorber **bushings.**

However, dirt is a conductor of electricity especially when wet. Therefore, the dirt acts as an electrical conductor and allows electrical current to flow through the suspension system *through the bearing* to the en-

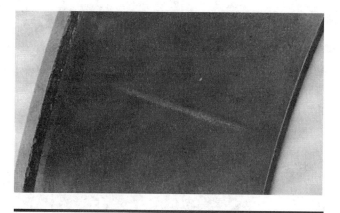

Figure 4–42 These dents resulted from the rollers "hammering" against the race, a condition called brinelling. (Courtesy of SKF USA Inc.)

Figure 4–43 This condition resulted from an improperly grounded arc welder. Replace the bearing. (Courtesy of SKF USA Inc.)

TECH TIP ✔

What's That Sound?

Defective wheel bearings usually make noise. The noise most defective wheel bearings make sounds like noisy off-road or aggressive tread, or mud and snow tires. Wheel bearing noise will remain constant while driving over different types of road surfaces while tire tread noise usually changes with different road surfaces. In fact, many defective bearings have been ignored by the vehicle owners and technicians because it was thought that the source of the noise was the aggressive tread design of the mud and snow tires. Always suspect defective wheel bearings whenever you hear what seems to be extreme or unusually loud tire noise.

gine block where the main starter ground cable connects to the battery negative (−) terminal.

Therefore, whenever any bearing is replaced in the chassis or driveline systems such as wheel bearings, U-joints, or drive axle shaft bearings, always check to see that the ground wires between the body of the vehicle and the engine block or negative (−) terminal of the battery are okay and the connections at both ends are clean and tight. If there is any doubt as to whether the body ground wires are okay, additional wires can always be added between the body and the engine without causing any harm.

■ SUMMARY

1. Wheel bearings support the entire weight of a vehicle and are used to reduce rolling friction. Ball and straight roller-type bearings are nonadjustable while **tapered** roller-type bearings must be adjusted for proper clearance.

2. Most front-wheel-drive vehicles use sealed bearings, either two preloaded tapered roller bearings or double row ball bearings.

3. Most wheel bearings are standardized sizes.

4. A defective bearing can be caused by metal fatigue that leads to **spalling** or caused by shock loads that cause **brinelling,** bearing damage from electrical arcing due to poor body ground wires or improper electrical welding on the vehicle.

5. Bearing grease is an oil with a thickener. The higher the NLGI number of the grease, the thicker or harder the grease consistency.

6. Tapered wheel bearings must be adjusted by hand tightening the spindle nut after properly seating the bearings. A new cotter key must always be used.

7. Defective wheel bearings usually make more noise while turning because more weight is applied to the bearing as the vehicle turns.

8. All bearings must be serviced, replaced, and/or adjusted using the vehicle manufacturer's recommended procedures as stated in the service manual.

PHOTO SEQUENCE Wheel Bearing Service

PS4–1 After safely hoisting the vehicle, remove the wheel(s) and then the dust (grease) cap.

PS4–2 Remove the old cotter key and discard it.

PS4–3 Remove the spindle nut and the washer.

PS4–4 Gently wiggle the disc brake rotor slightly to help free the outer wheel bearing.

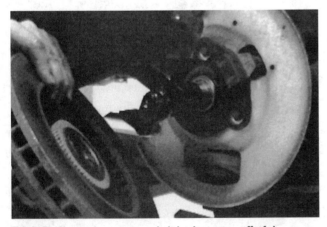

PS4–5 Grasp the rotor and slide the rotor off of the spindle.

PS4–6 Use a seal puller to remove the old seal. After the grease seal has been removed, remove the inner wheel bearing.

Wheel Bearing Service—continued

PS4–7 Thoroughly clean the wheel bearings. Cleaning solvent often leaves a residue on the surface of the bearings that should be removed using denatured alcohol. Brake cleaner can also be used. Thoroughly inspect the bearings for damage. Discard any bearing if a fault is discovered.

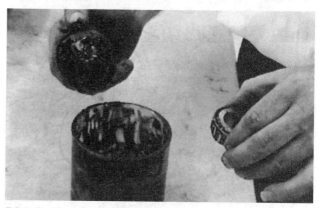

PS4–8 After the bearing has been thoroughly cleaned, it can be repacked using a bearing packer.

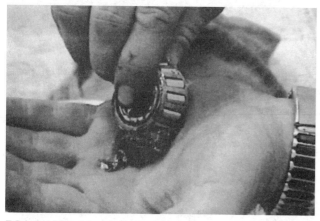

PS4–9 Wheel bearings can also be packed by hand. Place wheel bearing grease into your palm and force the grease between the inner and outer race of the bearing.

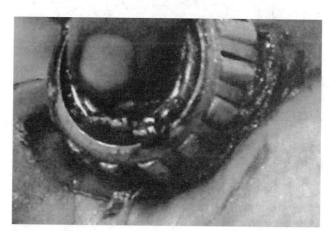

PS4–10 The grease should squirt out from between the roller bearing cage as shown.

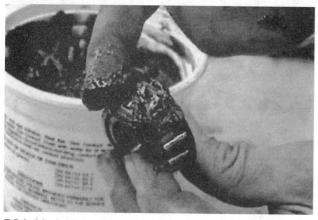

PS4–11 Add some grease to the outer surfaces of the bearing.

PS4–12 Place the inner bearing back into the rotor after applying a thin layer of grease to the outer race. Install a new grease seal using a hammer on a grease seal installation tool to properly seat the outside rim of the seal.

Wheel Bearing Service—continued

PS4–13 Apply a thin layer of grease to the outer bearing race.

PS4–14 Apply a thin layer of grease to the spindle.

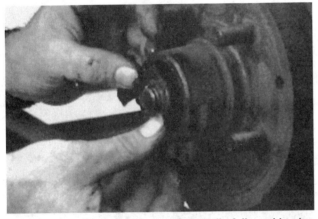

PS4–15 Install the rotor onto the spindle followed by the outer bearing, washer, and spindle nut.

PS4–16 Tighten the spindle nut snugly while rotating the disc brake rotor to seat the bearings. Loosen the nut and, while still rotating the rotor, finger tighten the nut.

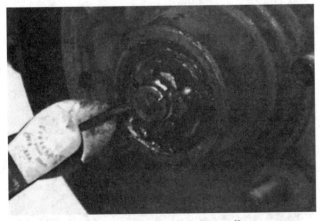

PS4–17 Install a new cotter key and cut off any excess.

PS4–18 Carefully install the dust (grease) cap. Avoid denting the cap.

■ REVIEW QUESTIONS

1. List three common types of automotive antifriction bearings.
2. Explain the adjustment procedure for a typical tapered roller wheel bearing.
3. List four symptoms of a defective wheel bearing.
4. Describe how the rear axle is removed from a C-clip-type axle.

■ ASE CERTIFICATION-TYPE QUESTIONS

1. Which type of automotive bearing can withstand radial and thrust loads, yet must be adjusted for proper clearance?
   a. Roller bearing
   b. Tapered roller bearing
   c. Ball bearings
   d. Needle roller bearing

2. Most sealed bearings used on the front wheels of front-wheel-drive vehicles are usually which type?
   a. Roller bearing
   b. Single tapered roller bearing
   c. Double row ball bearing
   d. Needle roller bearing

3. On a bearing that has been shock loaded, the race (cup) of the bearing can be dented. This type of bearing failure is called:
   a. Spalling
   b. Arcing
   c. Brinelling
   d. Fluting

4. The bearing grease most often specified is rated NLGI:
   a. #00
   b. #0
   c. #1
   d. #2

5. A non-drive-wheel bearing adjustment procedure includes a final spindle nut tightening torque of:
   a. Finger tight
   b. 5 in. lb.
   c. 12–30 lb. ft.
   d. 10–15 lb. ft. plus 1/16 turn

6. After a non-drive-wheel bearing has been properly adjusted, the wheel should have how much end play?
   a. Zero
   b. 0.001″ to 0.005″
   c. 0.10″ to 0.30″
   d. 1/16″ to 3/32″

7. The differential cover must be removed before removing the rear axle on which type of axle?
   a. Retainer plate
   b. C-clip
   c. Press fit
   d. Welded tube

8. What part *must* be replaced when servicing a wheel bearing on a non-drive wheel?
   a. The bearing cup
   b. The grease seal
   c. The cotter key
   d. The retainer washer

9. Technician A says that a defective wheel or axle bearing often makes a growling or rumbling noise. Technician B says that a defective wheel or axle bearing often makes a noise similar to a tire with an aggressive mud or snow design. Which technician is correct?
   a. Technician A only
   b. Technician B only
   c. Both Technician A and B
   d. Neither Technician A nor B

10. Two technicians are discussing differentials. Technician A says all differentials are vented. Technician B says that a clogged vent can cause the rear axle seal to leak. Which technician is correct?
    a. Technician A only
    b. Technician B only
    c. Both Technician A and B
    d. Neither Technician A nor B

Drum Brake Operation, Diagnosis, and Service

Objectives: After studying Chapter 5, the reader should be able to:

1. Identify drum brake component parts.
2. Describe the operation of dual-servo and leading–trailing brakes.
3. Discuss the procedure recommended for brake drum removal.
4. Discuss the inspection and lubrication points of the backing plate.
5. Explain the importance of proper drum brake hardware.
6. Disassemble and reassemble a drum brake assembly.

Drum brakes were the first type of brakes used on motor vehicles. Even today, over 100 years after the first "horseless carriages," drum brakes are still used on the rear of most vehicles, as shown in Figure 5–1.

■ DRUM BRAKE PARTS

Drum brakes use two **brake shoes** mounted on a stationary **backing (back) plate,** also called a **support plate** (see Figures 5–2 and 5–3). Hydraulic force from the master cylinder to the **wheel cylinder** pushes brake shoes against the rotating drum as shown in Figure 5–4 on page 112.

■ DUAL-SERVO (DUO-SERVO) DRUM BRAKES

Drum brakes use outward expanding brake shoes that contact the rotating brake drum when the driver depresses the brake pedal. Since the wheels of the vehicle are attached to the drums, the wheels also slow and stop when the brakes are applied. Because of the curved surface of the brake lining and the rotating brake drum, a wedging action occurs whenever the brakes are applied. This action is called **self-energizing** and increases the amount of force applied to the drums beyond that provided by hydraulic pressure alone. During braking, the primary lining wedges into the drum and tends to pivot in the direction of rotation. This movement is transmitted through a lower connecting link to the secondary lining, which is forced into the drum with even greater pressure. This type of braking action is called servo-self-energizing or **dual-servo** or **Duo-Servo** (Duo-Servo is a trade name of the Bendix Corporation). See Figures 5–5, 5–6, and 5–7 on page 112–113.

The self-energizing effect depends on the free movement of the linings against the backing plate. This is why the rear (secondary) lining is usually longer and made from a different mix of materials to be able to handle the greater forces and heat (see Figures 5–8, 5–9, and 5–10) on page 114.

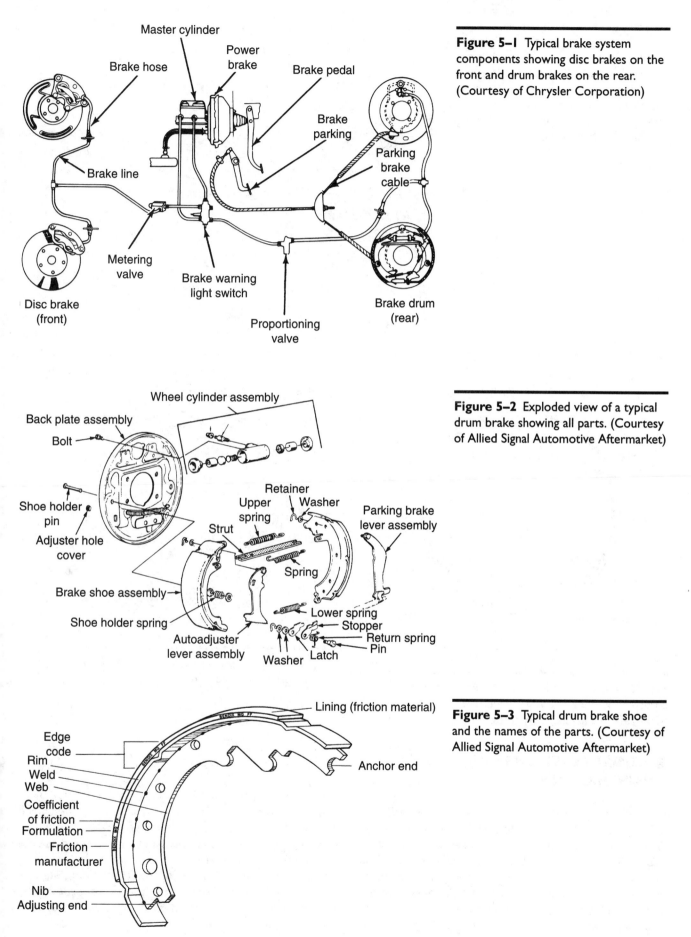

Figure 5–1 Typical brake system components showing disc brakes on the front and drum brakes on the rear. (Courtesy of Chrysler Corporation)

Master cylinder
Power brake
Brake hose
Brake pedal
Brake parking
Brake line
Parking brake cable
Metering valve
Brake warning light switch
Disc brake (front)
Proportioning valve
Brake drum (rear)

Figure 5–2 Exploded view of a typical drum brake showing all parts. (Courtesy of Allied Signal Automotive Aftermarket)

Wheel cylinder assembly
Back plate assembly
Bolt
Shoe holder pin
Adjuster hole cover
Retainer
Upper spring
Washer
Parking brake lever assembly
Strut
Brake shoe assembly
Spring
Shoe holder spring
Lower spring
Stopper
Return spring
Pin
Autoadjuster lever assembly
Washer
Latch

Figure 5–3 Typical drum brake shoe and the names of the parts. (Courtesy of Allied Signal Automotive Aftermarket)

Lining (friction material)
Edge code
Rim
Weld
Web
Coefficient of friction
Formulation
Friction manufacturer
Anchor end
Nib
Adjusting end

Figure 5–4 The drum rotates with the wheels. The brake shoes are attached to the vehicle. When the brake shoes expand outward, friction between the brake shoes and the rotating brake drum slows and stops the wheels. (Courtesy of Allied Signal Automotive Aftermarket)

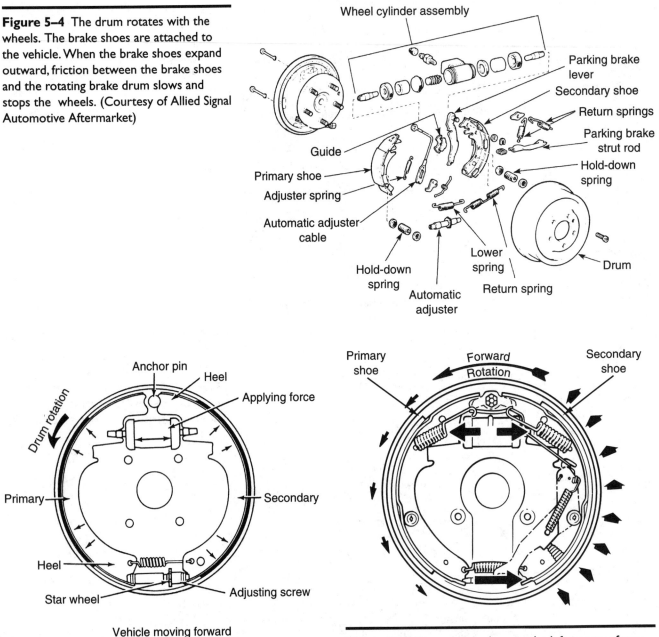

Figure 5–4 labels: Wheel cylinder assembly, Parking brake lever, Secondary shoe, Return springs, Parking brake strut rod, Hold-down spring, Drum, Return spring, Automatic adjuster, Lower spring, Hold-down spring, Automatic adjuster cable, Primary shoe, Adjuster spring, Guide

Figure 5–5 labels: Anchor pin, Heel, Applying force, Drum rotation, Primary, Secondary, Heel, Star wheel, Adjusting screw, Vehicle moving forward

Figure 5–5 The rotation of the brake drum causes the curved brake shoe to wedge tighter into the drum. (Courtesy of Chrysler Corporation)

Figure 5–6 labels: Primary shoe, Forward Rotation, Secondary shoe

Figure 5–6 The primary shoe on the left exerts a force on the secondary shoe on the right.

■ LEADING–TRAILING DRUM BRAKES

In a leading–trailing drum brake system, the forward shoe is held stationary at the bottom and pushed against the drum by the wheel cylinder at the top. As the drum rotates, this leading shoe is pulled tighter into the drum and tends to rotate with the drum; but because the shoe is anchored at the bottom, the shoe simply wedges itself into the drum. This **leading shoe** is also called the **forward shoe** or the **energized shoe** (see Figure 5–11 on page 114).

The **trailing shoe** is attached to the backing plate at the leading end of the shoe and pushed against the drum at the trailing end of the shoe. When the wheel cylinder pushes against the trailing shoe, the drum rotation tends to push the shoe away from the drum, reducing the application pressure. The trailing shoe is also called the **deenergized shoe** or **reverse shoe.** Leading–trailing drum brakes are also called a **non-servo brake.**

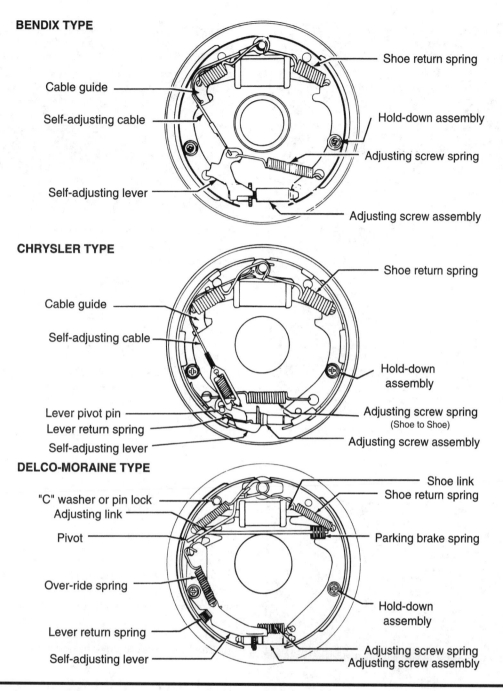

Figure 5–7 Typical drum brake assemblies. (Courtesy of Gibson Products, A Division of Rolero, Inc.)

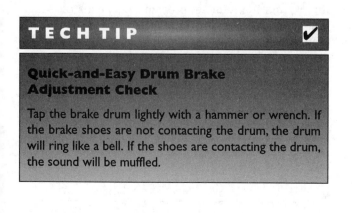

TECH TIP ✔

Quick-and-Easy Drum Brake Adjustment Check

Tap the brake drum lightly with a hammer or wrench. If the brake shoes are not contacting the drum, the drum will ring like a bell. If the shoes are contacting the drum, the sound will be muffled.

■ ADVANTAGES AND DISADVANTAGES OF DRUM BRAKES

Advantages of drum brakes include:

1. Commonly known by many service people
2. Common parts available
3. Generally low-cost parts
4. Few special tools or equipment required
5. Special tools readily available
6. Parking brake easily used and serviced

Figure 5–8 Brake lining on the assembly line at Delphi (Delco) brake systems. The darker color linings are the secondary shoes.

Figure 5–9 This brake lining can easily be broken by hand because it has not yet been baked (cured).

Disadvantages of drum brakes include:

1. Many small and separate parts to check, service, clean, handle, and lubricate
2. Fades easily when hot and drum temperature expands the drum away from the lining material

Figure 5–10 Molds used to bake brake lining. Each size has its own molds.

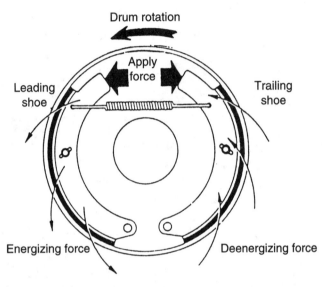

Figure 5–11 A leading–trailing design drum brake uses two brake shoes, both of the same length and not connected. The applying force is provided by the wheel cylinder.

3. Water reduces braking action when it gets between the lining and the drum.

■ BRAKE DRUM REMOVAL

The drum has to be removed before inspection or repair of a drum brake can begin. There are two basic types of drums, and the removal procedure depends on which type is being serviced. With either type it is usually recommended that the drums be marked with an "L" for left or an "R" for right so that they can be replaced in the same location.

> **CAUTION:** Proper precaution should be taken to prevent any asbestos that may be present in the brake system from becoming airborne. Removal of the brake drum should occur inside a sealed vacuum enclosure equipped with a hepa filter or washed with water or solvent. See Figure 5–12.

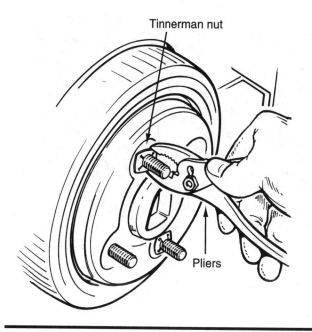

Figure 5–13 Tinnerman nuts are used at the vehicle assembly plant to prevent the brake drum from falling off until the wheels can be installed. These sheet metal retainers can be discarded after removal.

Figure 5–12 Before removing the brake drum, a liquid soaking solvent, such as brake cleaner, should be used to wet the linings. The purpose of wetting the lining material while the drum is still on the vehicle is to prevent the possibility of asbestos from the lining from becoming airborne. Asbestos is only hazardous when asbestos dust is airborne and is breathed in during brake system service.

Hub or Fixed Drums   A fixed or hub-mounted drum is often used on the rear of front-wheel-drive vehicles. The drum has a hub for inner and outer bearings and is retained by a spindle nut. To remove the brake drum, remove the dust cap and cotter key that is used to retain the spindle nut. Remove the spindle nut and washer and then the brake drum can be carefully pulled off the spindle. See Chapter 4 for details on wheel bearings, grease, and bearing adjustment.

Hubless or Floating Drums   Floating or hubless drums are usually used on the rear of a rear-wheel-drive vehicle. The drums are secured to the axle flange by the wheel and lug nuts. New vehicles have tinnerman nuts (clips), also called speed nuts, on the stud when the vehicle is being assembled. These thin sheet-metal nuts keep the brake drum from falling off during shipping and handling prior to installation of the rear wheels (see Figure 5–13). The tinnerman nuts can be discarded because they are not needed after the vehicle leaves the assembly plant. After removing the wheels, the drum should move freely on the hub and slip off over the brake shoes. Two situations that can prevent the drum from being removed include:

1. Drum is rusted to the hub. The fit between the drum and the hub is very close because it is this

Figure 5–14 The arrows indicate the area that can be struck to help break loose a broke drum that is stuck to the axle flange. The maximum diameter is stamped or cast into the brake drum.

center pilot hole in the drum that centers the drum on the axle. Rust and corrosion often cause the drum to seize to the hub. Striking the area inside the wheel studs will usually break the drum loose from the hub (see Figure 5–14). Sometimes a torch has to be used to expand the pilot hole.

HINT: Use of an air hammer with a flat-headed driver against the hub also works well to break the drum loose from the hub.

Figure 5–15 Access to the star-wheel adjuster is through adjuster plugs, often called knock-out plugs because they have to be knocked out to reach the adjuster. Sometimes these plugs are in the drum itself rather than in the backing plate.

> **CAUTION:** Overheating or not allowing the drum to cool slowly can cause the brake drum to distort. Using a puller can also damage a drum.

2. Brake shoes are worn into the drum. Even if the pilot hole is loose, many brake drums cannot be removed because the inner edge of the brake drum catches on the lining. Pulling outward on the drum often bends the backing plate or breaks some of the mounting hardware. To prevent damage, remove the adjuster plug from the backing plate or drum and back off the adjuster (see Figures 5–15 and 5–16).

TECH TIP ✔

Cutting the Nails Trick

Many times a brake drum cannot be removed because the linings have worn a groove into the drum. Attempting to adjust the brakes inward is often a frustrating and time-consuming operation. The easy solution is to use a pair of diagonal side-cut pliers and cut the heads off the hold-down pins (nails) at the backing plate. This releases the brake shoes from the backing plate and allows enough movement of the shoes to permit removal of the brake drum without bending the backing plate.

The hold-down pins (nails) must obviously be replaced, but they are included in most drum brake hardware kits. Since most brake experts recommend replacing all drum brake hardware anyway, this solution does not cost any more than normal, may save the backing plate from damage, and saves the service technician lots of time (see Figure 5–17).

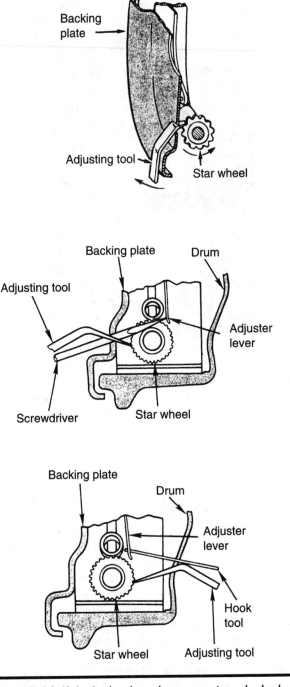

Figure 5–16 If the brake shoes have worn into the brake drum, the adjuster can be backed in after removing the access plug. After removing the plug, use another wire or screwdriver to move the adjusting lever away from the star wheel, then turn the star wheel with a brake adjusting tool, often called a brake "spoon." (Courtesy of Allied Signal Automotive Aftermarket)

> **NOTE:** Be sure to reinstall the adjuster opening plugs. These plugs help keep water and debris out of the brakes.

Figure 5–17 Use side-cut pliers to cut the heads off the hold-down spring pins (nails) from the backing plate to release the drum from the shoes.

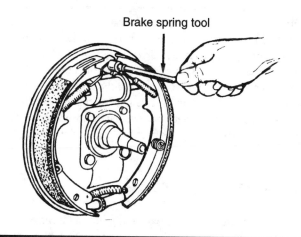

Brake spring tool

Figure 5–18 Use a brake spring tool to release a return (retracting) spring from the anchor pin.

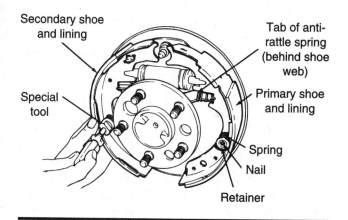

Secondary shoe and lining

Special tool

Tab of anti-rattle spring (behind shoe web)

Primary shoe and lining

Spring

Nail

Retainer

Figure 5–19 A special tool called a hold-down spring tool is used to depress and rotate the retainer. (Courtesy of Chrysler Corporation)

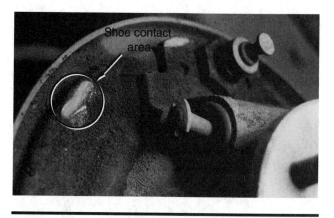

Shoe contact area

Figure 5–20 The brake shoes rest on the backing plate on raised pads called the **shoe contact area** or **shoe ledge.** As the shoes move, these raised areas can wear. Lack of lubrication in this area often causes a squeaking sound when the brake pedal is depressed or released.

After removing the brake drums, they should be cleaned, inspected, measured, and possibly machined before being returned to service. See Chapter 8 for measuring and machining procedures.

■ DRUM BRAKE DISASSEMBLY

After removal of the brake drum, the brake shoes and other brake hardware should be wetted down with a solvent or enclosed in an approved evacuation system to prevent possible asbestos release into the air. Usually, the first step in the disassembly of a drum brake system is removal of the return (retracting) springs (see Figure 5–18).

After the return springs have been removed, the hold-down springs and other brake hardware can be removed (see Figure 5–19).

NOTE: There are generally no "exact" disassembly or reassembly procedures specified by the manufacturer. The order in which the parts are disassembled or reinstalled is based on experience and the personal preference of the technician.

■ INSPECTING THE BACKING PLATE

The backing plate supports the parts of the drum brake and helps to keep water from getting onto the brake shoes. The backing plate bolts to the rear axle or spindle and is made from stamped steel. Backing plates are plated (usually cadmium) or painted to prevent rusting. When brakes are serviced, the six raised contact surfaces, called **pads, ledges,** or **shoe contact area,** of the backing plate should be inspected because they rub against the sides of the shoes (see Figure 5–20).

Figure 5–21 Since the backing plate is the foundation of the drum brake, it is important that it be square with the axle and flat. A homemade gauging tool can be made to check quickly how even the raised contact areas are to each other.

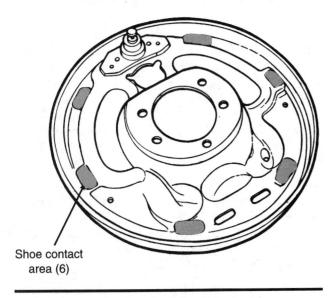

Shoe contact area (6)

Figure 5–22 Most drum brakes use six shoe contact areas. (Courtesy of Chrysler Corporation)

If the pads are worn more than 1/16″ (1.5 mm), the backing plate should be replaced. The backing plate must be inspected for looseness or bending. Backing plates should also be inspected to ensure that they are parallel with the axle flange. A simple gauge or dial indicator (gauge) can be used, as shown in Figure 5–21. The raised pads should be cleaned and lubricated (see Figure 5–22). Lithium high-temperature brake grease, synthetic brake grease, or antiseize should be used to lubricate drum brake parts (see Figure 5–23).

Figure 5–23 Lithium high-temperature brake grease is used by many service technicians to lubricate metal-to-metal contact surfaces of a drum brake. A small metal-handled acid brush is stuck through a hole cut into the lid of this container of grease to make the application of grease easy and less messy. Avoid using too much grease. Excessive grease can get onto the friction surfaces of the brake shoes or drum and affect braking performance.

■ LABYRINTH SEAL

The outer edge of most backing plates is bent outward to form a lip. This lip is designed to line up with a groove on the brake drum, to prevent water and dirt from entering from outside the brake (see Figure 5–24).

This type of seal is called a labyrinth seal. The term *labyrinth* means "a maze or complex passageway." As the brake drum rotates, any water that comes into contact with the brake drum would be thrown off by centrifugal force before the water has a chance to flow through and around the passages in the drum and backing plate.

> **CAUTION:** Water can still get into drum brakes, especially when stopped or when driving slowly through deep water. Water in a drum brake results in no friction between the brake linings and the drum. If a vehicle is driven through deep water, the driver should keep the brake pedal depressed slightly to help keep water from getting between the brake shoes and the drum. After driving out of deep water, apply the brakes to check for proper operation.

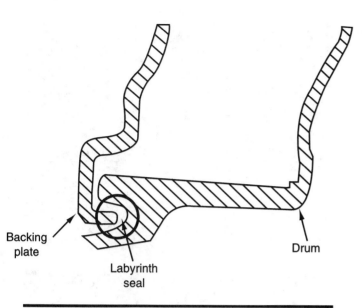

Figure 5–24 The flange on the backing plate is designed to come close to a notch or groove on the brake drum, forming a type of seal that helps prevent debris and water from getting onto the drum brake.

Figure 5–25 Cracked brake lining must be replaced.

■ DRUM BRAKE LINING INSPECTION

Both primary (front facing) and secondary (rear facing) lining material must be thicker than 0.060″ (1.5 mm).

> **HINT:** Most vehicle and brake lining manufacturers recommend replacing worn brake lining when the thickness of the riveted lining reaches 0.060″ or less. An American nickel is about 0.060″ thick, so simply remember that you must always have at least "a nickel's worth of lining."

The lining must be replaced if cracked as shown in Figure 5–25. Some vehicles are equipped with holes in the backing plate that allow for a visual inspection of the thickness of the lining. Most experts agree that the best possible inspection involves removing the brake drum and making a thorough visual inspection of the entire brake instead of just looking at the thickness of the remaining lining. If a riveted brake lining is cracked between rivets, the lining should be replaced. Some brake manufacturers recommend riveted replacement linings because of reduced brake noise. These manufacturers say that the recessed rivet holes allow brake dust to pocket away from the lining surface and thus help prevent the linings from glazing (see Figure 5–26). Most experts agree that high-quality linings purchased from a known brake manufacturer will help ensure that the brake performance is returned to original equipment standards.

■ RETURN SPRING INSPECTION

Each lining has a return spring (retracting spring) that returns the brake shoes back from the drums whenever the brakes are released. The springs are called primary and secondary return springs. The primary return spring attaches to the primary brake shoe and the secondary return spring attaches to the secondary brake shoe. These springs should be tested prior to a brake overhaul, especially when uneven lining wear is discovered as shown in Figure 5–27.

Some drum brakes use a spring that connects the primary and secondary shoes and is commonly called a shoe-to-shoe spring. Return springs can get weak due to heat and time and can cause the linings to remain in contact with the drum. See the following Tech Tip for one testing method.

(a)

(b)

(c)

Figure 5–26 (a) Riveted drum brake lining. (b) New steel brake shoes awaiting attachment (riveting) on the brake lining. (c) Typical brake lining rivet machine. Note that two rivets are attached at the same time.

Figure 5–27 Brake lining worn at the top edge near the anchor pin is one indication that the return (retracting) springs are weak.

TECH TIP ✔

The Drop Test

Brake return (retracting) springs can be tested by dropping them to the floor. A good spring should "thud" when the spring hits the ground. This noise indicates that the spring has not stretched and that all coils of the springs are touching each other. If the spring "rings" when dropped, the spring should be replaced because the coils are not touching each other (see Figure 5–28).

Although this drop test is often used, many experts recommend replacing all brake springs every time the brake linings are replaced. Heat generated by the brake system often weakens springs enough to affect their ability to retract brake shoes, especially when hot, yet not "ring" when dropped.

■ **HOLD-DOWN SPRINGS**

Hold-down springs (one on each shoe) are springs used with a retainer and a hold-down spring pin (or nail) to keep the linings on the backing plate (see Figure 5–29). Other types of hold-down springs include U-shape, flat spring

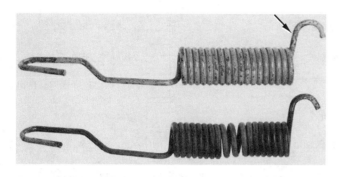

Figure 5–28 The top spring is a good-looking spring because all coils of the spring are touching each other. The bottom spring is stretched and should be discarded. The arrow points to the back side of the spring, which goes into a hole in the brake shoe. The open loop of the spring is not strong enough to keep from straightening out during use. Using the back side of the hook provides a strong, long-lasting hold in the brake shoe.

steel type, and the combination return-and-hold spring as shown in Figure 5–30. These springs still allow the freedom of movement necessary for proper braking operation.

■ CONNECTING SPRING (ADJUSTING SCREW SPRING)

The connecting spring attaches to the lower portion and connects the two shoes together as shown in Figure 5–31.

■ ANCHOR PIN

The anchor pin, which is located at the top of the backing plate, supports the top of both linings and provides

an anchor for both return springs. Covering the linings over the anchor pin is a shoe guide plate, also called an anchor pin support plate or butterfly (see Figure 5–32 on page 123).

■ SELF-ADJUSTING MECHANISMS

In the early 1960s, vehicle manufacturers began adding self-adjusting parts to drum brakes. The first to introduce self-adjusting brakes was Ford, which used an adjusting cable attached to the anchor pin going to an adjusting lever over a cable guide. The operation of the adjusting lever on the star-wheel adjuster involves applying the brakes while driving in reverse (see Figures 5–33 and 5–34 on pages 123–124).

Because of the free movement built into drum brakes, the force causes the secondary lining to become the primary lining in reverse, which causes rotation of the linings. This action pulls on the adjusting lever, and upon release of the brakes causes this lever to move one tooth of the star-wheel adjuster if there was enough movement (slack) to necessitate adjustment. Some details and precautions of self-adjusting brakes include:

1. Self-adjusting brakes will adjust only if there is enough clearance between the lining and the drum to require adjustment.
2. Star-wheel adjusters are threaded for left- or right-side operation. Make certain that the correct-side star-wheel adjuster is always used. If the incorrect star wheel were used, the brakes would tend to adjust inward rather than outward toward the drum.

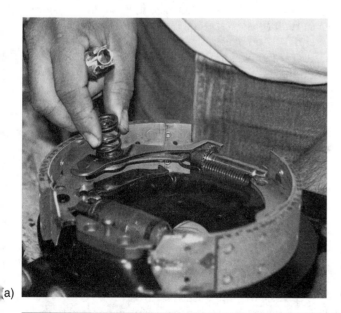

(a)

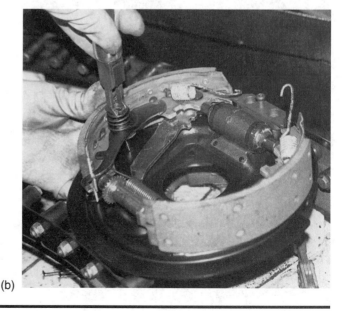

(b)

Figure 5–29 (a) A typical hold-down spring being installed on a drum brake on an assembly line at the factory. (b) The hold-down spring retainer is being pushed down and rotated using a special hold-down spring tool.

Figure 5–30 The large retracting spring (number 4) is used in this drum brake design as both the retracting spring and a hold-down spring for both brake shoes. This clever design uses fewer parts, but learning how to remove and reinstall this one large spring can be tricky. (Courtesy of Oldsmobile)

1	Adjuster socket
2	Adjuster screw
3	Pivot nut
4	Retractor spring
5	Adjuster shoe and lining
6	Wheel cylinder
7	Bleeder valve
8	Bolt

9	Access hole plug
10	Backing plate
11	Park brake shoe and lining
12	Park brake lever
13	Actuator spring
14	Adjuster actuator
15	Adjusting screw assemby

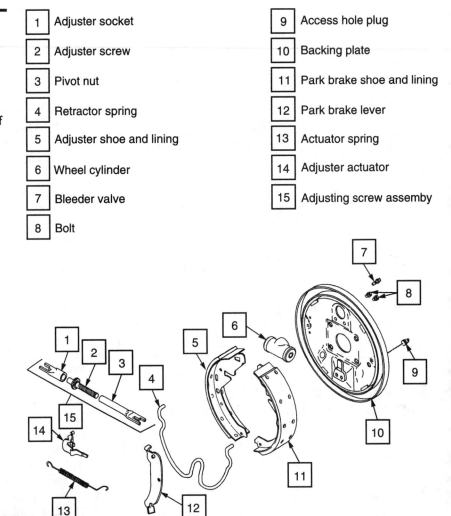

Figure 5–31 The adjusting screw spring is also called a **shoe-to-shoe spring** or a **shoe connecting spring** or simply a **shoe spring.**

3. Self-adjusting parts can be purchased individually or in a self-adjusting kit that includes all self-adjuster parts. The star-wheel adjuster can be purchased separately and should be replaced if the "points" of the star wheel are rounded. When purchasing self-adjusting parts, you must specify left (driver's side) or right (passenger side) (see Figures 5–35, 5–36, and 5–37 on pages 124–125).

4. Be careful backing up when drums are hot. Hot drums have expanded outward and the self-adjusting mechanism will try to adjust to this larger drum if the brakes are applied several times. This could overadjust the brakes and cause lockup after the drums have cooled.

5. GM does not use a cable to operate their self-adjusters but, rather, a steel lever called a activating lever, which is connected to the anchor pin by the actuator link and adjusts the star-wheel adjusting screw by an adjusting lever called a pawl.

6. Some manufacturers use the parking brake to act as the self-adjusting mechanism. Whenever the parking brake is used, a lever or a ratchet mechanism works to maintain the proper brake-shoe-to-brake-drum clearance to compensate for wear.

7. On some vehicles there is a spring connected to the self-adjusting mechanism which prevents binding of the mechanism in case the star-wheel adjuster cannot rotate. This spring is called an override spring.

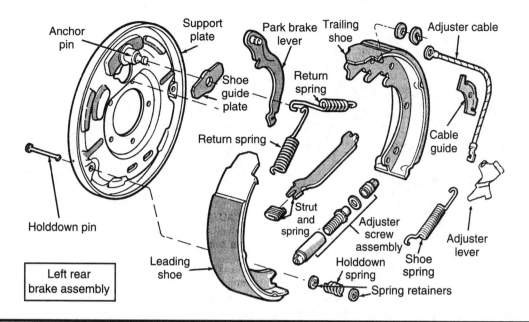

Figure 5–32 Typical drum brake showing support plate (backing plate), anchor pin, and shoe guide plate. (Courtesy of Chrysler Corporation)

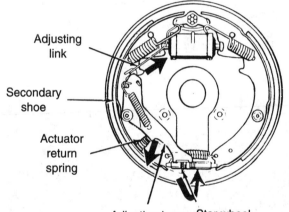

Figure 5–33 This self-adjusting mechanism operates only when the brake pedal is being depressed while traveling in reverse. If the secondary brake shoe travels far enough, the adjusting lever is raised up enough to cause the star wheel to move when the brake pedal is released. (Courtesy of EIS Brake Parts)

■ DRUM BRAKE HARDWARE KIT

If any spring is found to be defective, it is possible to purchase most parts individually or in pairs. However, for best results, many brake suppliers sell drum brake hardware kits. These kits usually include the items listed below for two drum brakes (axle set):

1. Primary and secondary return springs
2. Connecting spring
3. Hold-down springs

TECH TIP ☑

Time—Not Mileage—Is Important

Many brake experts recommend rebuilding or replacing wheel cylinders at every other brake job. Some experts recommend that the wheel cylinders be overhauled or replaced every time the brake linings are replaced. If the wheel cylinders are found to be leaking, they must be replaced or overhauled. The most important factor is time, not mileage, when determining when to repair or replace hydraulic components.

The longer the time, the more moisture is absorbed by the brake fluid. The greater the amount of moisture absorbed by the brake fluid, the greater the corrosion to metal hydraulic components. For example, the brakes will probably wear out much sooner on a vehicle that is used all day every day than on a vehicle driven only a short distance every week. In this example the high-mileage vehicle may need replacement brake linings every year, whereas the short-distance vehicle will require several years before replacement brakes are needed. The service technician should try to determine the amount of time the brake fluid has been in the vehicle. The longer the brake fluid has been in the system, the greater the chances that the wheel cylinders need to be replaced or overhauled.

---

4. Hold-down spring retainers
5. Hold-down spring pins (nails)

■ WHEEL CYLINDERS

Hydraulic pressure is transferred from the master cylinder to each wheel cylinder through brake fluid. The

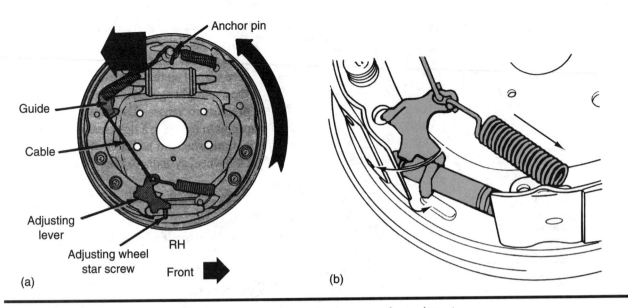

(a)

(b)

Figure 5–34 (a) Dual-servo adjusting mechanism using a cable between the anchor pin and the adjusting lever. A cable guide is used on the secondary brake shoe and is held in position by the secondary return spring. Note the arrows showing how the secondary shoe is moved off the anchor pin during a brake application when the vehicle is moving backward. As the shoe moves away from the anchor pin, the shoe guide pulls upward on the cable, which raises the adjusting lever. (b) When the brakes are released, the tension on the cable is released and the adjusting lever is returned by the spring. As the lever moves downward, the lever rotates the star wheel. (Courtesy of Ford Motor Company)

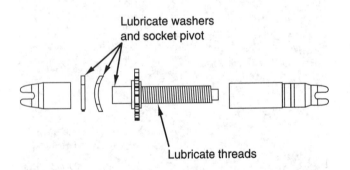

Figure 5–35 Star-wheel adjusters are designed with left- and right-handed threads. They are not interchangeable from side to side! Using an adjuster on the wrong side of the vehicle would cause the brake to self-adjust inward (farther from the brake drum) instead of closer to the brake drum. The wavy washer acts on the flat thrust washer to help prevent noise. The threads and end caps should be cleaned and lubricated before reuse.

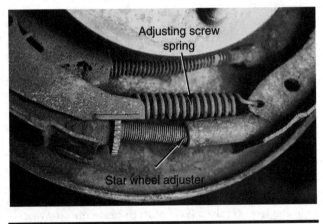

Figure 5–36 Note how this star-wheel adjuster came completely unthreaded.

force exerted on the brake fluid by the driver forces the piston inside the wheel cylinder to move outward. Through pushrods or links, this movement acts on the brake shoes, forcing them outward against the brake drum (see Figures 5–38, 5–39, and 5–40).

Drum brake wheel cylinders are cast iron with a bore (hole) drilled and finished to provide a smooth finish for the wheel cylinder seals and pistons. This special finish is called a bearingized finish. The final

step in manufacture of the wheel cylinder is to force a hardened steel ball through the bore to bend over the "grain" of the metal and to smooth the inner surface. This process provides a smooth porous-free surface over which the sealing caps will travel. It is this bearingized surface finish on the inside of the wheel cylinder that is often destroyed when a wheel cylinder is honed. The hone stone used to refinish the inside bore of a wheel cylinder often opens up the end grain of the cast iron. As a result, the sealing cups do not seal as well. The brake fluid can penetrate the

Figure 5–37 This star-wheel adjuster is damaged and must be replaced. A lack of proper lubrication can cause the star wheel to become frozen in one place and not adjust properly.

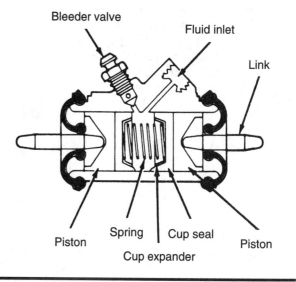

Figure 5–39 Cross section of a wheel cylinder that shows all of its internal parts. The brake line attaches to the fluid inlet. The cup expander prevents the cup seal lip from collapsing when the brakes are released.

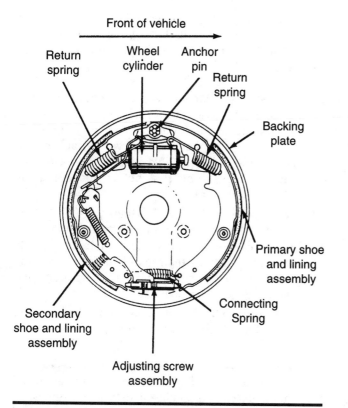

Figure 5–38 Notice that all of the self-adjuster mechanism operates off the secondary (rearward) brake shoe. This fact makes it easier for beginning technicians to remember which part goes where and the proper direction of the star wheel.

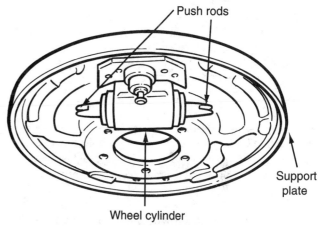

Figure 5–40 The pushrods are held in place by the rubber dust boots. As the wheel cylinder pistons move outward, the pushrods transfer the movement to the brake shoes. (Courtesy of Chrysler Corporation)

> **CAUTION:** It is because of this bearingized surface finish that most vehicle manufacturers do not recommend that wheel cylinders be honed. Be sure to follow the vehicle manufacturer's recommended procedures. Some manufacturers state that the wheel cylinders can be overhauled using new (replacement) sealing cups and dust shields after cleaning the cylinder bore only.

porous cast iron. This porous condition can cause the brake fluid to seep through the wheel cylinder, thus causing the outside of the wheel cylinder to become wet with brake fluid.

Outside each wheel cylinder piston are dust boots installed to keep dirt out of the cylinder bore. Between both piston seals is a spring with piston seal expanders to keep the seals from collapsing toward each other and to keep pressure exerted on the lips of both seals to ensure proper sealing (see Figure 5–41).

Figure 5–41 Exploded view of a typical wheel cylinder. Note how the flat part of the cups touch the flat part of the piston. The cup expander and spring go between the cups. (Courtesy of Chrysler Corporation)

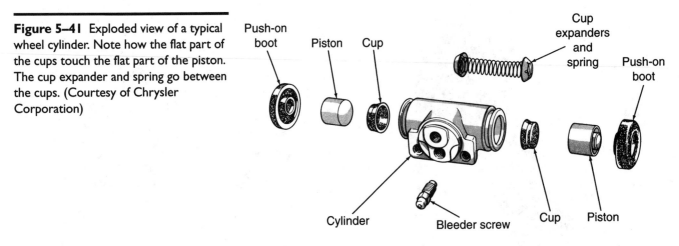

Figure 5–42 Many wheel cylinders are bolted to the support plate (backing plate). The O-ring seal helps keep water and dirt out of the drum brake. (Courtesy of Chrysler Corporation)

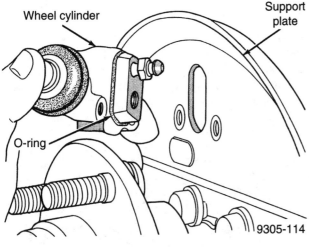

On the back of each wheel cylinder is a threaded hole for the brake line and a bleeder valve that can be loosened to remove (bleed) air from the hydraulic system. The wheel cylinder is bolted or clipped to the backing plate (see Figures 5–42 and 5–43).

The wheel cylinders should be checked regularly for possible brake fluid leakage past the piston seals. With a dull tool, pry the wheel cylinder dust boots aside slightly and check for wetness. Remember, the dust boots are not designed to hold hydraulic pressure, but they do act as a small reservoir for seeping fluid.

> **NOTE:** When inspecting a drum brake wheel cylinder, look for brake fluid under the dust boot. According to vehicle manufacturers, a slight amount of brake fluid behind the boot is normal and serves to lubricate the pistons. However, if there is enough fluid to run or spill out when the boot is pried back, excessive leakage is indicated and the wheel cylinder must be rebuilt or replaced.

■ OVERHAUL OF THE WHEEL CYLINDERS

If defective or leaking, wheel cylinders can be overhauled if recommended by the vehicle manufacturer. The following steps and procedures should be followed:

Step 1 Loosen the bleeder valve. If unable to loosen the bleeder valve without having it break off, a new replacement wheel cylinder is required. To help prevent broken bleeder valves, attempt to tighten the bleeder valve while tapping on the valve to loosen the rust before loosening the valve.

Step 2 To remove the wheel cylinder, the brake line must first be removed from the wheel cylinder. Unbolt or remove the wheel cylinder retainer clip. Be careful not to twist the brake line when removing the line from the wheel cylinder or the brake line will also require replacement.

Step 3 If the bleeder valve can be removed, remove all internal parts of the wheel cylinder.

> **NOTE:** With some vehicles, the wheel cylinder must be unbolted from the backing plate to enable removal of the seals and piston.

Step 4 Clean and/or hone a wheel cylinder as specified by the manufacturer to remove any rust and corrosion (see Figure 5–44).

Step 5 Install the pistons (usually not included in a wheel cylinder overhaul kit), seals, spring, and dust boots. Install on the vehicle and bleed the system.

(a)

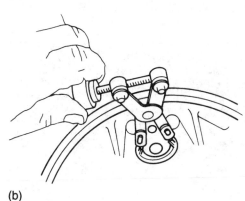

(b)

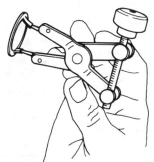

Figure 5–43 (a) Some wheel cylinders are simply clipped to the backing plate. (b) This special tool makes it a lot easier to remove the wheel cylinder clip. A socket (1 1/8″, 12 point) can be used to push the clip back onto the wheel cylinder. (Courtesy of General Motors)

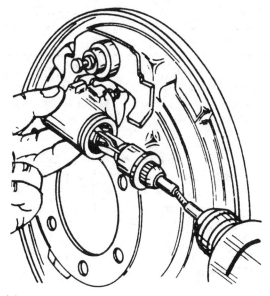

(a)

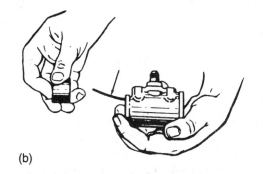

(b)

Figure 5–44 (a) A wheel cylinder hone being turned with an electric drill. Use brake fluid to lubricate the hone stones during the honing operation. Clean the wheel cylinder thoroughly using a soft cloth and clean brake fluid. (b) Use a narrow [1/4″ (6 mm)] (feeler) gauge 0.005″ (0.13 mm) thick held into the wheel cylinder. If the cylinder piston fits, the wheel cylinder bore is too large and the wheel cylinder must be replaced. Typical piston-to-wall clearance should range from 0.001″ to 0.003″ (0.03 to 0.08 mm).

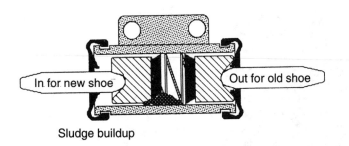

Figure 5–45 When new, thicker materials are installed, the pistons and cups are forced back into the wheel cylinder and pushed through the sludge that is present in every cylinder.

> **NOTE:** Even though the wheel cylinder is not leaking, many brake experts recommend replacing or rebuilding the wheel cylinder every time new replacement linings are installed. Any sludge buildup in the wheel cylinder can cause the wheel cylinder to start to leak shortly after a brake job. When the new, thicker replacement linings are installed, the wheel cylinder piston may be pushed inward enough to cause the cup seals to ride on a pitted or corroded section of the wheel cylinder. As the cup seal moves over this rough area, the seal can lose its ability to maintain brake fluid pressure and an external brake fluid leak can occur (see Figure 5–45).

■ INSPECTING THE DRUM BRAKE SHOES

Carefully inspect the replacement brake shoes. Check all of the following:

1. Check that the replacements are exactly the same size (width and diameter) as the original. Hold the replacement shoes up against the old shoes to make the comparison.
2. Check for sound rivets (if rivet type). The friction material should also be snug against the metal brake shoe backing.

After checking that the replacement brake lining is okay, place the old shoes into the new linings' box. This helps ensure proper credit for the old shoes (called the core) as well as protection against asbestos contamination exposure.

■ REASSEMBLING THE DRUM BRAKE

Carefully clean the backing plate. Check the anchor pin for looseness. Lubricate the shoe contact surfaces (shoe pads) with antiseize, brake grease, or synthetic grease. Reassemble the primary and secondary shoes and brake strut along with all springs.

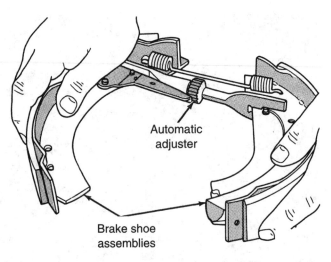

Figure 5–46 Preassembly of the star-wheel adjuster with its connecting spring often helps when reassembling a drum brake. (Courtesy of Chrysler Corporation)

TECH TIP ✔

Brake Parts Cleaning Tips

Denatured alcohol or "brake clean" should only be used to clean brake parts that are disassembled. When individual parts are cleaned, they can dry in the air before being assembled. Never clean or flush assembled brake components with denatured alcohol or brake clean. Often, the alcohol cannot evaporate entirely from an assembled component. This trapped alcohol will evaporate inside the brake system, causing contamination. The trapped alcohol vapors also act like trapped air in the braking system and can cause a spongy brake pedal. Always clean assembled brake components with brake fluid.

> **HINT:** Many technicians preassemble the primary and secondary shoes with the connecting (lower retracting) spring as a unit before installing them onto the backing plate (see Figures 5–46 and 5–47).

Finish assembling the drum brake being careful to note the correct location of all springs and parts. Most self-adjusters operate off the rear (secondary) shoe and should therefore be assembled toward the rear of the vehicle (see Figure 5–48).

■ ADJUSTING DRUM BRAKES

Most drum brakes are adjusted by rotating a star-wheel or rotary adjuster. As the adjuster is moved, the brake shoes move toward the drum. If the brakes have been

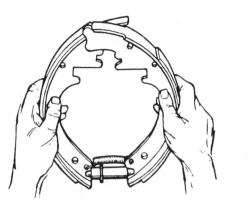

Figure 5–47 Sometimes it is necessary to cross the shoes when preassembling the star-wheel adjuster and connecting spring. (Courtesy of Allied Signal Automotive Aftermarket)

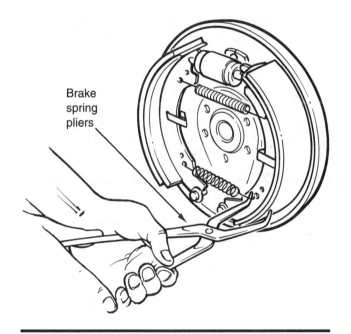

Brake spring pliers

Figure 5–48 Installing a shoe-to-shoe spring using brake spring pliers.

assembled correctly and with the parking brake fully released, both brake shoes should make contact with the anchor pin at the top. See Figure 5–49 for an example where one shoe does not make contact with the anchor pin. See Chapter 7 for details on parking brake operation and adjustment procedures.

If the clearance between the brake shoes and the brake drum is excessive, a low brake pedal results. The wheel cylinder travel may not be adequate to cause the lining to contact the drums. Often, the driver has to pump the brakes to force enough brake fluid into the wheel cylinder to move it enough for braking action to occur.

Many technicians use a brake shoe clearance gauge to adjust the brake shoes before installing the drum (see Figure 5–50).

> *CAUTION:* Before installing the brake drum, be sure to clean any grease off the brake lining. Some experts warn not to use sandpaper on the lining to remove grease. The sandpaper may release asbestos fiber into the air. Cover the linings with masking tape prior to installation on the vehicle to help protect the lining. Grease on the linings can cause the brakes to grab.

■ LUBRICATION CHECKLIST

For proper operation, the following points should be lubricated with approved brake lubricant:

> *CAUTION:* Do not use wheel bearing or chassis grease on a braking system. Use only approved brake lubricant such as molybdenum disulfide (moly) grease, synthetic grease, lithium-based brake grease, or antiseize compound.

1. The star-wheel adjuster threads and under end caps
2. The backing plate contact areas (pads or ledges)
3. Anchor pins

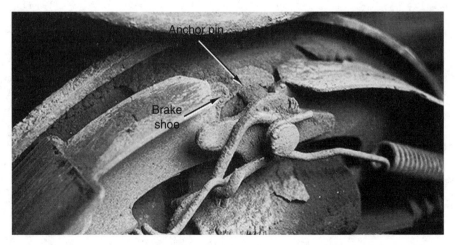

Anchor pin

Brake shoe

Figure 5–49 Notice that the brake shoe is not contacting the anchor pin. This often occurs when the parking brake cable is stuck or not adjusted properly.

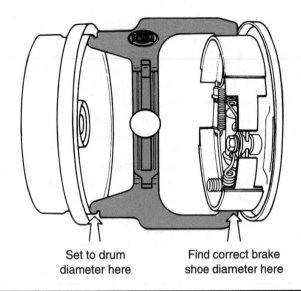

Set to drum diameter here

Find correct brake shoe diameter here

Figure 5–50 A brake shoe clearance gauge is first placed in the drum and the knob tightened to maintain the measured distance. The gauge is then turned around and the outside arm of the tool can be used as a gauge to adjust the shoes. When the shoes touch the gauge, the brakes are correctly matched to the brake drum. (Courtesy of Ford Motor Company)

Also, be sure to check and lubricate the parking brake cable, if necessary. See Chapter 7 for details.

■ DRUM BRAKE TROUBLESHOOTING GUIDE

Low Pedal or the Pedal Goes to the Floor

Possible causes:

1. Excessive clearance between linings and drum
2. Automatic adjusters not working
3. Leaking wheel cylinder
4. Air in the system

Springy, Spongy Pedal

Possible causes:

1. Drums worn below specifications
2. Air in the system

Excessive Pedal Pressure Required to Stop the Vehicle

Possible causes:

1. Grease or fluid-soaked linings
2. Frozen wheel cylinder pistons
3. Linings installed on wrong shoes

Light Pedal Pressure— Brakes Too Sensitive

Possible causes:

1. Brake adjustment not correct
2. Loose backing plate
3. Lining loose on the shoe
4. Excessive dust and dirt in the drums
5. Scored, bell-mouthed, or barrel-shaped drum
6. Improper lining contact pattern

Brake Pedal Travel Decreasing

Possible causes:

1. Weak shoe retracting springs
2. Wheel cylinder pistons sticking

Pulsating Brake Pedal (Parking Brake Apply Pulsates Also)

Possible cause:

1. Drums out-of-round

Brakes Fade (Temporary Loss of Brake Effectiveness When Hot)

Possible causes:

1. Poor lining contact
2. Drums worn below the discard dimension
3. Charred or glazed linings

Shoe Click

Possible causes:

1. Shoes lift off the backing plate and snap back
2. Hold-down springs weak
3. Shoe bent
4. Grooves in the backing plate pads

Snapping Noise in the Front End

Possible causes:

1. Grooved backing plate pads
2. Loose backing plates

Thumping Noise When Brakes Are Applied

Possible causes:

1. Cracked drum; hard spots in the drum
2. Retractor springs unequal—weak

Grinding Noise

Possible causes:

1. Shoe hits the drum
2. Bent shoe web
3. Brake improperly assembled

One Wheel Drags

Possible causes:

1. Weak or broken shoe retracting springs
2. Brake-shoe-to-drum clearance too tight—brake shoes not adjusted properly
3. Brake assembled improperly
4. Wheel cylinder piston cups swollen and distorted
5. Pistons sticking in the wheel cylinder
6. Drum out-of-round
7. Loose anchor pin/plate
8. Parking brake cable not free
9. Parking brake not adjusted properly

Vehicle Pulls to One Side

Possible causes:

1. Brake adjustment not correct
2. Loose backing plate
3. Linings not of specified kind; primary and secondary shoes reversed or not replaced in pairs
4. Water, mud, or other material in brakes
5. Wheel cylinder sticking
6. Weak or broken shoe retracting springs

7. Drums out-of-round
8. Wheel cylinder size different on opposite sides
9. Scored drum

Wet Weather: Brakes Grab or Will Not Hold

Possible causes:

1. Bent backing plate flange
2. Incorrect or abused shoe and linings

Brakes Squeak

Possible causes:

1. Backing plate is bent or shoes twisted
2. Shoes scraping on backing plate pads
3. Weak or broken hold-down springs
4. Loose backing plate, anchor, or wheel cylinder
5. Glazed linings
6. Dry shoe pads and hold-down pin surfaces

Brakes Chatter

Possible causes:

1. Incorrect lining-to-drum clearance
2. Loose backing plate
3. Weak or broken retractor spring
4. Drums out-of-round
5. Tapered or barrel-shaped drums
6. Improper lining contact pattern

PHOTO SEQUENCE   Drum Brake Service

PS5–1 Hoist the vehicle safely and remove the wheels before removing the brake drum.

PS5–2 Carefully inspect and measure the brake drum. Machine or replace the brake drum as necessary.

PS5–3 One way to disassemble the General Motors leading–trailing drum brake is to first remove the self-adjusting spring (also called an actuator spring).

PS5–4 This advanced design drum brake uses one large retracting spring that also works to hold the shoes against the backing plate. Start removing the retracting spring by prying the end of the spring from the hole in the brake shoe.

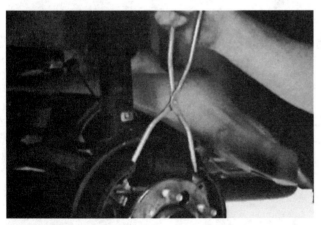

PS5–5 Using special pliers for this brake design, spread the shoes apart at the top.

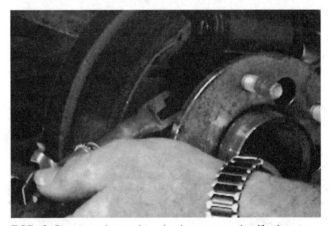

PS5–6 Remove the parking brake strut and self-adjusting actuator.

Drum Brake Service—continued

PS5–7 Continue the removal of the large U-shaped retracting spring.

PS5–8 Remove the leading brake shoe.

PS5–9 Remove the trailing brake shoe.

PS5–10 After cleaning the backing plate with a wire brush, apply brake grease to the shoe ledges of the backing plate.

PS5–11 Attach the new trailing brake shoe to the parking brake lever.

PS5–12 Install the leading brake shoe.

Drum Brake Service—continued

PS5–13 Using the special pliers, spread the shoes apart enough at the top to reinstall the strut and self-adjusting actuator.

PS5–14 Use needle-nose pliers to reattach the self-adjusting actuator spring.

PS5–15 Before installing the brake drum, use a brake drum/shoe clearance gauge and adjust to the inside diameter of the drum.

PS5–16 Turn the gauge to the other end and use the gauge as a guide to determine how much the shoes should be adjusted to provide the proper clearance between the shoes and the drum.

PS5–17 Turn the star-wheel adjuster as necessary to achieve the proper clearance.

PS5–18 After cleaning off any greasy fingerprints from the linings, double-check that everything is correct and install the brake drum.

■ SUMMARY

1. Brake shoes are forced outward against a brake drum by hydraulic action working on the brake shoes by the piston of a wheel cylinder.

2. The curved arch of the brake shoe causes a wedging action between the brake shoe and the rotating drum. This wedging action increases the amount of force applied to the drum.

3. Dual-servo brakes use primary and secondary brake shoes that are connected at one end. The wedge action on the front (primary) shoe forces the secondary shoe into the drum with even greater force. This action is called servo-self-energizing action.

4. Leading–trailing brakes use two brake shoes that are not connected. Leading–trailing brakes operate on a more linear basis and are therefore more suited than dual-servo brakes for ABS.

5. Care should be exercised when removing a brake drum so as not to damage the drum, backing plate, or other vehicle components.

6. After disassembly of the drum brake component, the backing plate should be inspected and cleaned.

7. Most experts recommend replacing the wheel cylinder as well as all brake springs as part of a thorough drum brake overhaul.

■ REVIEW QUESTIONS

1. Describe the difference between a dual-servo and a leading–trailing drum brake system.

2. List all the parts of a typical drum brake.

3. List all items that should be lubricated on a drum brake.

4. Explain how a self-adjusting brake mechanism works.

■ ASE CERTIFICATION-TYPE QUESTIONS

1. Technician A says that the tinnerman nuts used to hold on the brake drum should be reinstalled when the drum is replaced. Technician B says that a drum should be removed inside a sealed vacuum enclosure or washed with water or solvent to prevent the release of possible asbestos dust into the air. Which technician is correct?
   a. Technician A only
   b. Technician B only
   c. Both Technician A and B
   d. Neither Technician A nor B

2. The backing plate should be replaced if the shoe contact areas (pads or ledges) are worn more than
   a. 1/2″ (13 mm)
   b. 1/4″ (7 mm)
   c. 1/8″ (4 mm)
   d. 1/16″ (2 mm)

3. Technician A says that the labyrinth seal keeps water from ever getting onto a drum brake. Technician B says that only synthetic brake grease, lithium brake grease, or antiseize compound should be used as a brake lubricant. Which technician is correct?
   a. Technician A only
   b. Technician B only
   c. Both Technician A and B
   d. Neither Technician A nor B

4. Most brake experts and vehicle manufacturers recommend replacing brake lining when the lining thickness is
   a. 0.030″ (0.8 mm)
   b. 0.040″ (1.0 mm)
   c. 0.050″ (1.3 mm)
   d. 0.060″ (1.5 mm)

5. Technician A says that star-wheel adjusters use different threads (left- and right-handed) for the left and right sides of the vehicle. Technician B says that the threads and end caps of the adjusters should be lubricated with brake grease before being installed. Which technician is correct?
   a. Technician A only
   b. Technician B only
   c. Both Technician A and B
   d. Neither Technician A nor B

6. Technician A says that many vehicle manufacturers recommend that wheel cylinders not be honed because of the special surface finish inside the bore. Technician B says that seal expanders are used to help prevent the lip of the cup seal from collapsing when the brakes are released. Which technician is correct?
   a. Technician A only
   b. Technician B only
   c. Both Technician A and B
   d. Neither Technician A nor B

7. Most manufacturers recommend that brake parts should be cleaned with
   a. Carburetor cleaner
   b. Denatured alcohol
   c. Stoddard solvent
   d. Detergent and water

8. Old brake shoes are often returned to the manufacturer where new friction material is installed. These old shoes are usually called the
   a. Core
   b. Web
   c. Rim
   d. Nib

9. After assembling a drum brake, it is discovered that the brake drum will not fit over the new brake shoes. Technician A says that the parking brake cable may not have been fully released. Technician B says to check to see if both shoes are contacting the anchor pin. Which technician is correct?
   a. Technician A only
   b. Technician B only
   c. Both Technician A and B
   d. Neither Technician A nor B

10. Technician A says to use masking tape temporarily over the lining material to help prevent getting grease on the lining. Technician B says that grease on the brake lining can cause the brakes to grab. Which technician is correct?
    a. Technician A only
    b. Technician B only
    c. Both Technician A and B
    d. Neither Technician A nor B

Disc Brake Operation, Diagnosis, and Service

Objectives: After studying Chapter 6, the reader should be able to:

1. Describe how disc brakes function.
2. Name the parts of a typical disc brake system.
3. Identify the types of disc brake pads.
4. Explain how to disassemble and reassemble a disc brake caliper assembly.
5. Describe how to prevent disc brake noise.

Disc brakes use a piston(s) to squeeze friction material (pads) on both sides of a rotating disc (rotor). Disc may be spelled "disk" by some manufacturers, but *disc* is the SAE (Society of Automotive Engineers) term and the most commonly used spelling in the industry. The rotor is attached to and stops the wheel.

■ DISC BRAKE ADVANTAGES

Disc brakes do not have a self-energizing feature; therefore, disc brakes require greater pressures between the pads and the rotor than are required by drum brakes. Except for this disadvantage, disc brakes have the following advantages over drum brakes:

1. More **fade resistant**—The disc and pads are usually mounted where air can quickly cool the parts. In fact, over 80 percent of the rotor is exposed to the air. Also, as the rotor becomes hotter, the rotor expands toward the friction pads, not away

from the shoes as happens with drum brakes (see Figure 6–1).
2. **Even, straight stops**—The friction of disc brakes is directly proportional to the pressure applied. Drum brakes, however, tend to give uneven braking

Figure 6–1 Disc brakes can absorb and dissipate a great deal of heat. During this demonstration, the brakes were gently applied as the engine drove the front wheels until the rotor became cherry red. During normal braking, the rotor temperature can exceed 350°F (180°C) and about 1500°F (800°C) on a race vehicle.

Check the Tire Size for a Pulling Problem

If an unequal braking problem is being diagnosed, check that the front tires match and that the rear tires match. Brakes slow and stop wheels. Unequal diameter tires create an unequal braking force. The result may be a pulling toward one side while braking. Tire diameter can vary from one tire manufacturer to another even though the size designation is the same. Even slight differences in the wear of tires can cause a different tire diameter and, therefore, a different braking force.

Wax the Wheels?

Brake dust from semimetallic brake pads often discolors the front wheels. Customers often complain to service technicians about this problem, but it is normal for the front wheels to become dirty because the iron and other metallic and nonmetallic components wear off the front disc brake pads and adhere to the wheel covers. A coat of wax on the wheels or wheel covers helps prevent damage and makes it easier to wash off the brake dust.

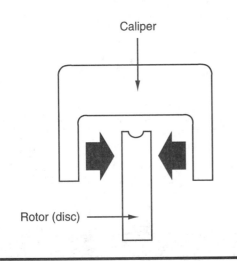

Figure 6–2 A fixed caliper disc brake uses two or four pistons with one or two on each side of the rotating rotor (disc).

because the self-energizing action tends to be uneven side to side.

3. **Wet stopping is possible**—The water simply runs off the vertical rotor surface and the pads constantly rub against the rotor surface effectively preventing water buildup and wet brake fade.

4. **Fewer service parts**—Because of fewer actual parts, most disc brake service is often easier than similar drum brake service.

■ SWEPT AREA

The greater the area that the brake pads contact the rotor measured in square inches (or square centimeters), the greater the stopping ability. The larger the disc brake pad, the greater the stopping ability. A large-diameter disc brake rotor allows more stopping power because of the leverage the caliper exerts on the rotor. The further out from the center of the wheel, the more effective the brakes. Large-diameter rotors, however, require larger diameter wheels to provide the necessary

clearance. This is the major reason why high-performance vehicles use 16″- and 17″-diameter wheels. Some vehicles can be equipped with standard or "heavy-duty" brakes. Often the disc brake pads and/or rotors are different for each type and are not interchangeable. The service technician often has to guess whether the vehicle being serviced has heavy-duty brakes. Many technicians simply order brake parts required for both styles and return to the parts store the parts not used.

■ FIXED CALIPERS

The first disc brakes on American vehicles often used four pistons, two on each side of the rotors. The caliper (containing the four pistons with rubber piston seals on each) was bolted directly to the steering knuckle and did not move. This is called a **fixed caliper** (see Figures 6–2 and 6–3).

When the brake pedal is depressed, hydraulic brake fluid is forced into the caliper cylinder bores. This forces the pistons outward and against the pads as shown in Figure 6–4.

Because of Pascal's Law, all four pistons received the same pressure and because of the large surface area of the four pistons combined, the pressure was great enough to stop big, heavy American vehicles. However, because of the greater pressures required, many disc brake-equipped vehicles also required vacuum-operated power brake boosters to reduce driver effort.

When the brake pedal is released, a small amount of brake fluid returns to the master cylinder lowering the hydraulic pressure on the piston. The clamping action of the brake pads against the rotor is released and the caliper pistons retract slightly back into the caliper bore (see Figure 6–5).

■ FIXED CALIPER OPERATION

A fixed disc brake caliper contains two or four pistons. If two pistons are used, the caliper uses one piston on each side of the rotor. If four pistons are used, the caliper uses two pistons on each side of the rotor.

Figure 6–3 Four-piston fixed caliper assembly on a race vehicle.

APPLY

Hydraulic pressure exerted on brake fluid by the master cylinder forces the pistons outward from the caliper and against the back of the disc brake friction pads. The square-cut O-ring inside the caliper bore is distorted as the caliper piston moves outward.

NOTE: This O-ring is the caliper seal and acts as the return "spring" for the piston.

The force on the backside of the pads pushes the friction material against the rotor. The friction of the pads against the rotor slows and stops the wheels.

RELEASE

When the brake pedal is released, pressure is removed from behind the caliper pistons. The piston is drawn back from its applied position by the square-cut caliper O-ring. The rubber O-ring has a "memory" and exerts a force onto the surface of the caliper piston as it returns to its original shape (see Figure 6–6).

FLOATING CALIPERS

Most modern disc brake calipers use only one large piston in a caliper which moves slightly, allowing it to squeeze the rotor between the two disc pads. This type of caliper is called a **single piston floating caliper** (see Figure 6–7).

When the brakes are applied, the hydraulic pressure in the caliper bore is exerted equally against the bottom of the piston and on the back of the caliper itself. (Remember, Pascal's Law.) See Figures 6–8 and 6–9 on page 141.

The pressure on the piston forces the inside pad against the rotor. At the same time the piston is pushing against the rotor, the caliper itself is being forced toward the center of the vehicle. Since the outboard pad

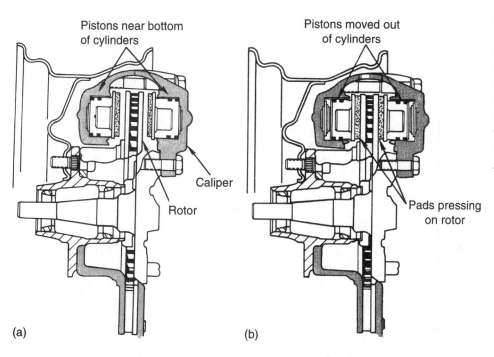

Figure 6–4 (a) Fixed caliper in the released position. (b) When the brake pedal is depressed, brake fluid from the master cylinder is applied behind the caliper piston forcing the friction pads against the rotor. (Courtesy of Allied Signal Automotive Aftermarket)

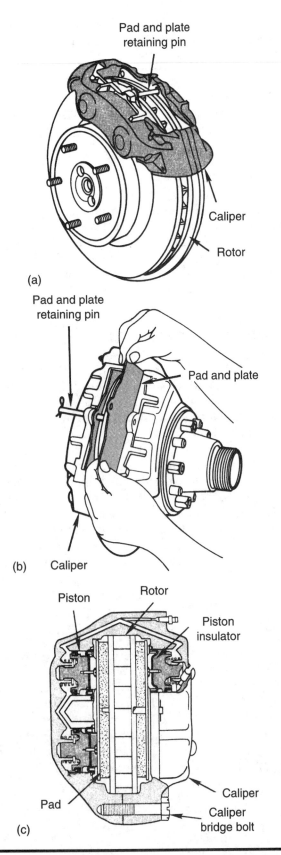

(a)

(b)

(c)

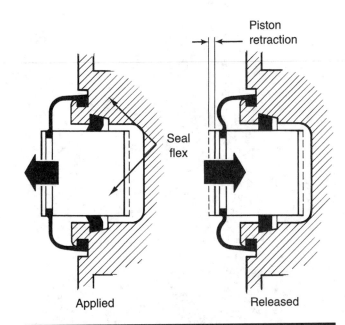

Figure 6–6 The square-cut O-ring not only seals hydraulic brake fluid, but also retracts the caliper piston when the brake pedal is released.

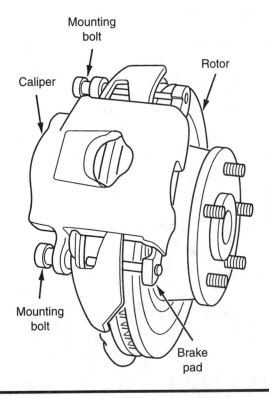

Figure 6–7 A typical single-piston floating caliper. In this type of design, the entire caliper moves when the single piston is pushed out of the caliper during a brake application. When the caliper moves, the outboard pad is pushed against the rotor. (Courtesy of General Motors)

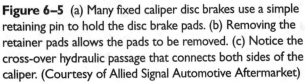

Figure 6–5 (a) Many fixed caliper disc brakes use a simple retaining pin to hold the disc brake pads. (b) Removing the retainer pads allows the pads to be removed. (c) Notice the cross-over hydraulic passage that connects both sides of the caliper. (Courtesy of Allied Signal Automotive Aftermarket)

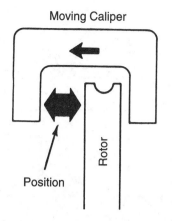

Moving Caliper

Position

Rotor

Figure 6–8 In a floating caliper, a piston on one side applies force to both the rotor and the caliper causing the caliper to move. (Courtesy of Ford Motor Company)

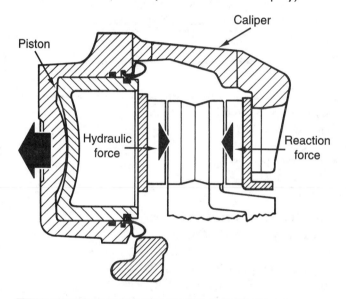

Piston

Caliper

Hydraulic force

Reaction force

Figure 6–9 Hydraulic force on the piston (left) is applied to the inboard pad and the caliper housing itself. The reaction of the piston pushing against the rotor causes the entire caliper to move toward the inside of the vehicle (large arrow). Since the outboard pad is retained by the caliper, the reaction of the moving caliper applies the force of the outboard pad against the outboard surface of the rotor.

is attached to this inward moving caliper, it contacts the outer surface of the rotor with the same force that is being exerted on the inboard pad as shown in Figure 6–10.

■ FLOATING CALIPER OPERATION

Brake fluid pressure is exerted on the back of a caliper piston or pistons (if two or more pistons are used in a caliper). This force pushes the brake pad against the ro-

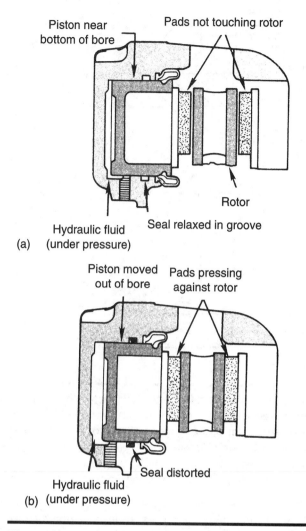

Piston near bottom of bore

Pads not touching rotor

Rotor

Hydraulic fluid

Seal relaxed in groove

(a) (under pressure)

Piston moved out of bore

Pads pressing against rotor

Hydraulic fluid

Seal distorted

(b) (under pressure)

Figure 6–10 (a) Single-piston floating caliper brake in the released position. (b) When the brake pedal is depressed, hydraulic fluid, under pressure, moves the caliper piston outward pressing the disc brake pads against the rotor bringing the vehicle to a stop. (Courtesy of Allied Signal Automotive Aftermarket)

TECH TIP ✔

The Bleed and Squirt Test

If you suspect a brake is not being fully released, simply loosen the bleeder valve. If brake fluid squirts out under pressure, then the brake is being kept applied. Look for a defective flexible brake hose.

If the vehicle is off the ground, the wheels should be able to be rotated with the brakes off. If a wheel is difficult or hard to turn by hand and is easy to turn after opening the bleeder valve, then there is a brake fluid restriction between the master cylinder and the brake.

tor. The same force that is pushing against the pad and rotor is exerted on the caliper itself. This reaction force was first described by Newton and is called the first law

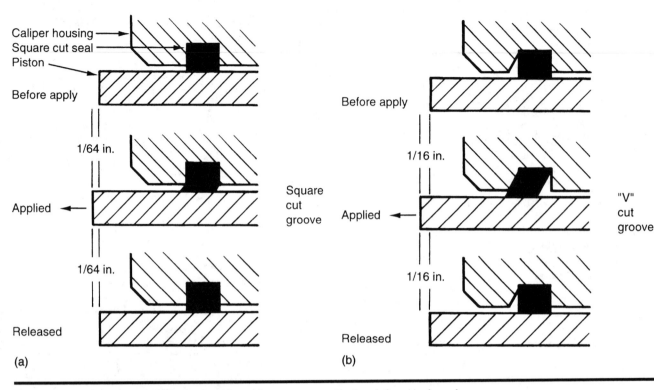

Figure 6–11 In a standard disc brake caliper, the square-cut O-ring deforms when the brakes are applied and returns the piston to its original (released) position due to the elastic properties of the rubber seal. In a low-drag caliper design, the groove for the square-cut O-ring is V-shaped allowing for more retraction. When the brake pedal is released, the piston is moved away from the rotor further, resulting in less friction between the disc brake pads and the rotor when the brakes are released.

of motion which states: "For every action, there is an opposite and equal reaction." It is this reaction against the force of the rotor that causes the entire caliper to slide or move toward the center of the vehicle. Since the outbound friction pads are attached to the caliper, as the caliper moves, it pushes the outbound pads against the outside surface of the rotor. If the caliper is properly lubricated and free to move, the force pushing against the outside of the rotor is the same as the force pushing against the inside of the rotor.

When the brake pedal is released, the hydraulic force against the piston is released. The caliper seal that was deformed during the brake application forces the piston to return to its original at-rest position (see Figure 6–11).

The entire caliper then returns to its released position and all pressure against the brake pads is removed.

> **NOTE:** If a floating caliper is stuck and cannot easily move when the brakes are applied, the inboard pad will wear more than the outboard pad. Uneven pad wear will also occur if the piston is stuck ("frozen") inside the caliper. Therefore, when uneven disc brake pad wear occurs, carefully inspect the caliper piston(s) and caliper slides.

■ BRAKE PAD WEAR COMPENSATION

As the disc brake pad wears, the caliper piston moves out closer to the rotor (see Figure 6–12).

The square-cut "O"-ring piston seal allows the piston to move as well as acts as a piston return. As the brake pad wears, the piston is forced to move through the caliper seal to make up for any pad wear. The surface finish on the piston must be clean to allow the piston to slide past this seal. Moisture accumulation inside the caliper often causes the piston to rust. These rust pits can cut or groove the caliper seal. In severe cases, the damaged seal allows brake fluid leakage past the seal and onto the friction pads. Excessive friction between the caliper piston and the caliper bore can prevent the piston from retracting. If the force of the caliper seal is not strong enough, the piston stays in the applied position. Since the brake pads are still in contact with the rotor, one or both pads will show excessive wear. To summarize:

Normal Operation—The piston moves just enough to distort the caliper seal and returns to original position when the brake pedal is released.

Wear Compensation—The piston moves more than the caliper seal can distort. The piston moves through

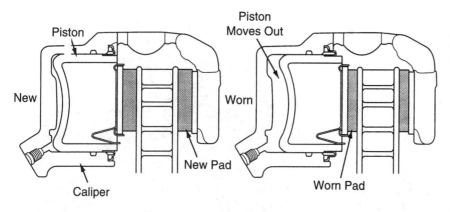

Figure 6–13 Riveted disc brake pad with a wear sensor.

the seal until the pad contacts the rotor. The caliper piston returns to the released position by the seal distortion, the same as during normal operation, except now in a different, more applied position.

As the wear occurs and the piston moves, additional brake fluid is needed behind the piston. This additional brake fluid comes from the master cylinder and the brake fluid level drops as the disc brake pads wear.

■ DISC BRAKE PADS

Disc brake pads have friction material attached to a steel backing. See Chapter 2 for details on friction materials composition. There are three methods used to attach the friction material to the steel backing.

Riveted—Holes are drilled through the friction material block, and brass rivets hold the block to the steel backing (see Figure 6–13).

Bonded—Friction blocks are glued to the steel backing.

Integrally Molded—The friction material is molded with the steel backing rather than molded separately, then attached to the steel backing. Integral molded linings use holes in the steel backing to allow the friction material to become a part of the steel backing. This process results in a brake pad that has a lot of strength and is resistant to shearing the friction material from the steel backing (see Figure 6–14).

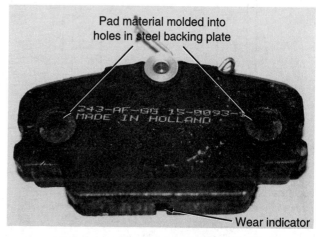

Figure 6–14 These replacement pads have a wear indicator groove and are also integrally molded.

Figure 6–15 Wear indicator groove. When the groove is no longer visible, the pads should be replaced.

■ WEAR SENSORS

Many disc brake pads are equipped with a groove or notch molded into the pad as shown in Figure 6–15.

When the pads are worn to the depth of the notch, the pads should be replaced. Another type of

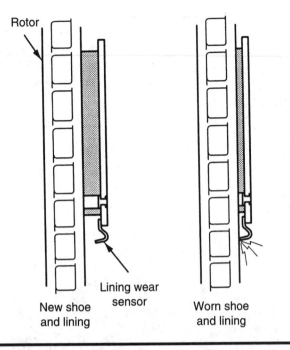

Figure 6–16 Typical pad wear sensor operation. It is very important that the disc brake pads are installed on the correct side of the vehicle to be assured that the wear sensor will make a noise when the pads are worn. If the pads with a sensor are installed on the opposite side of the vehicle, the sensor tab is turned so that the rotor touches it going the opposite direction. Usually the correct direction is where the rotor contacts the sensor before contacting the pads when the wheels are being rotated in the forward direction. (Courtesy of General Motors)

wear indicator uses a soft metal tang that contacts the rotor when the pad is worn to the thickness requiring replacement. These wear indicators make a "chirp, chirp" sound when the wheels are rotating and the ends of the metal tang are rubbing against the rotor (see Figure 6–16).

NOTE: With many vehicles, the wear indicator noise *stops* when the brakes are applied. The fact that the noise disappears when the brakes are applied has wrongly convinced many drivers (and some service technicians) that the problem is *not* due to the brakes. Some vehicles have indicators that only make noise while the vehicle is being driven in reverse. Other vehicles have sensors that tend to make the most noise during braking. Any noise while driving should be investigated.

Some manufacturers position the sensors on the brake pads so that the rotor touches the sensor before passing across the friction material. Other manufacturers position the sensor on the trailing edge of the pad (see Figure 6–17).

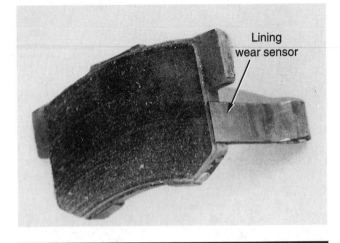

Figure 6–17 Typical disc brake pad wear sensor. This pad came off a rear disc brake that made a horrible, loud noise while backing up. The noise did not occur when driving forward. The very loud noise did an excellent job of notifying the driver of a possible problem.

■ ELECTRICAL BRAKE WEAR INDICATORS

Some vehicle manufacturers use electrical brake lining wear indicators. A typical installation involves an electrical wire leading to a sensor at the edge of the friction pad. When the lining material wears to the point of replacement, the electrical sensor touches the disc brake rotor. When the sensor touches the metal rotor, the electrical circuit is completed and lights a dash warning lamp.

Whenever servicing this type of system, be sure to purchase the correct pads for the vehicle that uses the electrical sensor. Failure to reinstall the original equipment sensor-type pads could cause the lining to be completely worn until metal-to-metal contact occurs between the steel backing plate of the disc brake pads and the rotor (see Figure 6–18).

TECH TIP

Be Sure to Have a Nickel's Worth of Linings

While the *exact* thickness of allowable brake lining varies with vehicle manufacturer, most experts agree that the lining should be thicker than the thickness of an American nickel coin. This is about 1/16" (0.060") or 1.5 mm.

Another rule of thumb that is easily used is to replace the brake pads if the thickness of the friction material is the same or less than the thickness of the steel backing of the disc brake pad.

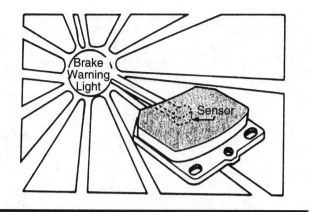

Figure 6–18 Some vehicles use an electrical wear sensor. When the pads wear enough, the typical electrical sensor touches the metal rotor and completes the electrical connection to light a dash warning lamp. (Courtesy of Allied Signal Automotive Aftermarket)

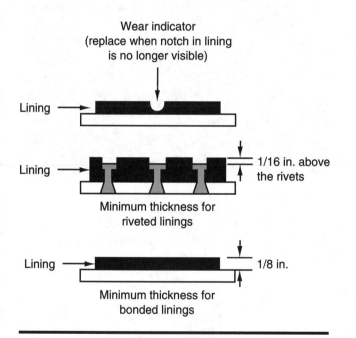

Figure 6–19 Minimum thickness for various types of disc brake pads. Disc brake pads can, of course, be replaced before they wear down to the factory-recommended *minimum* thickness.

■ VISUAL INSPECTION

Even with operating wear-indicating sensors, a thorough visual inspection is very important (see Figure 6–19).

A lining thickness check alone should not be the only inspection performed on a disc brake. **A thorough visual inspection can only be accomplished by removing the friction pads.** See Figure 6–20 for an example of a disc brake pad that shows usable lining thickness, but is severely cracked and *must* be replaced.

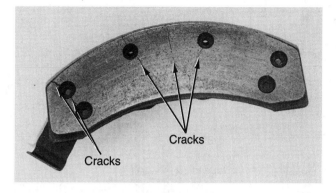

Figure 6–20 This cracked disc brake pad must be replaced even though it is thicker than the minimum allowed by the vehicle manufacturer.

NOTE: Some disc brake pads use a heat barrier (thermo) layer between the steel backing plate and the friction material. The purpose of the heat barrier is to prevent heat from transferring into the caliper piston where it may cause the brake fluid to boil. Do not confuse the thickness of the barrier as part of the thickness of the friction lining material. The barrier material is usually a different color and usually can be distinguished from the lining material.

■ TAPERED PAD WEAR

Some disc brake pads may show more wear on the end of the pad that first contacts the rotor as compared with the trailing end of the pad. This uneven wear is caused by the force between the pad and the abutment (slide area). In designs that place the caliper piston exactly in the center of the leading edge of the pad that first contacts the rotor as it is revolving through the caliper, pressures are often one-third higher than the average pressure exerted on the entire pad. The result of this higher pressure is greater wear.

Brake engineers design brakes to minimize or eliminate tapered pad wear by offsetting the piston more toward the trailing edge of the shoe or by other caliper/pad mounting designs.

One method used to help reduce tapered pad wear is the design that offsets the friction material off center. Be certain to position the pads correctly or severe tapered pad wear will occur (see Figures 6–21, 6–22, and 6–23).

■ BRAKE FADE

Brake fade is a term used to describe the decrease in braking effectiveness as the temperature of the brakes increases. In severe cases, the brake pedal can go to the

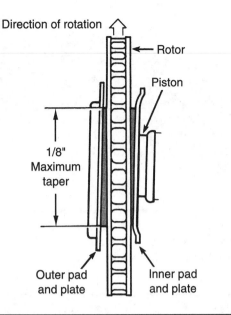

Figure 6–21 Tapered disc brake pad wear is sometimes discovered during a brake inspection. Many vehicle manufacturers specify a maximum taper as shown of 1/8″ (3 mm). (Courtesy of Allied Signal Automotive Aftermarket)

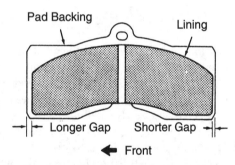

Figure 6–22 Be careful to observe the direction in which replacement linings are facing. Some vehicle manufacturers offset the friction material on the steel backing to help prevent or minimize tapered pad wear. (Courtesy of Wagner Division, Cooper Industries Inc.)

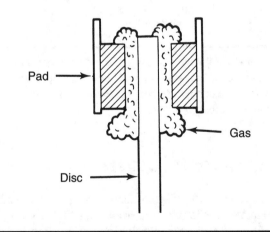

Figure 6–23 Most disc brake calipers have a brake inspection opening. For a thorough inspection, however, the caliper should be removed and the entire braking system thoroughly inspected.

Figure 6–24 One cause of brake fade occurs when the phenolic resin, a part of the friction material, gets so hot that it vaporizes. The vaporized gas from the disc brake pads gets between the rotor (disc) and the friction pad. Because the friction pad is no longer in contact with the rotor, no additional braking force is possible. (Courtesy of Raybestos Brake Parts Inc.)

floor and not have any braking force at all. Brake fade occurs when the temperature of the brake rotors or drums gets high enough that they cannot dissipate the heat away from the friction material. Often the temperature of the brake lining gets so hot that the resins in the friction material vaporize and create a layer of gas between the rotor and the friction pads as shown in Figure 6–24.

■ DISC BRAKE CALIPERS

Removal

Hoist the vehicle and remove the wheel(s). Note the caliper mount position as shown in Figure 6–26 before removing the caliper.

Knowing whether the caliper is "rear mount" position or "forward mount" position is often needed when purchasing replacement calipers.

Remove the caliper following the steps in Figures 6–27 through 6–35 on pages 147–150.

Figure 6–25 A high-performance disc brake rotor that has been designed to be drilled to provide additional cooling needed during severe braking conditions such as motorsport racing.

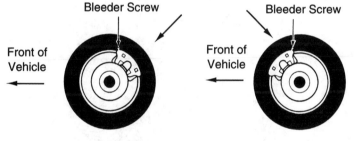

Rear-Mount Caliper Position   **Forward-Mount Caliper Position**

Figure 6–26 Both rear- and forward-mounted calipers have the bleeder valve at the top. Some calipers *will* fit on the wrong side of the vehicle, yet not be able to be bled correctly because the bleeder valve would point down, allowing trapped air to remain inside the caliper bore. If both calipers are being removed at the same time, mark them "left" and "right."

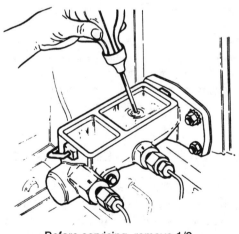

Before servicing, remove 1/2 fluid from reservoir

Figure 6–27 Many manufacturers recommend removing one-half of the brake fluid from the master cylinder before servicing disc brakes. Use a squeeze bulb and dispose of the used brake fluid correctly. (Courtesy of Wagner Division, Cooper Industries Inc.)

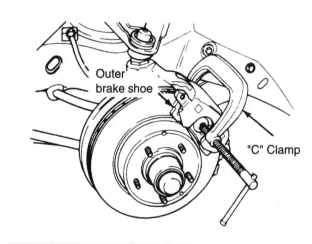

Figure 6–28 Use a C-clamp on the outboard pad and the caliper housing to squeeze the disc brake caliper piston back into its bore. Be sure to open the bleeder valve when performing the operation to help prevent old, dirty brake fluid from being forced back up into the master cylinder and/or ABS hydraulic unit. (Courtesy of Wagner Division, Cooper Industries Inc.)

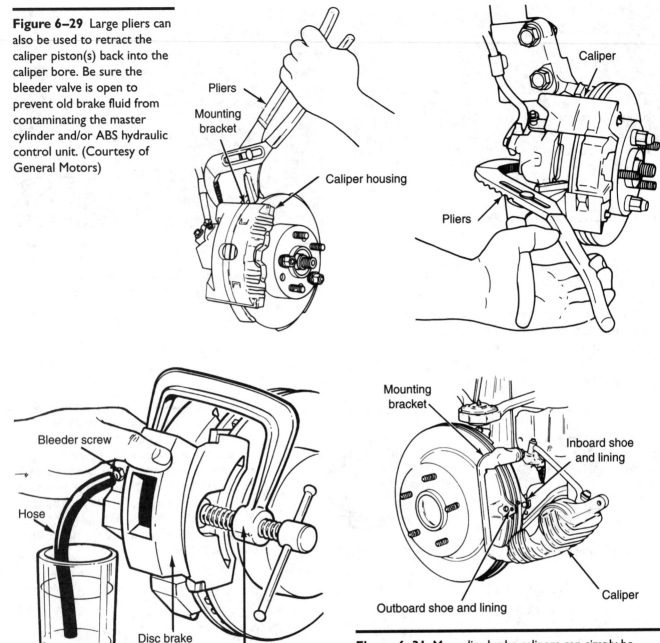

Figure 6–29 Large pliers can also be used to retract the caliper piston(s) back into the caliper bore. Be sure the bleeder valve is open to prevent old brake fluid from contaminating the master cylinder and/or ABS hydraulic control unit. (Courtesy of General Motors)

Figure 6–30 Most manufacturers recommend that the bleeder valve be opened and the brake fluid forced into a container rather than back into the master cylinder reservoir. This helps prevent contaminated brake fluid from being forced into the master cylinder where the dirt and contamination could cause problems.

Figure 6–31 Many disc brake calipers can simply be pivoted upward or downward on one of the mounting bolts to gain access to the disc brake pads. (Courtesy of General Motors)

Inspection and Disassembly

Check for brake fluid in and around the piston boot area. If the boot is damaged or a fluid leak is visible, then repair or a caliper assembly replacement is required (see Figures 6–36 and 6–37 on page 150).

■ PHENOLIC CALIPER PISTONS

Phenolic caliper pistons are made from a phenol-formaldehyde resin combined with various reinforcing fibers. Phenolic brake caliper pistons were first used in the 1970s on many Chrysler vehicles. The results were not good and the problem was blamed on "those *darn* plastic pistons." What was happening was that the pistons were becoming stuck in the caliper which caused the brake pads to remain applied. This caused the brake pads to wear out very rapidly. The problem occurred because the phenolic pistons absorbed moisture and swelled in size.

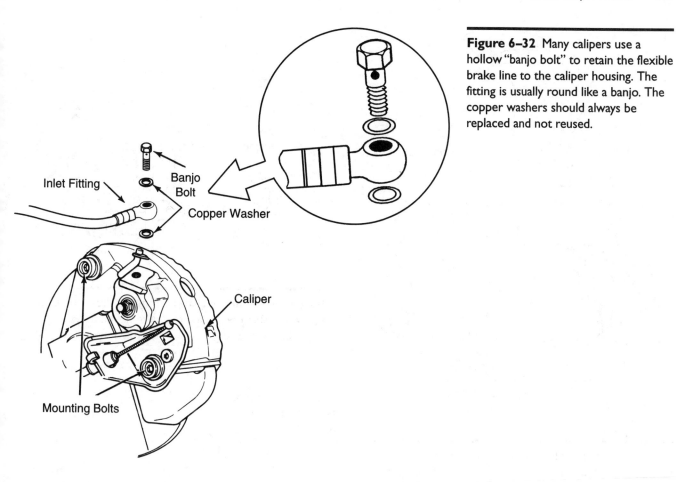

Figure 6–32 Many calipers use a hollow "banjo bolt" to retain the flexible brake line to the caliper housing. The fitting is usually round like a banjo. The copper washers should always be replaced and not reused.

Inlet Fitting

Banjo Bolt

Copper Washer

Caliper

Mounting Bolts

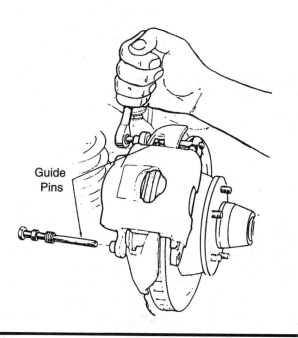

Guide Pins

Figure 6–33 Caliper retaining bolts are often called **guide pins**. These guide pins are used to retain the caliper to the steering knuckle. These pins also slide through metal bushings and rubber O-rings. (Courtesy of EIS Brake Parts)

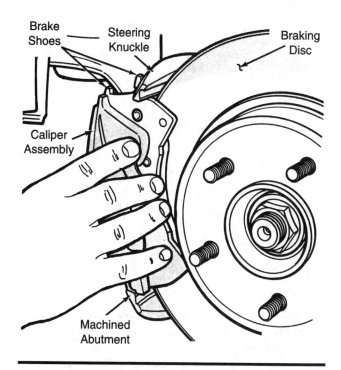

Brake Shoes

Steering Knuckle

Braking Disc

Caliper Assembly

Machined Abutment

Figure 6–34 After compressing the caliper piston back into the caliper bore and removing the caliper retaining bolts, the caliper assembly can be removed. (Courtesy of Chrysler Corporation)

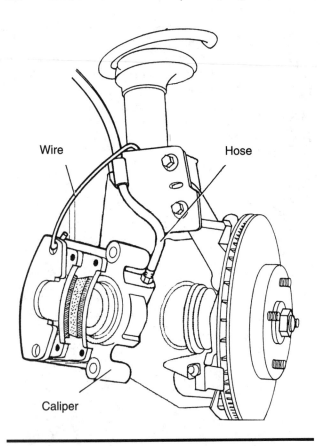

Figure 6–35 If the caliper is not being removed, it must be supported properly so that the weight of the caliper is not pulling on the flexible rubber brake line. A suitable piece of wire such as a coat hanger may be used.

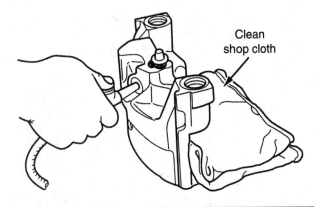

Figure 6–36 With the caliper removed from the vehicle, the caliper piston can be removed by applying compressed air into the inlet port with the bleeder valve closed. The compressed air will force the piston out of the caliper. A cloth or other soft material should be used to prevent damage to the piston as it is being forced out. Obviously, hands and fingers should also be kept out of the path of the piston. (Courtesy of General Motors)

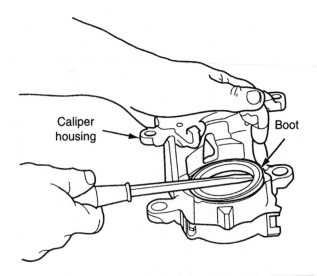

Figure 6–37 After the piston is removed from the caliper housing, the dust boot can often be removed using a straight-blade screwdriver. (Courtesy of General Motors)

Cracks, chips, gouges may not enter dust boot groove

Cracks, chips, gouges may be 1/2" long and may go inward almost to piston seal groove.

If no cracks, chips, gouges, or any other surface damage on ground seal surface (piston o.d.), the pistons are acceptable.

Figure 6–38 Phenolic (plastic) pistons should be carefully inspected. (Courtesy of Allied Signal Automotive Aftermarket)

NOTE: Brake engineers in the 1970s did not realize that phenolic materials were hygroscopic (absorbed moisture). As the phenolic material absorbed water over a long period of time, the diameter of the piston grew until it became stuck in the caliper bore.

By reducing the diameter of the pistons 0.001″ to 0.002″ (0.025 to 0.050 mm) and improving the caliper boot seal, the sticking problem has been solved. Since the mid-1980s, phenolic caliper pistons have been used as original equipment by many vehicle manufacturers. Phenolic caliper pistons are natural thermal insulators and help keep heat generated by the disc brake pads from transferring through the caliper piston to the brake fluid. Phenolic brake caliper pistons are also lighter in weight than steel caliper pistons and are usually brown in color (see Figure 6–38).

■ STEEL CALIPER PISTONS

Many manufacturers still use steel pistons. The stamped steel pistons are plated first with nickel, then chrome to achieve the desired surface finish (see Figure 6–39).

Unlike phenolic caliper pistons, steel pistons can transfer heat from the brake pads to the brake fluid. The surface finish on a steel piston is critical. Steel can rust and corrode. Any surface pitting can cause the piston to stick.

> **NOTE:** Care should be taken when cleaning steel pistons. Use crocus cloth to remove any surface staining. Do not use sand paper or emery cloth or any other substance that may remove or damage the chrome surface finish.

(a)

(b)

Figure 6–39 The outside surface of caliper pistons should be carefully inspected. The square-cut O-ring inside the caliper rides on this outside surface of the piston. Sometimes dirty pistons can be cleaned and reused. If there are any surface flaws such as rust pits on the piston, it should be replaced. (a) Dirty piston before cleaning at a remanufacturing plant. (b) Typical piston after cleaning.

Diagnostic Story

Three Brake Jobs in 40,000 Miles

A service technician was asked to replace the front disc brake pads on a Pontiac Grand Am because the sensors were touching the rotors and making a squealing sound (see Figure 6–40). This was the third time that the front brakes needed to be replaced. Previous brake repairs had been limited to replacement of the front disc brake pads only.

When the caliper was removed and the pads inspected, it was discovered that a part of one pad had broken and a piece of the lining was missing (see Figure 6–41). Further inspection of the pads indicated that the pads were worn on a taper—indicating a possible problem with the caliper mounts or dragging pads caused by a stuck caliper piston (see Figure 6–42). Then the technician spotted something at the rear of the vehicle that told the whole story—a trailer hitch (see Figure 6–43). The owner confirmed that a heavy jet ski was towed in hilly terrain. The technician recommended overhauling the front disc brake calipers to prevent the possibility of the front pads dragging. The technician also recommended an inspection of the rear brakes. The rear brakes were glazed and out of adjustment. The technician received permission to replace the rear brakes, overhaul both front calipers, and install quality disc brake pads. When the customer returned, the technician advised the customer to use the transmission on long downhill roads to help keep the brakes from overheating and failing prematurely.

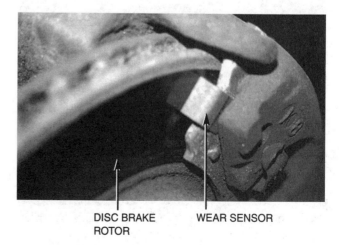

DISC BRAKE ROTOR   WEAR SENSOR

Figure 6–40 The customer wanted new front disc brake pads because the wear sensors were touching the rotor.

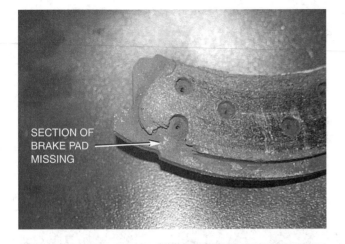

Figure 6–41 The pads were found to be cracked and a section was missing from a part of one pad.

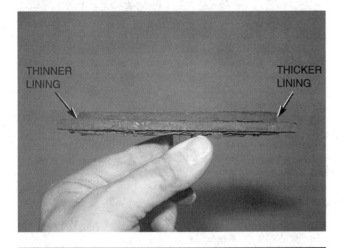

Figure 6–42 The front disc brake pads had also worn in a tapered shape indicating a possible stuck caliper piston that could have caused the pads to rub constantly against the rotor.

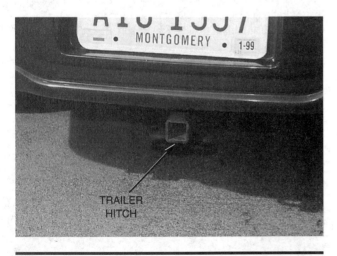

Figure 6–43 The observant technician noticed the trailer hitch indicating that the owner may have been towing a trailer which can cause more stress than normal on the braking system.

■ REASSEMBLING DISC BRAKE CALIPERS

After disassembly, the caliper should be thoroughly cleaned in denatured alcohol and closely examined (see Figure 6–44).

If the caliper bore is rusted or pitted, some manufacturers recommend that a special hone be used as shown in Figure 6–45.

Some manufacturers do *not* recommend honing the caliper bore because the actual sealing surface in the caliper is between the piston seal and the piston itself. This is the reason why the surface condition of the piston is so important.

Carefully clean the caliper bore with clean brake fluid from a sealed container. Coat a new piston seal with clean brake fluid and install it in the groove inside the caliper bore as shown in Figure 6–46. Check the piston-to-caliper bore clearance. Typical piston-to-caliper bore clearance is:

steel piston—0.002″–0.005″ clearance (0.05-0.13 mm)

phenolic piston—0.005″–0.010″ clearance (0.13-0.25 mm)

Coat a new piston boot with brake fluid or brake assembly fluid (see Figure 6–47). Install the piston into the caliper piston as shown in Figures 6–48 and 6–49 on page 154.

Some caliper boots require a special boot seating tool as shown in Figure 6–50 on page 154.

Always lubricate caliper bushings, shims, and other brake hardware as instructed by the manufacturer (see Figure 6–51 on page 155).

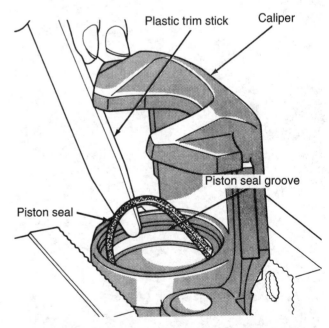

Figure 6–44 Removing the square-cut O-ring seal from the caliper bore. Use a wooden or plastic tool to prevent damage to the seal groove. (Courtesy of Chrysler Corporation)

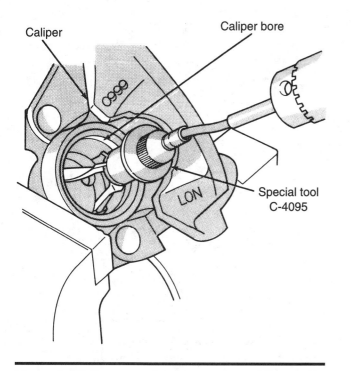

Figure 6–45 Some manufacturers recommend cleaning the inside of the caliper bore using a honing tool as shown. Even though the caliper piston does not contact the inside of this bore, removing any surface rust or corrosion is important to prevent future problems. If the honing process cannot remove any pits or scored areas, the caliper should be replaced. (Courtesy of Chrysler Corporation)

Figure 6–47 Brake assembly fluid or clean brake fluid from a sealed container can be used to lubricate the caliper seal and caliper pistons before assembly.

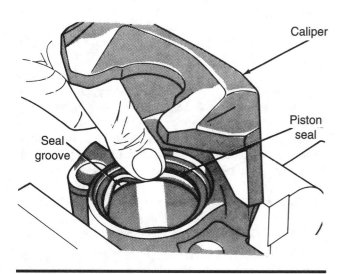

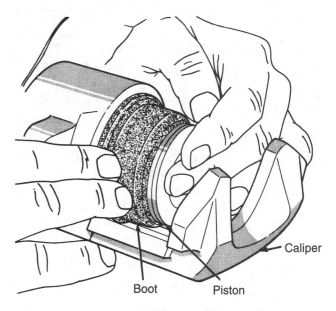

Figure 6–46 Installing a new piston seal. Never reuse old rubber parts. (Courtesy of Chrysler Corporation)

Figure 6–48 Installing the caliper piston. Many calipers require that the dust boot be installed in the groove of the piston and/or caliper before installing the piston. (Courtesy of Chrysler Corporation)

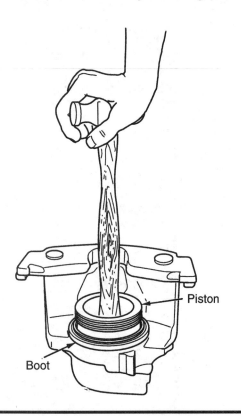

Figure 6–49 Installing a piston into a caliper. Sometimes a C-clamp is needed to install the piston. Both the piston and the piston seal should be coated in clean brake fluid before assembly. (Courtesy of General Motors)

TECH TIP ✔

Using "Loaded Calipers" Saves Time

Many technicians find that disassembly, cleaning, and rebuilding calipers can take a lot of time. Often the bleeder valve breaks off or the caliper piston is too corroded to reuse. This means that the technician has to get a replacement piston, caliper overhaul kit (piston seal and boot), plus the replacement friction pads and hardware kit.

To save time (and sometimes money), many technicians are simply replacing the old calipers with "loaded calipers." Loaded calipers are remanufactured calipers that include (come loaded) with the correct replacement friction pads and all the necessary hardware (see Figure 6–55 on page 156). Therefore, only one part number is needed for each side of the vehicle for a complete disc brake overhaul.

The pads should also be securely attached to the caliper as shown in Figures 6–52, 6–53, and 6–54 on pages 155–156.

CAUTION: Installing disc brake pads on the wrong side of the vehicle (left versus right) will often prevent the sensor from making noise when the pads are worn.

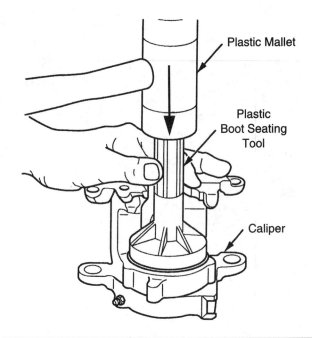

Figure 6–50 Seating the dust boot into the caliper housing using a special plastic seating tool.

■ CALIPER MOUNTS

When the hydraulic force from the master cylinder applies pressure to the disc brake pads, the entire caliper tends to be forced in the direction of rotation of the rotor. All calipers are mounted to the steering knuckle or axle housing (see Figure 6–56 on page 157).

All braking force is transferred through the caliper to the mount. The places where the caliper contacts the caliper mount are called the **abutments, reaction pads,** or **ways.** The sliding surfaces of the caliper support should be cleaned with a wire brush and coated with a synthetic grease or antiseize compound according to manufacturer's recommendations (see Figure 6–57 on page 157). As the vehicle ages and the brakes are used thousands of times, these abutments (pads) can wear, causing too much clearance between the caliper and the mounting. When this occurs, the caliper often rotates against the abutment when the brakes are first applied, making a loud "knocking" noise. If this occurs, the service technician can repair this type of wear two ways:

Method 1—Replace the entire steering knuckle or caliper mount. This is the recommended method and also the more expensive. Replacement caliper mounts or knuckles may also be difficult to locate.

Method 2—Some aftermarket brake supply companies offer "abutment repair kits" that include oversize slides.

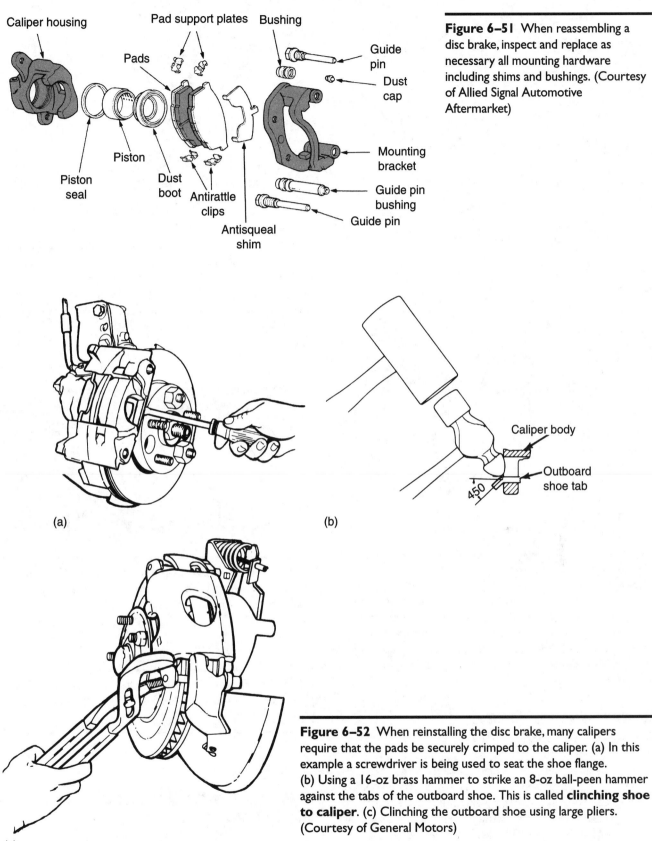

Caliper housing

Pad support plates   Bushing

Pads

Guide
pin

Dust
cap

Piston

Mounting
bracket

Piston
seal

Dust
boot   Antirattle
clips

Guide pin
bushing

Guide pin

Antisqueal
shim

Figure 6–51 When reassembling a disc brake, inspect and replace as necessary all mounting hardware including shims and bushings. (Courtesy of Allied Signal Automotive Aftermarket)

(a)

(b)

Caliper body

Outboard
shoe tab

450

(c)

Figure 6–52 When reinstalling the disc brake, many calipers require that the pads be securely crimped to the caliper. (a) In this example a screwdriver is being used to seat the shoe flange. (b) Using a 16-oz brass hammer to strike an 8-oz ball-peen hammer against the tabs of the outboard shoe. This is called **clinching shoe to caliper**. (c) Clinching the outboard shoe using large pliers. (Courtesy of General Motors)

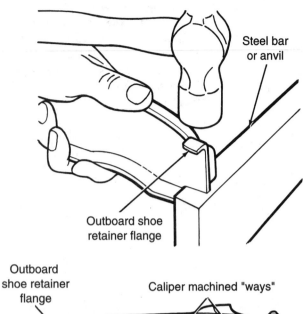

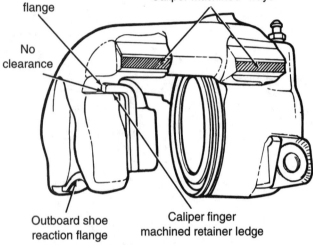

Figure 6–53 Often, a hammer is necessary to bend the retainer flange to make certain that the pads fit tightly to the caliper. If the pads are loose, a "click" may be heard every time the brakes are depressed. This click occurs when the pad(s) move and then hit the caliper or caliper mount. If the pads are loose, a clicking noise may be heard while driving over rough road surfaces. (Courtesy of Chrysler Corporation)

■ TEST-DRIVE AFTER BRAKE REPLACEMENT

After installing replacement disc brake pads or any other brake work, depress the brake pedal several times before driving the vehicle. This is a very important step! New brake pads are installed with the caliper piston pushed all the way into the caliper. The first few brake pedal applications usually result in the brake pedal going all the way to the floor. The brake pedal must be depressed ("pumped") several times before enough brake fluid can be moved from the master cylinder into the calipers to move the piston tight against the pads and the pads against the rotors.

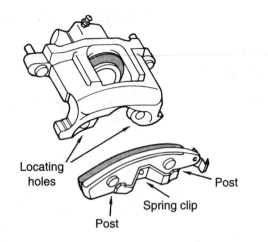

Figure 6–54 In this style of disc brake, the posts must be seated into the matching holes in the caliper housing. The spring clip that is riveted to the outboard shoe plate will hold the pad in position after it is seated. (Courtesy of Allied Signal Automotive Aftermarket)

Figure 6–55 A loaded caliper includes all hardware and shims with the correct pads all in one convenient package ready to install on the vehicle.

CAUTION: Never allow a customer to be the first to test-drive the vehicle after brake work has been performed.

■ BEDDING-IN REPLACEMENT BRAKE PADS

Some manufacturers recommend that their replacement brake pads be "bedded-in" or "burnished" before returning the vehicle to the owner. This break-in process varies with manufacturer, but usually involves stopping the vehicle from 30 mph (48 km/h) up to thirty

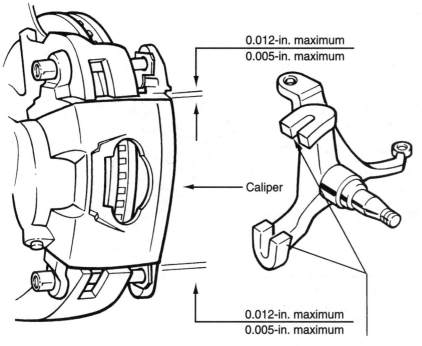

0.012-in. maximum
0.005-in. maximum

Caliper

0.012-in. maximum
0.005-in. maximum

File Adjustments (reaction pools)
if necessary to obtain clearance

Figure 6–56 Floating calipers must be able to slide during normal operation. Therefore, there must be clearance between the caliper and the caliper mounting pads (abutments). Too little clearance will prevent the caliper from sliding and too much clearance will cause the caliper to make a clunking noise when the brakes are applied.

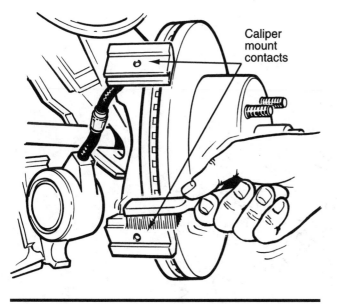

Caliper mount contacts

Figure 6–57 All caliper mounting surfaces should be cleaned and lubricated according to manufacturer recommendations.

times, allowing the brakes to cool two to three minutes between stops. This break-in procedure helps the replacement pads to conform to the rotor and helps cure the resins used in the manufacture of the pads. Failure to properly break in new pads according to the manufacturer's recommended procedure could result in a hard brake pedal complaint from the driver and/or reduced braking effectiveness.

Even if the brake pad manufacturer does not recommend a break-in procedure, high-speed stops and overheating of the brakes should be avoided as much as possible during the first 50 to 100 stops.

■ REAR DISC BRAKES

Rear disc brakes are used on the rear of many vehicles. A parking brake is more difficult to use with disc brakes; therefore, rear disc brakes are commonly found on high performance or more expensive vehicles. Most vehicles equipped with rear disc brakes use one of two different styles of parking brake.

Style 1—An integral parking brake built into the piston assembly (see Figures 6–58, 6–59, and 6–60 on pages 158–159).

Style 2—A more conventional disc brake that uses a small drum brake for the parking brake function (see Figures 6–61 and 6–62 on pages 159–160).

■ CAUSES OF DISC BRAKE SQUEAL

Disc brakes tend to create brake noise (squeal). The cause and correction of brake noise is a major concern for both the vehicle manufacturers and the service technicians. The greatest customer complaint about brake work involves brake noise. Noise is caused by moving air and the air is moved by movement of the brake components.

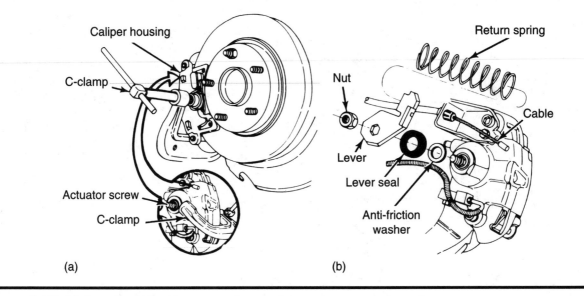

(a)   (b)

Figure 6–58 (a) Care should be taken not to damage the actuator screw when using a
C-clamp on a rear disc brake. (b) Carefully note the location of the seal and washer
when disassembling a rear disc brake. (Courtesy of General Motors)

1. Nut
2. Lever
3. Return spring
4. Bolt
5. Bracket
6. Sleeve
7. Bushing
8. Bolt
9. Copper washer
10. Fitting
11. Bushing
12. Caliper housing
13. Shaft seal
14. Thrust washer
15. Balance spring
16. Actuator screw
17. Piston seal
18. Piston assembly
19. Two-way check valve
20. Bleeder valve
21. Anti-friction washer
22. Lever seal
23. Mounting bolt
24. Boot
25. Inboard shoe & lining
26. Wear sensor
27. Outboard shoe & lining
28. Shoe dampening spring

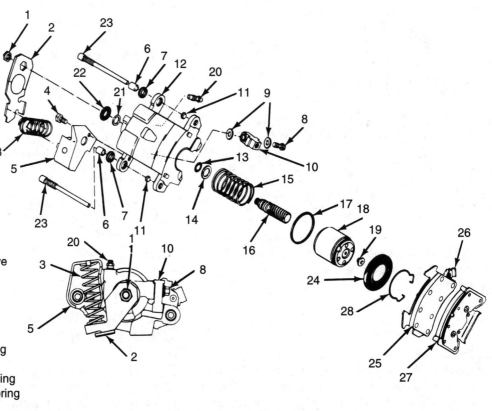

Figure 6–59 Exploded view of a typical rear disc brake with an integral parking brake.
The parking brake lever mechanically pushes the caliper piston against the rotor.
(Courtesy of General Motors)

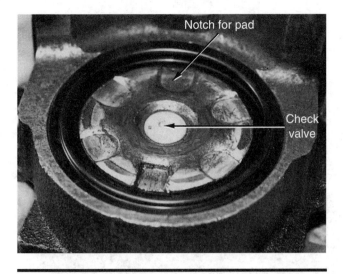

Figure 6–60 Many rear disc brakes have a notched piston as shown. The disc brake pad must fit into the notch to keep the piston from rotating inside the caliper bore when the parking brake is applied. The two-way check valve should be pried out. If there is brake fluid under the valve, the caliper should be overhauled or replaced because the inside caliper seal has failed. Slight dampness should be considered normal.

■ CORRECTING DISC BRAKE SQUEAL

Brake squeal can best be *prevented* by careful attention to details whenever servicing any disc brake. Some of these precautions include:

Keeping the Disc Brake Pads Clean

Grease on brake lining material causes the friction surface to be uneven. When the brakes are applied, this uneven brake surface causes the brake components to move.

Use Factory-Type Clips and Anti-Squeal Shims

The vehicle manufacturer has designed the braking system to be as quiet as possible. To ensure that the brakes are restored to like-new performance, all of the original hardware should be used. Many original equipment brake pads use **constrained layer shims (CLS)** on the back of the brake pads. These shims are constructed with dampening material between two layers of steel (see Figure 6–63).

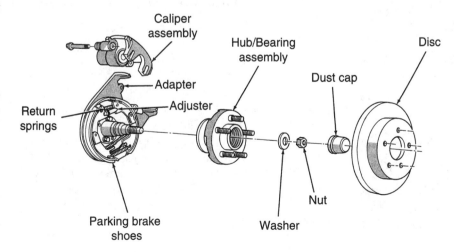

Figure 6–61 Typical rear disc brake that uses a small drum brake as the parking brake. The drum brake shoes move outward and contact the inner surface (hat) section of the rotor. (Courtesy of Chrysler Corporation)

(a)

(b)

Figure 6–62 (a) Removing the disc brake rotor from this Chrysler minivan reveals a small drum brake used for the parking brake. (b) The inside "hat" of the rotor is the friction surface for the drum brake shoes.

TECH TIP ✔

Increasing Pad Life

Many vehicles seem to wear out front disc brakes more often than normal. Stop-and-go city-type driving is often the cause. Driving style, such as rapid stops, also causes a lot of wear to occur.

The service technician can take some actions to increase brake pad life that is easier than having to cure the driver's habits. These steps include:

1. Make sure the rear brakes are properly adjusted and working correctly. If the rear brakes are not functioning, all of the braking is accomplished by the front brakes alone.

> **HINT:** Remind the driver to apply the parking brake regularly to help maintain proper rear brake clearance on the rear brakes.

2. Use factory brake pads or premium brake pads from a known manufacturer. Tests performed by vehicle manufacturers show that many aftermarket replacement brake pads fail to deliver original equipment brake pad life.

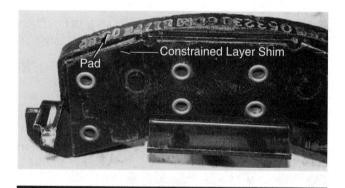

Figure 6–63 Many original equipment (OE) disc brake pads are equipped with noise-reducing constrained layer (dampening) shims.

> **NOTE:** Many aftermarket disc brake pads do *not* include replacement hardware that usually includes noise-reducing shims and clips. One of the advantages of purchasing original equipment (OE) disc brake pads is that they usually come equipped with all necessary shims and often with special grease that is recommended to be used on metal shims.

Figure 6–64 Most vehicle manufacturers recommend the use of silicone grease for brake lubrication. Silicone grease can be used to lubricate metal or rubber parts. Antiseize compound should only be used on metal-to-metal contacts.

Lubricate All Caliper Slide Points as Per Manufacturer's Recommendation

Lubrication of moving or sliding components prevents noise being generated as the parts move over each other. Many vehicle manufacturers recommend one or more of the following greases:

1. **lithium-based brake grease**
2. **silicone grease**
3. **molybdenum disulfide (MOS$_2$) grease ("Molykote")**
4. **synthetic grease** (usually **polyalphaolefin [PAO]**) sometimes mixed with graphite, Teflon, and/or MOS$_2$
5. **antiseize compound**

The grease should be applied on both sides of shims used between the pad and the caliper piston. See Figure 6–64.

> **CAUTION:** Grease should only be applied to the nonfriction (steel) side of the disc brake pads.

Machine the Brake Rotor as Little as Possible and with the Correct Surface Finish

Machining the brake rotor reduces its thickness. A thinner rotor will vibrate at a different frequency than a thicker rotor. (See Chapter 8 for details on rotor machining and surface finish.) Factors that can help or hurt brake squeal include (see Figure 6–65):

Factor	Increase noise	Reduce noise
Brake pad thickness	Thinner (worn) pads	Thicker (new) pads
rotor (disc) thickness	Thinner (worn) rotor	Thicker (new) rotor
brake pad material	Harder	Softer

Factor	Increase noise	Reduce noise
Lubrication of parts	Dry—not lubricated	Properly lubricated
Dampening	No dampening	Dampening material behind the pads
Pad mounting	Pad tabs not bent over	Pad tabs securely crimped
Anti-rattle clips	Worn, defective or not lubricated	New and properly lubricated

Vehicle manufacturers also change brake pad (lining) composition and the shape of the pads to help eliminate brake noise. The change of shape thus changes the frequency of the sound. Noise is vibration, but much of the vibration generated is not heard because the noise is beyond the normal frequency to be heard. Most people can hear from 20 to 20,000 cycles per second (called hertz). To stop brake noise, the manufacturer can change the frequency of the vibration to above or below the hertz range that can be heard (see Figure 6–66).

> **NOTE:** All metal-to-metal contacts *must* be lubricated to help prevent brake noise.

■ ROTATING PISTONS BACK INTO THE CALIPER

Many disc brake calipers used on the rear wheels require that the piston be rotated to reseat the pistons. When the parking brake is applied, the actuating screw moves the piston outward forcing the pads against the disc brake rotor. The piston is kept from rotating because of an anti-rotation device or notches on the inboard pad and piston.

When the disc brake pads are being replaced, use a special tool to rotate the piston back into the brake calipers. Insert the tip of the tool in the holes or slots in

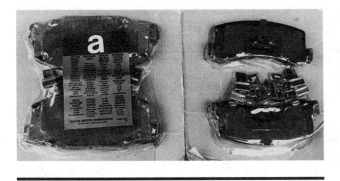

Figure 6–65 Many factory replacement disc brake pads come equipped with all new replacement hardware. The letter "a" on this package indicates that the pads contain asbestos.

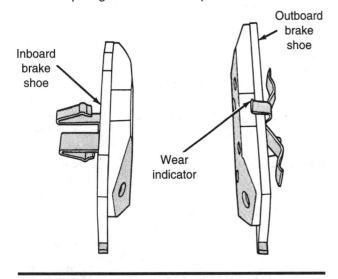

Figure 6–66 Notice the beveled pads. The shape of the pad helps determine the frequency of any vibration in the brakes. (Courtesy of Chrysler Corporation)

the piston. Exert inward pressure while turning the piston. Make sure that the piston is retracting into the caliper and continue to turn the piston until it bottoms out.

NOTE: Some pistons are activated with left-handed threads.

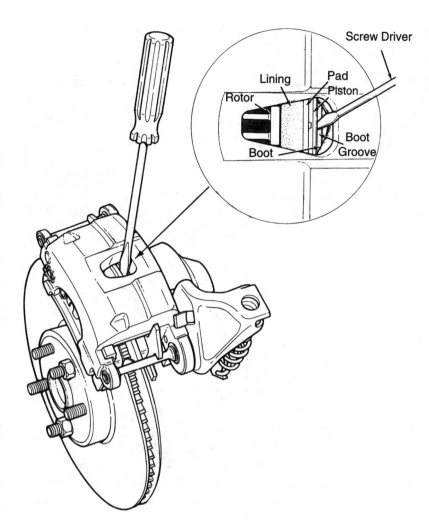

Figure 6–67 The screwdriver blade is used to keep the piston applied to allow self-adjustment to occur when the brake pedal is released.

After replacing the pads back into the caliper, check that the clearance does not exceed 1/16″ (1.5 mm) from the rotor. Clearance greater than 1/16″ may allow the adjuster to be pulled out of the piston when the service brake is applied. If the clearance is greater than 1/16″, readjust by rotating the piston outward to reduce the clearance (see Figure 6–68).

■ DISC BRAKE TROUBLESHOOTING GUIDE
Pulls to One Side During Braking

Possible causes:

1. Incorrect or unequal tire pressures
2. Front end out of alignment
3. Unmatched tires on the same axle
4. Restricted brake lines or hoses
5. Stuck or seized caliper or caliper piston
6. Defective or damaged shoe and lining (grease or brake fluid on the lining, or a bent shoe)
7. Malfunctioning rear brakes
8. Loose suspension parts
9. Loose calipers

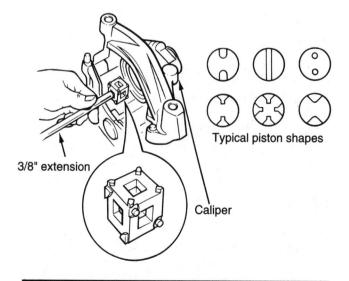

Figure 6–68 Determine which face of the special tool best fits the holes or slots in the piston. Sometimes needle-nose pliers can be used to rotate the piston back into the caliper bore.

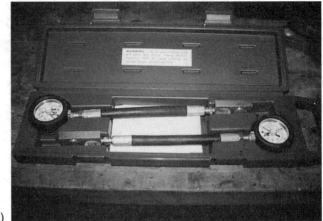

(a)

(b)

Figure 6–69 (a) A brake pressure tester. (b) The small "pads" can be placed between the caliper piston and the rotor to check for applied pressure and inserted between the caliper and the rotor on the outside of the rotor to test the pressure—the pressure should be the same if the caliper is able to slide on its pins or slides.

TECH TIP ☑

Pressure Testing Can Help Find Problems

A stuck caliper or caliper slide is often difficult to see or diagnose as a problem because the movement of the broken pads is so little. Using a pressure gauge between the caliper piston and the rotor (inboard) or between the rotor and the caliper (outboard) can tell the service technician if there is a difference between the left and the right side brakes (see Figure 6–69).

Brake Roughness or Chatter (Pedal Pulsates)

Possible causes:

1. Excessive lateral runout of rotor
2. Parallelism of the rotor not within specifications
3. Wheel bearings not adjusted correctly
4. Rear drums out of round
5. Brake pads worn to metal backing plate

Excessive Pedal Effort

Possible causes:

1. Binding or seized caliper suspension
2. Binding brake pedal mechanism
3. Improper rotor surface finish
4. Malfunctioning power brake
5. Partial system failure
6. Excessively worn shoe and lining
7. Piston in the caliper stuck or sluggish
8. Fading brakes due to incorrect lining

Excessive Pedal Travel

Possible causes:

1. Partial brake system failure
2. Insufficient fluid in the master cylinder
3. Air trapped in the system
4. Bent shoe and lining
5. Excessive pedal effort
6. Excessive parking brake travel (four-wheel disc brakes, except Corvette)

Dragging Brakes

Possible causes:

1. Pressure trapped in the brake lines (To diagnose, momentarily open the caliper bleeder valve to relieve the pressure.)
2. Restricted brake tubes or hoses
3. Improperly lubricated caliper suspension system
4. Improper clearance between the caliper and torque abutment surfaces

5. Check valve installed the outlet of the master cylinder to the disc brakes

Front Disc Brakes Very Sensitive to Light Brake Applications

Possible causes:

1. Metering valve not holding off the front brake application
2. Incorrect lining material
3. Improper rotor surface finish
4. Check other causes listed under "PULLS"

Rear Drum Brakes Skidding under Hard Brake Applications

Possible causes:

1. Proportioning valve
2. Contaminated rear brake lining
3. Caliper or caliper piston stuck or corroded

PHOTO SEQUENCE GM Disc Brake Service

PS6–1 After safely hoisting the vehicle, remove the wheels. To help break loose a bleeder valve, tap on the caliper at the base of the bleeder valve.

PS6–2 Often a blow to the top of the bleeder valve is also necessary to "break the taper" at the base of the bleeder valve.

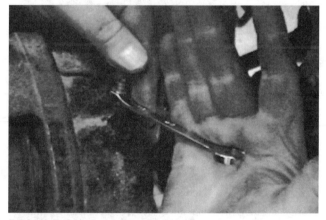

PS6–3 Before loosening the bleeder valve, attempt to tighten the valve first. Again, this helps break the bleeder valve loose.

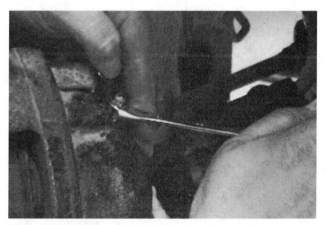

PS6–4 The bleeder valve should be able to be loosened without breaking.

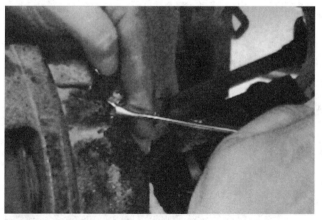

PS6–5 With the bleeder valve open, use a pry bar or screwdriver against the inboard pad to force the caliper piston back into its bore to provide clearance so that the caliper can be removed.

PS6–6 A C-clamp can also be used to compress the caliper piston. Be sure the bleeder valve is open to prevent the old brake fluid from being forced up into the ABS hydraulic unit and/or the master cylinder.

GM Disc Brake Service—continued

PS6–7 After the caliper piston has been pushed back into its bore, the caliper guide pins (caliper retaining pins) can be removed.

PS6–8 It may be necessary to use a screwdriver or pry bar to lift the caliper off of its support.

PS6–9 Lift the caliper assembly off of the rotor.

PS6–10 Hang the caliper by a wire or, in this case, the service technician simply hung the caliper on the strut. This support is necessary to prevent damage to the flexible brake line that could occur if the caliper were allowed to hang by the hose.

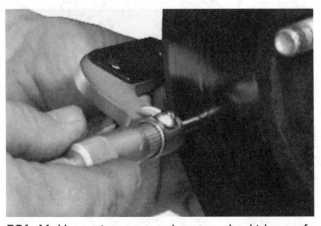

PS6–11 Use a micrometer and measure the thickness of the rotor. Machine or replace the rotor as necessary.

PS6–12 Remove the disc brake pads.

GM Disc Brake Service—continued

PS6–13 If necessary, open the bleeder valve and use a C-clamp to push the caliper piston all the way into the caliper.

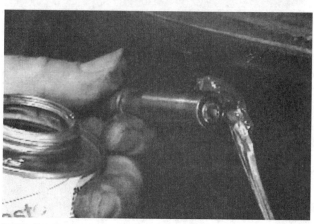

PS6–14 During reassembly, use silicone brake grease to lubricate any part(s) that contains both rubber and metal, such as this guide pin.

PS6–15 Thoroughly clean the caliper slides.

PS6–16 Apply disc brake dampening material on the back of the pads especially if they are not equipped with noise-dampening shims.

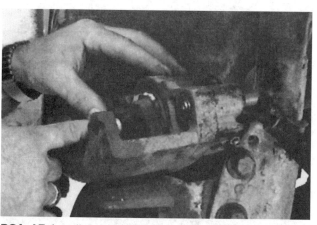

PS6–17 Install the pads. Be sure to use all the clips and noise reduction shims and install properly.

PS6–18 Install the caliper and torque the guide pins (or caliper retaining bolts) to specifications. Be sure to depress the brake pedal several times before test-driving the vehicle.

PHOTO SEQUENCE Honda Disc Brake Service

PS6–19 After properly setting the hoist pads under the vehicle, raise the vehicle to chest level and remove the lug nuts.

PS6–20 Remove the wheel/tire assembly and place it where it will not get in the way or be damaged.

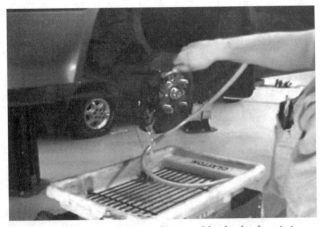

PS6–21 Before starting to disassemble the brakes, it is recommended that the entire brake assembly be washed using a commercially available cleaner to avoid the possibility of allowing brake dust to become airborne (may contain harmful asbestos).

PS6–22 If a commercial brake cleaning unit is not available, use brake cleaner from an aerosol or pressurized container.

PS6–23 To service the front disc brake pads on this Honda, loosen the upper caliper retainer bolt and remove the lower bolt.

PS6–24 After the lower caliper bolt has been removed, the caliper assembly can be lifted upward pivoting on the upper retaining bolt.

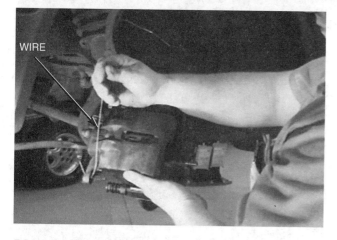

PS6–25 Use mechanic's wire to hold the caliper in the raised position to allow access to the disc brake pads.

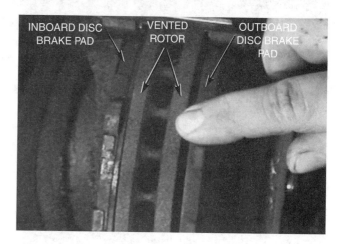

PS6–26 Notice that both the inboard and outboard pad remain attached to the steering knuckle. The pads and shims can be lifted off.

PS6–27 To install the thicker replacement disc brake pads, the caliper piston must be pushed back into the caliper. A C-clamp can be used to push the piston into the caliper, but be sure to open the bleeder valve first.

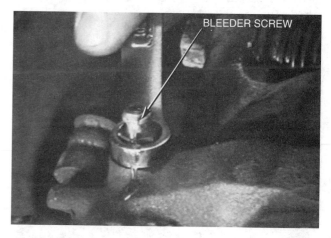

PS6–28 The bleeder valve should be opened to allow the old brake fluid to flow out of the caliper and not be forced up into the ABS hydraulic unit or master cylinder where it could cause harm to the seals or solenoid valves. Dispose of the old brake fluid properly. Resurface or replace the rotors as needed.

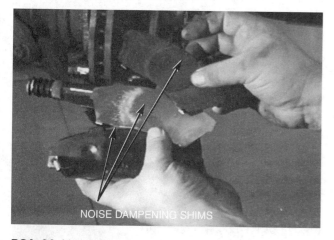

PS6–29 Honda factory replacement disc brake pads include noise-dampening shims, anti-rattle clips, and special moly disc brake grease that is to be used on the shims as specified in the instructions that come with the replacement brake pads.

PS6–30 All hardware including this anchor shim should be replaced.

Honda Disc Brake Service—continued

PS6–31 Install new shims after thoroughly cleaning the steering knuckle area of any rust using a wire brush or other suitable tool.

PS6–32 After coating the shims with the supplied moly grease, the replacement disc brake pads are installed next to the rotor and held in place by the tension of the anchor shims.

PS6–33 After double-checking that all shims, clips, and spacers are correctly installed, lower the calipers and install the lower attaching bolt.

PS6–34 Torque the retaining bolts to factory specifications. Repeat the process on the other side and bleed the hydraulic system.

PS6–35 Reinstall the wheel/tire assembly.

PS6–36 Torque the lug nuts to factory specifications or use a torque-limiting adjuster as shown with an air impact. Be sure to test-drive the vehicle before returning it to the customer.

■ SUMMARY

1. Disc brakes are used on the front and rear wheels on many vehicles. Disc brake calipers are either fixed or floating.

2. When a disc brake is applied, the square-cut O-ring is deformed. When the brakes are released, the rubber O-ring returns to its original shape and draws the caliper piston back into the caliper and away from the rotor.

3. As the disc brake pad wears, the caliper piston moves through the square-cut O-ring to compensate for the wear. Because the piston is now moved outward, brake fluid fills the space and the brake fluid level in the master cylinder drops.

4. Disc brake wear indicators can be a metal tang that touches the rotor and makes noise or can be a groove molded into the pad itself. Some wear indicators are electrical and light a dash indicator lamp when the brakes are worn.

5. Caliper pistons are either chrome-plated steel or plastic (phenolic). Any damaged piston must be replaced. Both the square-cut O-ring and the dust boot must be replaced when the caliper is disassembled.

6. All metal-to-metal contact points of the disc brake assembly should be coated with an approved brake lubricant such as synthetic grease, moly grease, or antiseize compound.

7. After a brake overhaul, the brake pedal should be depressed several times until a normal brake pedal is achieved before performing a thorough test drive.

8. Many rear disc brake systems use an integral parking brake. Regular use of the parking brake helps maintain proper rear brake clearance.

■ REVIEW QUESTIONS

1. Describe how a single caliper works.
2. List what parts are included in a typical overhaul kit for a single piston floating caliper.
3. List three types of disc brake pad wear sensors.
4. Describe how to remove caliper pistons and perform a caliper overhaul.
5. Explain what causes disc brake squeal and list what a technician can do to reduce or eliminate the noise.

■ ASE CERTIFICATION-TYPE QUESTIONS

1. Uneven disc brake pad wear is being discussed. Technician A says the caliper piston may be stuck. Technician B says the caliper may be stuck on the slides and unable to "float." Which technician is correct?

   a. Technician A only
   b. Technician B only
   c. Both Technician A and B
   d. Neither Technician A nor B

2. A "chirping" noise is heard while the vehicle is moving forward, but stops when the brakes are applied. Technician A says that the noise is likely caused by the disc brake pad wear sensors. Technician B says the noise is likely a wheel bearing because the noise stops when the brakes are applied. Which technician is correct?

   a. Technician A only
   b. Technician B only
   c. Both Technician A and B
   d. Neither Technician A nor B

3. What part causes the disc brake caliper piston to retract when the brakes are released?

   a. Return (retracting) spring
   b. The rotating rotor (disc) pushes the piston back
   c. The square-cut O-ring
   d. The caliper bushings

4. Two technicians are discussing the reason why the brake fluid level in the master cylinder drops. Technician A says that it may be normal due to the wear of the disc brake pads. Technician B says that a low brake fluid level may indicate a hydraulic leak somewhere in the system. Which technician is correct?

   a. Technician A only
   b. Technician B only
   c. Both Technician A and B
   d. Neither Technician A nor B

5. Technician A says that disc brake pads should be replaced when worn to the thickness of the steel backing. Technician B says the pads should be removed and inspected whenever there is a brake performance complaint. Which technician is correct?

   a. Technician A only
   b. Technician B only
   c. Both Technician A and B
   d. Neither Technician A nor B

6. A typical disc brake caliper overhaul (OH) kit usually includes what parts?

   a. Square-cut O-ring seal and dust boot
   b. Replacement caliper piston and dust boot
   c. Dust boot, return spring, and caliper seal
   d. Disc brake pad clips, dust boot, and caliper piston assembly

7. Technician A says that a lack of lubrication on the back of the disc brake pads can cause brake noise. Technician B says that pads that are not correctly crimped to the caliper housing can cause brake noise. Which technician is correct?

   a. Technician A only
   b. Technician B only
   c. Both Technician A and B
   d. Neither Technician A nor B

8. Two technicians are discussing ways of removing a caliper piston. Technician A says to use compressed air. Technician says to use large pliers. Which technician is correct?
    a. Technician A only
    b. Technician B only
    c. Both Technician A and B
    d. Neither Technician A nor B

9. Which is *not* a recommended type of grease to use on brake parts?
    a. Silicone grease
    b. Wheel bearing (chassis) grease
    c. Synthetic grease
    d. Antiseize compound

10. Technician A says that many rear disc brake caliper pistons must be turned to retract before installing replacement pads. Technician B says that some vehicles equipped with rear disc brakes use a small drum brake as the parking brake. Which technician is correct?
    a. Technician A only
    b. Technician B only
    c. Both Technician A and B
    d. Neither Technician A nor B

Parking Brake Operation, Diagnosis, and Service

Objectives: After studying Chapter 7, the reader should be able to:

1. Describe what is required of a parking brake.
2. Describe the parts and operation of the parking brake as used on a rear drum brake system.
3. Describe how a parking brake functions when the vehicle is equipped with rear disc brakes.
4. Explain how to adjust a parking brake properly.

Before 1967, most vehicles had only a single master cylinder operating all four brakes. If the fluid leaked at just one wheel, the operation of all brakes was lost. This required the use of a separate method to stop the vehicle in case of an emergency. This alternative method required that a separate mechanical method be used to stop the vehicle using two of the four wheel brakes. After 1967, federal regulations required the use of dual or tandem master cylinders where half of the braking system has its own separate hydraulic system. In case one-half of the system fails, a dash brake warning lamp lets the driver know that a failure has occurred. The term *parking brake* has replaced the term *emergency brake* since the change to dual master cylinder design.

■ PARKING BRAKE STANDARDS

According to Federal Motor Vehicle Safety Standard (FMVSS) 105, the parking brake must hold a fully loaded (laden) vehicle stationary on a slope of 30 percent for a manual-transmission-equipped vehicle, or a slope of 20 percent if equipped with an automatic transmission. The hand force required cannot exceed 80 lb. (18 N) or a foot force greater than 100 lb. (22 N). See Figure 7–1 for a typical parking brake system.

■ PARKING BRAKE LEVER

Parking brakes can be applied using either a hand lever or foot-operated pedal (see Figure 7–2). Some foot-operated parking brakes use a ratchet mechanism that requires that the driver push the pedal down several times to apply. This type of parking brake is commonly called *pump to set*. The lever or foot-pedal mechanism is designed to apply the required force on the parking brake using normal driver effort (see Figure 7–3 on page 175).

All parking brakes lock into a slot or notch that keeps the parking brake applied until it is released. Some vehicles are equipped with a mechanism connected to the shifter mechanism that releases the parking brake automatically when the transmission is moved from park to a drive gear (either forward or reverse). See the service manual for the exact service procedures.

Figure 7–1 Typical parking brake cable system showing the foot-operated parking brake lever and cable routing. (Courtesy of Chrysler Corporation)

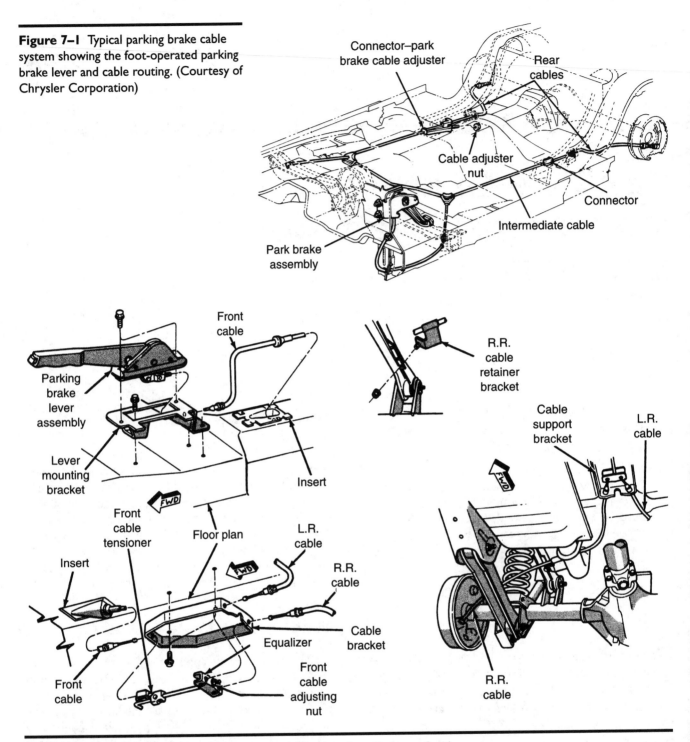

Figure 7–2 Typical hand-operated parking brake. Note that the adjustment for the cable is underneath the vehicle at the equalizer. (Courtesy of Chrysler Corporation)

■ PARKING BRAKE WARNING LAMP

Whenever the parking brake is engaged, a red BRAKE warning lamp lights on the dash. On most vehicles, this is the same lamp that lights when there is a hydraulic or brake fluid level problem. The warning lamp for the parking brake warns the driver that the parking brake is applied or partially applied. This warning helps pre-vent damage or overheating to the brake drums and linings that could occur if the vehicle was driven with the parking brake applied. If the red BRAKE warning lamp is on, check the parking brake to see if it is fully released. If the BRAKE lamp is still on, the parking brake switch may be defective, out of adjustment, or there may be a hydraulic problem. See Chapter 3 for further details on troubleshooting the BRAKE dash warning lamp.

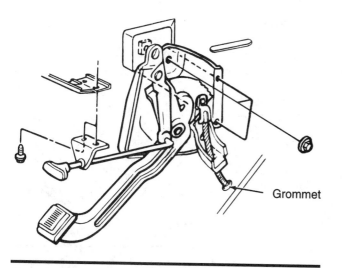

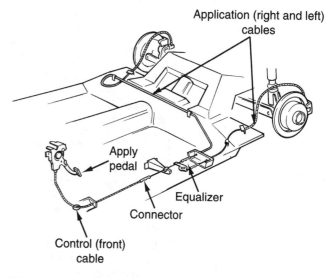

Figure 7–4 The parking brake control cable on this vehicle runs under the carpet next to the sill. Under the front seat, the cable exits through the floor of the vehicle to an equalizer and a cable to each rear wheel brake.

■ PARKING BRAKE CABLES

Parking brake cables run through protective housing. The cable attaches to the hand lever on foot-operated pedals and runs to a junction. This front section of parking brake cable is usually called the control cable (see Figure 7–4). The control cable then attaches to an equal-

Figure 7–5 The cable from the activating lever to the equalizer is commonly called the **control cable.** From the equalizer, the individual brake cables are often called **application cables.** These individual cables can usually be purchased separately.

izer to a second cable or pair of cables that runs to each rear brake. These individual wheel brake cables are often called application cables or left or right parking brake cables (see Figure 7–5). The parking brake equalizer is normally located under the vehicle. Most vehicles manufactured since the mid-1980s use wire strand cables covered with nylon for corrosion resistance. The housing or conduit contains plastic seals that help keep out dirt and water to prevent the cables from sticking and to reduce parking brake effort.

■ PARKING BRAKE ON DRUM BRAKES

Most parking brakes move steel woven cables attached to the rear brakes only and operate the lining through the parking brake lever, which is attached to the cable and the secondary lining. The parking brake force is transferred to the primary lining through a steel flat bar called a parking brake strut. Around the end of the slotted strut is a spring called an antirattle spring (or strut spring), which prevents the strut from rattling whenever the parking brake is not applied (see Figure 7–6).

■ FRONT AND REAR ENTRY PARKING BRAKE CABLES

The parking brake standard requires that the vehicle be held stationary on a 30 degree grade facing either uphill or downhill. Many drum parking brake systems attach the parking brake lever on the secondary (rearward) shoe and push the primary (forward facing) brake shoe

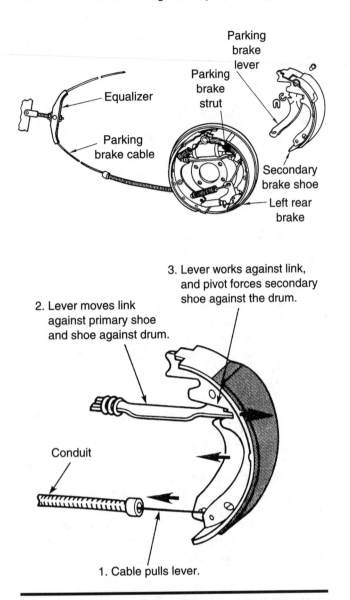

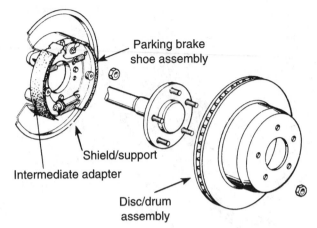

Figure 7-7 Many vehicles equipped with rear disc brakes have a small drum brake inside the rear rotor. When the brake shoes expand, they contact the inner surface of the rotor. (Courtesy of Allied Signal Automotive Aftermarket)

3. Lever works against link, and pivot forces secondary shoe against the drum.

2. Lever moves link against primary shoe and shoe against drum.

Conduit

1. Cable pulls lever.

Figure 7-6 Notice the spring at the end of the parking brake strut. This anti-rattle spring keeps tension on the strut. The parking brake lever is usually attached with a pin and spring (wavy) washer and retained by a horseshoe clip.

against the drum. The parking brake cable enters the backing plate from the front of the vehicle (front entry). Because the primary shoe is attached to the secondary shoe on dual-servo brakes, any forward motion of the vehicle tends to wedge the primary shoe into the brake drum *and* force the rear secondary lining also against the drum.

Applying only the forward brake shoe tends to hold the vehicle best when the vehicle is being held on a hill with the front pointing downward. To help provide the same holding power for a vehicle being held from backing up, some vehicles reverse the parking brake arrangement for the right side. Instead of having the parking brake cable enter the backing plate from the front, this style has the cable entering from the rear (rear entry). In this case the right rear brake has the parking brake lever installed on the *primary* shoe.

HINT: An easy way to remember how to reassemble a drum brake is to realize that the parking brake lever is usually attached to the secondary (rearward) brake shoe. The parking brake strut attaches between the shoes with the spring toward the front of the vehicle (remember, "spring forward").

■ AUXILIARY DRUM PARKING BRAKES

Equipping a vehicle with a parking brake that has rear disc brakes is expensive. One commonly used method is to use a small brake drum inside the "hat" section of the rear disc brake rotor. This method is used on many Chevrolet Corvettes and Toyota Supras. Although this method costs more and adds weight to the vehicle, the operation of the brake shoes by the parking brake cable is independent of the rear disc brakes (see Figure 7-7).

Because the parking brake is generally used only for holding a stopped vehicle, the parking brake shoes wear little, if at all.

NOTE: Some new vehicles equipped with this style of brake require that the service technician "burnish" or "bed-in" the parking brake lining by driving the vehicle a specified speed and stopping the vehicle using the parking brake alone. Repeating this procedure the specified number of times wears the parking brake lining to the drum for maximum contact. Until or unless this procedure is performed, the parking brake may not hold on a steep incline.

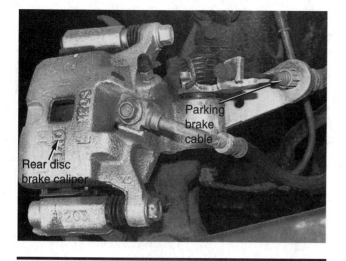

Figure 7–8 Typical rear disc brake with an integral (built-in) parking brake.

■ INTEGRAL DISC BRAKE PARKING BRAKE

Many vehicles equipped with rear disc brakes use a lead screw mechanism to apply the piston on the rear disc brakes. Most styles use conventional parking brake cables to activate a lever on the back of the caliper. The hydraulic part of the rear disc brake operates the same as a conventional disc brake. The parking brake lever rotates an actuator screw. As the screw rotates, the nut

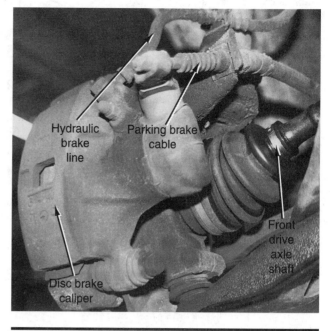

Figure 7–9 Subaru front disc brake caliper with parking brake.

of the screw does not rotate but instead, moves against the inside of the piston. As the piston moves, it presses on the inboard brake pad. When the inboard pad contacts the disc brake rotor, the reaction force slides the caliper assembly and applies the outboard pad (see Figures 7–8 through 7–20 on pages 177–179).

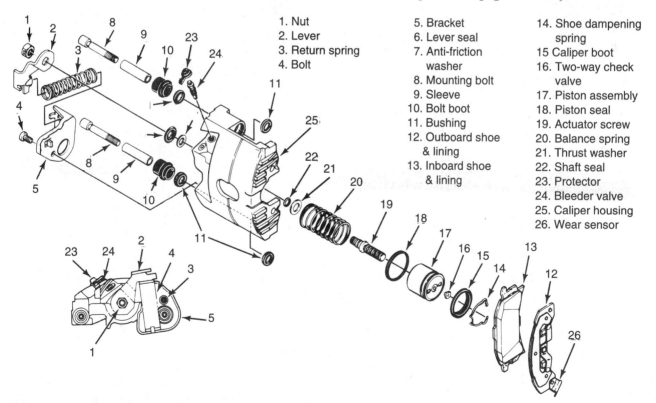

1. Nut
2. Lever
3. Return spring
4. Bolt
5. Bracket
6. Lever seal
7. Anti-friction washer
8. Mounting bolt
9. Sleeve
10. Bolt boot
11. Bushing
12. Outboard shoe & lining
13. Inboard shoe & lining
14. Shoe dampening spring
15. Caliper boot
16. Two-way check valve
17. Piston assembly
18. Piston seal
19. Actuator screw
20. Balance spring
21. Thrust washer
22. Shaft seal
23. Protector
24. Bleeder valve
25. Caliper housing
26. Wear sensor

Figure 7–10 Typical General Motors rear disc brake with an integral parking brake. (Courtesy of General Motors)

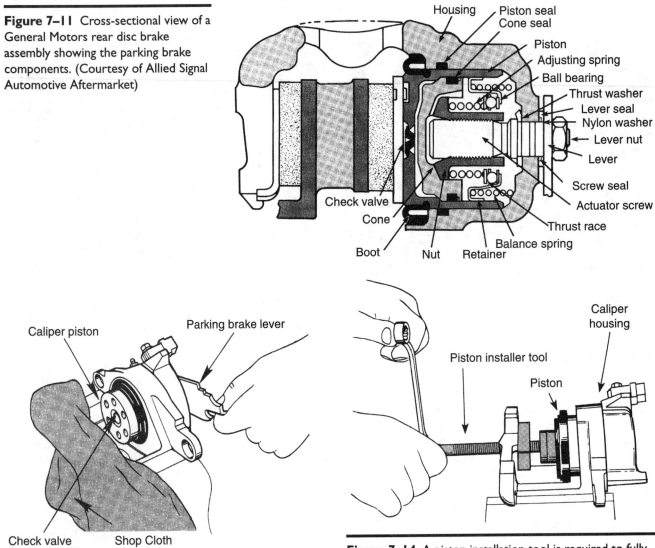

Figure 7–11 Cross-sectional view of a General Motors rear disc brake assembly showing the parking brake components. (Courtesy of Allied Signal Automotive Aftermarket)

Housing
Piston seal
Cone seal
Piston
Adjusting spring
Ball bearing
Thrust washer
Lever seal
Nylon washer
Lever nut
Lever
Screw seal
Actuator screw
Thrust race
Balance spring
Retainer
Nut
Boot
Cone
Check valve

Caliper piston
Parking brake lever
Check valve
Shop Cloth

Figure 7–12 Removing the piston from a typical General Motors rear disc brake caliper. (Courtesy of Allied Signal Automotive Aftermarket)

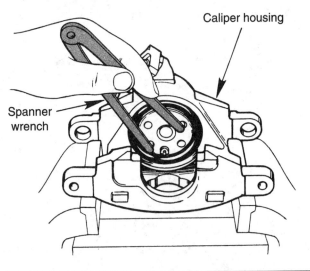

Caliper housing
Piston installer tool
Piston

Figure 7–14 A piston installation tool is required to fully install the piston into a General Motors rear disc brake caliper. (Courtesy of Allied Signal Automotive Aftermarket)

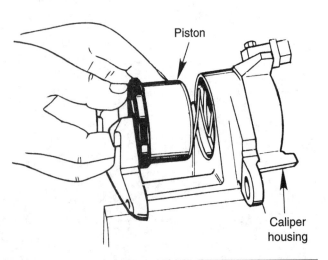

Piston
Caliper housing

Figure 7–13 Installing the piston into a General Motors rear disc brake caliper.

Caliper housing
Spanner wrench

Figure 7–15 A spanner wrench (or needle-nose pliers) can be used to rotate the caliper piston prior to installing the disc brake pads. A notch on the piston must line up with a tab on the back of the brake pad to keep the piston from rotating when the parking brake is applied. (Courtesy of Allied Signal Automotive Aftermarket)

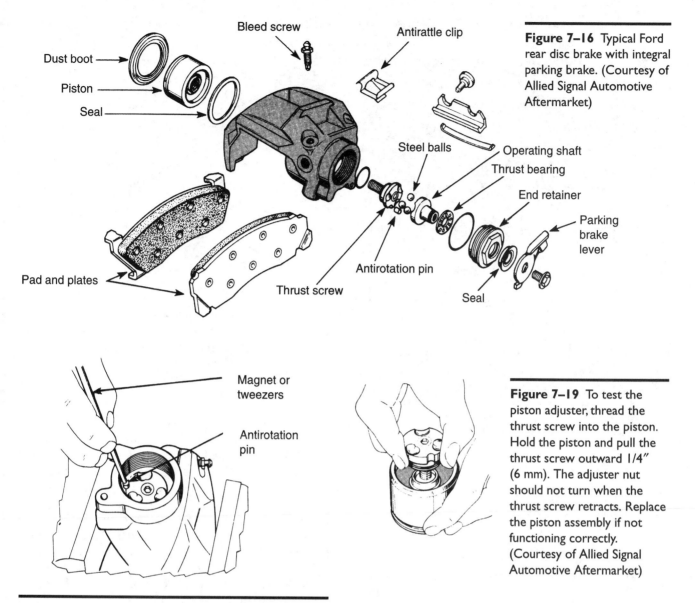

Dust boot

Piston

Seal

Bleed screw

Antirattle clip

Steel balls

Operating shaft

Thrust bearing

End retainer

Parking brake lever

Pad and plates

Thrust screw

Antirotation pin

Seal

Figure 7–16 Typical Ford rear disc brake with integral parking brake. (Courtesy of Allied Signal Automotive Aftermarket)

Magnet or tweezers

Antirotation pin

Figure 7–17 After removing the parking brake lever and thrust bearing, remove the anti-rotation pin. (Courtesy of Allied Signal Automotive Aftermarket)

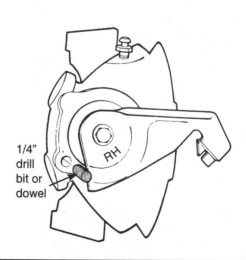

Figure 7–19 To test the piston adjuster, thread the thrust screw into the piston. Hold the piston and pull the thrust screw outward 1/4″ (6 mm). The adjuster nut should not turn when the thrust screw retracts. Replace the piston assembly if not functioning correctly. (Courtesy of Allied Signal Automotive Aftermarket)

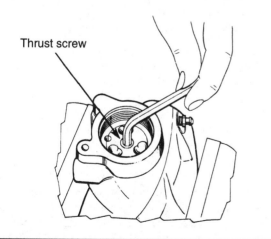

Thrust screw

Figure 7–18 Unscrew the thrust screw from the piston with an Allen (hex) wrench. After removing the thrust screw, push the piston out of the caliper bore. (Courtesy of Allied Signal Automotive Aftermarket)

1/4″ drill bit or dowel

RH

Figure 7–20 To adjust the parking brake cable on a Ford vehicle equipped with rear disc brakes, start by loosening the cable adjustment until the cables to the calipers are slack. Tighten until the caliper lever moves. Position a 1/4″ drill bit or dowel into the caliper alignment hole. Adjustment is correct if the parking brake lever does not hit the 1/4″ dowel.

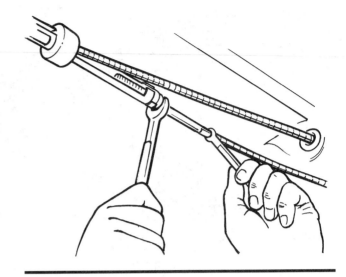

TECH TIP ✔

The Parking Brake "Click" Test

When diagnosing any brake problem, apply the parking brake and count the "clicks." This method works for both hand- and foot-operated parking brakes. Most vehicle manufacturers specify a maximum of ten clicks. If the parking brake travel exceeds this amount, the rear brakes may be worn or out of adjustment.

> **CAUTION:** Do not adjust the parking brake cable until the rear brakes have been thoroughly inspected and adjusted.

If the rear brake lining is usable, check for the proper operation of the self-adjustment mechanism. If the rear brakes are out of adjustment, the service brake pedal will also be low. This ten-click test is a fast and easy way to determine if the problem is due to rear brakes.

Figure 7–21 After checking that the rear brakes are okay and properly adjusted, the parking brake cable can be adjusted. Always follow the manufacturer's recommended procedure.

■ PARKING BRAKE CABLE ADJUSTMENT

Most manufacturers specify a minimum of three or four and a maximum of eight to ten clicks when applying the parking brake. Consult the service manual for the vehicle being serviced on the exact specification and adjustment procedures. Most vehicle manufacturers specify that the rear brakes be inspected and adjusted correctly before attempting to adjust the parking brake cable. Always follow the manufacturer's recommended procedure exactly.

Below is a general procedure for parking brake adjustment.

1. Make certain that the rear service brakes are adjusted correctly and the lining is serviceable.
2. With the drums installed, apply the parking brake three or four clicks. There should be a slight drag on both rear wheels.
3. Adjust the cable at the equalizer (equalizes one cable's force to both rear brakes) if necessary until there is a slight drag on both rear brakes (see Figures 7–21 through 7–23).
4. Release the parking brake. Both rear brakes should be free and not dragging. Repair or replace rusted cables or readjust as necessary to ensure that the brakes are not dragging.

> **NOTE:** The rear parking brake adjustment should always be checked whenever replacing the rear brake linings. It may be necessary to loosen the parking brake cable adjustment to allow clearance to get the drum over the new linings. This could happen because someone may have adjusted the parking brake cable during the life of the rear linings (see Figure 7–24). With new thicker linings, the parking brake adjustment can keep the brake shoes pushed outward toward the drum.

To prevent possible parking brake cable adjustment problems when installing new rear brakes, always observe the following:

1. Both brake shoes should make contact with the anchor pin at the top. If not, check the parking brake cable for improper adjustment or improper installation of the brake shoes.
2. Feel the tension of the parking brake cable underneath the vehicle. It should be slightly loose (with the parking brake "off").
3. Lubricate the parking brake cable to ensure that water or ice will not cause rust or freezing of the cable. This is necessary because even though the parking brake lever is released inside the vehicle, a stuck parking brake cable could cause the linings to remain out against the drums.

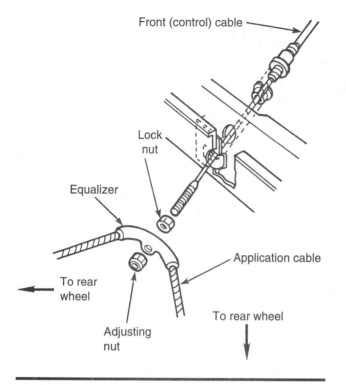

Front (control) cable

Lock nut

Equalizer

To rear wheel

Adjusting nut

Application cable

To rear wheel

Figure 7–22 Most parking brake cables are adjusted at the equalizer where the front (control) cable attaches to the individual (application) cable(s).

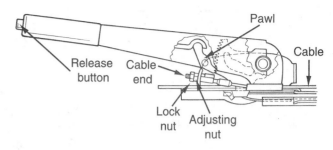
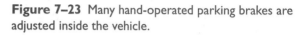

Pawl

Cable

Release button

Cable end

Lock nut

Adjusting nut

Figure 7–23 Many hand-operated parking brakes are adjusted inside the vehicle.

TECH TIP ✔

The Hose Clamp or Wrench Trick

It is often difficult to remove a parking brake cable from the backing plate due to the design of the retainer. The many fingers used to hold the cable to the backing plate can be squeezed all at once if a hose clamp is used to compress the fingers. A wrench as shown in Figure 7–27 can also be used.

NOTE: Some vehicles are equipped with an automatic adjusting parking brake lever/cable. Simply cycling the parking brake on/off/on three times is often all that is required to adjust the parking brake cable.

4. If the parking brake needs to be adjusted (will not hold on a hill or requires excessive lever movement), always check and adjust the rear brake adjustment before adjusting the parking brake cable (see Figure 7–25).

5. Replace any stuck, corroded, or broken parking brake cable (see Figures 7–26 and 7–27).

Figure 7–24 Always check that the brake shoes contact the anchor pin.

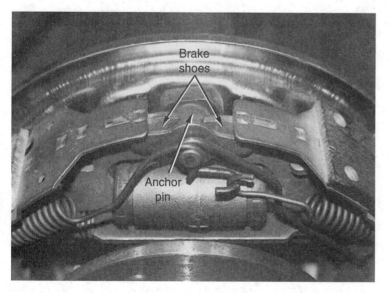

Brake shoes

Anchor pin

Figure 7–25 An 1/8″ (3 mm) drill bit is placed through an access hole in the backing plate to adjust this General Motors leading–trailing rear parking brake. Adjust the parking brake cable until the drill can just fit between the shoe web and the parking brake lever.

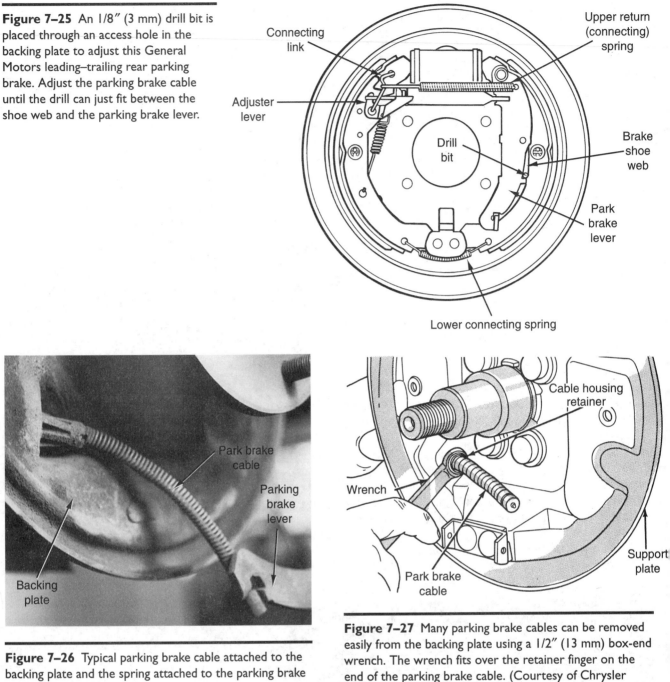

Figure 7–26 Typical parking brake cable attached to the backing plate and the spring attached to the parking brake lever.

Figure 7–27 Many parking brake cables can be removed easily from the backing plate using a 1/2″ (13 mm) box-end wrench. The wrench fits over the retainer finger on the end of the parking brake cable. (Courtesy of Chrysler Corporation)

■ SUMMARY

1. Government regulation requires that the parking brake be able to hold a fully loaded vehicle on a 30 percent grade.

2. The typical parking brake uses either a hand-operated lever or a foot-operated pedal to activate the parking brake.

3. On a typical drum brake system, the parking brake cable moves a parking brake lever attached to the secondary brake shoe. The primary shoe is applied through force being transferred through the strut.

4. All parking brake cables should move freely. The rear brakes should be adjusted properly before the parking brake is adjusted.

■ REVIEW QUESTIONS

1. Describe how a typical parking brake functions on a vehicle equipped with rear drum brakes.

2. Describe how a typical parking brake functions on a vehicle equipped with an integral rear disc brake system.

3. Explain how to adjust a parking brake properly.

■ ASE CERTIFICATION-TYPE QUESTIONS

1. Technician A says that the parking brake cable should be adjusted at each wheel. Technician B says that the parking brake cable adjustment is usually done after adjusting the rear brakes. Which technician is correct?
   a. Technician A only
   b. Technician B only
   c. Both Technician A and B
   d. Neither Technician A nor B

2. Technician A says that the parking brake hand lever can turn on the red brake warning lamp. Technician B says that a foot-operated parking brake can turn on the red brake warning lamp. Which technician is correct?
   a. Technician A only
   b. Technician B only
   c. Both Technician A and B
   d. Neither Technician A nor B

3. Technician A says that if the parking brake cable is adjusted too tight, the rear brakes may drag and overheat. Technician B says that the parking brake is adjusted properly if the cable is tight when in the released position. Which technician is correct?
   a. Technician A only
   b. Technician B only
   c. Both Technician A and B
   d. Neither Technician A nor B

4. On most drum brake systems, the parking brake lever and the strut transfer the pulling force of the parking brake cable against the
   a. Primary shoe
   b. Secondary shoe

5. On most vehicles, the anti-rattle spring (strut spring) should be installed on the parking brake strut toward the _____ of the vehicle.
   a. Front
   b. Rear

6. In a typical integral rear disc brake caliper, the parking brake cable moves the
   a. Caliper
   b. Actuator screw
   c. Auxiliary piston
   d. Rotor

7. The rear brakes should be inspected and adjusted if necessary if the parking brake requires more than
   a. 5 clicks
   b. 10 clicks
   c. 15 clicks
   d. 20 clicks

8. A rear drum brake is being inspected. The primary shoe is not contacting the anchor pin at the top. Technician A says that this is normal. Technician B says that the parking brake cable may be adjusted too tight or is stuck. Which technician is correct?
   a. Technician A only
   b. Technician B only
   c. Both Technician A and B
   d. Neither Technician A nor B

9. Technician A says that a hose clamp can be used to compress the retainer fingers of a parking brake cable in order to remove it from the backing plate. Technician B says a box-end wrench can be used instead of a hose clamp. Which technician is correct?
   a. Technician A only
   b. Technician B only
   c. Both Technician A and B
   d. Neither Technician A nor B

10. The wrong replacement rear disc brake pads were installed on a vehicle that used an integral parking brake. The inboard pad did not have a pin that fits into a notch on the caliper piston. Technician A says that the brakes will likely overadjust. Technician B says that the parking brake will not work. Which technician is correct?
    a. Technician A only
    b. Technician B only
    c. Both Technician A and B
    d. Neither Technician A nor B

Machining Brake Drums and Rotors

Objectives: After studying Chapter 8, the reader should be able to:

1. Discuss the construction of brake drums and rotors.
2. Explain the formation of hard spots in drums and rotors.
3. Describe how to measure and inspect drums and rotors before machining.
4. Discuss how surface finish is measured and its importance to satisfactory brake service.
5. Demonstrate how to machine a brake drum and rotor correctly.

Brake drums and rotors are the major energy-absorbing parts of the braking system. Friction between the friction material and the drum or rotor creates heat. This heat is absorbed by the drum or rotor and travels from the friction surface to the remainder of the drum or rotor by heat **convection.** As energy continues to be absorbed, the drum or rotor increases in temperature. Airflow across the drum or rotor helps to dissipate the heat and keep the temperature rise under control. See Figure 8–1 through 8–4 for examples of how drums and rotors are cooled.

■ BRAKE DRUMS

Brake drums are constructed of cast iron where the lining contacts the drum with mild steel centers. The drum is drilled for the lug studs. Cast iron contains approxi-

mately 3 percent carbon, which makes the drum hard, yet brittle. For this reason it is recommended that any pounding needed to remove drums be done on the center mild steel portion, which due to its material characteristics can take this force without damage. This 3 percent carbon content of the cast iron also acts as a lubricant which prevents noise during braking. Also, the rubbing surface can be machined without the need of a coolant (as would be required if constructed of mild steel). Because of these properties, cast iron is used on the friction surface of all drums (see Figure 8–5).

Figure 8–1 An aluminum brake drum with a cast iron friction surface. The cooling fins around the outside help dissipate the heat from the friction surface to the outside air. Note the "MAX DIA 243.5 mm" cast into the drum.

Figure 8–2 The airflow through cooling vents helps brakes from overheating. (Courtesy of General Motors)

Air scoops for front brakes

Figure 8–4 Most race cars are equipped with scoops to direct air past the brakes to dissipate the heat quickly. The cooler the brakes; the more efficient and effective they are.

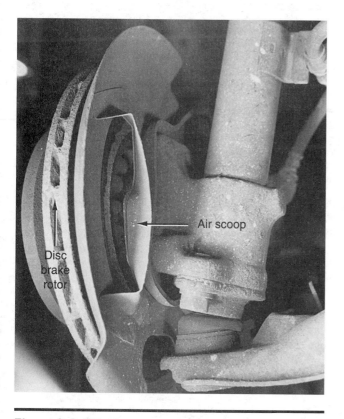

Air scoop

Disc brake rotor

Figure 8–3 This air scoop is part of the water/dirt shield attached next to the rotor.

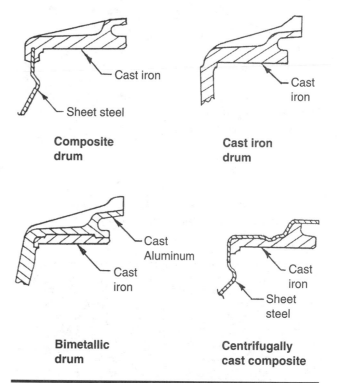

Cast iron

Sheet steel

Composite drum

Cast iron

Cast iron drum

Cast Aluminum

Cast iron

Bimetallic drum

Cast iron

Sheet steel

Centrifugally cast composite

Figure 8–5 Types of brake drums. Regardless of the design, all types use cast iron as a friction surface.

Even aluminum brake drums use cast iron for the friction surface area. Besides saving weight, aluminum brake drums transfer heat to the surrounding air faster than cast iron or steel. Metal clips called **tinnerman nuts** are installed at the factory to keep the brake drums from falling off during vehicle assembly. These clips can be removed and do not need to be reinstalled since the wheel lug nuts hold onto the brake drum. See Chapter 5 for additional information on brake drum removal.

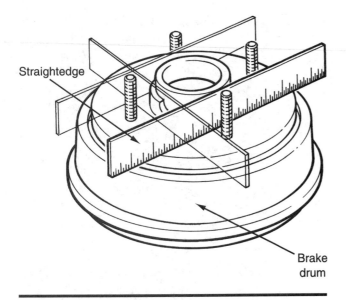

Figure 8–6 A straightedge can be used to check for brake drum warpage.

The first inspection step after removing a brake drum is to check it for warpage using a straightedge as shown in Figure 8–6.

A warped drum is often a source of vibration. A brake drum that is out-of-round can cause a brake pedal pulsation during braking.

> **HINT:** To help diagnose if the front brakes or rear brakes are the cause of the vibration, try slowing the vehicle using the parking brake. If vibration occurs, the problem is due to the rear brakes.

■ HARD SPOTS

Hard spots are created by heat. Vehicles that are stopped from high speed, or long braking down a hill or mountain, can generate excessive temperatures. The

TECH TIP ✔

Mark It to Be Sure

Most experts recommend that brake rotors, as well as drums and wheels, be marked before removing them for service. Many disc brake rotors are directional and will function correctly only if replaced in the original location. A quick-and-easy method is to use correction fluid. This alcohol-based liquid comes in small bottles with a small brush inside, making it easy to mark rotors with an "L" for left and an "R" for right. Correction fluid (also called "white-out" and "liquid paper") can also be used to make marks on wheel studs, wheels, and brake drums to help ensure reinstallation in the same location.

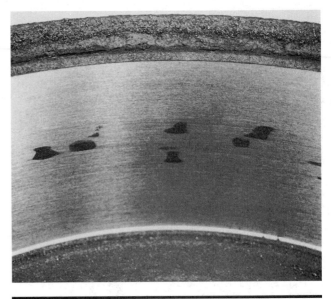

Figure 8–7 These dark hard spots are created by heat that actually changes the metallurgy of the cast iron drum. Most experts recommend replacement of any brake drum that has these hard spots.

metal on the surface, being at a much higher temperature, tends to expand and raise a small bump. This bump is then a source of high pressure between the brake lining and the drum or rotor. The greater the pressure, the greater the heat in this small area. Hard spots usually occur in brake drums, but can also occur on disc brake rotors. Hard spots usually appear in the center of the friction surface of the drum or rotor farthest from the edge. This is the area of greatest temperature because the heat generated in this part has the farthest distance to travel to the cooling air (see Figure 8–7). As the spot cools, the crystallized structure of the cast iron changes to a hard steel so that the metallurgy is actually different in the hard spot than in the surrounding areas. Regular brake lathe cutting tools have about the same hardness as these hard spots.

Some experts recommend using a grinding stone to remove hard spots. However, most experts and vehicle manufacturers agree that these hard spots have "memory" and will tend to return as soon as the brakes are subjected to severe service again and recommend that drums or rotors with hard spots be replaced.

■ "MACHINE TO" VERSUS "DISCARD"

Brake drums can usually be machined a maximum of 0.060″ (1.5 mm) oversize (for example, a 9.500″ drum new could wear or be machined to a maximum inside diameter of 9.560″) unless otherwise stamped on the drum. Most brake experts recommend that both drums on the same axle be within 0.010″ (0.25 mm) of each

TECH TIP ✔

Brake Drum Chamfer

Look at the chamfer on the outer edge of most brake drums. When the chamfer is no longer visible, the brake drum is usually at or past its maximum I.D. (see Figure 8–8). Although this chamfer is not an accurate gauge of the inside diameter of the brake drum, it still is a helpful indicator to the technician.

Figure 8–8 Most brake drums have a chamfer around the edge. If the chamfer is no longer visible, the drum is usually worn (or machined) to its maximum allowable inside diameter.

other. *The maximum specified inside diameter (I.D.) means the maximum wear inside diameter.* Always leave at least 0.015″ (0.4 mm) after machining (resurfacing) for wear. Many manufacturers recommend that 0.030″ (0.8 mm) be left for wear. See Appendix 8 for a chart of the drum and rotor machining specifications or factory technical information for the vehicle being serviced.

■ REASONS FOR EQUAL DRUM INSIDE DIAMETER

There are several reasons why the service technician should check and make sure that both brake drums on the same axle are close to the same inside diameter.

Reason 1. Since heat is generated by braking, if there is less material (larger I.D.), the drum will tend to expand more rapidly than a drum with more material (smaller I.D.).

Reason 2. If one drum expands more than the drum on the other side of the vehicle, unequal braking forces result.

Reason 3. The drum that is larger in I.D. will expand away from the brake linings more than the other side.

For example:

Left Drum	Right Drum
9.500″	9.560″

In this example, when the drums get hot (heavy braking), the vehicle will tend to pull to the left.

■ MEASURING AND INSPECTING BRAKE DRUMS

Brake drums are usually measured using a micrometer especially designed for brake drums (see Figure 8–9). The drum should be checked for roundness, bell mouth, taper, and deep scoring (see Figure 8–10).

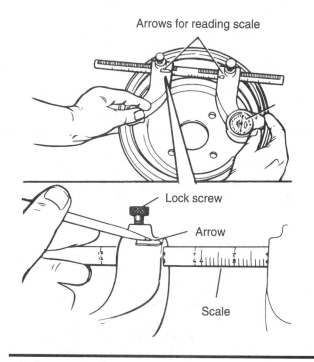

Figure 8–9 Typical needle dial brake drum micrometer. The left movable arm is set to the approximate drum diameter and the right arm to the more exact drum diameter. The dial indicator (gauge) reads in thousandths of an inch. (Courtesy of Ammco Tools, Inc.)

HINT: Hold a brake drum in the center with one hand and tap the outside of the drum with a light steel hammer. The drum should ring like a bell. If the drum sounds like a dull thud, the drum is probably cracked and needs to be replaced.

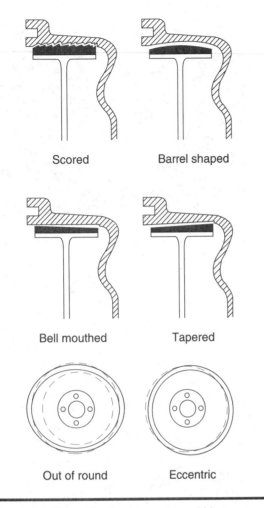

Scored   Barrel shaped

Bell mouthed   Tapered

Out of round   Eccentric

Figure 8–10 Typical brake drum wear problems.

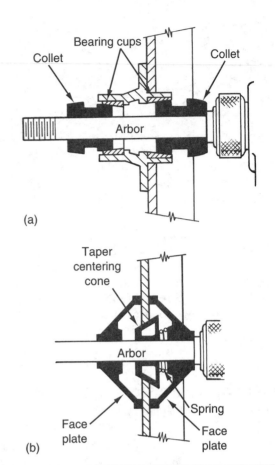

(a)

(b)

Figure 8–11 (a) A rotor or brake drum with a bearing hub should be installed on a brake lathe using the appropriate size collet that fit the bearing cups (races). (b) A hubless rotor or brake drum requires a spring and a tapered centering cone. A faceplate should be used on both sides of the rotor or drum to provide support.

■ MACHINING DRUMS

Always start any machining operation by making certain that the brake drum is clean and that excess grease is removed from the hub. If the drum has a hub with bearings, check the outer bearing races (cups) for wear and replace as necessary before placing the drum on the brake lathe. Also, carefully inspect and clean the lathe spindle shaft and cones before use. Use a **self-aligning spacer** (SAS) to be assured of even force being applied to the drum by the spindle nut. Always follow the instructions for the lathe you are using.

Hubless drums use a hole in the center of the brake drum for centering. Always check that the center hole is clean and free of burrs or nicks. Typical drum brake machining steps include:

Step 1 Mount the drum on the lathe and install the silencer band as shown in Figures 8–11 and 8–12.

Step 2 Turn the drum by hand before turning on the lathe to be sure everything is clean. Advance the tool bit manually until it just contacts the drum. This is called a **scratch cut** (see Figure 8–13).

Step 3 Stop the lathe and back off the tool bit. Loosen the arbor nut and rotate the drum one-half turn (180°) on the arbor and retighten the arbor nut (see Figure 8–14). Turn the lathe on and make a second scratch cut.
   a. If the scratch cuts are side by side, the lathe is okay and machining can begin.
   b. If the scratch cuts are opposite, remove the drum and check for nicks, burrs, or chips on the mounting surfaces.

Step 4 Start the lathe and set the depth of the cut (see Figures 8–15 and 8–16 on pages 189–190). The maximum rough cut depends on the lathe type. The minimum cut is usually specified as no less than 0.002″ (0.05 mm). A shallower cut usually causes the tool bit to slide over the surface of the metal rather than cut into the metal.

See Figure 8–17 on page 190 for an example of a drum machined without properly positioning the antichatter (vibration) strap.

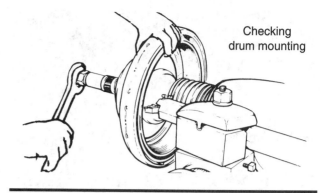

Checking
drum mounting

Figure 8–14 After making a scratch cut, loosen the retaining nut and rotate the drum on the lathe and make another scratch cut. If both cuts are in the same location, the drum is installed correctly on the lathe and drum machining can begin. (Courtesy of Ammco Tools, Inc.)

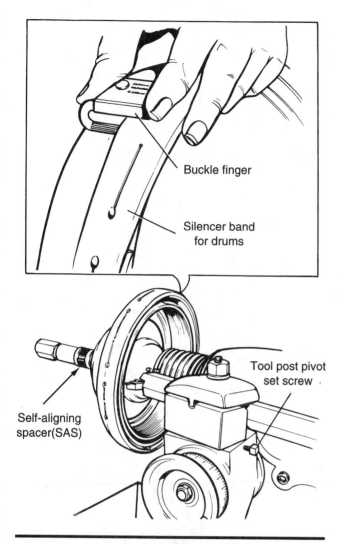

Buckle finger

Silencer band
for drums

Self-aligning
spacer(SAS)

Tool post pivot
set screw

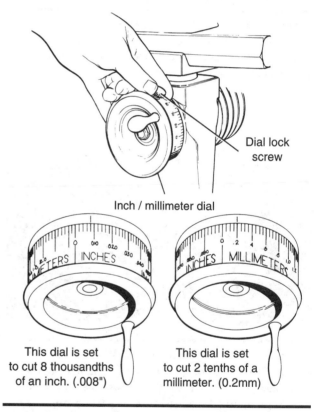

Dial lock
screw

Inch / millimeter dial

This dial is set
to cut 8 thousandths
of an inch. (.008")

This dial is set
to cut 2 tenths of a
millimeter. (0.2mm)

Figure 8–15 Set the depth of the cut indicator to zero just as the turning tool touches the drum. (Courtesy of Ammco Tools, Inc.)

Figure 8–12 A self-aligning spacer (SAS) should always be used between the drum or rotor and the spindle retaining nut to help ensure an even clamping force and to prevent the adapters and cone from getting into a bind. A silencer band should always be installed to prevent turning-tool chatter and to ensure a smooth surface finish. (Courtesy of Ammco Tools, Inc.)

■ POSITIVE RAKE VERSUS NEGATIVE RAKE BRAKE LATHES

Many lathes are capable of removing a large amount of material in one pass, thereby reducing the time necessary to refinish a drum or rotor. These lathes normally use a positive rake tool bit angle (see Figure 8–18). Other lathes that use six-sided reversible tool bits normally use a negative rake tool bit angle. Ammco is an example of a negative rake lathe; Perfect-Hofmann and Accu-turn are examples of positive rake lathes.

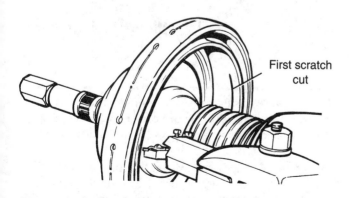

First scratch
cut

Figure 8–13 After installing a brake drum on the lathe, turn the cutting tool outward until the tool just touches the drum. This is called a **scratch cut.** (Courtesy of Ammco Tools, Inc.)

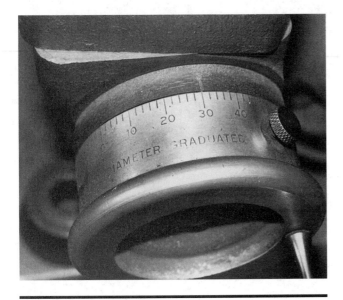

Figure 8–16 This lathe has a dial that is "diameter graduated." This means that a reading of 0.030″ indicates a 0.015″ cut that increases the inside diameter of the brake drum by 0.030″.

Figure 8–17 Notice the chatter marks at the edge of the friction-area surface of the brake drum. These marks were caused by vibration of the drum because the technician failed to wrap the dampening strap (silencer band) over the friction-surface portion of the brake drum.

■ CAST IRON DISC BRAKE ROTORS

Disc brake rotors use cast gray iron at the area that contacts the friction pad. Rotors, also called **discs** or **disks,** have mass (weight) that absorbs heat. The heavier the rotor, the more heat can be absorbed. Since the late 1970s, vehicle downsizing has resulted in the use of thinner and lighter-weight rotors. As the weight of the rotor decreases, the less heat the rotor can "store" or absorb, resulting in the rotor getting hotter. As the rotor gets hotter, the rotor expands and "grows" larger where it is the hottest. If the rotor is allowed to cool gradually, the rotor simply returns

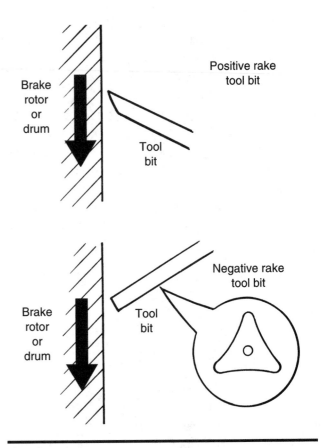

Figure 8–18 Most positive rake brake lathes can cut any depth in one pass, thereby saving time. A typical negative rake lathe uses a three-sided turning tool that can be flipped over, thereby giving six cutting edges.

Figure 8–19 This excessively worn (thin) rotor was removed from the vehicle in this condition. It is amazing that the vehicle was able to stop with such a thin rotor.

to its original shape. If, however, the rotor is exposed to water, it may cool rapidly, causing the rotor to distort.

Rotors are made in several styles, including:

1. **Solid.** Used on the rear of many vehicles equipped with rear disc brakes and on the front of some small and midsize vehicles. Solid rotors are usually

Figure 8–20 Severely worn vented disc brake rotor. The owner brought the vehicle to a repair shop because of a "little noise in the front." Notice the straight vane design.

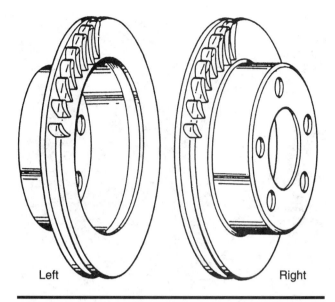

Figure 8–22 Directional vane vented disc brake rotors. Note that the fins angle toward the rear of the vehicle. It is important that this type of rotor be reinstalled on the correct side of the vehicle. (Courtesy of Allied Signal Automotive Aftermarket)

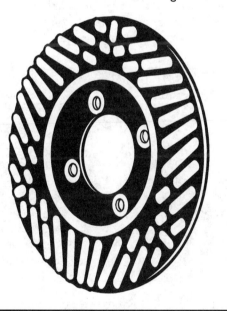

Figure 8–21 Some vented disc brake rotors use asymmetrical vents to direct the air between the friction surfaces.

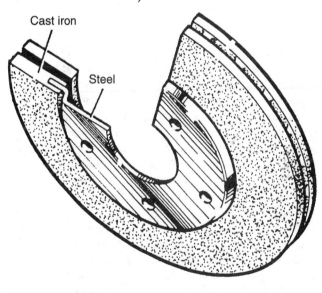

Figure 8–23 Typical composite rotor that uses cast iron friction surfaces and a steel center section.

used on the rear where only 20 to 40 percent of the braking occurs. Solid rotors are much thinner than vented rotors. See Figure 8–19 for an example of an excessively worn solid rotor.

2. **Vented.** Used on the front of most vehicles. The internal vanes allow air to circulate between the two friction surfaces of the rotor. Rotors can either be straight vane design, as shown in Figures 8–20 and 8–21, or directional vane design, as shown in Figure 8–22.

   Composite rotors use a steel center section with a cast iron wear surface. These composite rotors are lighter in weight than conventional cast iron rotors (see Figure 8–23). The light weight of composite rotors makes them

popular with vehicle manufacturers. However, technicians should be aware that full-contact adapters that simulate the actual wheel being bolted to the rotor must be used when machining composite rotors. If composite rotors are machined incorrectly, they must usually be replaced.

■ ALUMINUM METAL MATRIX COMPOSITE ROTORS

Some disc brake rotors are manufactured from an aluminum metal matrix composite alloy reinforced with 20 percent silicon carbide particulate. Aluminum

Figure 8–24 An aluminum metal matrix composite rear rotor for a Chrysler Plymouth Prowler. (Courtesy of Duralcan, USA)

composites combine the light weight and thermal conductivity of aluminum with the stiffness and wear resistance of a ceramic to create a disc brake rotor with excellent heat dissipation and service life.

These rotors can be distinguished from conventional cast iron rotors in several ways. At first glance the rotors are silver gray with a dark gray or black transfer layer (from the brake pad) on the rubbing surface. Unlike cast iron, these rotors will show no signs of rust and are nonmagnetic. When removed from the vehicle, the aluminum composite rotors can be further distinguished by their light weight [usually under 6 lb. (2.7 kg) versus over 12 lb. (5.4 kg) for cast iron rotors on the typical passenger vehicle] (see Figure 8–24).

Servicing these rotors is slightly different from cast iron rotors. The dark transfer layer on the rubbing surface does not harm rotor performance and should not be removed unless the rotor needs to be machined for dimensional reasons (warped, etc.). *Aluminum composite disc brake rotors cannot be machined with steel cutting tools!* Carbide tools can be used to machine a single set of aluminum composite rotors. If a shop receives these rotors on a regular basis, a polycrystalline diamond (PCD) tipped tool is a good investment. Although more expensive initially, the PCD tool can last 100 times longer than a carbide tool.

■ LATERAL RUNOUT

A disc brake rotor should have a maximum of 0.002″ to 0.005″ (0.05 to 0.13 mm), depending on the manufacturer's specifications for total lateral runout.

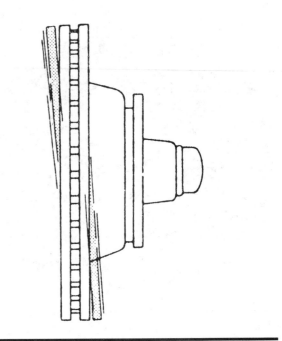

Figure 8–25 Excessive lateral runout can cause uneven wear. To help prevent excessive runout, always use a torque wrench or torque-absorbing adapters with an impact wrench when tightening lug nuts.

TECH TIP ✔

Think of a Human Hair

Measurements and specifications do not seem to mean much unless you can visualize the size compared to something with which you are familiar. The diameter of a human hair is from 0.002″ to 0.004″ (2 to 4 thousandths of an inch).

The maximum lateral runout of a rotor is usually within this same dimension. Students ask why we have to use a dial indicator to measure runout, and the answer is that you cannot see runout that is as small as a human hair.

See Figure 8–25. Excessive rotor runout is also called **wobble** and causes disc brake rotor wear that can cause uneven thickness variations. The procedure to check lateral runout follows:

1. If the rotor is installed on a wheel where bearings are adjustable, temporarily tighten the wheel bearings to remove all end play as shown in Figure 8–26. With a hubless rotor, install and torque the lug nuts to retain the rotor as shown in Figure 8–27.
2. Attach a dial indicator to the end of the spindle and observe the reading through one complete revolution as shown in Figure 8–28.
3. Total dial indicator movement should not exceed the specifications. If greater than specifications, machine the rotor.
4. Readjust the front wheel bearing for proper end play.

Dial indicator
(gauge)

Disc brake caliper

Torque
wrench

Disc brake
rotor

Figure 8–26 Before measuring lateral runout with a dial indicator (gauge), remove any wheel bearing end play by torquing the spindle nut to 10 to 20 lb. ft. with a torque wrench. This step helps prevent an inaccurate reading. If the vehicle is to be returned to service, be sure to loosen the spindle nut and retighten to specifications (usually, finger tight) to restore proper bearing clearance.

Figure 8–27 When checking a hubless rotor for runout, install and torque lug nuts to specifications.

Dial indicator
(gauge)

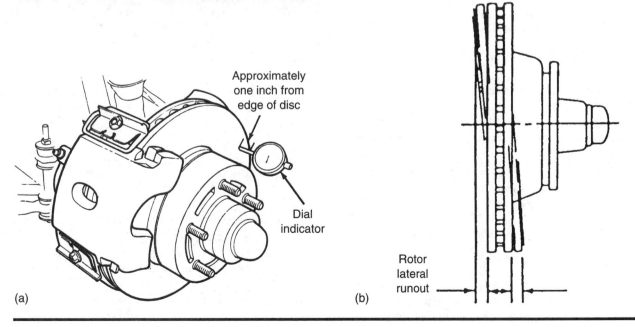

Approximately
one inch from
edge of disc

Dial
indicator

Rotor
lateral
runout

(a)

(b)

Figure 8–28 (a) Rotate the disc brake rotor one complete revolution while observing the dial indicator (gauge). (Courtesy of Chrysler Corporation) (b) Most vehicle manufacturers specify a maximum runout of about 0.003″ (0.08 mm).

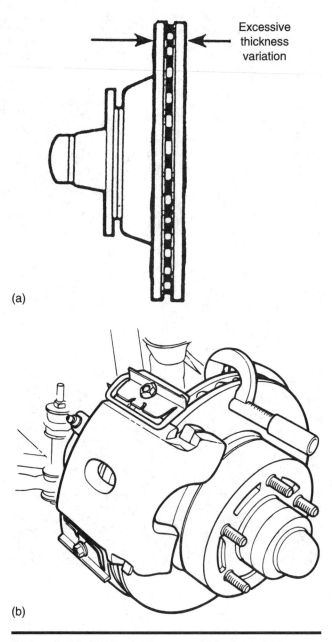

Braking Vibration Could Be Due to the Tires

A vibrating condition (roughness) during braking is usually caused by disc brake rotor thickness variation or an out-of-round brake drum. Both conditions should be investigated. However, the tires and/or road conditions can also cause the same vibrations.

Tests performed by vehicle and tire manufacturing engineers have shown that tires, and tires alone, could be the cause. If no other problem can be isolated, install a different brand of tire on the vehicle and retest. The cause of the tire vibration seems to be due to distortion or movement of the tire tread. A different brand of tires would have a different tread rubber compound, carcass body ply angles, etc.

(a)

(b)

Figure 8–29 (a) Disc brake rotor thickness variation (parallelism). (b) The rotor should be measured with a micrometer at four or more equally spaced locations around the rotor. (Courtesy of Chrysler Corporation)

■ ROTOR THICKNESS (PARALLELISM)

Excessive rotor runout does lead to rotor thickness variations as the rotor wears. Measure rotor thickness, using a micrometer, at four or more equally spaced locations of the rotor (see Figure 8–29).

Each measurement must not vary more than 0.0005″ [1/2 of 1 thousandth of an inch (0.013 mm)] It is the excessive rotor thickness variation that causes brake shudder or steering wheel shimmy (see Figure 8–28).

NOTE: Some manufacturers specify that eight or more measurements be made to check for parallelism (see Figure 8–30).

■ MINIMUM THICKNESS

Most rotors have a minimum thickness cast or stamped into the rotor. This thickness is minimum wear thickness. At least 0.015″ (0.4 mm) must remain after machining to allow for wear. [Some vehicle manufacturers, such as General Motors, specify that 0.030″ (0.8 mm) be left for wear.] See Figure 8–31. Whenever machining (resurfacing) a rotor, an equal amount of material must be removed from each side.

■ WHEN THE ROTORS SHOULD BE MACHINED

According to brake design engineers, a worn rotor has a very smooth friction surface that is ideal for replacement (new) disc brake pads. Often when the rotors are machined, the surface finish is not as smooth as specified. Therefore, a rotor should be machined only if one of the following conditions exists:

1. Deep grooves deeper than 0.060″ (1.5 mm). This is the approximate thickness of a U.S. nickel! See Figure 8–32.
2. Thickness variation exceeding specifications and a brake pedal pulsation complaint.
3. Heavy rust that has corroded the friction surface of the rotor, as shown in Figure 8–33.

Therefore, if there is no complaint of a pulsating brake pedal during braking and the rotor is not deeply grooved or rusted, it should not be machined. New disc brake pads perform best against a smooth surface, and a used disc brake rotor is often smoother than a new rotor.

Figure 8–30 Measuring the thickness of a rotor using a micrometer.

Brown = Semimetallic

Brake rotors that have used semimetallic brake pads during operation are brown on the friction surface. The reason for the brown color is the rust from the steel used in the manufacture of the pads (see Figure 8–34). If the friction surface of the disc brake rotor is shiny, then organic (asbestos), nonasbestos organic (NAO), or nonasbestos synthetic (NAS) pads have been used on the rotor.

This information is helpful to know, especially if the vehicle being serviced is to be equipped with semimetallic pads as specified by the manufacturer and the rotors are shiny. In this case the incorrect lining may have been installed during a previous service. Friction surface color is a quick-and-easy way to determine whether semimetallic pads have been used.

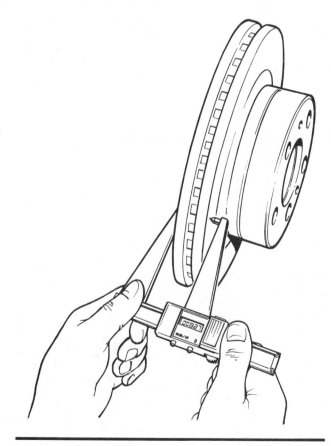

Figure 8–31 A digital readout rotor micrometer is an accurate tool to use when measuring a rotor. Both fractional inches and metric millimeters are generally available.

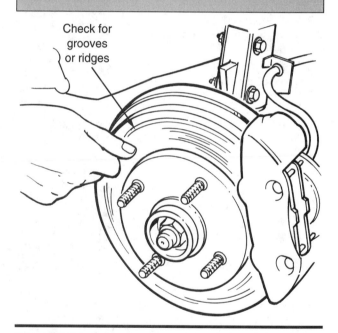

Check for grooves or ridges

Figure 8–32 If a fingernail catches on a groove in the rotor, the rotor should be machined.

Figure 8–33 This rusted rotor should be machined.

■ ROTOR FINISH

The smoothness of the rotor is called rotor finish or surface finish. Surface finish is measured in units called microinches, abbreviated μ in., where the symbol in front of "in." is the Greek lowercase letter μ (mu). One microinch equals 0.000001″ [0.025 micrometer (mm)]. The finish classification of microinch means the distance between the highest peaks and the deepest valley. The usual method of expressing surface finish is the arithmetic average roughness height, abbreviated Ra, which is the average of all peaks and valleys from the mean (average) line. This surface finish is measured using a machine with a diamond stylus, as shown in Figure 8–35.

Figure 8–34 The rotor on the left is shiny, indicating that nonmetallic pads have been used, whereas the rotor on the right is brown, indicating that semimetallic pads have been used.

Figure 8–35 (a) Electronic surface finish machine. The reading shows about 140 μ in. This is much too rough for use but is typical for a rough cut surface. (b) The stylus is moved over the surface by the machine and the readout gives the average of all the high and low ridges.

TECH TIP ✔

The Ballpoint Pen Test

A smooth friction surface on a drum or rotor is necessary for proper brake operation. To quickly determine if the friction surface of a brake drum or rotor is not smooth enough, draw a ballpoint pen across the surface. If the surface is smooth enough, a solid ink line will be observed. If the line drawn by the pen is not solid, then the surface is not smooth enough.

Another classification of surface finish that is becoming obsolete is the root mean square (RMS). The RMS method gives a slightly higher number and can be obtained by multiplying Ra $\times$ 1.11 = RMS.

Often, a machined rotor will not be as smooth as a new rotor, resulting in a hard stopping complaint after new brakes have been installed. A rough rotor has less surface area touching the new brake pads, resulting in a hard brake pedal and reduced braking effectiveness. Most new rotors have a surface finish of 45 to 60 μ in. Ra.

■ MACHINING A DISC BRAKE ROTOR

Before machining a rotor, be sure that it can be machined by comparing the minimum thickness specification and the measured thickness of the rotor.

> **CAUTION:** Some original equipment and replacement disc brake rotors are close to the minimum allowable thickness when new. Often, these rotors cannot be safely machined at all!

Following is an example of the steps necessary to machine a disc brake rotor. Always follow the instructions for the equipment you are using.

Step 1 Mount the disc brake rotor to the spindle of the lathe using the cones and adapters recommended (see Figures 8–36 and 8–37 on pages 198–199).

Step 2 Install a rotor damper and position the cutting tools close to the rotor surface as shown in Figure 8–38 on page 199.

> **NOTE:** Failure to install the damper causes vibrations to occur during machining that create a rough surface finish.

Step 3 Make a scratch cut on the rotor face as shown in Figure 8–39 on page 199.

Step 4 To check that the rotor is mounted correctly, loosen the retaining nut and turn the rotor one-half

turn (180°) and retighten the nut. Make another scratch cut.

  a. The second scratch cut should be side-by-side with the first scratch cut if the rotor is properly installed, as shown in Figure 8–40 on page 200.
  b. If the second scratch cut is on the opposite side (180°) from the first scratch cut, the rotor may not be installed on the lathe correctly.

> **NOTE:** The runout as measured with a dial indicator on the brake lathe should be the same as the runout measured on the vehicle. If the runout is not the same, the rotor is not installed on the brake lathe correctly.

After proper installation of the disc brake rotor on the brake lathe, proceed with machining the rotors. For best results do not machine any more material from the rotor than is absolutely necessary. Always follow the recommendations and guidelines as specified by the vehicle manufacturer.

Rough Cut A rough cut on a lathe involves cutting 0.005 in. per side with a feed of 0.008″ per revolution and 150 rpm spindle speed. This usually results in a very coarse surface finish of about 150 μ in. Ra.

Finish Cut A finish cut means removing 0.002″ per side with a feed of 0.002″ per revolution and 150 rpm spindle speed. Although this cut usually looks smooth, the surface finish is about 90 to 100 μ in. Ra. Even a typical finish cut is still not nearly as smooth as a new rotor.

> **NOTE:** Measure the thickness of the rotor after the finish cut and compare with manufacturer's specifications. Be sure to allow for wear. See the chart in Figure 8–41 on page 200 for a metric/fractional measurement chart.

Nondirectional Finish Most vehicle and brake component manufacturers recommend a nondirectional finish to help prevent the grooves machined into the rotor from acting like record grooves that can force the pads to move outward while the rotor rotates.

> **CAUTION:** Some nondirectional finish tools such as those that use Scotch Brite (a registered trademark) plastic pads often do not make the rotor as smooth as new, even though the finish has been swirled (see Figure 8–42 on page 201).

Surface-Finishing the Rotor The goal of any brake repair or service should be to restore the braking effectiveness to match new vehicle brakes. This means that the rotor finish should be as smooth or smoother

Typical rotor mounting configurations

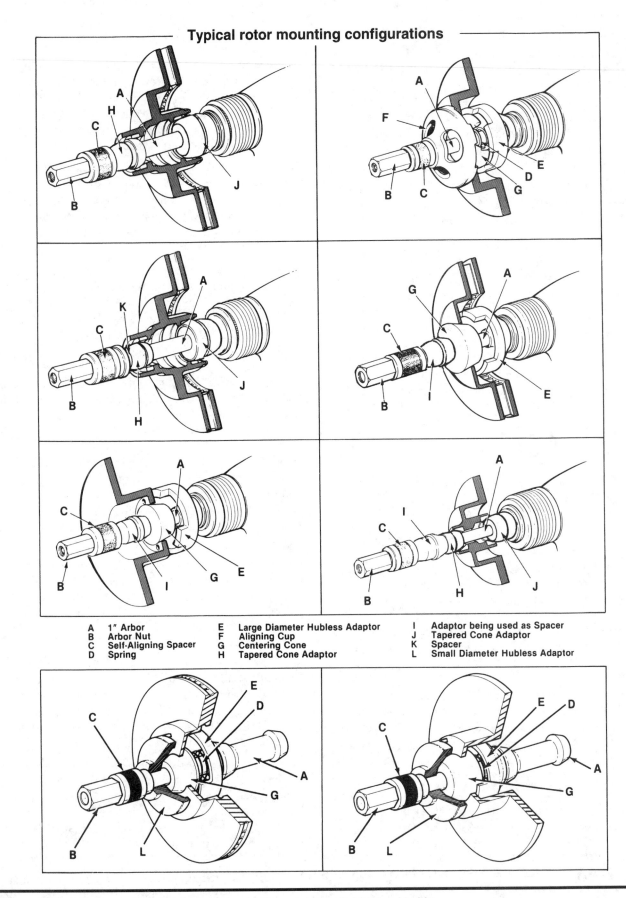

A	1″ Arbor	E	Large Diameter Hubless Adaptor	I	Adaptor being used as Spacer
B	Arbor Nut	F	Aligning Cup	J	Tapered Cone Adaptor
C	Self-Aligning Spacer	G	Centering Cone	K	Spacer
D	Spring	H	Tapered Cone Adaptor	L	Small Diameter Hubless Adaptor

Figure 8–36 Recommended adapters and location for machining hubbed and hubless rotors. (Courtesy of Ammco Tools, Inc.)

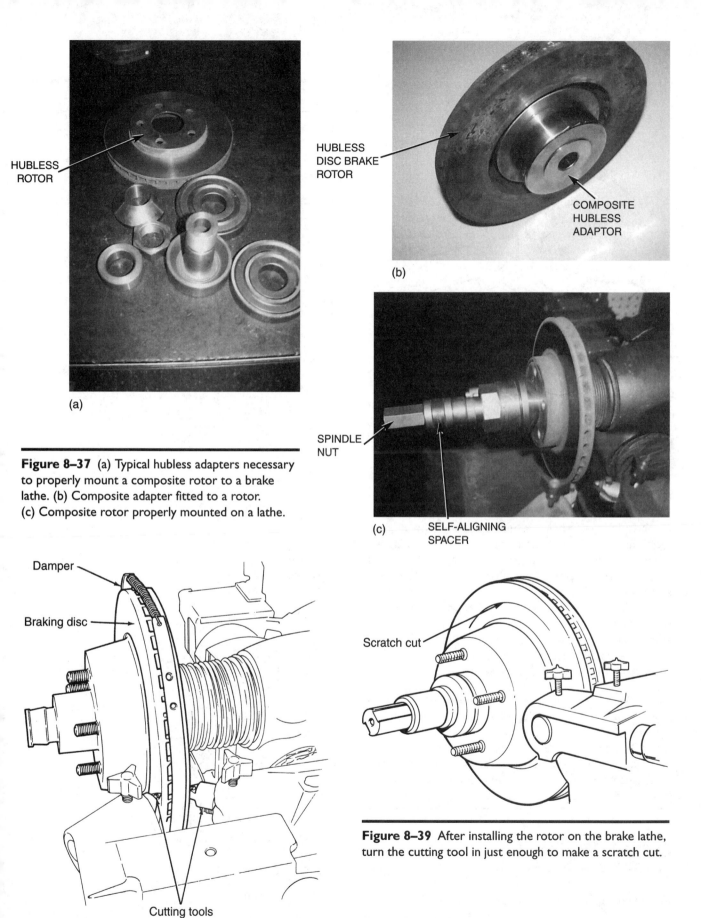

HUBLESS ROTOR

(a)

HUBLESS DISC BRAKE ROTOR

COMPOSITE HUBLESS ADAPTOR

(b)

SPINDLE NUT

(c)

SELF-ALIGNING SPACER

Figure 8–37 (a) Typical hubless adapters necessary to properly mount a composite rotor to a brake lathe. (b) Composite adapter fitted to a rotor. (c) Composite rotor properly mounted on a lathe.

Damper

Braking disc

Cutting tools

Figure 8–38 A damper is necessary to reduce cutting-tool vibrations that can cause a rough surface finish. (Courtesy of Chrysler Corporation)

Scratch cut

Figure 8–39 After installing the rotor on the brake lathe, turn the cutting tool in just enough to make a scratch cut.

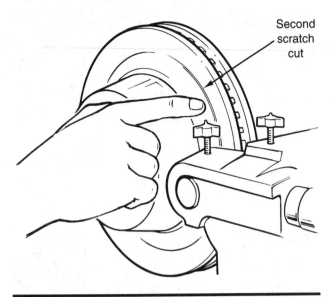

Second scratch cut

Figure 8–40 After making a scratch cut, loosen the retaining nut and rotate the rotor on the spindle of the lathe one-half turn. Tighten the nut and make a second scratch cut. The second scratch cut should be side-by-side with the first scratch if the rotor is installed correctly on the brake lathe.

than a new rotor for maximum brake pad contact. Research conducted at Delphi has shown that like-new rotor finish can easily be accomplished by using a block and sandpaper. After completing the finish cut, place 150-grit aluminum oxide sandpaper on a block and apply steady pressure against the rotor surface for sixty seconds on each side of the rotor (see Figure 8–43). The aluminum oxide is hard enough to remove the highest ridges left by the lathe cutting tool. This results in a surface finish ranging from 20 to 80 μ in. and usually less than 40 μ in., which is smoother than a new rotor (see Figure 8–44 on page 202).

> **NOTE:** Many commercial rotor-finish products may also give a smooth surface finish (see Figures 8–45 and 8–46 on page 202). Always compare rotor finish to that of a new rotor. Microinch finish is often hard to distinguish unless you have a new rotor with which to compare.

■ ON-THE-VEHICLE ROTOR MACHINING

Many vehicle manufacturers recommend on-the-vehicle machining for rotors if the disc brake rotor must be machined due to deep scoring or pulsating brake pedal complaint. This is especially true of composite rotors or for vehicles such as many Honda vehicles that require major disassembly to remove the rotors.

Inch	Decimal Inch	Millimeter
1/64	0.015625	0.396785
1/32	0.03125	0.79375
3/64	0.046875	1.190625
1/16	0.0625	1.5875
5/64	0.078125	1.984375
3/32	0.09375	2.38125
7/64	0.109375	2.778125
1/8	0.125	3.175
9/64	0.140625	3.571875
5/32	0.15625	3.96875
11/64	0.171875	4.365625
3/16	0.1875	4.7625
13/64	0.203125	5.159375
7/32	0.21875	5.55625
15/64	0.234375	5.953125
1/4	0.25	6.35001
17/64	0.265625	6.746875
9/32	0.28125	7.14375
19/64	0.296875	7.540625
5/16	0.3125	7.9375
21/64	0.328125	8.334375
11/32	0.34375	8.73125
23/64	0.359375	9.128125
3/8	0.375	9.525
25/64	0.390625	9.921875
13/32	0.40625	10.31875
27/64	0.421875	10.715625
7/16	0.4375	11.1125
29/64	0.453125	11.509375
15/32	0.46875	11.90625
31/64	0.484375	12.303125
1/2	0.50	12.7
33/64	0.515625	13.096875
17/32	0.53125	13.49375
35/64	0.546875	13.890625
9/16	0.5625	14.2875
37/64	0.578125	14.684375
19/32	0.59375	15.08125
39/64	0.609375	15.478125
5/8	0.625	15.875
41/64	0.640625	16.271875
21/32	0.65625	16.66875
43/64	0.671875	17.065625
11/16	0.6875	17.4625
45/64	0.703125	17.859375
23/32	0.71875	18.25625
47/64	0.734375	18.653125
3/4	0.75	19.05
49/64	0.765625	19.446875
25/32	0.78125	19.84375
51/64	0.796875	20.240625
13/16	0.8125	20.6375
53/64	0.828125	21.034375
27/32	0.84375	21.43125
55/64	0.859375	21.828125
7/8	0.875	22.225
57/64	0.890625	22.621875
29/32	0.90625	23.01875
59/64	0.921875	23.415625
15/16	0.9375	23.8125
61/64	0.953125	24.209375
31/32	0.96875	24.60625
63/64	0.984375	25.003125
1	1.00000	25.4

Figure 8–41 Metric/fractional chart

Figure 8–42 A proper sanding disc for removing material and providing the proper surface finish.

(a)

(b)

Figure 8–43 (a) This technician uses two sanding blocks each equipped with 150-grit aluminum-oxide sandpaper. (b) With the lathe turned on, the technician presses the two sanding blocks against the surface of the rotor after the rotor has been machined, to achieve a smooth microinch surface finish.

TECH TIP ✔

Turn or Machine?

When asked about what was done to their vehicle, a common response is, "They rotated my rotors." Many customers do not understand the terms that are commonly used in the vehicle service industry. Try to use terms that are technically correct and avoid slang when talking to customers. For example, the term "machined the rotors" indicates an operation, whereas the term "turned the rotors" may be misinterpreted by some customers as simply meaning using your hand and moving (rotating) the rotor. "Resurfacing," "refinishing," and "reconditioning" are other terms that could be used to describe a drum or rotor machining operation.

NOTE: All on-the-vehicle lathes require that the wheel be removed. For best results, always use a torque wrench when tightening lug nuts or lathe adapters. Unequal torque on the bolts causes stress and distortion that can cause warped rotors and a pulsating brake pedal.

Caliper mount, on-the-vehicle lathes require that the disc brake caliper be removed. The cutter attaches to the steering knuckle or caliper support in the same location as the caliper (see Figure 8–47 on page 203).

Hub mount, on-the-vehicle lathes attach to the hub using the lug nuts of the vehicle. To achieve a proper cut, the hub mount must be calibrated for any runout caused by the hub bearings and the outside surface face of the rotor. See Figures 8–48 and 8–49 on page 203.

(a)

(b)

Figure 8–44 (a) After machining and sanding the rotor, it should be cleaned. In this case brake cleaner from an air pressurized spray can is used. (b) With the lathe turning, the technician stands back away from the rotor and sprays both sides of the rotor to clean it of any remaining grit from the sanding process. This last step ensures a clean, smooth surface for the disc brake pads and a quality brake repair. Sanding each side of the rotor surface for one minute using a sanding block and 150-grit aluminum oxide sandpaper after a finish cut gives the rotor the proper smoothness and finish.

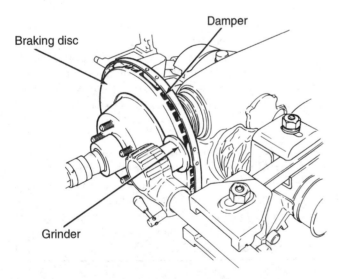

Figure 8–45 A grinder with sandpaper can be used to give a smooth nondirectional surface finish to the disc brake rotor. (Courtesy of Chrysler Corporation)

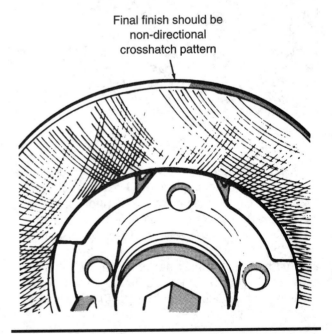

Figure 8–46 The correct final surface finish should be smooth and nondirectional. (Courtesy of Chrysler Corporation)

(a)

(b)

(c)

Figure 8–47 (a) Typical on-the-vehicle disc brake rotor lathe. (b) This lathe mounts to the steering knuckle in the same location as the caliper and is called a caliper mount lathe. (c) Close-up of the machining operation from below.

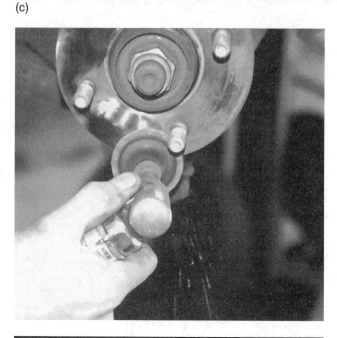

Figure 8–48 Rust should always be cleaned from both the rotor and the hub whenever the rotors are machined or replaced. An air-powered die grinder with a sanding disc makes quick work cleaning this hub.

Figure 8–49 A typical hub-mount on-the-vehicle lathe. This particular lathe oscillates while machining the rotor thereby providing a smooth and nondirectional finish at the same time.

PHOTO SEQUENCE Machining a Drum

PS8–1 Before starting to machine a brake drum, check the drum for any obvious damage such as heat cracks or hard spots.

PS8–2 Lightly tap the drum. It should ring like a bell. If a dull thud is heard, the drum may be cracked and should be discarded.

PS8–3 Use a drum micrometer to measure the inside diameter of the drum and compare this measurement with specifications to be sure that the drum can be safely machined.

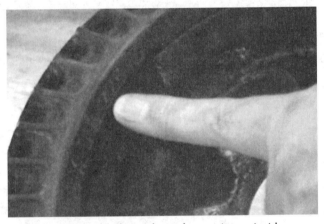

PS8–4 Most brake drums have the maximum inside diameter cast into the drum as shown.

PS8–5 Thoroughly clean the outside and inside of the drum.

PS8–6 Be sure the center hole in the drum is clean and free from any burrs that could prevent the drum from being properly centered on the shaft of the brake lathe.

Machining a Drum—continued

PS8–7 A typical brake lathe used to machine drums.

PS8–8 Locate a tapered, centering cone that best fits inside the hole of the brake drum.

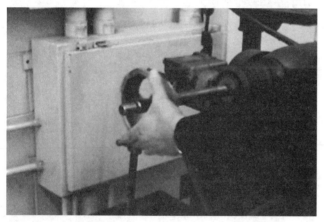

PS8–9 Slide the large face plate over the shaft of the brake lathe.

PS8–10 Slide the tapered centering cone onto the shaft with the spring between the face plate and the centering cone.

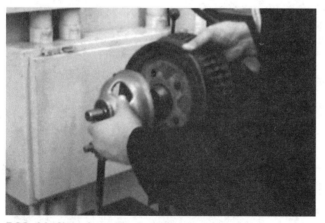

PS8–11 Slide the other face plate onto the shaft.

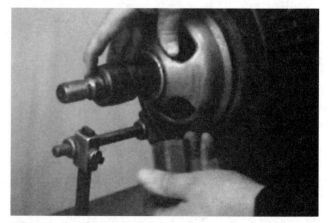

PS8–12 Install the self-aligning spacer (SAS) and left-hand-thread spindle nut.

Machining a Drum—continued

PS8–13 Tighten the spindle nut.

PS8–14 Loosen the turning bar retainer.

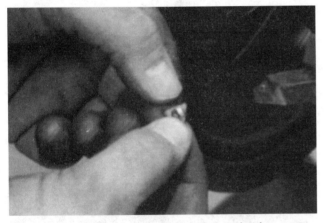

PS8–15 Carefully check the cutting bits and either rotate the bit to a new cutting point or replace it with a new part as necessary.

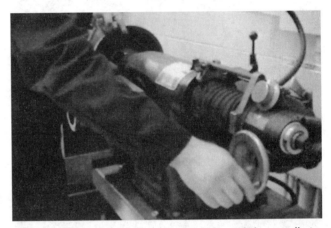

PS8–16 Turn the spindle control knob until the spindle is as short as possible (the drum as close to the machine as possible) to help reduce vibration as much as possible.

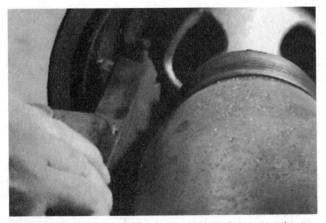

PS8–17 Position the cutting bar so that the cutting bit is located at the back surface of the drum.

PS8–18 Install the silencer band (vibration dampener strap).

Machining a Drum—continued

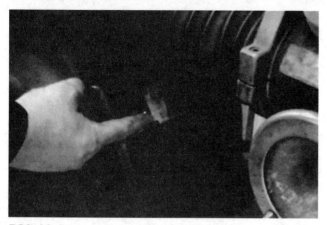

PS8–19 Be sure the tool bit and clothing are away from the drum and turn on the brake lathe.

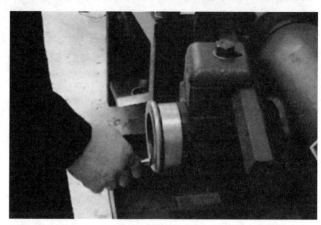

PS8–20 Center the bit on the center of the brake surface of the drum and slowly rotate the control knob that moves the bit into contact with the drum friction surface. This should produce a light scratch cut.

PS8–21 Turn off the lathe.

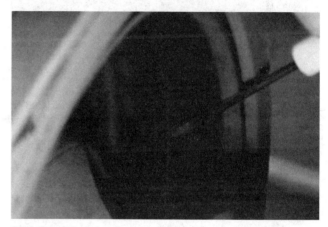

PS8–22 Observe the scratch cut.

PS8–23 Loosen the spindle nut.

PS8–24 Rotate the drum 180 degrees (one-half turn) on the spindle.

Machining a Drum—continued

PS8–25 Tighten the spindle nut.

PS8–26 Turn on the lathe and rotate the control knob and run the cutter into the drum for another scratch cut.

PS8–27 Observe the scratch cut. If the second scratch cut is in the same place as the first scratch cut or extends all the way around the drum, the drum is correctly mounted on the lathe and machining can continue.

PS8–28 Adjust the depth gauge to zero when the cutter just touches the drum.

PS8–29 Run the cutter all the way to the back surface of the drum.

PS8–30 Adjust the depth of the cut and lock it in position by turning the lock knob. Most vehicle manufacturers recommend a rough cut depth should be 0.005"–0.010"

Machining a Drum—continued

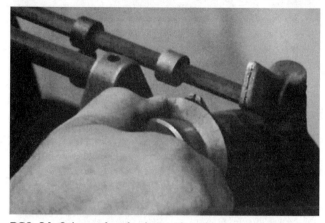

PS8–31 Select a fast-feed rate if performing a rough cut (0.006″–0.010″ per revolution).

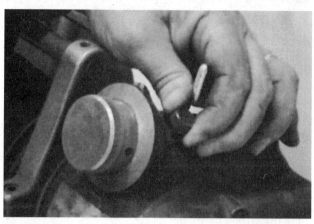

PS8–32 Turn the lock knob to keep the feed adjustment from changing.

PS8–33 Engage the automatic feed.

PS8–34 The drum will automatically move as the tool bit remains stationary to make the cut.

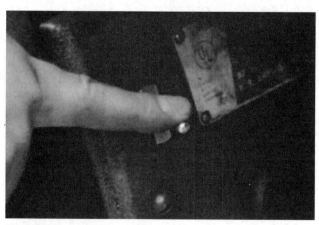

PS8–35 Turn off the lathe.

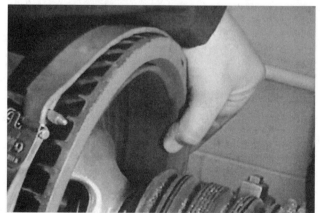

PS8–36 Observe the machined surface. If the feed rate was low and the surface is smooth on all portions of the friction surface, the drum can be removed. If additional material must be removed, proceed with the finish cut.

Machining a Drum—continued

PS8–37 Turn the lathe back on.

PS8–38 Move the cutter back into position to start the finish cut.

PS8–39 Loosen the lock to allow the depth of cut to be adjusted for the finish cut.

PS8–40 Adjust the cutting depth to a maximum of 0.002″ for a good finish cut.

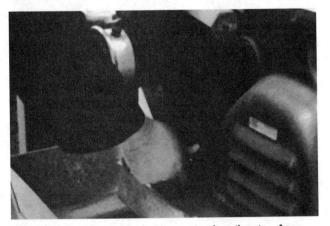

PS8–41 Tighten the lock to prevent the vibration from changing the adjustment.

PS8–42 Adjust the feed to the lowest rate for the finish cut (0.002″ per revolution).

Machining a Drum—continued

PS8–43 Engage the automatic feed.

PS8–44 Observe the machining process.

PS8–45 Turn off the lathe when the machining is completed and move the drum away from the cutting bit.

PS8–46 Remove the silencer band.

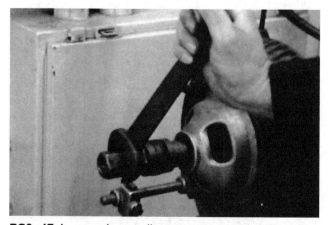

PS8–47 Loosen the spindle retaining nut and remove the drum from the lathe.

PS8–48 Carefully inspect and clean the drum before installing it on the vehicle.

PHOTO SEQUENCE   Machining a Rotor

PS8–49 Before machining any rotor, use a micrometer and measure the thickness of the rotor.

PS8–50 Check the specifications for the minimum allowable thickness.

PS8–51 Visually check the rotor for evidence of heat cracks or hard spots which would require replacement (rather than machining) of the rotor.

PS8–52 After removing the grease seal and bearings, remove the grease from the bearing races.

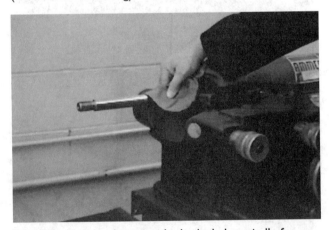

PS8–53 Clean and inspect the brake lathe spindle for damage or burrs that could affect its accuracy.

PS8–54 Select a tapered cone adapter that fits the inner bearing race.

Machining a Rotor—continued

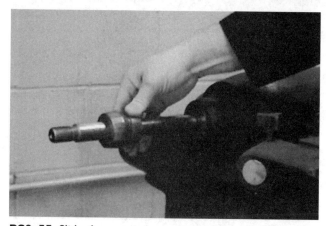

PS8–55 Slide the cone adapter onto the brake lathe spindle.

PS8–56 Select the proper size tapered cone adapter for the smaller outer wheel bearing race.

PS8–57 Place the rotor onto the large cone adapter and then slide the small cone adapter into the outer wheel bearing race.

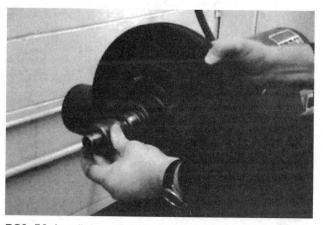

PS8–58 Install the self-aligning spacer (SAS) and spindle nut.

PS8–59 Tighten the spindle nut (usually left-hand threads).

PS8–60 If a hubless rotor is being machined, be sure to thoroughly clean the inside surface.

Machining a Rotor—continued

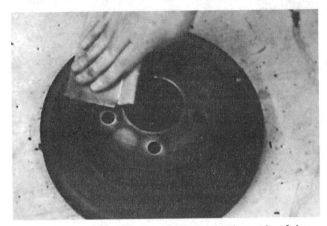

PS8–61 Also remove all rust from the other side of the hubless rotor.

PS8–62 Select the proper centering cone for the hole in the center of the hub.

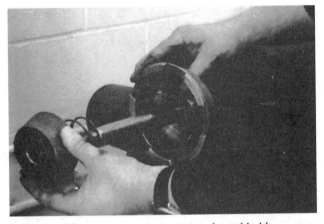

PS8–63 Select the proper size cone-shaped hubless adapter and the tapered centering cone with a spring in between.

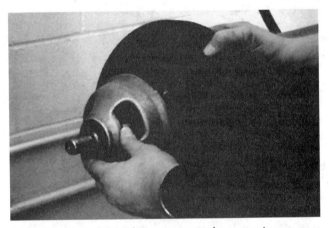

PS8–64 After sliding the rotor over the centering cone, install the matching hubless adapter.

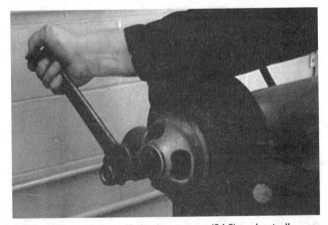

PS8–65 Install the self-aligning spacer (SAS) and spindle nut.

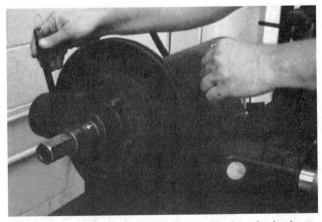

PS8–66 After the rotor has been secured to the brake lathe spindle, install the noise silencer band (dampener).

Machining a Rotor—continued

PS8–67 Carefully inspect the cutting bits and replace if necessary.

PS8–68 Loosen the tool holder arm.

PS8–69 Adjust the twin cutter arm until the rotor is centered between the two cutting bits.

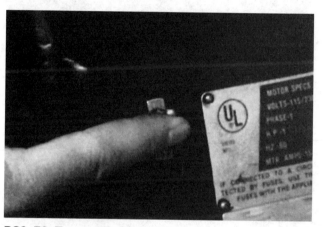

PS8–70 Turn on the lathe.

PS8–71 Move the cutter arm toward the center of the rotor placing the cutting bits in about the center of the friction surface.

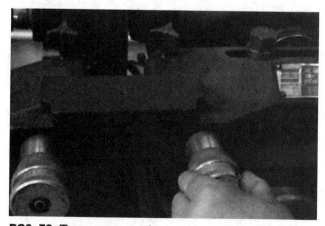

PS8–72 Turn one cutting bit into the surface of the rotor to make a scratch cut.

Machining a Rotor—continued

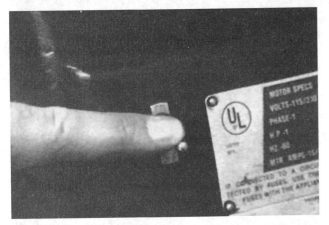

PS8–73 Turn off the lathe.

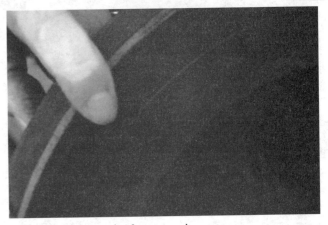

PS8–74 Observe the first scratch cut.

PS8–75 Loosen the spindle retaining nut.

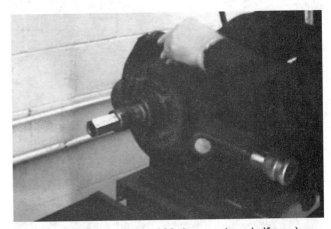

PS8–76 Rotate the rotor 180 degrees (one-half turn) on the spindle of the brake lathe.

PS8–77 Tighten the spindle nut.

PS8–78 Turn the lathe back on and turn the cutting bit slightly into the rotor until a second scratch cut is made.

Machining a Rotor—continued

PS8–79 Observe the location of the second scratch cut. If the second scratch cut is in the same location as the first scratch cut or extends all around the surface of the rotor, then the rotor is properly installed on the lathe and machining can begin.

PS8–80 Start the machining process by moving the twin cutters to about the center of the rotor friction surface.

PS8–81 Turn the cutting bits inward until they touch the rotor and zero the depth adjustment.

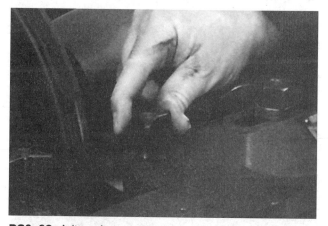

PS8–82 Adjust the twin cutters to the inside of the rotor (toward the hub), then dial in the amount of depth (0.005″–0.010″ per side for a rough cut) and lock the adjustment so that vibration will not change the setting.

PS8–83 Turn the feed control knob until the desired feed rate is achieved for the first or rough cut (0.006″– 0.010″ per revolution) or finish cut (0.002″ per revolution) depending on the condition of the rotor and the amount of material that can be safely removed.

PS8–84 Engage the automatic feed.

Machining a Rotor—continued

PS8–85 Observe the machining operation.

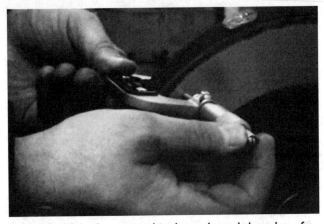

PS8–86 After the cutting bits have cleared the edge of the rotor, turn off the lathe and measure the thickness of the rotor.

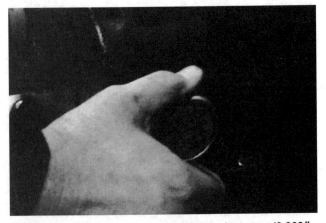

PS8–87 Readjust the feed control to a slow rate (0.002″ per revolution or less) for the finish cut.

PS8–88 Reposition the cutting bits for the finish cut.

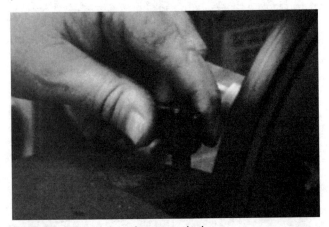

PS8–89 Loosen the adjustment locks.

PS8–90 Turn the depth of the cut for the finish cut (0.002″ maximum)

Machining a Rotor—continued

PS8–91 Lock the adjustment.

PS8–92 Engage the automatic feed.

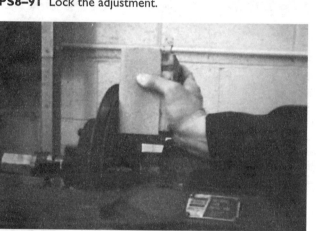

PS8–93 After the last machining operation, use 150-grit aluminum oxide sandpaper on a block of wood for sixty seconds per side or a grinder to give a nondirectional and smooth surface to both sides of the rotor.

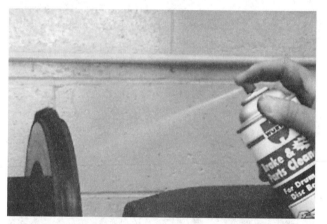

PS8–94 After the sanding or grinding operation, thoroughly clean the machined surface of the rotor to remove any and all particles of grit that could affect the operation and life of the disc brake pads.

PS8–95 Remove the silencer band.

PS8–96 Loosen the spindle retaining nut and remove the rotor.

PHOTO SEQUENCE **Using an On-the-Vehicle Lathe**

PS8–97 Prepare to machine a disc brake rotor using an on-the-vehicle lathe by properly positioning the vehicle in the stall and hoisting the vehicle to a good working height.

PS8–98 Remove the wheels and place them out of the way.

PS8–99 Remove the disc brake caliper and use a wire to support the caliper out of the way of the rotor.

PS8–100 Measure the rotor thickness and compare it with factory specifications before machining. If a discard thickness is specified, be sure to allow an additional 0.015″ for wear

PS8–101 Install the hub adapter onto the hub and secure it using the wheel lug nuts.

PS8–102 Engage the drive unit by aligning the hole in the drive plate with the raised button on the adapter.

Using an On-the-Vehicle Lathe—continued

PS8–103 Use the thumb wheel to tighten the drive unit to the adapter.

PS8–104 Attach a dial indicator to a secure part on the vehicle and position the dial indicator on a flat portion of the lathe to measure the lathe runout.

PS8–105 Rotate the wheel or turn on the lathe motor and measure the amount of runout.

PS8–106 Use a wrench to adjust the runout using the four numbers stamped on the edge of the drive flange as a guide. The manufacturer of this on-the-vehicle lathe specifies that the total runout of the lathe itself should be less than 0.005″.

PS8–107 After the hub runout is adjusted to 0.005″ or less, remove the dial indicator from the vehicle.

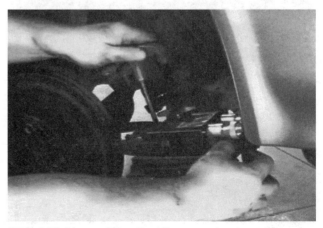

PS8–108 Using a T-handle Allen wrench, adjust the cutter arms until they are centered on the disc brake rotor.

Using an On-the-Vehicle Lathe—continued

PS8–109 Move the cutters to the center of the rotor.

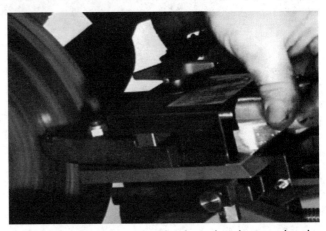

PS8–110 Adjust the cutter depth until each cutter barely touches the rotor.

PS8–111 Position the cutters to the inside edge of the rotor surface and adjust the cutters to the desired depth of cut.

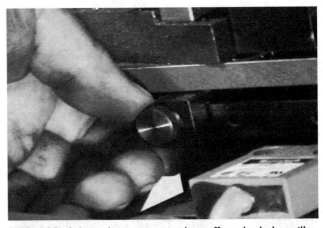

PS8–112 Adjust the automatic shut-off so the lathe will turn itself off at the end of the cut.

PS8–113 Turn on the lathe by depressing the start button.

PS8–114 Monitor the machining operations as the lathe automatically moves the cutters from the center toward the outside edge of the rotor.

Using an On-the-Vehicle Lathe—continued

PS8–115 After the lathe reaches the outside edge of the rotor, the drive motor should stop.

PS8–116 Measure the thickness of the rotor after machining to be certain that the rotor thickness is within service limits.

PS8–117 While this brand of on-the-vehicle lathe produces a nondirectional surface finish to the rotor, the technician is using 150-grit aluminum oxide sandpaper and a wood block for sixty seconds on each side of the rotor to provide a smooth surface finish.

PS8–118 After completing the machining and resurfacing of the rotor, unclamp the drive unit from the hub adapter and clean the rotor using brake cleaner.

PS8–119 After the drive unit has been removed, remove the lug nuts holding the adapter to the rotor hub.

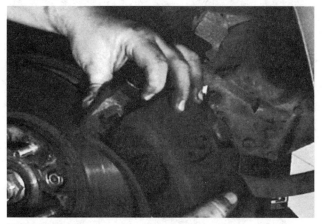

PS8–120 After removing the hub adapter, the caliper can be reinstalled.

Using an On-the-Vehicle Lathe—continued

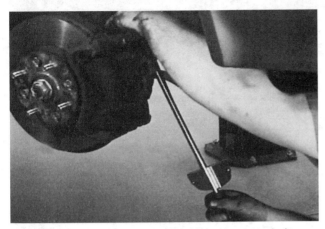

PS8–121 Be sure to torque the caliper retaining bolts.

PS8–122 Install the wheel and wheel cover. On this vehicle, the wheel cover must be installed before the lug nuts because the lug nuts hold the wheel cover on the wheel.

PS8–123 Always use a torque wrench or a torque-limiting adapter with an air impact as shown here when tightening lug nuts.

PS8–124 Be sure to clean the wheel covers of any grease or fingerprints before returning the vehicle to the customer.

PS8–125 Pump the brake pedal several times to restore proper brake pedal height and check and add brake fluid as necessary before moving the vehicle.

PS8–126 Carefully back out of the stall and test-drive the vehicle to be assured of proper brake operation before returning the vehicle to the customer.

■ SUMMARY

1. Brake drums and rotors must absorb the heat generated by the friction of slowing and stopping a vehicle.

2. All rotors should be marked before removing them from the vehicle to ensure that they will be reinstalled in the same position and on the same side of the vehicle.

3. All brake drums should be machined only enough to restore proper braking action. Brake drums should be the same size on the same axle to help prevent unequal braking.

4. Disc brake rotors should be machined and allow up to 0.030″ (0.8 mm) for wear.

5. To ensure proper braking, all rotors should be machined to a very smooth surface of less than 60 μ in. finish.

■ REVIEW QUESTIONS

1. Explain the difference between "machine to" specifications and "discard."

2. List the steps for machining a brake drum.

3. Describe how to measure a disc brake rotor for lateral runout and thickness variation.

4. List the steps for machining a disc brake rotor.

5. Describe what is necessary to achieve "like new" disc brake rotor finish.

■ ASE CERTIFICATION-TYPE QUESTIONS

1. Technician A says that aluminum brake drums use cast iron friction surfaces. Technician B says that up to 0.030″ (0.8 mm) should be left after machining a drum to allow for wear. Which technician is correct?
   a. Technician A only
   b. Technician B only
   c. Both Technician A and B
   d. Neither Technician A nor B

2. Technician A says that hard spots in a brake drum should be removed using a carbide-tip machining tool. Technician B says that the drum should be replaced if hard spots are discovered. Which technician is correct?
   a. Technician A only
   b. Technician B only
   c. Both Technician A and B
   d. Neither Technician A nor B

3. Technician A says that brake drums on the same axle should be close to the same inside diameter for best brake balance. Technician B says that a brake drum may be cracked if it rings like a bell when tapped with a light steel hammer. Which technician is correct?
   a. Technician A only
   b. Technician B only
   c. Both Technician A and B
   d. Neither Technician A nor B

4. A hubless brake drum cannot be machined because it cannot be held in a lathe.
   a. True
   b. False

5. The major reason for brake pedal pulsation during braking is due to excessive rotor thickness variation.
   a. True
   b. False

6. Rotor finish is measured in
   a. Millimeters
   b. Inches
   c. Microinches
   d. Centimeters

7. The lower the Ra of a rotor, the _____ the surface.
   a. Smoother
   b. Rougher
   c. Higher
   d. Lower

8. A disc brake rotor is being installed on a lathe for machining. During the setup a scratch test is performed. The scratch extended all the way around the rotor. Technician A says that the rotor should be loosened, rotated 180 degrees, and retightened. Technician B says that the rotor is not warped. Which technician is correct?
   a. Technician A only
   b. Technician B only
   c. Both Technician A and B
   d. Neither Technician A nor B

9. Typical maximum rotor runout specifications are
   a. 0.0003″ to 0.0005″ (0.008 to 0.013 mm)
   b. 0.003″ to 0.005″ (0.08 to 0.13 mm)
   c. 0.030″ to 0.050″ (0.8 to 1.3 mm)
   d. 0.300″ to 0.500″ (8.0 to 13 mm)

10. Typical maximum rotor thickness variation (parallelism) specifications are
   a. 0.0003″ to 0.0005″ (0.008 to 0.013 mm)
   b. 0.003″ to 0.005″ (0.08 to 0.13 mm)
   c. 0.030″ to 0.050″ (0.8 to 1.3 mm)
   d. 0.300″ to 0.500″ (8.0 to 13 mm)

Power Brake Unit Operation, Diagnosis, and Service

Objectives: After studying Chapter 9, the reader should be able to:

1. List the parts of a vacuum brake booster.
2. Describe how a vacuum brake booster operates.
3. Explain how to test a vacuum brake booster.
4. Describe how a hydraulic or electrohydraulic brake booster operates.

Power-assisted brakes reduce the effort of the driver to apply the necessary stopping forces of the vehicle. Power-assisted brakes, once considered a luxury, were available first on large, heavy cars and trucks. Without power-assisted brakes, the entire braking force was achieved by mechanical and hydraulic leverage, as explained in Chapter 2 (see Figure 9–1). The use of disc brakes required greater forces because disc brakes are not self-energizing. With most drum brakes, a little increase in pedal effort resulted in much greater stopping power being exerted against the brake drums, due to the wedging action of the shoes and the rotation of the drum. To double the stopping power of a disc brake, the driver must double the force on the brake pedal. This is the reason why most vehicles equipped with disc brakes are power assisted, even on small, lightweight vehicles. The use of semimetallic brake pads also requires greater force. The most commonly used power-assisted units are vacuum operated.

■ VACUUM BOOSTER OPERATION

Most power brake boosters are vacuum operated, getting vacuum from the intake manifold of the engine. As any gasoline-powered engine runs, vacuum is created in the intake manifold. A vacuum is pressure below atmospheric pressure. Vacuum is measured in units of **inches of mercury.** The chemical symbol for mercury is **Hg.** Therefore, the abbreviation is commonly written **in. Hg.** A well-running engine should produce between 17 and 21 in. Hg vacuum.

NOTE: Most manufacturers specify that the minimum engine vacuum necessary for proper operation of a vacuum power-assist unit is 15 in. Hg. If the engine is producing less than 15 in. Hg at idle, the cause of the low vacuum should be found and repaired before further brake system diagnosis is performed. See the following Tech Tip for an example of how vacuum affects braking performance.

■ CHARCOAL FILTER

The vacuum hose leading from the engine to the power booster should run downward without any low places in the hose. If a dip or sag occurs in the vacuum hose, condensed fuel vapors and/or moisture can accumulate that can block or restrict the vacuum to the booster. Many manufacturers use a small charcoal filter in the vacuum line between the engine and booster, as shown in Figure 9–2. The charcoal filter attracts and holds

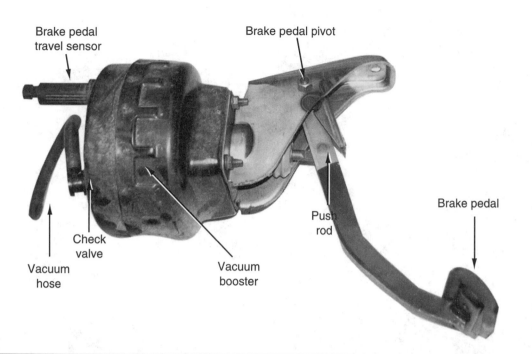

Figure 9–1 Typical vacuum brake booster assembly. The vacuum hose attaches to the intake manifold of the engine. The brake pedal travel sensor is an input sensor for the antilock braking system.

Check the Vacuum, Then the Brakes

A customer complained of a very rough idle and an occasional pulsating brake pedal. The customer was certain that the engine required serious work since there were over 100,000 miles on the vehicle. During the troubleshooting procedure, a spray cleaner was used to find any vacuum (air) leaks. A large hole was found melted through a large vacuum hose next to the vacuum hose feeding the vacuum-operated power brake booster.

After repairing the vacuum leak, the vehicle was test driven again to help diagnose the cause of the pulsating brake pedal. The engine idled very smoothly after the vacuum leak was repaired and the brake pulsation was also cured. The vacuum leak resulted in lower-than-normal vacuum being applied to the vacuum booster. During braking, when engine vacuum is normally higher (deceleration), the vacuum booster would assist, then not assist when the vacuum was lost. This on-and-off supply of vacuum to the vacuum booster was noticed by the driver as a brake pulsation. Always check the vacuum at the booster whenever diagnosing any brake problems. Most vehicle manufacturers specify a maximum of 15 in. Hg of vacuum at the booster. The booster should be able to provide at least two or three stops even with no vacuum. The booster should also be checked to see if it can hold a vacuum after several hours. A good vacuum booster, for example, should be able to provide power assist after sitting all night without starting the engine.

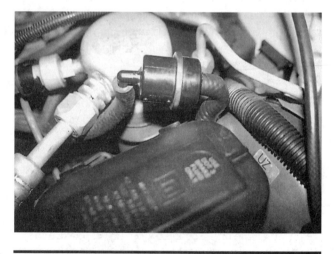

Figure 9–2 The charcoal filter traps gasoline vapors that are present in the intake manifold and prevents them from getting into the vacuum chamber of the booster.

gasoline vapors and keeps fumes from entering the vacuum booster. Without this filter, gasoline fumes can enter the vacuum booster, where it can deteriorate the rubber diaphragm and other rubber components of the booster.

■ VACUUM CHECK VALVE

All vacuum boosters use a one-way vacuum check valve. This valve allows air to flow in only one direction—from the booster toward the engine. This valve prevents loss of vacuum when the engine stops. Without this check

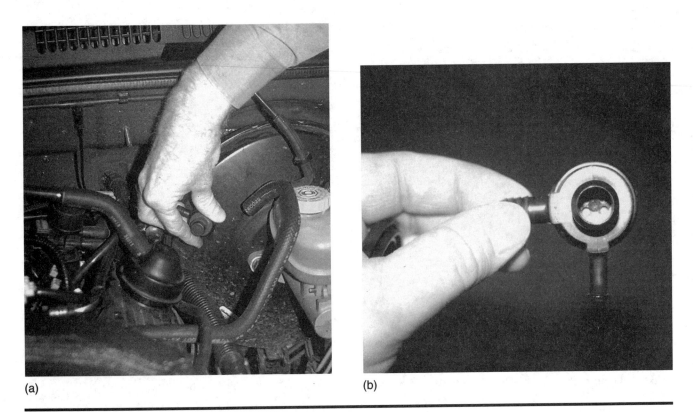

(a)   (b)

Figure 9–3 (a) Many vacuum-brake-booster check valves are located where the vacuum hose from the engine (vacuum source) attaches to the vacuum booster. (b) This one-way valve prevents the loss of vacuum when the engine is off. The diaphragm inside allows air to flow in one direction only.

valve, the vacuum stored in the vacuum booster would simply be lost through the hose and intake manifold of the engine (see Figures 9–3 and 9–4).

> **CAUTION:** Sometimes an engine backfire can destroy or blow the vacuum check valve out of the booster housing. If this occurs, all power assist will be lost and a much greater-than-normal force must be exerted on the brake pedal to stop the vehicle. Be sure to repair the cause of the backfire before replacing the damaged or missing check valve. Normal causes of backfire include an excessively lean air/fuel ratio or incorrect firing order or ignition timing.

■ VACUUM BRAKE BOOSTER

A vacuum power-brake booster contains a rubber diaphragm(s) connected to the brake pedal at one end and to the master cylinder at the other end. When the brakes are off or released, there is equal vacuum on both sides of the diaphragm.

The vacuum power unit contains the power-piston assembly, which houses the control valve and reaction mechanism, and the power-piston return spring. The control valve is composed of the air valve (valve plunger), the floating control-valve assembly, and the pushrod. The reaction mechanism consists of a hydraulic piston reaction plate and a series of reaction levers. An air filter, air silencer, and filter retainer are assembled around the valve operating rod, filling the cavity inside the hub of the power piston. The pushrod that operates the air valve projects out of the end (see Figure 9–5).

Released-Position Operation

At the released position (brake pedal up), the air valve is seated on the floating control valve, which shuts off the air. The floating control valve is held away from the valve seat in the power-piston insert. Vacuum from the engine is present in the space on both sides of the power piston. Any air in the system is drawn through a small passage in the power piston, over the seat in the power-piston insert, and through a passage in the power-piston insert. There is a vacuum on both sides of the power piston and it is held against the rear of the housing by the power-piston return spring. At rest, the hydraulic reaction plate is held against the reaction retainer. The air-valve spring holds the reaction lever against the hydraulic reaction plate and holds the air valve against its stop in the tube of the power piston. The floating control-valve assembly is held against the

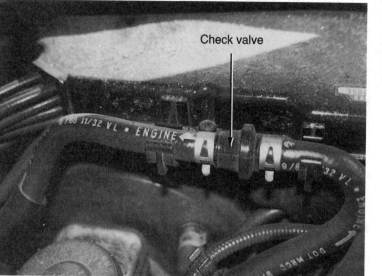

Figure 9–4 Not all check valves are located at the vacuum line to the booster housing connection. This vehicle uses an inline check valve located between the intake manifold of the engine and the vacuum brake booster.

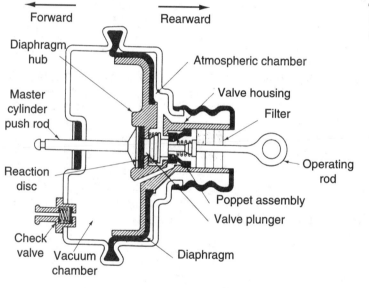

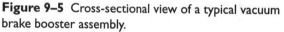

Figure 9–5 Cross-sectional view of a typical vacuum brake booster assembly.

air-valve seat by the floating control-valve spring (see Figures 9–6 and 9–7).

Applied-Position Operation

As the brake pedal is depressed, the valve pushrod moves the air valve away from the floating control valve. The floating control valve will follow until it is in contact with the raised seat in the power-piston insert. When this occurs, vacuum is shut off to the rear of the power piston, and air under atmospheric pressure enters through the air filter and travels past the seat of the air valve and through a passage into the housing at the rear of the power piston. Since there is still vacuum on the front side of the power piston, the atmospheric air pressure at the rear of the piston will force the power piston to travel forward.

NOTE: This movement of air into the rear chamber of the brake booster may be heard inside the vehicle as a hissing noise. The loudness of this airflow varies from vehicle to vehicle and should be considered normal.

As the power piston travels forward, the master cylinder pushrod pushes the master cylinder primary and secondary pistons forward. As back pressure builds up on the end of the master cylinder piston, the hydraulic reaction plate is moved off its seat on the power piston and presses against the reaction levers. The reaction lever pushes against the end of the air-valve rod assembly. Approximately 30 percent of the load on the hydraulic master cylinder piston is transferred back through the reaction system to the brake pedal. This gives the driver a feel

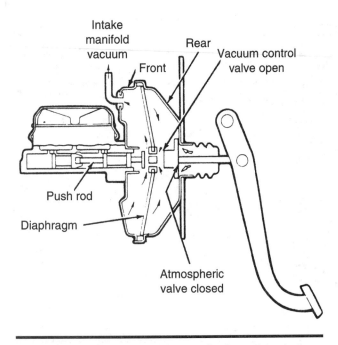

Figure 9–6 In the release position (brake pedal up), the vacuum is directed to both sides of the diaphragm. (Courtesy of Chrysler Corporation)

that is proportional to the degree of brake application (see Figures 9–8 and 9–9).

Hold-Position Operation

When the desired brake pedal force is reached, the power piston moves forward until the floating control valve, which is still on the power piston, again seats on the air valve. The power piston will now remain stationary until force is either applied or released at the brake pedal. As the force at the brake pedal is released, the air-valve spring forces the air valve back to its stop on the power piston. As it returns, the air valve pushes the floating control valve off its seat on the power-piston insert. The air valve seating on the floating control valve has shut off the outside air source. When it lifts the floating control valve from its seat on the power-piston insert, it opens the space at the rear of the power-piston insert to the vacuum source. The power-piston return spring will return the piston to its released position against the rear housing, since

Figure 9–7 Vacuum booster in released position showing the vacuum port open and the atmospheric port closed. The brake pedal is up and no force is being applied to the master cylinder. (Courtesy of Chrysler Corporation)

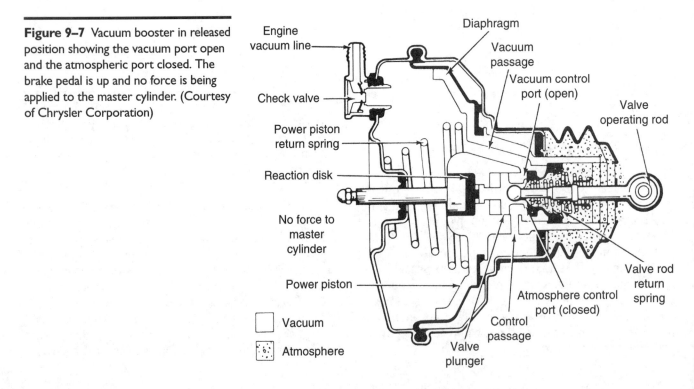

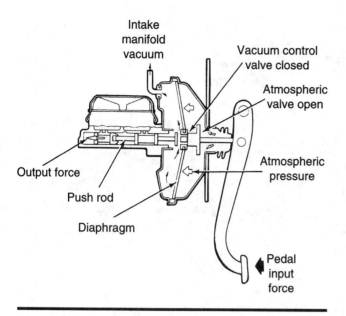

Figure 9–8 Simplified diagram of a vacuum brake booster in the apply position. Notice that the atmospheric valve is open and air pressure is being applied to the diaphragm. (Courtesy of Chrysler Corporation)

both sides of the piston are now under vacuum. As this occurs, the master cylinder releases its pressure and the brakes are released (see Figure 9–10).

Vacuum-Failure Mode

In case of vacuum source interruption, the brake operates as a standard brake as follows: As the pedal is pushed down, the end of the air valve contacts the reaction levers and pushes, in turn, against the hydraulic reaction plate, which is fastened to the master cylinder piston rod, which applies pressure in the master cylinder. For safety in the event of a stalled engine and a loss of vacuum, a power brake should have adequate storage of vacuum for several power-assisted stops.

■ DUAL- (TANDEM-) DIAPHRAGM VACUUM BOOSTERS

To provide power assist, air pressure must work against a rubber diaphragm. The larger the area of the diaphragm,

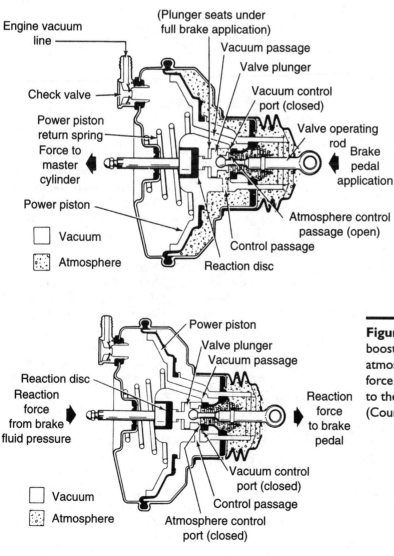

Figure 9–9 Cross-sectional view of a vacuum brake booster in the apply position, showing force being transferred and increased through the booster assembly. (Courtesy of Chrysler Corporation)

Figure 9–10 Cross section of a vacuum brake booster in hold position with both vacuum and atmospheric valves closed. Note that the reaction force from the brake fluid pressure is transferred back to the driver as a reaction force to the brake pedal. (Courtesy of Chrysler Corporation)

Figure 9–11 Cutaway showing a dual-diaphragm (tandem) vacuum brake booster.

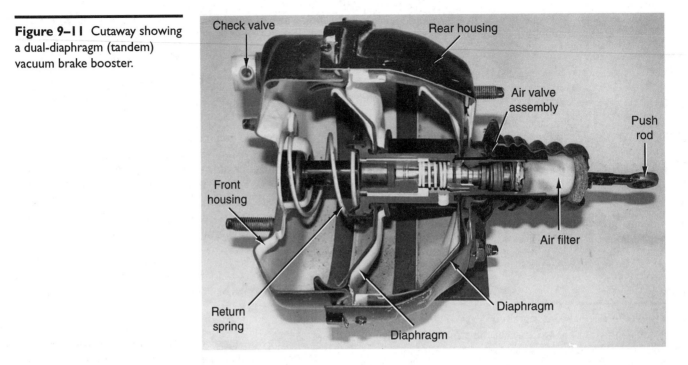

the more force can be exerted. The usual method of increasing the area of the vacuum diaphragm was to increase the diameter of the vacuum booster. However, a larger vacuum booster took up too much room under the hood of many vehicles. Instead of increasing the diameter, vacuum booster manufacturers used two smaller-diameter diaphragms and placed one in front of the other. These designs increased the total area without increasing the physical diameter of the booster. This style is called a **dual-diaphragm** or **tandem-diaphragm** vacuum booster (see Figure 9–11).

■ VACUUM BOOSTER OPERATION TEST

With the engine "off," apply the brakes several times to deplete the vacuum. With your foot on the brake pedal, start the engine. The brake pedal *should* drop. If the brake pedal does *not* drop, check for proper vacuum source to the booster. If there is proper vacuum, repair or replacement of the power booster is required.

■ VACUUM BOOSTER LEAK TEST

To test if the vacuum booster can hold a vacuum, run the engine to build up a vacuum in the booster, then turn the engine off. Wait one minute, then depress the brake pedal several times. There should be two or more power-assisted brake applications.

If applications are not power assisted, either the vacuum check valve or the booster is leaking. To test the check valve, remove the valve from the booster and

blow through the check valve. If air passes through, the valve is defective and must be replaced. If the check valve is okay, the vacuum booster is leaking and should be repaired or replaced based on the manufacturer's recommendations.

■ HYDRAULIC SYSTEM LEAK TEST

An internal or external hydraulic leak can also cause a brake system problem. To test if the hydraulic system (and not the booster) is leaking, depress and release the brake pedal (service brakes) several times. This should deplete any residual power assist. On some ABS units, this may require depressing the brake pedal twenty or more times!

After depleting the power-assist unit, depress and then hold the brake pedal depressed with medium force (20 to 35 lb. or 88 to 154 N). The brake pedal should *not* fall away. If the pedal falls, the hydraulic brake system is leaking. Check for external leakage at wheel cylinders, calipers, hydraulic lines, and hoses. If there is no external leak, there may be an internal leak inside the master cylinder. Repair or replace components as needed to correct the leakage.

■ PUSHROD CLEARANCE ADJUSTMENT

Whenever the vacuum brake booster or master cylinder is replaced, the pushrod length should be checked. The length of the pushrod must match correctly with the

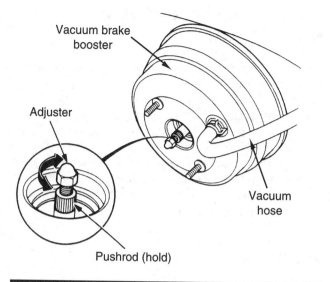

Figure 9–12 Typical adjustable pushrod. This adjustment is critical for the proper operation of the braking system. If the pushrod is too long, the brakes may be partially applied during driving. If the rod is too short, the brake pedal may have to be depressed farther down before the brakes start to work.

master cylinder (see Figure 9–12). If the pushrod is too long and the master cylinder is installed, the rod may be applying a force on the primary piston of the master cylinder even though the brake pedal is not applied. This can cause the brakes to overheat, causing the

brake fluid to boil. If the brake fluid boils, a total loss of braking force can occur. Obviously, this pushrod clearance check and adjustment is very important. A gauge is often used to measure the position of the master cylinder piston, and then the other end of the gauge is used to determine the proper pushrod clearance (see Figure 9–13).

■ VACUUM BOOSTER DISASSEMBLY AND SERVICE

Some vehicle manufacturers recommend that the vacuum brake booster be disassembled and overhauled if defective.

> **CAUTION:** Some vehicle manufacturers recommend that the vacuum brake booster be replaced as an assembly if tested to be leaking or defective. Always follow the manufacturer's recommendations.

A special holding fixture should be used before rotating (unlocking) the front and rear housing because the return spring is strong (see Figure 9–14). Disassemble the vacuum brake booster according to the manufacturer's recommended procedures for the specific unit being serviced (see Figure 9–15). A rebuilding kit is available that includes all necessary parts and the proper silicone grease. The manufacturer warns that all parts included in the kit be replaced.

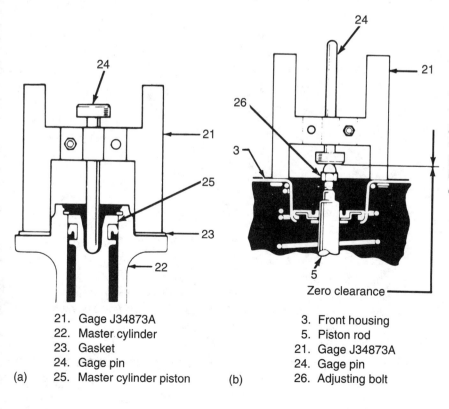

Figure 9–13 Typical vacuum brake booster pushrod gauging tool. (a) The tool is first placed against the mounting flange of the master cylinder and the depth of the piston determined. (b) The gauge is then turned upside down and used to gauge the pushrod length. Some vacuum brake boosters do not use adjustable pushrods. If found to be the incorrect length, a replacement pushrod of the correct length should be installed.

21. Gage J34873A
22. Master cylinder
23. Gasket
24. Gage pin
25. Master cylinder piston

3. Front housing
5. Piston rod
21. Gage J34873A
24. Gage pin
26. Adjusting bolt

(a)

(b)

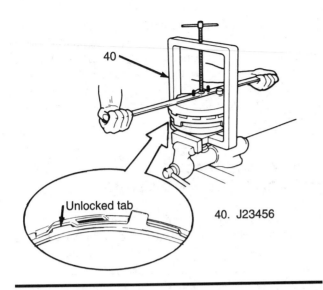

40. J23456

Figure 9–14 A holding fixture and a long tool being used to rotate the two halves of a typical vacuum brake booster. (Courtesy of General Motors)

■ POWERMASTER POWER BRAKE UNIT

The Powermaster unit is a complete, integral power brake apply system. It combines the functions of the booster (vacuum or hydraulic) and master cylinder. The Powermaster uses brake fluid as its only fluid medium and eliminates dependence on external pumps, fluids, and vacuum sources.

The Powermaster consists of an electrohydraulic (E-H) pump, fluid accumulator, pressure switch, fluid reservoir, and a hydraulic booster with an integral dual master cylinder (see Figure 9–16).

■ POWERMASTER OPERATION

The nitrogen-charged accumulator stores fluid at 510 to 685 psi (3500 to 4700 kPa) for hydraulic booster operation. The 12-volt E-H pump operates between pressure switch limits with the ignition "on." When the pressure switch senses accumulator pressure below 510 psi (3500 kPa), the E-H pump operates to increase accu-

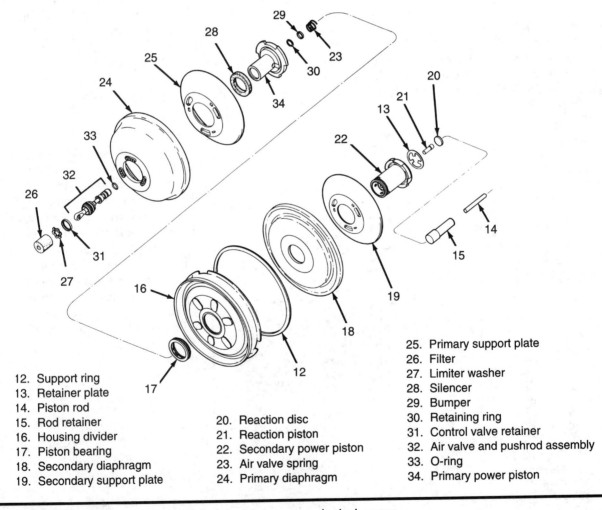

12. Support ring
13. Retainer plate
14. Piston rod
15. Rod retainer
16. Housing divider
17. Piston bearing
18. Secondary diaphragm
19. Secondary support plate

20. Reaction disc
21. Reaction piston
22. Secondary power piston
23. Air valve spring
24. Primary diaphragm

25. Primary support plate
26. Filter
27. Limiter washer
28. Silencer
29. Bumper
30. Retaining ring
31. Control valve retainer
32. Air valve and pushrod assembly
33. O-ring
34. Primary power piston

Figure 9–15 Exploded view of a typical dual diaphragm vacuum brake booster assembly. (Courtesy of General Motors)

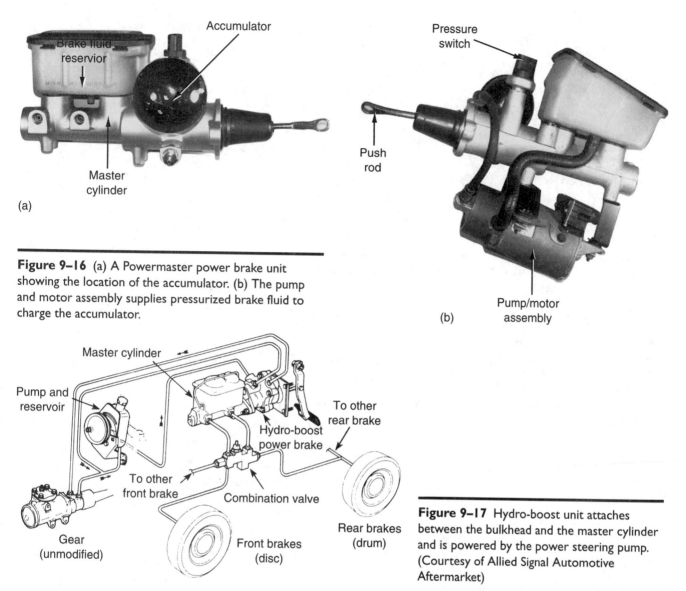

(a)

Figure 9–16 (a) A Powermaster power brake unit showing the location of the accumulator. (b) The pump and motor assembly supplies pressurized brake fluid to charge the accumulator.

(b)

Figure 9–17 Hydro-boost unit attaches between the bulkhead and the master cylinder and is powered by the power steering pump. (Courtesy of Allied Signal Automotive Aftermarket)

mulator pressure to 685 psi (4700 kPa). This is accomplished by transferring brake fluid from the pump reservoir into the accumulator, compressing the nitrogen, causing the pressure to rise. When the brake pedal is depressed, pressurized fluid from the accumulator acts on the power piston to provide assist to the master cylinder, which functions in the same manner as a conventional dual master cylinder. When the brake pedal is released, this fluid is transferred back into the pump reservoir. Additional pedal applications will reduce the pressure in the accumulator to approximately 510 psi (3500 kPa). This will again cause the E-H pump to operate to increase the accumulator pressure.

■ POWERMASTER DIAGNOSIS

The first step in the diagnostic procedure is to discharge the accumulator fully by making ten medium brake applications with the ignition "off." Inspect for fluid leakage at the brake pedal pushrod, reservoir cover, hose and pipe connections, reservoir attaching points, pres-

sure switch, and accumulator. The reservoir should be at least half full. Check for fluid leaks.

Remove the pressure switch from the Powermaster and install the pressure gauge and adapter in the pressure switch port. Reinstall the pressure switch in the test adapter. Close the bleed valve and route the tubing into the pump side of the reservoir.

Turn the ignition "on." The E-H pump should run and then shut off. (Do not allow the pump to run more than twenty seconds. Excess run time could severely damage the pump.)

■ HYDRO-BOOST HYDRAULIC BRAKE BOOSTER

Hydro-boost is a hydraulically operated power-assist unit built by Bendix. The hydro-boost system uses the pressurized hydraulic fluid from the vehicle's power steering pump as a power source rather than using engine vacuum as is used with vacuum boosters (see Figures 9–17 and 9–18).

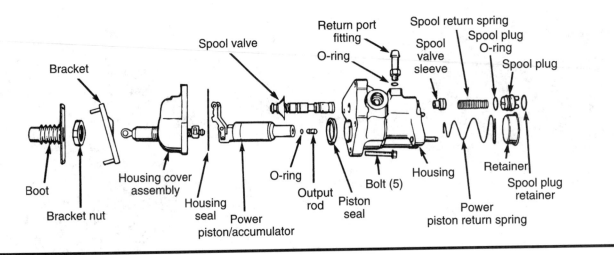

Figure 9–18 Exploded view of the hydro-boost unit. (Courtesy of Allied Signal Automotive Aftermarket)

Figure 9–19 Simplified drawing of a hydro-boost power brake unit. Note that the hydraulic pressure from the power steering pump enters the unit and goes around the primary valve assembly, then back out and goes to the steering gear.

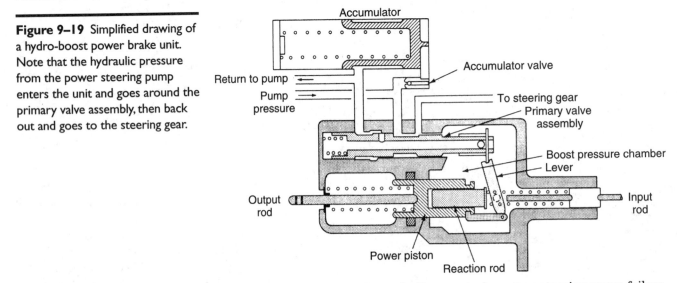

The hydro-boost unit is used on vehicles that lack enough engine vacuum, such as turbo-charged or diesel engine vehicles. During operation, diesel engines do not produce vacuum in the intake manifold. As a result, diesel engines must use accessory engine-driven vacuum pumps to operate vacuum accessories. Turbo-charged and supercharged engines do not create engine vacuum during periods of acceleration. Even though vacuum is available when the engine is decelerating, some vehicle manufacturers elect to install a hydro-boost system rather than equip the vehicle with an accessory engine-driven vacuum pump.

Operation

Fluid pressure from the power steering pump enters the unit and is directed by a spool valve (see Figures 9–19 and 9–20). When the brake pedal is depressed, the lever and primary valve are moved. The valve closes off the return port, causing pressure to build in the boost pressure chamber. The hydraulic pressure pushes on the power piston, which then applies force to the output rod that connects to the master cylinder

piston. In the event of a power steering pump failure, power assist is still available for several brake applications. During operation, hydraulic fluid under pressure from the power steering pump pressurizes an accumulator. While some units use a spring inside the accumulator, most hydro-boost units use nitrogen gas. The fluid trapped in the accumulator under pressure is used to provide power-assisted stops in the event of a hydraulic system failure.

Diagnosis

The power source for hydro-boost units comes from the power steering pump. The first step of troubleshooting is to perform a thorough visual inspection, including:

1. Checking for proper power steering fluid level
2. Checking for leaks from the unit or power steering pump
3. Checking the condition and tightness of the power steering drive belt
4. Checking for proper operation of the base brake system

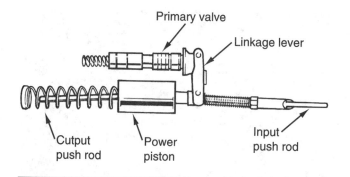

Figure 9–20 Operating linkages and levers used on a hydro-boost unit.

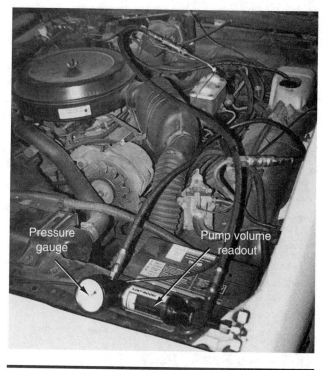

After checking all of the visual components, check for proper pressure and volume from the power steering pump using a power steering pump tester as shown in Figures 9–21 and 9–22. The pump should be capable of producing a minimum of 2 gallons (7.5 liters) with a maximum pressure of 150 psi (1000 kPa) with the steering in the straight-ahead position. With the engine "off," the accumulator should be able to supply a minimum of two power-assisted brake applications.

Figure 9–22 Power steering pump/gear tester being used on a hydro-boost power brake unit.

■ HYDRO-BOOST FUNCTION TEST

With the engine off, apply the brake pedal several times until the accumulator is depleted completely. Depress the service brake pedal and start the engine. The pedal should fall and then push back against the driver's foot.

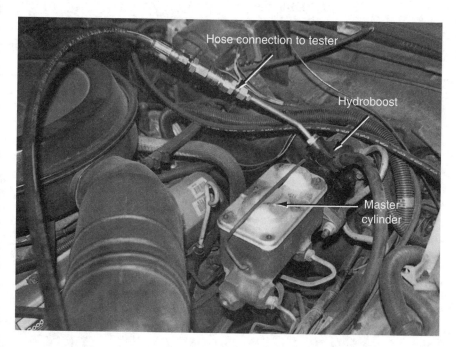

Figure 9–21 Typical hydro-boost assembly being tested.

TECH TIP ✔

The Hydro-Boost Accumulator Test

The accumulator stores hydraulic fluid under pressure to provide a reserve in the event of a failure of the power steering system. The accumulator is designed to provide three or more power-assisted stops with the engine off. See Figure 9–23. If the accumulator fails, it does not hold pressure. To easily check whether the accumulator has lost its charge, simply grasp the accumulator with your hand and try to twist or move it. The accumulator should have so much pressure on it that it should not move or wiggle. If the accumulator moves, it has lost its ability to hold pressure and the hydro-boost unit should be replaced.

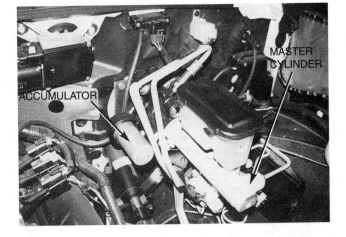

Figure 9–23 The accumulator should be able to hold pressure and feel tight when hand force is used to try to move it.

■ HYDRO-BOOST TROUBLESHOOTING GUIDE

Excessive Brake Pedal Effort

Possible causes:

1. Loose or broken power steering pump belt
2. No fluid in the power steering reservoir
3. Leaks in the power steering, booster, or accumulator hoses
4. Leaks at tube fittings, power steering, booster, or accumulator connections
5. External leakage at the accumulator
6. Faulty booster piston seal, causing leakage at the booster flange vent
7. Faulty booster cover seal with leakage between housing and cover
8. Faulty booster spool plug seal

Slow Brake Pedal Return

Possible causes:

1. Excessive seal friction in the booster
2. Faulty spool action

3. Broken piston return spring
4. Restriction in the return line from the booster to the pump reservoir
5. Broken spool return spring

Grabby Brakes

Possible causes:

1. Broken spool return spring
2. Faulty spool action caused by contamination in the system

Booster Chatters— Pedal Vibrates

Possible causes:

1. Power steering pump belt slipping
2. Low fluid level in the power steering pump reservoir
3. Faulty spool operation caused by contamination in the system

PHOTO SEQUENCE   *Checking a Vacuum Power Brake Booster*

PS9–1 Start the diagnosis of the vacuum power brake booster by performing a thorough visual inspection. Check the condition of the hose. Carefully check the hose at the end where it attaches to the intake manifold of the engine. Engine heat can damage rubber hose.

PS9–2 Carefully inspect the check valve for damage. The check valve prevents the loss of vacuum from the booster when the engine is off.

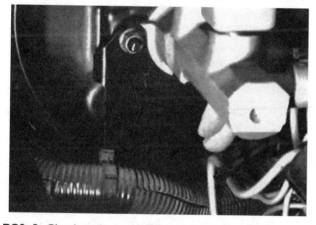

PS9–3 Check under the master cylinder for signs of brake fluid leakage that could get into and damage the rubber parts of the booster assembly.

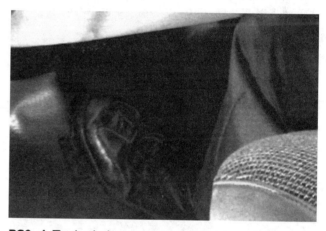

PS9–4 To check the operation of the vacuum power brake booster, depress the brake pedal four or more times until all of the vacuum has been released from the booster and the brake pedal feels hard.

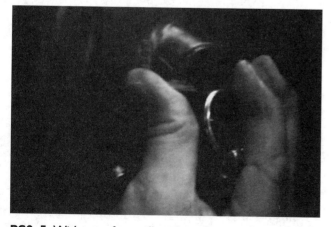

PS9–5 With your foot still applying force to the brake pedal, start the engine.

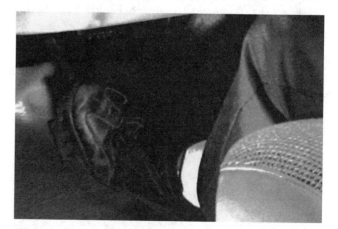

PS9–6 The brake pedal should drop if the vacuum booster is functioning correctly.

■ SUMMARY

1. Vacuum brake boosters use air pressure acting on a diaphragm to assist the driver's force on the brake master cylinder.

2. At rest, there is vacuum on both sides of the vacuum booster diaphragm. When the brake pedal is depressed, atmospheric air pressure is exerted on the back side of the diaphragm.

3. The use of two diaphragms in tandem allows a smaller-diameter booster with the same area. The larger the area of the booster diaphragm, the more air pressure force can be applied to the master cylinder.

4. Hydraulic-operated brake boosters use either an electric motor–driven pump or the engine-driven power steering pump.

5. When replacing a vacuum brake booster, always check for proper pushrod clearance.

6. To be assured of power-assisted brake application in the event of failure, hydraulic power-assisted brake systems use an accumulator to provide pressure to the system.

■ REVIEW QUESTIONS

1. Describe the purpose and function of the one-way check valve used on vacuum brake booster units.

2. Explain how vacuum is used to assist in applying the brakes.

3. Describe how to perform a vacuum booster leak test and hydraulic system leak test.

4. Explain how a hydro-boost system functions.

■ ASE CERTIFICATION-TYPE QUESTIONS

1. Two technicians are discussing vacuum brake boosters. Technician A says that a low, soft brake pedal is an indication of a defective booster. Technician B says that there should be at least two power-assisted brake applications after the engine stops running. Which technician is correct?
   a. Technician A only
   b. Technician B only
   c. Both Technician A and B
   d. Neither Technician A nor B

2. Technician A says that to check the operation of a vacuum brake booster, the brake pedal should be depressed until the assist is depleted and then start the engine. Technician B says that the brake pedal should drop when the engine starts, if the booster is okay. Which technician is correct?
   a. Technician A only
   b. Technician B only

   c. Both Technician A and B
   d. Neither Technician A nor B

3. Brake pedal feedback to the driver is provided by the
   a. Vacuum check-valve operation
   b. Reaction system
   c. Charcoal filter unit
   d. Vacuum diaphragm

4. The proper operation of a vacuum brake booster requires that the engine be capable of supplying at least
   a. 15 in. Hg vacuum
   b. 17 in. Hg vacuum
   c. 19 in. Hg vacuum
   d. 21 in. Hg vacuum

5. The purpose of the charcoal filter in the vacuum hose between the engine and the vacuum brake booster is to
   a. Filter the air entering the engine
   b. Trap gasoline vapors to keep them from entering the booster
   c. Act as a one-way check valve to help keep a vacuum reserve in the booster
   d. Direct the vacuum

6. A defective vacuum brake booster will cause a
   a. Hard brake pedal
   b. Soft (spongy) brake pedal
   c. Low brake pedal
   d. Slight hiss noise when the brake pedal is depressed

7. An accumulator such as that used on electric or hydraulic brake boosters
   a. Reduces brake pedal noise
   b. Provides higher force being fed back to the driver's foot
   c. Provides a reserve in the event of a failure
   d. Works against engine vacuum

8. The first step in diagnosing a hydro-boost problem is
   a. A pressure test of the pump
   b. A volume test of the pump
   c. To tighten the power steering drive belt
   d. A thorough visual inspection

9. A brake pedal feels spongy when depressed. Technician A says that a defective hydraulic brake booster could be the cause. Technician B says that a defective vacuum brake booster could be the cause. Which technician is correct?
   a. Technician A only
   b. Technician B only
   c. Both Technician A and B
   d. Neither Technician A nor B

10. If the engine stops running, the hydro-boost will not be able to provide any power assist for the brakes.
    a. True
    b. False

ABS Components and Operation

Objectives: After studying Chapter 10, the reader should be able to:

1. Explain the reason for ABS.
2. Describe the purpose and function of the ABS components, such as wheel speed sensors, electrohydraulic unit, and electronic controller.
3. Discuss how the ABS components control wheel slippage.
4. Explain how the ABS components control acceleration traction control.

Antilock braking systems help prevent the wheels from locking during sudden braking, especially on slippery surfaces. This helps the driver maintain control.

■ THEORY OF OPERATION

When the wheels stop turning during a stop, the friction (traction) between the road surface and the tires decreases by almost 40 percent. At the surface of the road, a locked tire creates heat that generally softens the rubber of the tire. The tread rubber becomes almost liquid and loses its traction grip on the road surface.

A total loss of traction, called *100 percent slip*, occurs when the tire is sliding across the road surface with the wheels locked (see Figure 10–1). Maximum traction occurs when the slip is controlled to between 10 and 20 percent (see Figure 10–2). This is accomplished by

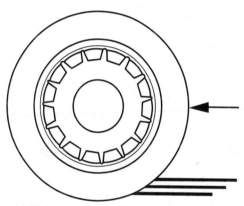

Vehicle moving-tire not rotating—100% slip

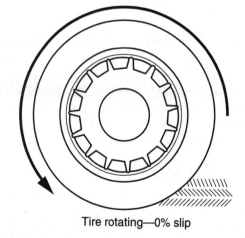

Tire rotating—0% slip

Figure 10–1 Maximum braking traction occurs when tire slip is between 10 and 20 percent. A rotating tire has 0 percent slip and a locked-up wheel has 100 percent slip.

Figure 10–2 Typical stop on a slippery road surface without antilock brakes. Notice that the wheels stopped rotating and skidded until the vehicle finally came to a stop.

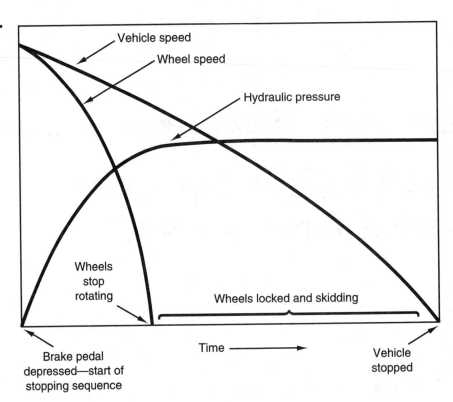

using electronic and hydraulic controls to monitor wheel slip and pulse the brakes on and off just the right amount to achieve maximum possible traction without wheel lockup. A typical ABS vehicle pulses the brakes on and off between ten and twenty times per second. This is much faster than drivers are capable of doing.

■ STEERING CONTROL

When a front tire loses traction, the vehicle cannot be steered. Steering a vehicle requires that the tires have traction, and a locked wheel has little or no traction with the road. As a result, the vehicle will continue traveling in a straight line even though the front wheels are being turned by the driver (see Figure 10–3).

■ SKID CONTROL

A vehicle can easily get into a skid if one or both *rear* wheels lock before the front wheels. If the rear wheels lock, the rear of the vehicle has less traction with the road surface than the front wheels. As a result, the rear of the vehicle wants to move faster than the front and this results in the rear end of the vehicle skidding around. Left uncontrolled, the skid results in the vehicle turning around and around, completely out of control. A vehicle equipped with ABS can still get into a skid;

Figure 10–3 Being able to steer and control the vehicle during rapid braking is one major advantage of an antilock braking system.

therefore, the term *skid control* is no longer used when describing antilock braking systems. ABS systems can prevent wheel lockup but cannot prevent the vehicle from skidding (see Figures 10–4 and 10–5).

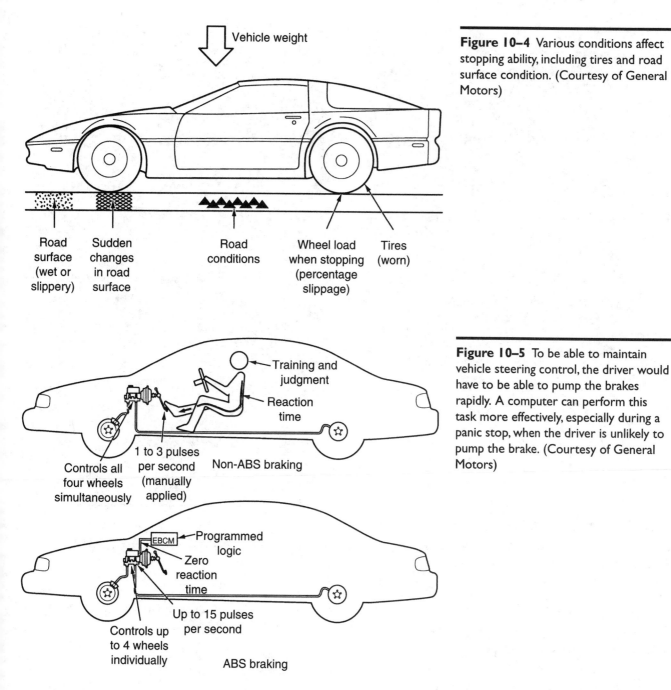

Figure 10–4 Various conditions affect stopping ability, including tires and road surface condition. (Courtesy of General Motors)

Figure 10–5 To be able to maintain vehicle steering control, the driver would have to be able to pump the brakes rapidly. A computer can perform this task more effectively, especially during a panic stop, when the driver is unlikely to pump the brake. (Courtesy of General Motors)

■ BRAKING DISTANCES

A vehicle equipped with ABS may or may not be able to stop in a shorter distance. It is the ability to *control* the vehicle during braking that ABS ensures. In deep snow, a vehicle with locked wheels may be able to stop a little sooner than a similar vehicle equipped with ABS. A locked wheel tends to act like a snow plow, building up a wedge of snow in front of the wheels. It is this snow wedge that helps stop a non-ABS vehicle. The same thing happens in loose sand or gravel (see Figure 10–6).

Rough roads present a stopping challenge for both ABS- and non-ABS-equipped vehicles. The advantage in stopping distance is usually without ABS. ABS systems

prevent wheel lockup; therefore, if a tire leaves the ground with the brake applied, the wheel would normally stop turning (lock) because it has no traction. With the wheel *unlocked*, the vehicle feels as if it is speeding up when the tire hits the road again because it is free to rotate without resistance.

NOTE: It is this "freewheeling" feeling that is very disturbing to some drivers new to the operating characteristics of ABS. Often, the service technician is asked to check the operation of the braking system because of customer experience on rough roads.

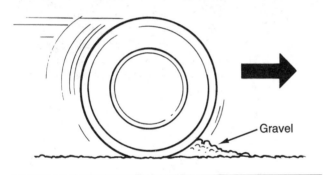

Figure 10–6 Sometimes a vehicle can stop in a shorter distance in loose gravel or deep snow without ABS because of the wedge of material that builds in front of the tires.

■ PURPOSE AND FUNCTION OF ABS COMPONENTS

All ABS systems use three basic subsystems:

1. **Wheel speed sensors.** These electromagnetic sensors produce a speed signal for the electronic controller (see Figure 10–7).
2. **Electronic control unit.** This is the brain, computer, or controller of any ABS unit. The controller receives wheel speed information from the wheels and controls the hydraulic control unit if one or more wheels are slowing down at a faster rate than the other wheels. The electronic control unit is also called a **controller antilock brake (CAB)** or **electronic brake control module (EBCM).**
3. **Electromechanical hydraulic unit.** This unit does the actual work of controlling brake line pressures to keep the wheels from locking during a stop (see Figures 10–8 and 10–9).

■ ABS HYDRAULIC OPERATION

All ABS units use solenoid valves or rotary valves to control the brake fluid pressure at the wheels. Three stages of ABS operation are controlled by the hydraulic control unit.

Pressure Buildup (Normal Braking)

The hydraulic system functions the same as any other hydraulic braking system. The driver has complete control of the pressure applied to the wheel cylinders and calipers. The inlet valve (solenoid) is open and the outlet valve (solenoid) is closed. When greater braking force is required, the driver simply depresses the brake pedal farther down, which increases hydraulic pressure buildup in the master cylinder and in all wheel cylinders and calipers. This greater pressure exerts more force on the friction shoes or pads against the brake drum or rotor, and the wheels slow and stop. When pressure is released from the brake pedal, the hydraulic pressure in the braking system decreases to zero and the brakes release. The hydraulic pressure control is *not* controlled by the hydraulic unit except for the rear brakes on the Teves Mark II system (see Chapter 11 for details on each

(a)   (b)

Figure 10–7 (a) A steering knuckle with a hub/bearing assembly. (b) When the hub/bearing is unbolted from the knuckle, the tone wheel for the ABS wheel speed sensor is visible.

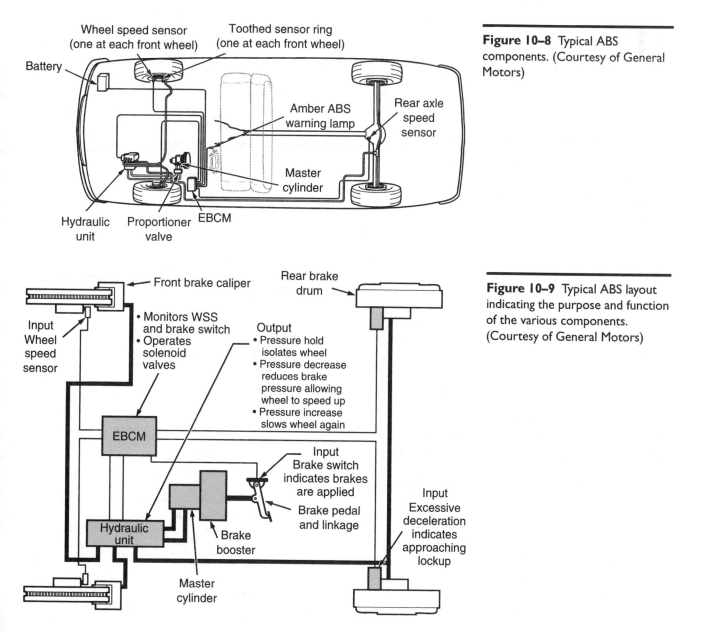

Figure 10–8 Typical ABS components. (Courtesy of General Motors)

Figure 10–9 Typical ABS layout indicating the purpose and function of the various components. (Courtesy of General Motors)

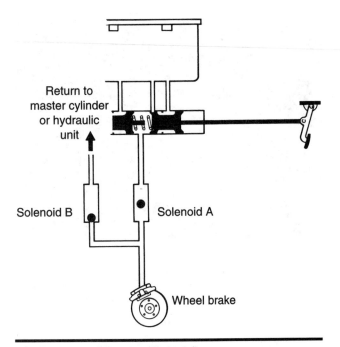

Figure 10–10 In a typical antilock braking system, the flow of brake fluid is controlled by valves or solenoids. During normal braking, solenoid A is open, allowing normal pressure building to occur from the master cylinder during a normal non-ABS stop. Solenoid B is closed to maintain master cylinder pressure at the wheel brake.

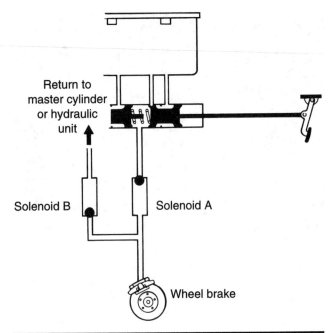

Figure 10–11 If a wheel is starting to slow too fast, the ABS controller will command that solenoid A block off the master cylinder from the wheel brake. This prevents the driver from exerting additional pressure to the wheel brake. This stage is called **pressure holding.** This solenoid is called the *inlet* or *isolating* solenoid because it is used to control the movement of brake fluid to the wheel brake and, if closed, isolate any pressure from the wheel brake.

system). This stage is also called **pressure increase** stage (see Figure 10–10).

> **NOTE:** Antilock braking systems cannot increase brake fluid pressure higher than the applied pressure by the driver.

Pressure Holding

Pressure holding means that the ABS controller has detected rapid slowing of a wheel during braking. To help prevent the wheel from locking, the controller commands that the inlet valve or solenoid be closed between the master cylinder and the wheel brake drum or caliper (see Figure 10–11).

By closing off the passage from the master cylinder, the pressure to the brake is held at the present level. Even if the driver pushes down farther on the brake pedal, the increase in pressure at the master cylinder is blocked. If the controller senses that the wheel is no longer in danger of locking up, the valve is opened to the master cylinder. This is called the **pressure holding stage.**

Pressure Reduction

The ABS controller can reduce hydraulic pressure on the wheel cylinder or caliper by opening the outlet valve

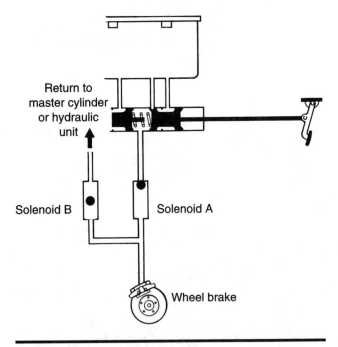

Figure 10–12 If a wheel is still slowing too fast and is about to lock up, solenoid B is opened, allowing the trapped pressurized brake fluid at the wheel brake to escape. This stage is called **pressure reduction** (release). The pressure reduction is also called **pressure decay,** or **pressure dump.**

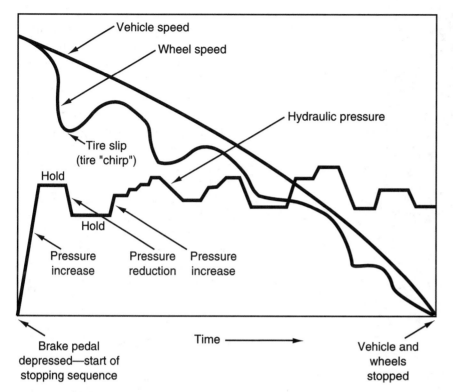

or solenoid and allowing the pressurized brake fluid to escape into a low-pressure area of the system. When this occurs, the pressure is reduced and is called the **pressure reduction, pressure decay,** or **pressure dump stage** (see Figure 10–12). See Figure 10–13 for a graph showing vehicle speed, wheel speed, and hydraulic pressure during a typical ABS stop.

The hydraulic pump delivers brake fluid to the master cylinder to decrease fluid pressure in the caliper. The accumulators (reservoir) temporarily store brake fluid returning from the calipers, as required in order to provide a smooth pressure decrease in the caliper (see Figure 10–14).

■ BRAKE PEDAL FEEDBACK

Many ABS units force brake fluid back into the master cylinder under pressure during an ABS stop. This pulsing brake fluid return causes the brake pedal to pulsate. Some vehicle manufacturers use the pulsation of the brake pedal to inform the driver that the wheels are tending toward lockup and that the ABS is pulsing the brakes.

NOTE: A pulsating brake pedal may be normal only during an ABS stop. It is not normal for a vehicle with ABS to have a pulsating pedal during normal braking. If the brake pedal is pulsating during a non-ABS stop, the brake drums or rotor may be warped (see Chapter 8 for details).

Figure 10–14 The brake fluid return pump sends brake fluid back to the reservoir during the pressure release stage (mode). (Courtesy of General Motors)

Some manufacturers use an isolation valve that prevents brake pedal pulsation even during an ABS stop.

T E C H T I P ✔

KISS

KISS means "Keep It Stock, Stupid" and it is important to remember when replacing tires. Vehicles equipped with antilock brakes are "programmed" to pulse the brakes at just the right rate for maximum braking effectiveness. A larger tire rotates at a slower speed and a smaller-than-normal tire rotates at a faster speed. Therefore, tire size affects the speed and rate of change in speed of the wheels as measured by the wheel speed sensors.

Although changing tire size will not prevent ABS operation, it will cause less effective braking during hard braking with the ABS activated. Using the smaller spare tire can create such a difference in wheel speed compared with the other wheels that a false wheel speed sensor code may be set and an amber ABS warning lamp on the dash may light. However, most systems will still function with the spare tire installed, but the braking performance will not be as effective. For best overall performance, always replace tires with the same size and type as specified by the vehicle manufacturer.

■ BRAKE PEDAL TRAVEL SWITCH (SENSOR)

Some ABS systems, such as the Teves Mark IV system, use a brake pedal travel switch (sensor). The purpose of the switch is to turn on the hydraulic pump when the brake pedal has been depressed 40 percent of its travel. The pump runs and pumps brake fluid back into the master cylinder, which raises the brake pedal until the switch closes again, turning off the pump.

NOTE: Some early antilock braking systems did not use a brake switch. The problem occurred when the ABS could be activated while driving over rough roads. The brake switch can be the same as the brake light switch or a separate switch.

The brake pedal switch is an input for the electronic controller. When the brakes are applied, the electronic controller "gets ready" to act if ABS needs to "initialize" the starting sequence of events.

CAUTION: If the driver pumps the brakes during an ABS event, the controller will reset and reinitialization starts over again. This resetting process can disrupt normal ABS operation. The driver need only depress and hold down the brake pedal during a stop for best operation.

■ WHEEL SPEED SENSORS

Wheel speed sensors are small electromagnetic generators. Wheel speed sensors are often abbreviated WSS. A toothed wheel is called a **tone ring, toothed ring,** or **reluctor** (see Figures 10–15 through 10–21 on pages 248–250).

The speed sensor contains a coil of wire surrounding a permanent magnet. As each tooth passes by the magnet, the magnetic field around the coil is increased. Then as the tooth moves away, the magnetic field strength weakens. It is this changing magnetic field strength that produces a changing voltage (electrical pressure) in the coil of wire surrounding the magnet. This rapidly changing voltage signal is sent to the electronic controller. The electronic controller uses the frequency of the high and low voltages as a measure of the wheel speed. Frequency means the number of times the voltage changes per second and is measured in hertz. One hertz (Hz) is one cycle

Figure 10–15 Typical toothed sensor ring (on the front wheel of a front-wheel-drive vehicle).

Toothed sensor ring

CV joint boot

Drive axle shaft

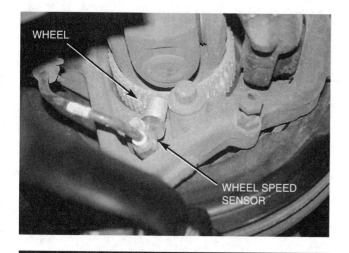

Figure 10–16 The wheel speed sensor and wiring are exposed on the front wheels of this four-wheel-drive vehicle. Road debris could damage the wiring or nick the tone wheel, especially if the vehicle is used off road.

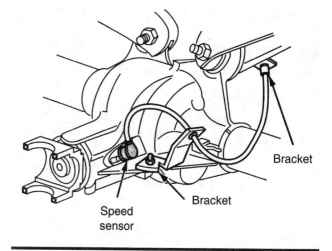

Figure 10–17 Many rear-wheel-drive vehicles use just one speed sensor at the differential to measure the speed of both rear wheels. (Courtesy of General Motors)

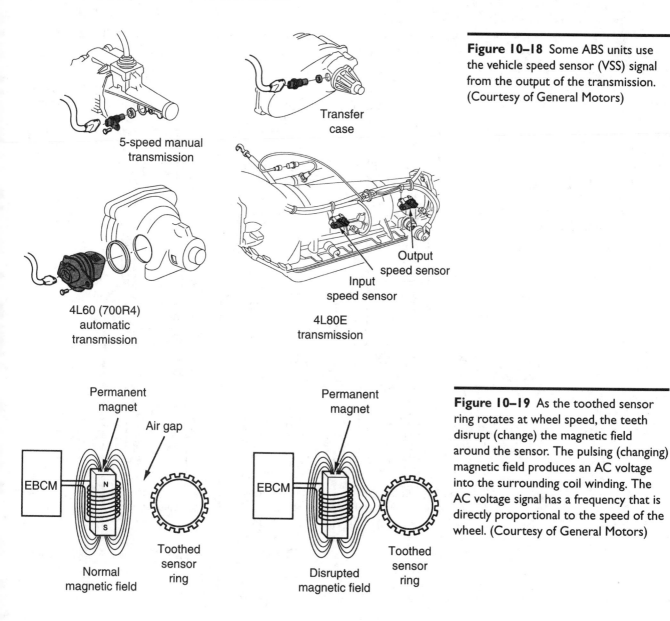

5-speed manual transmission

Transfer case

4L60 (700R4) automatic transmission

4L80E transmission

Input speed sensor

Output speed sensor

Figure 10–18 Some ABS units use the vehicle speed sensor (VSS) signal from the output of the transmission. (Courtesy of General Motors)

Permanent magnet

Air gap

EBCM

Normal magnetic field

Toothed sensor ring

Permanent magnet

EBCM

Disrupted magnetic field

Toothed sensor ring

Figure 10–19 As the toothed sensor ring rotates at wheel speed, the teeth disrupt (change) the magnetic field around the sensor. The pulsing (changing) magnetic field produces an AC voltage into the surrounding coil winding. The AC voltage signal has a frequency that is directly proportional to the speed of the wheel. (Courtesy of General Motors)

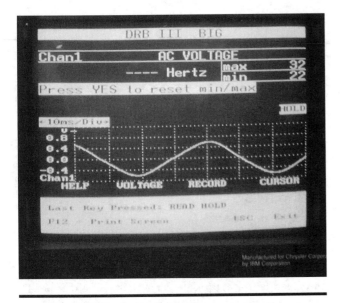

Figure 10–20 The wheel speed sensor generates a varying voltage as the wheel revolves. As the speed of the wheel increases, the voltage and the frequency (number of voltage cycles per second) also increase. This wheel speed sensor scope pattern was produced by simply rotating the tire by hand.

Figure 10–21 Wiring diagram (schematic) of a typical ABS wheel speed sensor circuit. Notice that all wiring is electrically shielded to prevent interference, such as from high-voltage spark plug wires, from affecting the wheel speed sensor signal to the electronic brake control module (EBCM). (Courtesy of General Motors)

per second. The electronic controller looks at the frequency of all wheel speed sensors and activates the antilock control if one or more sensors indicate that a wheel is slowing down a lot faster than the other wheel sensors.

■ LATERAL ACCELERATION SENSOR

Some ABS-equipped vehicles include a lateral acceleration sensor or switch that measures the vehicle's cornering force (see Figure 10–22). The signal is sent from the lateral acceleration sensor to the electronic brake control module (EBCM) to modify its control logic, accounting for hard cornering conditions.

■ ELECTRONIC CONTROLLER OPERATION

The electronic controller is the computer in the system that controls all parts of ABS operation, including:

1. **A self-test.** The controller runs a self-test of all its components every time the ignition is turned on.

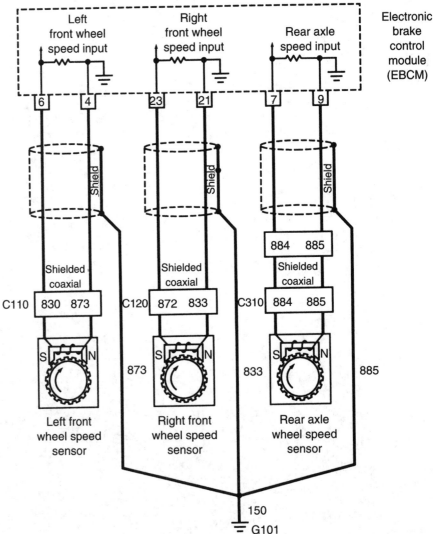

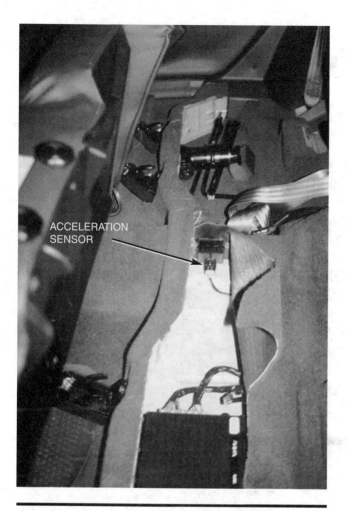

ACCELERATION
SENSOR

Figure 10–22 The acceleration sensor is located under the back seat of this Jeep. This sensor signals the antilock controller (computer) how rapidly the vehicle is decelerating.

NOTE: Since an antilock braking system is a safety-related system, if it malfunctions, people can be injured. This is one reason why the system does a complete "system check" every time the ignition is cycled (See Figure 10–23).

---

2. **The wheel hydraulic controls.** The controller looks at the rate of wheel deceleration and compares it with normal stopping rates using an internal computer program that is based on vehicle weight, tire size, etc. If a wheel is slowing down too fast, the controller activates the necessary hydraulic pressure controls (see Figures 10–24 through 10–27 on pages 252–253).

■ REAR-WHEEL ANTILOCK SYSTEMS

Antilock brakes are especially important for use on the rear wheels. Starting in the late 1960s and early 1970s, antilock braking systems were designed to pulsate the

rear brake only. Rear-wheel antilock systems are commonly used on pickup trucks, sport utility vehicles (SUVs), and vans (see Figure 10–28 on page 254). Rear-wheel antilock systems may be abbreviated:

RWAL: rear-wheel antilock
RABS: rear antilock braking system

Rear-wheel antilock systems will hold or decrease hydraulic pressure to both rear-wheel brakes if either wheel starts to lock up. In other words, both rear wheels are handled as one and it does not matter to the electronic controller which wheel brake is about to lock. This simplified system is lower cost, yet effective.

Empty pickup trucks tend to lock up the rear brake during rapid stops easier than most passenger vehicles because the lack of weight over the rear wheels limits the tires' traction with the road. Heavily loaded trucks have less tendency to suffer from rear wheel lockup during braking because the cargo adds weight to the rear of the vehicle that increases the force of the rear tires on the road. Rear-wheel antilock braking systems are also called one-channel systems because the hydraulic controls just one hydraulic circuit to both rear wheels.

■ THREE-CHANNEL SYSTEMS

Most rear-wheel-drive and many front-wheel-drive vehicles use a three-channel antilock braking system (see Figure 10–29 on page 254). Each front-wheel brake is controlled separately and both rear brakes are controlled together.

■ FOUR-CHANNEL SYSTEMS

Four-channel antilock braking systems control all four wheel brakes individually. This is the most expensive type of system and requires that each wheel have a wheel speed sensor (WSS) (see Figure 10–30 on page 254).

■ INTEGRAL ANTILOCK BRAKING SYSTEMS

Integral ABS means that the hydraulic control unit includes:

- A master cylinder with reservoir
- A hydraulic brake booster
- A brake pressure pump and motor
- A pressure accumulator
- Pressure-monitoring switches
- Brake pressure modulator valves
- A brake fluid level sensor

Because the system functions as a brake booster as well as an antilock braking unit, the hydraulic pump can

Figure 10–23 Typical inputs and outputs of an ABS computer.

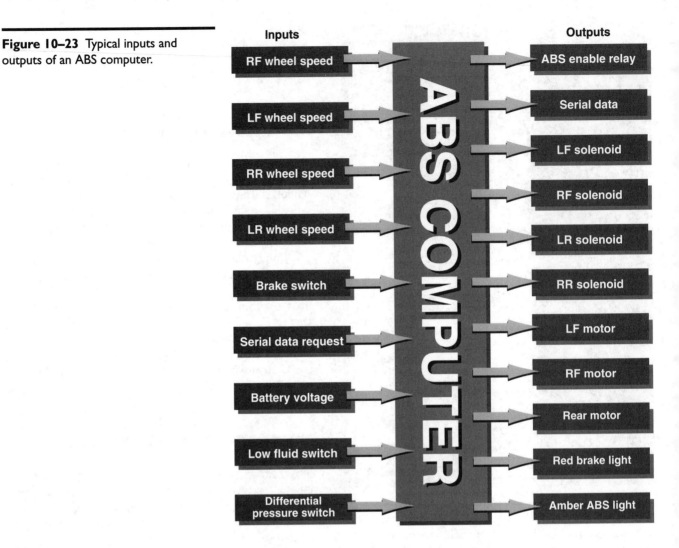

Inputs

- RF wheel speed
- LF wheel speed
- RR wheel speed
- LR wheel speed
- Brake switch
- Serial data request
- Battery voltage
- Low fluid switch
- Differential pressure switch

ABS COMPUTER

Outputs

- ABS enable relay
- Serial data
- LF solenoid
- RF solenoid
- LR solenoid
- RR solenoid
- LF motor
- RF motor
- Rear motor
- Red brake light
- Amber ABS light

Figure 10–24 An overvoltage protection relay is often used to power electronic brake control modules. The purpose of the relay is to supply electrical power to the controller and protect the electronics inside from damage if a high-voltage surge were to occur in the vehicle's electrical system. (Courtesy of General Motors)

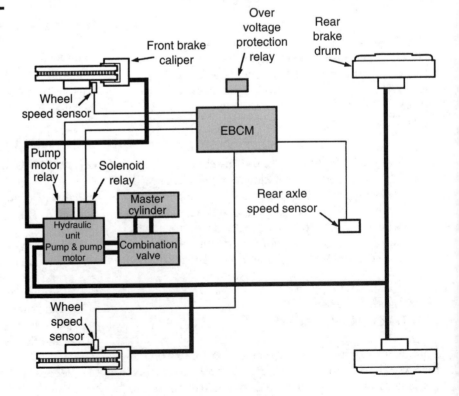

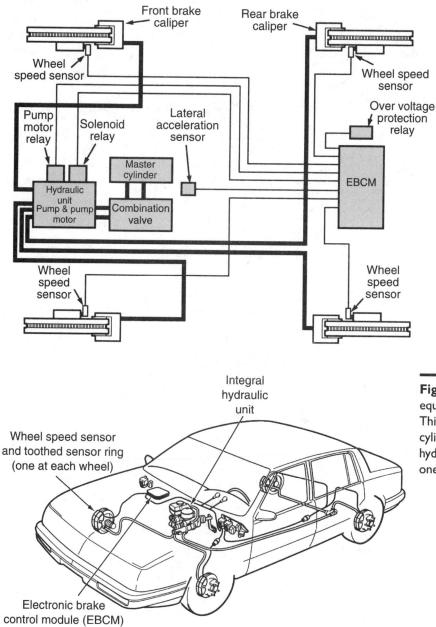

Front brake caliper

Rear brake caliper

Wheel speed sensor

Wheel speed sensor

Over voltage protection relay

Pump motor relay

Solenoid relay

Lateral acceleration sensor

Master cylinder

Hydraulic unit Pump & pump motor

Combination valve

EBCM

Wheel speed sensor

Wheel speed sensor

Figure 10–25 ABS layout for a vehicle with four-wheel disc brakes. Notice that each wheel has a wheel speed sensor. The EBCM is protected by an over-voltage protection relay and the vehicle has a lateral acceleration sensor to signal the controller when the vehicle is cornering. (Courtesy of General Motors)

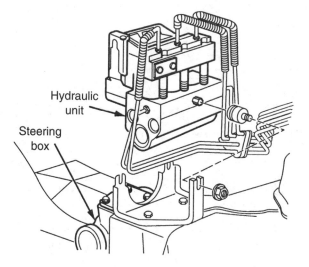

Integral hydraulic unit

Wheel speed sensor and toothed sensor ring (one at each wheel)

Electronic brake control module (EBCM)

Figure 10–26 A Teves Mark II ABS is equipped with four-wheel speed sensors. This integral-type ABS combines the master cylinder, hydraulic booster, and ABS hydraulic-control solenoids and valves in one unit. (Courtesy of General Motors)

Hydraulic unit

Steering box

Figure 10–27 This Bosch ABS hydraulic unit is remotely mounted under the hood near the master cylinder. (Courtesy of General Motors)

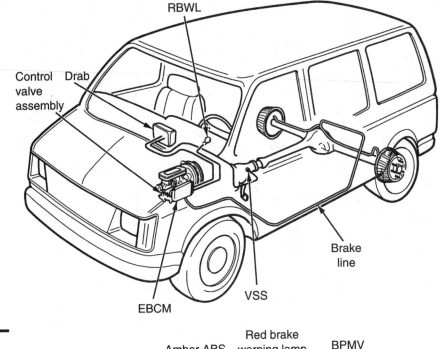

Figure 10–28 Typical Kelsey-Hayes rear-wheel antilock (rear ABS) unit that uses the vehicle speed sensor for speed information and controls both rear wheels together if one or both tend to slow too rapidly during a stop. (Courtesy of General Motors)

RBWL

Control valve assembly Drab

Brake line

VSS

EBCM

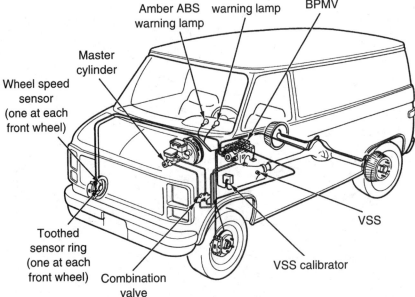

Figure 10–29 Typical Kelsey-Hayes four-wheel antilock (4WAL) ABS is a three-channel system that controls each front wheel individually but both rear wheels together. The BPMV is the brake pressure modulator valve, also referred to as the EHCU (electrohydraulic control unit). The VSS calibration can be changed if different size tires are used on the vehicle. This helps ensure maximum ABS effectiveness and correct vehicle speed being registered on the speedometer/odometer. (Courtesy of General Motors)

Amber ABS warning lamp

Red brake warning lamp

BPMV

Master cylinder

Wheel speed sensor (one at each front wheel)

VSS

Toothed sensor ring (one at each front wheel)

Combination valve

VSS calibrator

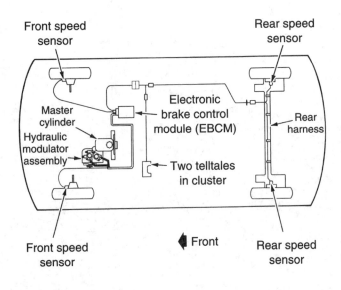

Figure 10–30 Delphi (Delco) ABS VI. This system uses high-speed bidirectional motors to reduce, hold, and apply hydraulic pressure. This is a three-channel system that controls each front wheel individually, but both rear wheels brake together even though each rear wheel has its own wheel speed sensor.

Front speed sensor

Rear speed sensor

Master cylinder

Electronic brake control module (EBCM)

Rear harness

Hydraulic modulator assembly

Two telltales in cluster

Front speed sensor

Front

Rear speed sensor

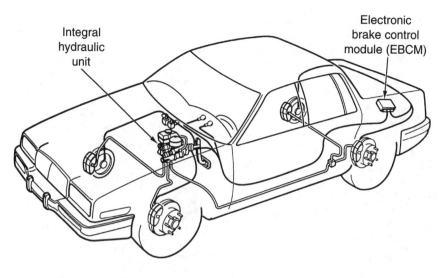

Integral
hydraulic
unit

Electronic
brake control
module (EBCM)

Figure 10–31 Typical integral ABS.
(Courtesy of General Motors)

run even in normal braking applications. If the pump fails, there will be no rear brakes and the brake pedal will be hard because of a lack of power assist (see Figures 10–31 and 10–32).

Integral ABS units are usually serviced as complete units as an assembly. The operation of each unit varies with individual vehicle and year. All integral systems are used on front-wheel-drive vehicles because if the rear brakes are lost, it is not as severe as with a rear-wheel-drive vehicle. On a front-wheel-drive vehicle, only about 20 percent of the braking force occurs on rear brakes. Teves Mark II and Delco Moraine III (Powermaster III) are examples of integral systems.

> **NOTE:** All ABS units use DOT 3 brake fluid. The brake fluid cools and lubricates all hydraulic parts.

■ NONINTEGRAL (REMOTE) ABS

Nonintegral systems are added to a base brake system and are often called "remote" or "add-on" ABS (see Figure 10–33). Their only function is to provide antilock braking. These systems use a hydraulic system that is remote (removed) from the master cylinder. The ABS hydraulic unit is added in series with the hydraulic brake lines. Some nonintegral systems use a hydraulic pump for fluid circulation. Bosch 2U/2S, Kelsey-Hayes RWAL/RABS, Kelsey-Hayes 4WAL, Teves Mark IV and 20, and Delphi VI are examples of nonintegral (remote) types of ABS.

■ TRACTION CONTROL

Antilock braking systems can often be used to limit wheel spin during acceleration. In a conventional

antilock braking system, the wheels are kept from locking (stopping) when the electronic controller senses one or more wheels slowing too rapidly. With traction control (TC), the electronic controller applies hydraulic pressure to the wheel brakes on the drive wheels if the wheels start to spin or slip during acceleration. This slipping during acceleration is referred to as positive slip. If the driving wheels are slipping, the vehicle will not move. If the vehicle is front-wheel drive, steering is impaired when the front wheels are spinning on slippery surfaces. Best acceleration is achieved when positive wheel slip is controlled to about 10 percent.

Low-speed traction control uses the braking system to limit positive slip up to a vehicle speed of about 30

Frequently Asked Question   ???

I Thought Traction Control Meant Additional Drive Wheels Were Engaged

When the term *traction control* is used, many people think of four-wheel-drive or all-wheel-drive vehicles and power trains. Instead of sending engine torque to other drive wheels, it is the purpose and function of the traction control system to prevent the drive wheel(s) from slipping during acceleration. A slipping tire has less traction than a non-slipping tire—therefore, if the tire can be kept from slipping (spinning), more traction will be available to propel the vehicle. Traction control works with the engine computer to reduce torque delivery from the engine as well as the ABS controller to apply the brakes to the spinning wheel if necessary to regain traction.

Figure 10–32 Integral ABS combines master cylinder, hydraulic booster, and ABS hydraulic control in one unit.

Figure 10–33 This Dodge Durango ABS unit is conveniently located under the hood. The controller antilock brake (CAB) has been removed from the top of the hydraulic unit. Notice the six solenoid plungers on the hydraulic unit. Two solenoids are used for each of the three channels controlled (two front wheels and the rear wheels controlled together).

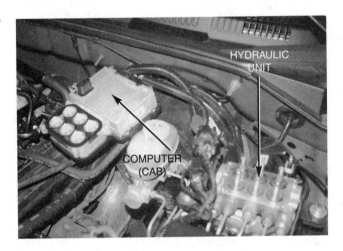

mph (48 km/h) (see Figure 10–34). All speed-traction control systems are capable of reducing positive wheel slip at all speeds. Most speed-traction control systems use accelerator reduction and engine power reduction to limit slip. For example, if a vehicle were being driven on an icy or snow-covered road, the brakes may become overheated if heavy acceleration is attempted. To help take the load off the brakes, the acceleration and power output from the engine is reduced. Many systems use accelerator pedal reduction and fuel injector cutout or ignition timing retardation individually or in combination to help match engine power output to the available tire traction. Traction control is also called acceleration slip regulation (ASR) (see Figures 10–35 and 10–36 on pages 257–258).

NOTE: The ABS controller supplies to the wheel brake only the pressure that is required to prevent tire slipping during acceleration. The amount of pressure varies according to the condition of the road surface and the amount of engine power being delivered to the drive wheels. A program inside the controller will disable traction control if brake system overheating is likely to occur. The driver should either wait for the brakes to cool or use less accelerator pedal while driving.

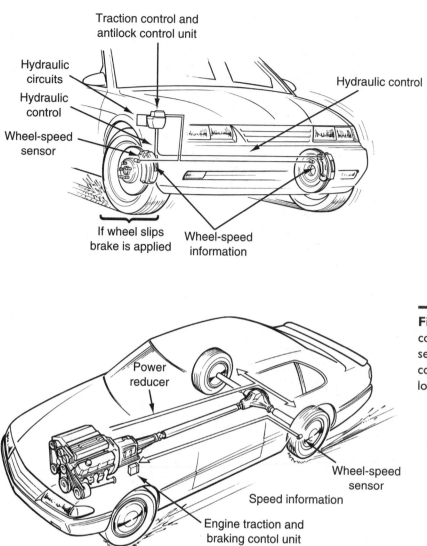

Traction control and
antilock control unit

Hydraulic
circuits

Hydraulic
control

Wheel-speed
sensor

Hydraulic control

If wheel slips
brake is applied

Wheel-speed
information

Figure 10–34 Typical low-speed
traction control design that uses wheel
speed sensor information and the
application of the drive-wheel brakes to
help reduce tire slippage during
acceleration.

Power
reducer

Wheel-speed
sensor

Speed information

Engine traction and
braking contol unit

Figure 10–35 Typical all-speed traction
control system that uses wheel speed
sensor information and the engine
controller to not only apply the brakes at
lower speeds but also reduce engine power.

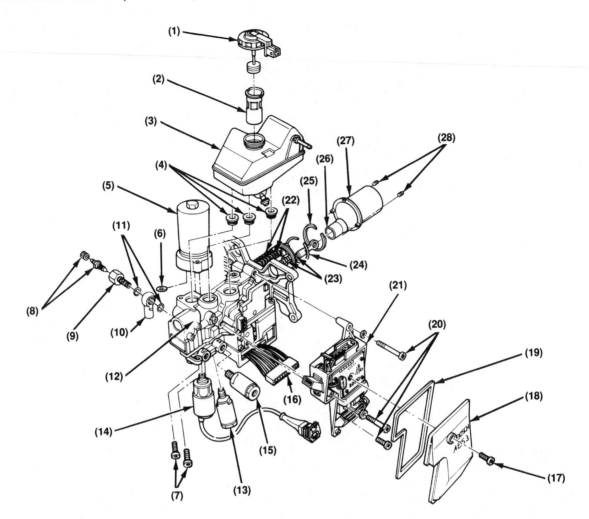

(1) Cap with fluid level switch
(2) Filter/strainer
(3) Reservoir
(4) Reservoir ring
(5) Accumulator
(6) O-ring seal
(7) Accumulator mounting bolts 6 N•m
(4 lbs. ft.)
(8) Bleed screw and cap 12 N•m (9 lbs. ft.)
(9) Banjo bolt-bleeder screw 15 N•m (11 lbs. ft.)
(10) High pressure fitting
(11) O-rings (2 required)
(12) Booster/master cylinder assembly
(13) LR proportioner valve 15 N•m (11 lbs. ft.)
(14) Control pressure switch 30 N•m (22 lbs. ft.)

(15) RR proportioner valve 15 N•m (11 lbs. ft.)
(16) Valve block conector
(17) Cover block
(18) Sensor block cover
(19) Gasket
(20) Sensor block mounting bolts 4 N•m
(35 lbs. ft.)
(21) Sensor block assembly
(22) Return springs
(23) Pushrod
(24) Cover seal spring
(25) Cover seal
(26) Pushrod boot
(27) Return spring cover
(28) Cover retaining screws

Figure 10–36 Exploded view of a Bosch III ABS/TC unit. (Courtesy of General Motors)

PHOTO SEQUENCE *Checking a Wheel Speed Sensor*

PS10–1 A tone ring and a wheel speed sensor on the rear of a Dodge Caravan.

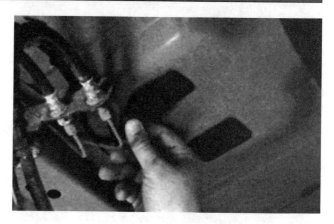

PS10–2 To test a wheel speed sensor, disconnect the sensor connector to gain access to the terminals. The connectors on this minivan are sealed from the weather under rubber grommets.

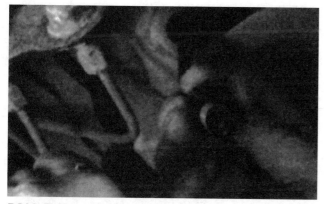

PS10–3 Pulling down the rubber seal reveals the connector.

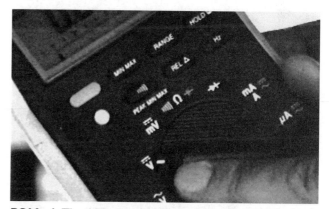

PS10–4 The ABS controller (computer) on this vehicle supplies a 2.5-volt reference signal to the wheel speed sensors. To check that the ABS computer is applying this voltage, select DC volts on the digital multimeter.

PS10–5 T-pins were used to gain access to the terminals of the computer end of the wheel speed sensor connector. Using anything larger than the male pin of the connector could cause harm by expanding the terminal, which could charge the connector.

PS10–6 The meter reads about 2.3 volts indicating that the ABS controller is supplying the voltage to the wheel speed sensor. This DC voltage is used for the diagnosis of the sensor circuit by the controller. If a sensor wire were to become open or grounded, the ABS controller would detect the fault.

Checking a Wheel Speed Sensor—continued

PS10–7 Select ohms (Ω) to measure the resistance of the wheel speed sensor.

PS10–8 The test probes are touched to the terminals leading to the wheel speed sensor and the resistance is 1.143 k ohms or 1143 ohms. This is about in the center of the specifications of 900 to 1300 ohms for this vehicle.

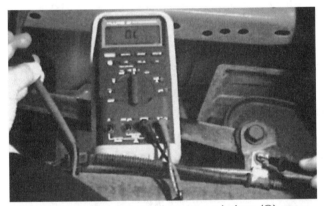

PS10–9 With the meter still set to read ohms (Ω), move one test terminal from the wheel speed sensor terminal to a good clean chassis ground. The meter should (and does) read "OL" indicating that the wheel speed sensor and pigtail wiring is not shorted to ground.

PS10–10 To measure the output of the wheel speed sensor, select AC volts on the digital multimeter.

PS10–11 Rotate the wheel and tire assembly by hand while observing the AC voltage output on the digital multimeter.

PS10–12 A good wheel speed sensor should be able to produce at least 100 mV (0.1 V) when the wheel is spun by hand. This wheel speed sensor is OK because it produces over 187 mV.

■ SUMMARY

1. Antilock brake systems are designed to limit the amount of tire slip by pulsing the wheel brake on and off up to twenty times per second.

2. Steering control is possible during an ABS stop if the tires maintain traction with the road surface.

3. The three stages of ABS operation are pressure buildup, pressure holding, and pressure reduction.

4. The heart of an antilock braking system is the electronic controller (computer). Wheel speed sensors produce an electrical frequency that is proportional to the speed of the wheel. If a wheel is slowing too fast, the controller controls the pressure of the wheel brake through an electro-hydraulic unit.

5. Both integral and nonintegral antilock braking systems control the rear wheels only, both front wheels individually and the rear as one unit (three-channel), or all four wheel brakes independently (four-channel).

6. Antilock braking systems that control the drive-wheel brakes can be used for acceleration traction control.

■ REVIEW QUESTIONS

1. Describe how an antilock braking system works.
2. List the three stages of ABS operation.
3. Explain how wheel speed sensors work.
4. Describe the difference between a three- and a four-channel system.
5. Explain how ABS can be used to prevent wheel slippage during acceleration.

■ ASE CERTIFICATION-TYPE QUESTIONS

1. Technician A says that the ABS system is designed so that the pressure to the wheel brakes is never higher than the pressure the driver is applying through the brake pedal. Technician B says that a pulsating brake pedal during normal braking is a characteristic feature of most ABS-equipped vehicles. Which technician is correct?
   a. Technician A only
   b. Technician B only
   c. Both Technician A and B
   d. Neither Technician A nor B

2. The maximum traction between a tire and the road occurs when the tire is:
   a. Locked and skidding
   b. Rotating freely
   c. Slipping 10 to 20 percent
   d. Slipping 80 to 90 percent

3. Technician A says that ABS-equipped vehicles can stop quickly and without skidding on all road surfaces even if covered with ice. Technician B says that steering is possible during an ABS stop. Which technician is correct?
   a. Technician A only
   b. Technician B only
   c. Both Technician A and B
   d. Neither Technician A nor B

4. A customer wanted the ABS checked because of tire chirp noise during hard braking. Technician A says that the speed sensors may be defective. Technician B says that tire chirp is normal during an ABS stop on dry pavement. Which technician is correct?
   a. Technician A only
   b. Technician B only
   c. Both Technician A and B
   d. Neither Technician A nor B

5. Two technicians are discussing ABS wheel speed sensors. Technician A says that some ABS systems use a sensor located in the rear-axle pinion gear area. Technician B says that all ABS systems use a wheel speed sensor at each wheel. Which technician is correct?
   a. Technician A only
   b. Technician B only
   c. Both Technician A and B
   d. Neither Technician A nor B

6. Technician A says that it may be normal for the hydraulic pump and solenoids to operate after the vehicle starts to move after a start. Technician B says that the ABS is disabled (does not function) below about 5 mph (8 km/h). Which technician is correct?
   a. Technician A only
   b. Technician B only
   c. Both Technician A and B
   d. Neither Technician A nor B

7. Technician A says that a scan tool may be necessary to bleed some ABS hydraulic units. Technician B says that only DOT 3 brake fluid should be used with an ABS. Which technician is correct?
   a. Technician A only
   b. Technician B only
   c. Both Technician A and B
   d. Neither Technician A nor B

8. Technician A says that traction control is available if a rear-wheel-drive vehicle is equipped with rear ABS only. Technician B says that hydraulic pressure from the electrohydraulic unit supplies brake fluid pressure to the wheel brake that is spinning during a traction control event. Which technician is correct?
   a. Technician A only
   b. Technician B only
   c. Both Technician A and B
   d. Neither Technician A nor B

9. The faster a wheel rotates, the higher the frequency produced by a wheel speed sensor.
   a. True
   b. False

10. Technician A says that some wheel speed sensors are enclosed in a wheel bearing assembly. Technician B says that some wheel speed sensors are exposed to possible damage from road debris. Which technician is correct?
    a. Technician A only
    b. Technician B only
    c. Both Technician A and B
    d. Neither Technician A nor B

ABS Diagnosis and Service

■ BRAKE WARNING LAMP OPERATION

The first step in the correct diagnosis of an antilock braking system problem is to check the status of the brake warning lamps.

Red Brake Warning Lamp This lamp warns of a possible dangerous failure in the base brakes, such as low brake fluid level or low pressure in half of the hydraulic system. The red brake warning lamp will also light if the parking brake is applied and may light due to an ABS failure such as low brake pressure on an integral system (see Figure 11–1).

Amber ABS Warning Lamp This lamp usually comes on after a start during the initialization or startup self-test sequence. The exact time the amber lamp re-

mains on after the ignition is turned on varies with the vehicle and the ABS design (see Figure 11–2 on page 265 for a typical example of a Teves Mark II integral ABS).

■ THOROUGH VISUAL INSPECTION

Many ABS-related problems can be diagnosed quickly if all the basics are carefully inspected (see Figure 11–3 on page 266). A thorough visual inspection should include the following items:

Brake fluid level	Check the conditions and level in the reservoir.
Brake fluid leaks	Check for cracks in flexible lines or other physical damage.
Fuses and fusible links	Check all ABS-related fuses.
Wiring and connections	Check all wiring, especially wheel speed sensor leads for damage.
Wheel speed sensors	Check that the sensor ring teeth are not damaged. Clean debris from the sensor if possible.

NOTE: Most wheel speed sensors are magnetic and therefore can attract and hold metallic particles. Be sure to remove any metallic debris from around the magnetic wheel speed sensor.

Figure 11–1 Typical brake warning lamp operation chart. Not all vehicles use the same light sequence. The top of the chart indicates normal warning lamp operation if the system is okay. (Courtesy of Ford Motor Company)

Symptom (With Parking Brake Released)	Warning Lamps	Ignition On	Cranking Engine	Engine Running	Vehicle Moving	Braking with/without Anti-Lock	Vehicle Stopped	Engine Idle	Ignition Off
Normal Light Sequence									
Normal Warning Lamps Sequences (System OK)	Check Anti-lock (Amber)	▨		▨					
	Brake (Red)		■						
Abnormal Warning Lamps Sequences									
● "Check Anti-Lock Brakes" Warning Lamp On Normal "Brake" Warning Lamp Sequence	Check Anti-lock (Amber)	▨▨		▨▨▨▨▨▨					
	Brake (Red)		■						
● "Check Anti-Lock Brakes" Warning Lamp On After Starting Engine Normal "Brake" Warning Lamp Sequence	Check Anti-lock (Amber)	▨		▨▨▨▨▨▨					
	Brake (Red)		■						
● "Check Anti-Lock Brakes" Warning Lamp Comes On Again After Vehicle Starts Moving Normal "Brake" Warning Lamp Sequence	Check Anti-lock (Amber)	▨		▨	▨▨▨▨▨				
	Brake Red		■						
● False Cycling of Anti-Lock System Normal Warning Lamp Sequence	Check Anti-lock (Amber)	▨		▨					
	Brake (Red)		■						
● "Check Anti-Lock Brakes" Warning Lamp and "Brake" Warning Lamp On ● No Boost (High Brake Pedal Effort)	Check Anti-lock (Amber)	▨▨		▨▨▨▨▨▨					
	Brake (Red)		████████████████						
● Pump Motor Runs More Than 60 Seconds Normal Warning Lamp Sequence	Check Anti-lock (Amber)	▨		▨					
	Brake (Red)		■						
● "Check Anti-Lock Brakes" Warning Lamp Intermittently On	Check Anti-lock (Amber)	▨		▨	▨ ▨▨				
	Brake (Red)		■						
● Normal "Check Anti-Lock Brakes" Warning Lamp Sequence "Brake" Warning Lamp On	Check Anti-lock (Amber	▨		▨					
	Brake (Red)		████████████████						
● No "Check Anti-Lock Brakes" Warning Lamp During Test Cycle ● Normal "Brake" Warning Lamp Sequence	Check Anti-lock (Amber)								
	Brake (Red)		■						
● Spongy Brake Pedal Normal Warning Lamp Sequence	Check Anti-lock (Amber)	▨		▨					
	Brake (Red)		■						
● Poor Vehicle Tracking During Anti-Lock Braking Normal Warning Lamp Sequence	Check Anti-lock (Amber)	▨		▨					
	Brake (Red)		■						

▨▨▨▨ "Check Anti-Lock Brakes" Warning Lamp On   ████ "Brake" Warning Lamp On

Base brake components All base brake components, such as disc brake calipers, drum brake wheel cylinders, and related components, must be in proper working condition.

Parking brake Check that the parking brake is correctly adjusted and fully released.

Wheel bearings All wheel bearings must be free of defects and adjusted properly.

Wheels and tires Check for correct size, proper inflation, and legal tread depth.

■ TEST-DRIVE AND VERIFY THE FAULT

A test drive is a very important diagnostic procedure. Many antilock braking systems and diagnostic trouble codes (DTC) will not set unless the vehicle is moving. Often the driver has noticed something like the self-test while driving and believed it to be a fault in the system.

> **NOTE:** Some ABS units, such as the Delphi VI, will cause the brake pedal to move up and down slightly during cycling of the valves during the self-test. Each system has unique features. The service technician will have to learn to avoid attempting to repair a problem that is not a fault of the system.

Before driving, start the engine and observe the red and amber brake warning lamps. If the red brake warning lamp is on, the base brakes may not be functioning correctly. Do not drive the vehicle until the base brakes are restored to proper operation.

> **NOTE:** Some systems are diagnosed by "antilock" and "brake" warning lamps, vehicle symptoms, and the use of a breakout box.

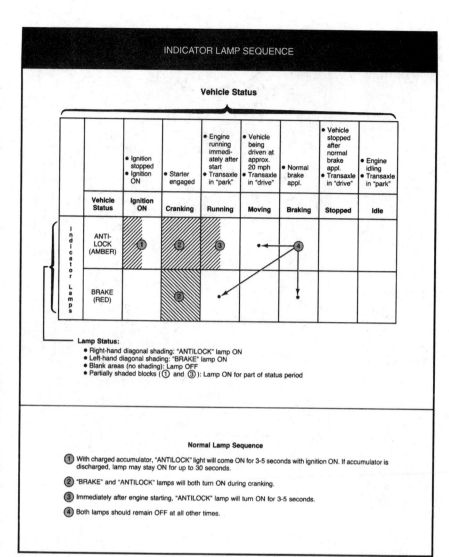

INDICATOR LAMP SEQUENCE

Vehicle Status

Vehicle Status	Ignition ON	Cranking	Running	Moving	Braking	Stopped	Idle
	• Ignition stopped • Ignition ON	• Starter engaged	• Engine running immediately after start • Transaxle in "park"	• Vehicle being driven at approx. 20 mph • Transaxle in "drive"	• Normal brake appl.	• Vehicle stopped after normal brake appl. • Transaxle in "drive"	• Engine idling • Transaxle in "park"
Indicator Lamps ANTI-LOCK (AMBER)	①	②	③	•	④		
BRAKE (RED)		②					

Lamp Status:
- Right-hand diagonal shading: "ANTILOCK" lamp ON
- Left-hand diagonal shading: "BRAKE" lamp ON
- Blank areas (no shading): Lamp OFF
- Partially shaded blocks (① and ③): Lamp ON for part of status period

Normal Lamp Sequence

① With charged accumulator, "ANTILOCK" light will come ON for 3-5 seconds with ignition ON. If accumulator is discharged, lamp may stay ON for up to 30 seconds.

② "BRAKE" and "ANTILOCK" lamps will both turn ON during cranking.

③ Immediately after engine starting, "ANTILOCK" lamp will turn ON for 3-5 seconds.

④ Both lamps should remain OFF at all other times.

Figure 11–2 Another example of a normal warning lamp sequence chart during normal (no-fault) operation. (Courtesy of General Motors)

■ RETRIEVING DIAGNOSTIC TROUBLE CODES

After performing a thorough visual inspection and after verifying the customer's complaint, retrieve any stored ABS-related diagnostic trouble codes (DTCs). The exact procedure varies with the type of ABS and with the make, model, and year of the vehicle (see Tables 11–1, 11–2, and 11–3 on page 267). Always consult factory service information for the vehicle being diagnosed. Some systems can only display flash codes (flashing ABS or brake lamp in sequence), whereas other systems can perform self-diagnosis and give all information to the technician through a scan tool.

NOTE: With some antilock braking systems, the diagnostic trouble code is lost if the ignition is turned "off" before grounding the diagnostic connector.

■ KELSEY-HAYES ANTILOCK (NONINTEGRAL)

The Kelsey-Hayes rear-wheel antilock uses two solenoids and valves to control the rear-wheel brakes (see Figure 11–4 on page 268). Kelsey-Hayes four-wheel antilock uses the computer to pulse the valves rather than turning them on or off. The pulsing is called pulse-width modulated (PWM) and the valve is called a PWM valve (see Figure 11–5 on page 269).

Retrieving Diagnostic Trouble Codes

A speed sensor signal is sent through a digital ratio adapter controller (DRAC), which is part of the instrument panel. If the axle ratio or tire size is changed, the DRAC must be replaced or recalibrated using the procedure described in the factory service manual. This

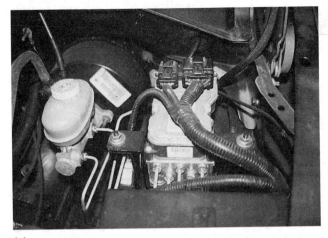

(a)

(b)

(c)

Figure 11–3 A thorough visual inspection should include carefully inspecting around the electrohydraulic unit for signs of obvious problems or the installation of aftermarket devices such as alarm systems. (a) Dodge truck ABS hydraulic control unit (b) Toyota Camry ABS hydraulic control unit (c) Plymouth Prowler ABS hydraulic control unit. Note that the ABS hydraulic unit is underneath the vehicle as it is with the Dodge, Plymouth, and Chrysler minivans.

TECH TIP ✔

Quick-and-Easy Wheel Speed Sensor Diagnosis

A fault in a wheel speed sensor (WSS) is a common ABS problem. A quick-and-easy test that works on most Bosch ABS systems (and perhaps others) involves the following steps:

Step 1 Hoist the vehicle safely.

Step 2 Turn on the ignition (engine off).

Step 3 Spin a tire by hand as fast as possible.

Step 4 The ABS amber warning light should come on indicating that a speed was detected but not by all the wheel speed sensors.

Step 5 Turn off the ignition to reset the ABS warning light.

Step 6 Repeat the test on each of the remaining wheels.

If any wheel fails to turn on the ABS light, carefully inspect the wheel speed sensor for proper resistance and the tone ring and wiring. If the ABS light is on all the time and does not reset when the ignition is turned off, the problem is not caused by a wheel speed sensor.

Frequently Asked Question ???

What's That Noise and Vibration?

Many vehicle owners and service technicians have been disturbed to hear and feel an occasional groaning noise. It is usually heard and felt through the vehicle after first being started and driven. Because it occurs when first being driven in forward or reverse, many technicians have blamed the transmission or related driveline components. This is commonly heard on many ABS vehicles as part of a system check. As soon as the ABS controller senses speed from the wheel speed sensors after an ignition cycles on, the controller will run the pump either every time or whenever the accumulator pressure is below a certain level. This can occur while the vehicle is being backed out of a driveway or being driven forward because wheel sensors can only detect speed—not direction. Before serious and major repairs are attempted to "cure" a noise, make sure that it is not the normal ABS self-test activation sequence of events.

Table 11–1 General Motors ABS Diagnostic Guide

Type of ABS System	Code Clearing Procedure	Scan Tool* Code Retrieval
Teves II integral	Not needed	Jumper key
Teves IV nonintegral	Yes	Yes
Bosch 2U nonintegral	Yes	Yes
Delphi (Delco) VI	Yes	Yes
Bosch 2S	Yes	Yes
Bosch III	Yes	Yes
Delco Powermaster III	Yes	Yes
Kelsey-Hayes RWAL	Yes or disconnect ABS fuse	Yes or flash codes
Kelsey-Hayes 4WAL	Yes	Yes

*A jumper key can be used for some systems. Not all scan tools can perform all functions.

Table 11–2 Ford ABS Diagnostic Guide

Type of ABS System	Code Clearing Procedure	Scan Tool* Code Retrieval
Teves II 32-pin integral	No codes available on this system	No codes available on this system
Teves II 35-pin integral	Drive vehicle after repair	Yes
Teves IV nonintegral	Drive vehicle after repair	Yes
Kelsey-Hayes RABS	Drive vehicle after repair	Flash codes
Teves 4WABS	Drive vehicle after repair	Yes

*A jumper wire can be used on some systems. Not all scan tools can perform all functions.

Table 11–3 Chrysler ABS Diagnostic Guide

Type of ABS System	Code Clearing Procedure	Scan Tool* Code Retrieval
Bosch III integral	Depress the brake	Turn the key off
Bendix 10 integral	Yes or disconnect the battery	Yes
Bendix 6 nonintegral	Yes or disconnect the battery	Yes
Bosch MMC	Yes	Yes
Bosch 2U nonintegral	No codes available on this system	No codes available on this system
Teves Mark II	Yes	Yes
Teves Mark IV	Yes	Yes
Kelsey-Hayes RWAL	Disconnect the battery	Flash codes
Kelsey-Hayes 4WAL	Yes	Yes

*A jumper wire can be used on some systems. Not all scan tools can perform all functions.

Figure 11–4 Kelsey-Hayes rear-wheel antilock (RWAL) system components. (Courtesy of General Motors)

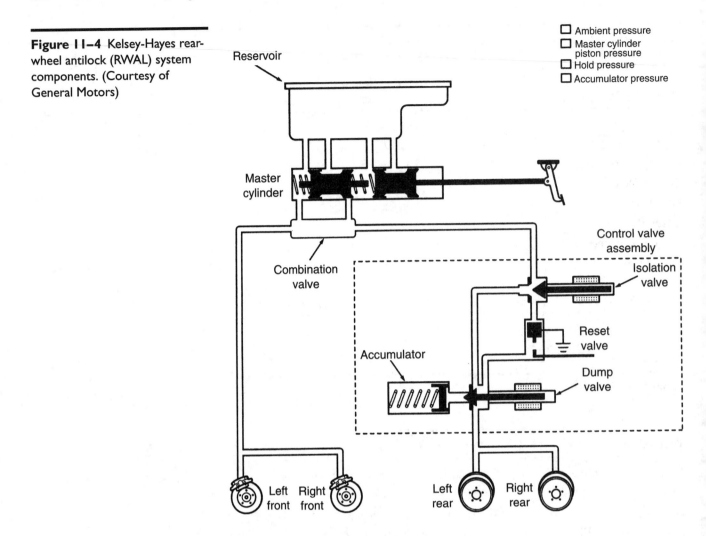

recalibration ensures that the speedometer and ABS will function correctly. The ABS system is usually disabled when the vehicle is in four-wheel drive (4WD).

GM trucks (RWAL). Flash codes and scan data through the use of OEM scan tool (Tech I/II) or connect H to A at DLC (see Figure 11–6 on page 270)

> **NOTE:** Be sure that the brake warning lamp is on before trying to retrieve diagnostic trouble codes. If the lamp is not on, a false code 9 could be set.

Ford trucks (RABS). Jumper lead flash codes only (see Figure 11–7 on page 270)

Chrysler light trucks. Ground diagnostic connections (see Figure 11–8 on page 270)

■ KELSEY-HAYES DIAGNOSTIC TROUBLE CODES

> **NOTE:** If the ignition is turned off, the failure code will be lost unless it is a hard code that will be present when the ignition is turned back on.

RWAL Diagnostic Codes

Code	Description
2	Open isolation valve solenoid circuit or malfunctioning EBCM/VCM
3	Open dump valve solenoid circuit or malfunctioning EBCM/VCM
4	Grounded valve reset switch circuit
5	Excessive actuations of dump valve during antilock braking
6	Erratic speed signal
7	Shorted isolation valve circuit or faulty EBCM/VCM
8	Shorted dump valve circuit or faulty EBCM/VCM
9	Open or grounded circuit to vehicle speed sensor
10	Brake switch circuit
12–17	Computer malfunction

> **NOTE:** A scan tool may or may not be able to retrieve or display diagnostic trouble codes. Check with the technical literature for the specific vehicle being scanned.

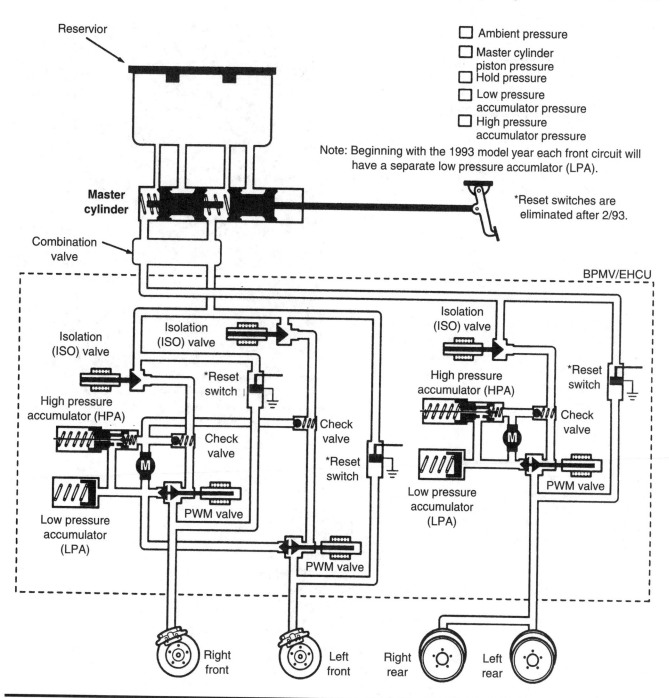

Figure 11–5 Kelsey-Hayes four-wheel antilock (4WAL) system components. (Courtesy of General Motors)

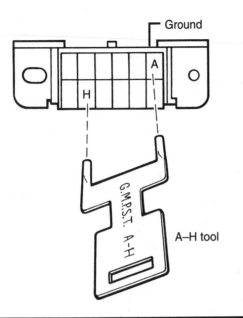

Figure 11–6 General Motors diagnostic connector. Flash codes are available by using a jumper wire to ground (terminal A) to terminal H. This connector is located under the dash near the steering column on most General Motors vehicles.

Diagnostic Story 📖

RWAL Diagnosis

The owner of an S-10 pickup truck complained that the red brake warning lamp on the dash remained on even when the parking brake was released. The problem could be:

1. A serious hydraulic problem
2. Low brake fluid
3. A stuck or defective parking brake switch
4. If the brake lamp is dim, RWAL trouble is indicated.

The technician found that the brake lamp was on dimly, indicating that an antilock braking problem was detected. The first step in diagnosing an antilock braking problem with a dash lamp on is to check for stored trouble codes. The technician used a jumper between terminals A and H on the DLC (ALCL), and four flashes of the brake lamp indicated a code 4.

Checking a service manual, code 4 was found to be a grounded switch inside the hydraulic control unit. The hardest part about the repair was getting access to and the replacement of the defective (electrically grounded) switch. After bleeding the system and a thorough test drive, the lamp sequence and RWAL functioned correctly.

Figure 11–7 Connecting a jumper wire from the diagnostic connector to ground. The exact location of this diagnostic connector varies with exact vehicle model and year. (Courtesy of Ford Motor Company)

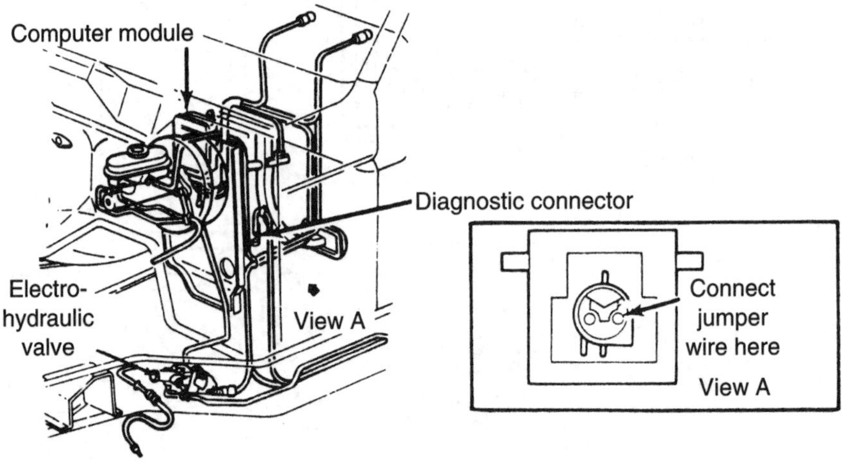

Figure 11–8 Chrysler diagnostic connector location varies with model and year. (Courtesy of Chrysler Corporation)

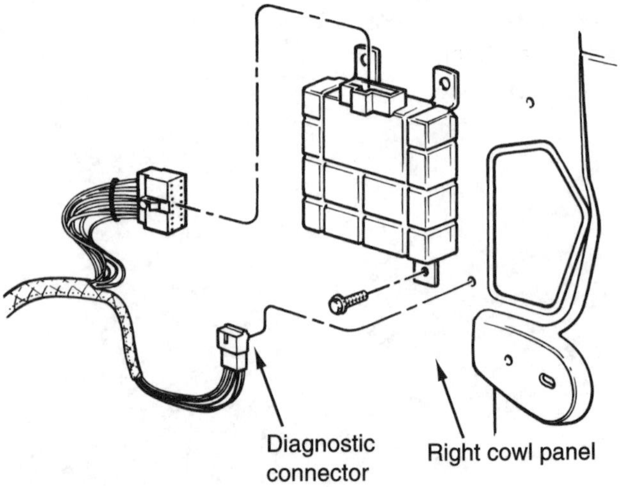

4WAL Diagnostic Trouble Codes

Code	Description
12	System normal (2WD applications)
13	System normal—brake applied (2WD applications)
14	System normal (4WD/AWD applications)
15	System normal—brake applied (4WD/AWD applications)
21 RF, 25 LF, 31 RR, 35 LR	Speed sensor circuit open.
35	VSS circuit open
22 RF, 26 LF, 32 RR, 36 LR	Missing speed sensor signal
36	Missing VSS signal
23 RF, 27 LF, 33 RR, 37 LR	Erratic speed sensor signal
37	Erratic VSS signal
28	Simultaneous dropout of front-wheel speed sensors
29	Simultaneous dropout of all speed sensors
35	Vehicle speed sensor circuit open
36	Missing LR or vehicle speed sensor signal
37	Erratic LR or vehicle speed sensor signal
38	Wheel speed error
41–66	Malfunctioning BPMV/EHCU
67	Open motor circuit or shorted EBCM output
68	Locked motor or shorted motor circuit
71–74	Memory failure
81	Open or shorted brake switch circuit
86	Shorted ABS warning lamp
88	Shorted red brake warning lamp (RBWL)

■ BOSCH 2 ABS (NONINTEGRAL)

The Bosch 2U/2S ABS is used on many domestic and imported brands of vehicles (see Figure 11–9).

Retrieving Diagnostic Trouble Codes

On General Motors vehicles, diagnostic trouble codes can be retrieved by connection A to H at the diagnostic link connection (DLC). On most Bosch 2 systems, a scan tool can and should be used if available to retrieve diagnostic trouble codes.

Bosch 2U/2S ABS Diagnostic Trouble Codes

Code	Description
12	Diagnostic system operational
21 RF, 25 LF, 31 RR, 35 LR	Wheel speed sensor fault

Code	Description
35	Rear-axle speed sensor fault
22 RF, 26 LF, 32 RR, 36 LR	Toothed wheel frequency error
36	Rear-axle toothed wheel frequency error
41 RF, 45 LF,	Valve solenoid fault
55	Rear valve solenoid fault
61	Pump motor or motor relay fault
63	Solenoid valve relay fault
71	Electronic brake control module fault
72	Serial data link fault
74	Low voltage
75	Lateral acceleration sensor fault
76	Lateral acceleration sensor fault

■ BOSCH III ABS (INTEGRAL)

The Bosch III integral is used on many different makes and models of vehicles including various models of General Motors (see Figure 11–10).

■ BOSCH III DIAGNOSTIC TROUBLE CODES

Code	Description
1	LF wheel circuit valve
2	RF wheel circuit valve
3	RR wheel circuit valve
4	LR wheel circuit valve
5	LF wheel speed sensor
6	RF wheel speed sensor
7	RR wheel speed sensor
8	LR wheel speed sensor
9	LF/RR wheel speed sensor
10	RF/LR wheel speed sensor
11	Replenishing valve
12	Valve relay
13	Circuit failure
14	Piston travel switches
15	Stoplight switch
16	ABCM error

Retrieving diagnostic trouble codes for a Bosch III antilock braking system varies with vehicle make, model, and year. Most codes are erased when the ignition is turned off; therefore, code retrieval must occur before key-off. If the amber ABS lamp is on, a trouble code has been set.

■ TEVES MARK II

Teves Mark II ABS is an integral system as shown in Figure 11–11 on page 273.

Retrieving Diagnostic Trouble Codes

On General Motors vehicles equipped with Teves Mark II ABS, diagnostic trouble codes can be retrieved by

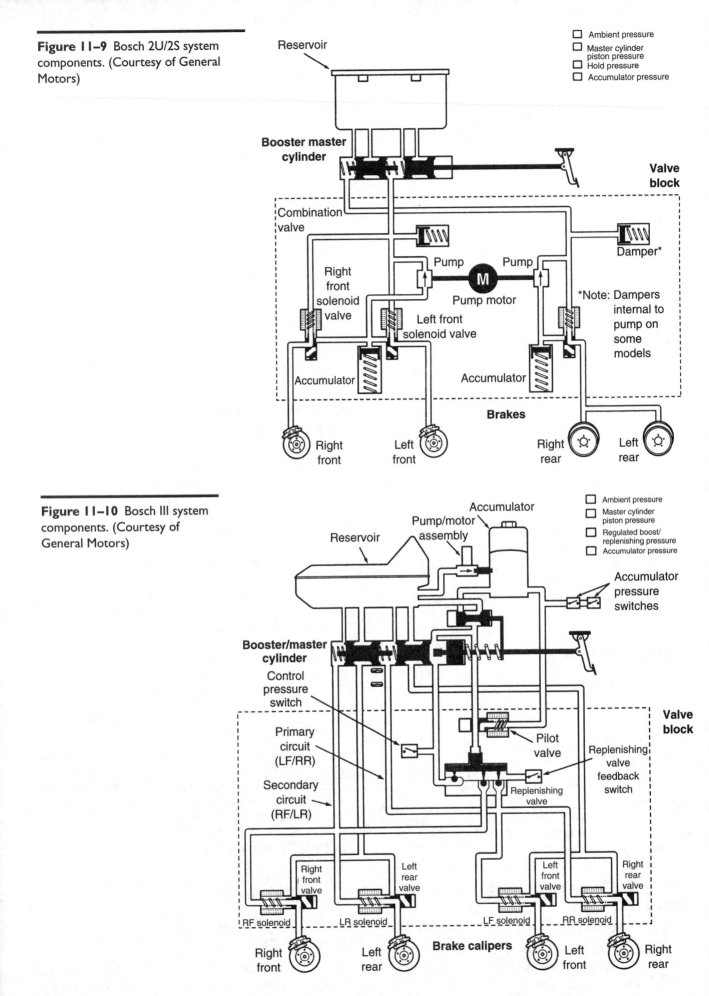

Figure 11–9 Bosch 2U/2S system components. (Courtesy of General Motors)

Reservoir

☐ Ambient pressure
☐ Master cylinder piston pressure
☐ Hold pressure
☐ Accumulator pressure

Booster master cylinder

Valve block

Combination valve

Damper*

Right front solenoid valve

Pump   Pump

M

Pump motor

Left front solenoid valve

*Note: Dampers internal to pump on some models

Accumulator   Accumulator

Brakes

Right front   Left front   Right rear   Left rear

Figure 11–10 Bosch III system components. (Courtesy of General Motors)

Accumulator

Pump/motor assembly

Reservoir

☐ Ambient pressure
☐ Master cylinder piston pressure
☐ Regulated boost/replenishing pressure
☐ Accumulator pressure

Accumulator pressure switches

Booster/master cylinder

Control pressure switch

Pilot valve

Replenishing valve feedback switch

Primary circuit (LF/RR)

Valve block

Secondary circuit (RF/LR)

Replenishing valve

Right front valve   Left rear valve   Left front valve   Right rear valve

RF solenoid   LR solenoid   LF solenoid   RR solenoid

Brake calipers

Right front   Left rear   Left front   Right rear

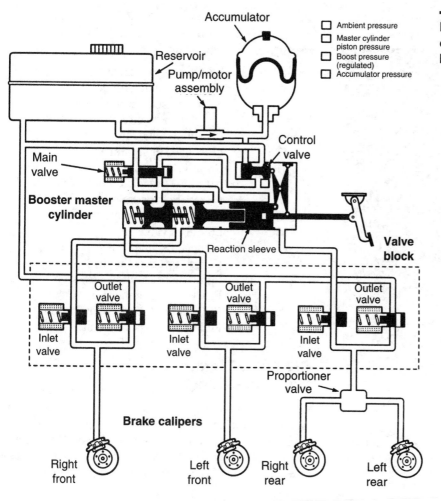

☐	Ambient pressure
☐	Master cylinder piston pressure
☐	Boost pressure (regulated)
☐	Accumulator pressure

Figure 11–11 Teves Mark II system components. (Courtesy of General Motors)

connecting terminals A and H at the data link connector (DLC). A scan tool can also be used on most General Motors vehicles to retrieve trouble codes. A scan tool is required to retrieve codes on other vehicle makes and models. Consult technical information for the exact vehicle being serviced.

Teves Mark II Diagnostic Trouble Codes

ABS Code	Description
11	EBCM
12	EBCM
21	Main valve
22	LF inlet valve
23	LF outlet valve
24	RF inlet valve
25	RF outlet valve
26	Rear inlet valve
27	Rear outlet valve
31	LF WSS
32	RF WSS
33	RR WSS
34	LR WSS
35	LF WSS
36	RF WSS
37	RR WSS

ABS Code	Description
38	LR WSS
41	LF WSS
42	RF WSS
43	RR WSS
44	LR WSS
45	Two sensors (LF)
46	Two sensors (RF)
47	Two sensors (rear)
48	Three sensors
51	LF outlet valve
52	RF outlet valve
53	Rear outlet valve
54	Rear outlet valve
55	LF WSS
56	RF WSS
57	RR WSS
58	LR WSS
61	EBCM "loop" circuit
71	LF outlet valve
72	RF outlet valve
73	Rear outlet valve
74	Rear outlet valve
75	LF WSS
76	RF WSS
77	RR WSS
78	LR WSS

Diagnostic Story

The Nervous Taurus

A customer complained that sometimes during normal braking, the ABS would be activated just before coming to a stop. The ABS light does not come on. The service technician was able to duplicate the condition and there were no diagnostic trouble codes (DTCs) stored. Using a scan tool to monitor the wheel speed sensors, the technician discovered that the left front wheel speed was slightly different than the others. A thorough visual inspection revealed that the tone wheel (sensor ring) was cracked. This crack created a different wheel speed signal to the ABS controller than the other wheels and the controller activated the ABS as it would normally—that is why there were no DTCs.

Other things that could have caused this problem include a bent wheel, mismatched tire sizes, or metal debris around the sensor.

Clearing Diagnostic Trouble Codes

After all stored codes have been received and problems corrected, the trouble code should be erased from the computer memory after driving above 25 mph (40 km/h).

■ TEVES MARK IV

The Teves Mark IV is a nonintegral (remote) ABS system (see Figure 11–12).

Retrieving Diagnostic Trouble Codes

Trouble codes are accessed only by a bidirectional scan tool such as a Tech I or II connected to the diagnostic link connector (DLC).

Teves Mark IV ABS Diagnostic Trouble Codes

ABS Code	Description
21	RF speed sensor circuit open
22	RF speed sensor signal erratic
23	RF wheel speed is 0 mph
25	LF speed sensor circuit open
26	LF speed sensor signal erratic
27	LF wheel speed is 0 mph
31	RR speed sensor circuit open
32	RR speed sensor signal erratic
33	RR wheel speed is 0 mph
35	LR speed sensor circuit open
36	LR speed sensor signal erratic
37	LR wheel speed is 0 mph

ABS Code	Description
41	RF inlet valve circuit
42	RF outlet valve circuit
43	RF speed sensor noisy
45	LF inlet valve circuit
46	LF outlet valve circuit
47	LF speed sensor noisy
51	RR inlet valve circuit
52	RR outlet valve circuit
53	RR speed sensor noisy
55	LR inlet valve circuit
56	LR outlet valve circuit
57	LR speed sensor noisy
61	Pump motor test fault
62	Pump motor fault in ABS stop
71	EBCM check sum error
72	TCC/antilock brake switch circuit
73	Fluid level switch circuit

Clearing Diagnostic Trouble Codes

A scan tool is required to clear diagnostic trouble codes on some vehicles. Driving the vehicle over 20 mph (32 km/h) will clear the codes on some vehicles. Disconnecting the battery will also clear the codes but will cause other "keep-alive" functions of the vehicle to be lost.

■ DELPHI (DELCO) ABS VI (NONINTEGRAL)

The Delphi (Delco) ABS VI is unique from all other antilock systems because it uses motor-driven ball screws and pistons for brake pressure reduce, hold, and apply (see Figures 11–13, 11–14, and 11–15 on pages 276–277).

Retrieving Diagnostic Codes

The Delphi (Delco) VI antilock braking system has extensive self-diagnostic capability. Access to this vast amount of information requires the use of a scan tool designed to interface (work) with the Delco VI system.

ABS Code	Description
11	ABS lamp open or shorted to ground
13	ABS lamp circuit shorted to battery
14	Enable relay contacts open, fuse open
15	Enable relay contacts shorted to battery
16	Enable relay coil circuit open
17	Enable relay coil shorted to ground
18	Enable relay coil shorted to B1 or 0 ohms
21	Left-front wheel speed 50
23	Left-rear wheel speed 50
24	Right-rear wheel speed 50
25	Excessive left-front wheel acceleration
26	Excessive right-front wheel acceleration

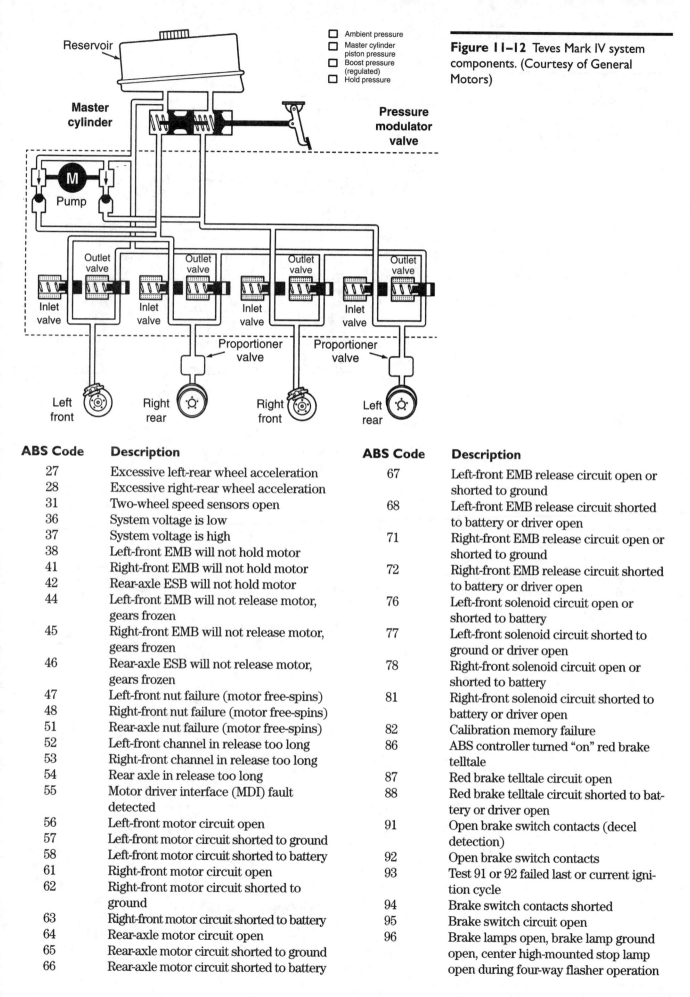

Reservoir

Master cylinder

Pressure modulator valve

□ Ambient pressure
□ Master cylinder piston pressure
□ Boost pressure (regulated)
□ Hold pressure

Figure 11–12 Teves Mark IV system components. (Courtesy of General Motors)

Pump

Outlet valve

Inlet valve

Proportioner valve

Left front

Right rear

Right front

Left rear

ABS Code	Description	ABS Code	Description
27	Excessive left-rear wheel acceleration	67	Left-front EMB release circuit open or shorted to ground
28	Excessive right-rear wheel acceleration	68	Left-front EMB release circuit shorted to battery or driver open
31	Two-wheel speed sensors open	71	Right-front EMB release circuit open or shorted to ground
36	System voltage is low		
37	System voltage is high	72	Right-front EMB release circuit shorted to battery or driver open
38	Left-front EMB will not hold motor		
41	Right-front EMB will not hold motor	76	Left-front solenoid circuit open or shorted to battery
42	Rear-axle ESB will not hold motor	77	Left-front solenoid circuit shorted to ground or driver open
44	Left-front EMB will not release motor, gears frozen	78	Right-front solenoid circuit open or shorted to battery
45	Right-front EMB will not release motor, gears frozen	81	Right-front solenoid circuit shorted to battery or driver open
46	Rear-axle ESB will not release motor, gears frozen	82	Calibration memory failure
47	Left-front nut failure (motor free-spins)	86	ABS controller turned "on" red brake telltale
48	Right-front nut failure (motor free-spins)	87	Red brake telltale circuit open
51	Rear-axle nut failure (motor free-spins)	88	Red brake telltale circuit shorted to battery or driver open
52	Left-front channel in release too long		
53	Right-front channel in release too long	91	Open brake switch contacts (decel detection)
54	Rear axle in release too long	92	Open brake switch contacts
55	Motor driver interface (MDI) fault detected	93	Test 91 or 92 failed last or current ignition cycle
56	Left-front motor circuit open	94	Brake switch contacts shorted
57	Left-front motor circuit shorted to ground	95	Brake switch circuit open
58	Left-front motor circuit shorted to battery	96	Brake lamps open, brake lamp ground open, center high-mounted stop lamp open during four-way flasher operation
61	Right-front motor circuit open		
62	Right-front motor circuit shorted to ground		
63	Right-front motor circuit shorted to battery		
64	Rear-axle motor circuit open		
65	Rear-axle motor circuit shorted to ground		
66	Rear-axle motor circuit shorted to battery		

Figure 11–13 Delphi (Delco) VI system components. Notice that each front brake is controlled by a separate piston whereas the rear brakes are controlled by the same piston. (Courtesy of General Motors)

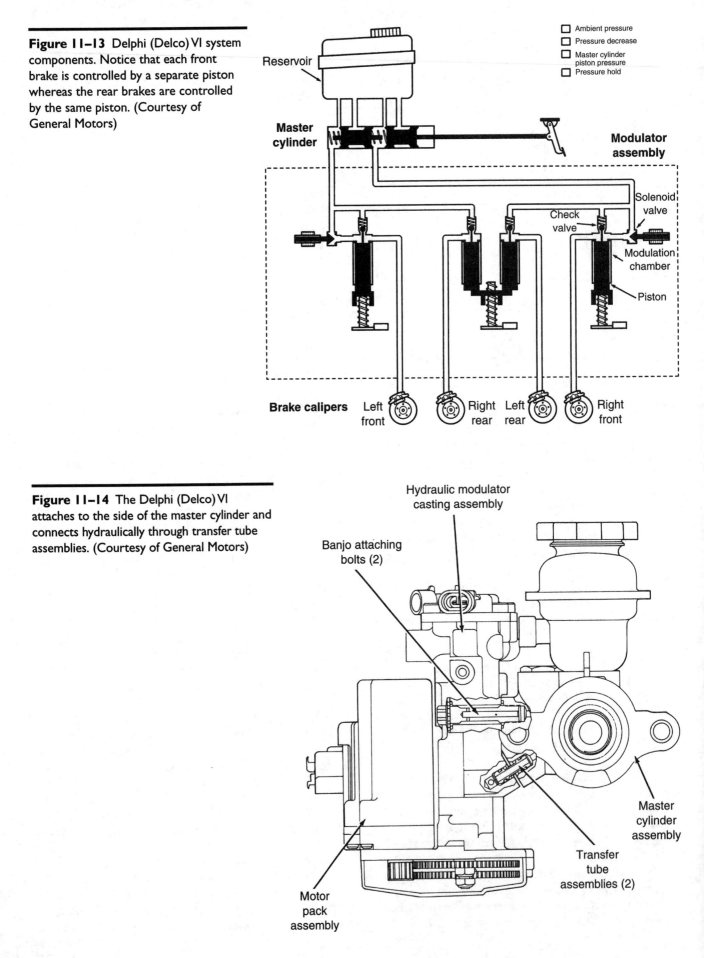

Figure 11–14 The Delphi (Delco) VI attaches to the side of the master cylinder and connects hydraulically through transfer tube assemblies. (Courtesy of General Motors)

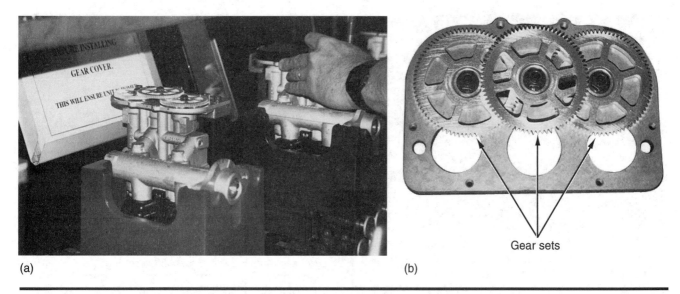

(a)

(b)

Gear sets

Figure 11–15 (a) Delphi (Delco) VI ABS units being assembled at the Delphi (Delco) chassis assembly plant in Dayton, Ohio. (b) These gears are turned by high-speed electric motors and move pistons up and down to control braking during an ABS stop.

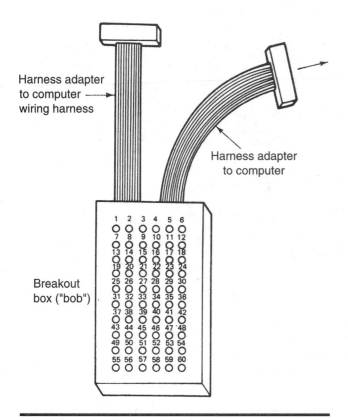

Harness adapter to computer wiring harness

Harness adapter to computer

Breakout box ("bob")

Figure 11–16 A breakout box is used to measure resistance and voltage in the antilock braking system by opening up the wiring between the components and the ABS controller. A digital multimeter can be connected to the appropriate terminal of the breakout box to measure the resistance or voltage according to the service information for the vehicle being serviced.

■ BREAKOUT BOX TESTING

Many antilock braking systems require the use of a breakout box (often abbreviated "BOB") to diagnose electrical components. A breakout box connects between the ABS controller (computer) and the wiring harness that leads to all of the input devices, such as the wheel speed sensors (see Figure 11–16). The breakout box uses electrical contact points for each circuit being used by the computer. With this easy access to all the electrical components, an electrical digital meter called a DMM (digital multimeter) can be used to check the electrical condition of the various ABS components. The meter is used to measure the electrical values of the input and output devices used in the system. By comparing the readings to what is specified, a fault in the system can be determined (see Figure 11–17).

A digital meter measures units of electricity. Electricity is the movement of electrons from one atom to another. Movement of electrons through a conductor is called electrical current (moving electricity). If an outside source of power, such as a battery, is connected to the ends of a conductor, a positive (1) charge (lack of electrons) is placed on one end of the conductor and a negative (2) charge is placed on the opposite end of the conductor. The negative (2) charge will repel the electrons from the atoms of the conductor, while the positive (1) charge on the opposite end of the conductor will attract electrons. As a result of this attraction of opposite charges and repulsion of like charges, electrons will flow through the conductor (see Figure 11–18).

Diagnostic Story

The Mystery ABS Amber Warning Light

The owner of an Acura Legend complained to a service technician that the ABS warning light would come on but only while driving down from a parking garage. When the driver turns off the ignition and restarts the engine, the ABS amber light is not on and does not come on again until the vehicle is again driven down the spiral parking garage ramp. The service technician used a scan tool and found that no diagnostic trouble codes had been stored.

> **NOTE:** Some ABS systems will not retain a diagnostic trouble code unless the problem is currently present and the ABS amber warning light is on.

All of the brakes were in excellent condition, but the brake fluid level was down a little. After topping off the master cylinder with clean DOT 3 brake fluid, the vehi-cle was returned to the customer with the following information:

- The ABS amber warning light may have been triggered by the brake fluid level switch. While driving down the steep parking garage ramp, the brake fluid moved away from the fluid level sensor.

> **NOTE:** While the brake fluid level sensor normally would turn on the red brake warning light, in some systems it turns on the amber ABS light if the brake level reaches a certain level in the ABS reservoir.

- The difference in wheel speed between the outboard and the inboard wheels could have triggered a fault code for a wheel speed sensor during the drive down the spiral parking garage ramp.

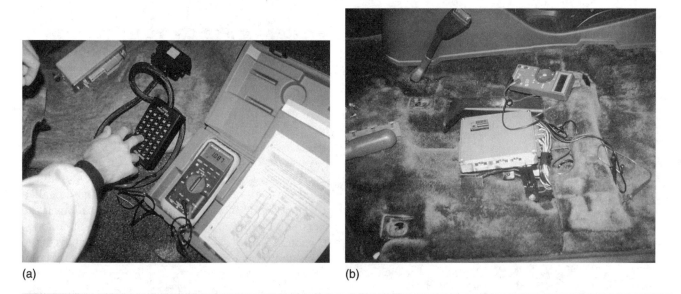

(a) (b)

Figure 11–17 (a) A breakout box is being used to diagnose an ABS problem. The controller (computer) is located in the trunk of this vehicle, and a digital multimeter is being used to measure resistance and voltage at various points in the system, following the service manual procedure. (b) Another vehicle being tested for an ABS fault. In this vehicle, the computer is located under the passenger seat, which has been removed to gain better access to the wiring and terminals.

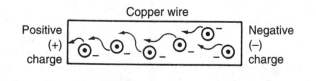

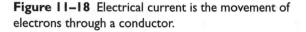

Figure 11–18 Electrical current is the movement of electrons through a conductor.

■ AMPERES

The ampere is the unit used throughout the world as a measure of the amount of current flow. One ampere is a unit that represents 6.28 billion electrons moving past a point in one second (see Figure 11–19). The ampere is the electrical unit for the amount of electron

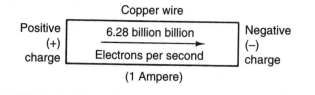

Copper wire
Positive (+) charge | 6.28 billion billion → Electrons per second | Negative (−) charge
(1 Ampere)

Figure 11–19 An ampere is the unit of electricity that measures the amount of current flow. One ampere is the movement of 6.28 billion billion electrons past a point in one second.

flow, just as "gallons per minute" is the unit that can be used to measure the quantity of water flow. It was named for a French physicist, André-Marie Ampère (1775–1836). The conventional abbreviations and measurement for ampere are summarized as follows:

1. The ampere is the unit of measurement of the amount of current flow.
2. "A" and "amps" are acceptable abbreviations for ampere.
3. Amperes are measured by an ammeter (not ampmeter).

■ VOLTS

A volt is the unit of measurement of electrical pressure. It is named for Alessandro Volta (1745–1827), an Italian physicist. The comparable unit using water as an example would be pounds per square inch (psi). Voltage is also called electrical potential because if voltage is present in a conductor, there is a potential (possibility) for current flow. Voltage does not flow through conductors, but voltage does cause current (in amperes) to flow through conductors. The conventional abbreviations and measurements for voltage are as follows:

1. The volt is the unit of measurement of the amount of electrical pressure or potential to do work.
2. Electromotive force (EMF) is another way of indicating voltage.
3. "V" is the generally accepted abbreviation for volts.
4. The symbol used in calculations is E, for electromotive force.
5. Volts are measured by a voltmeter.

■ OHMS

Resistance to the flow of current through a conductor is measured in units called ohms, named after a German physicist, Georg Simon Ohm (1787–1854). The resistance to the flow of electrons through a conductor results from the countless collisions the electrons

Note: Lines of force leave the north pole and enter the south pole

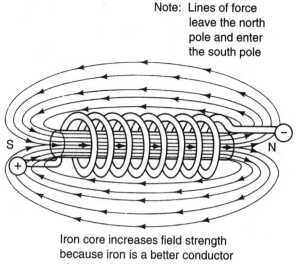

Iron core increases field strength because iron is a better conductor of magnetic lines of force than air

Figure 11–20 Any conductor (wire) carrying an electrical current has a magnetic field around it. When a wire is wrapped in a coil, its magnetic lines of force combine. An iron core is used to increase the strength of the magnetic field.

make within the atoms of the conductor. The conventional abbreviations and measurements for resistance are as follows:

1. The ohm is the unit of measurement of electrical resistance.
2. The symbol for ohms is Ω (Greek capital letter omega), the last letter of the Greek alphabet.
3. Ohms are measured by an ohmmeter.

■ ELECTRICITY AND MAGNETISM

Whenever there is electricity flowing through a conductor, magnetic lines of force are produced around the conductor. Whenever there is a conductor near a moving magnetic field, electricity is produced in the conductor. A magnetic field created by current flow is called electromagnetism. If a wire (conductor) is coiled and current is sent through the wire, the same magnetic field that surrounds a straight wire combines to form one larger magnetic field with true north and south poles (see Figures 11–20 and 11–21).

In 1831, Michael Faraday (1791–1867) discovered that electrical energy can be induced from one circuit to another by using magnetic lines of force. When a conductor is moved through a magnetic field, a difference of potential is set up between the ends of the conductor and a voltage is induced. This action is called electromagnetic induction. This voltage exists only when the magnetic field or the conductor is in motion.

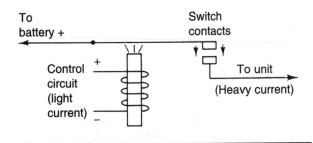

Figure 11–21 Electromagnetic switch. A light current (low amperes) produces an electromagnet and causes the contact points to close. The contact points then conduct a heavy current (high amperes) to an electrical unit.

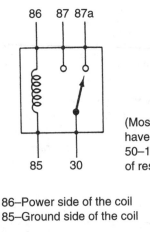

(Most relay coils have between 50–150 ohms of resistance.)

86—Power side of the coil
85—Ground side of the coil

30—Common power for relay contacts
87—Normally open output (N.O.)
87a—Normally closed output (N.C.)

Figure 11–23 Most relays that have five terminals are labeled with this standardized identification. Four-terminal relays do not have a terminal for 87a (normally closed position).

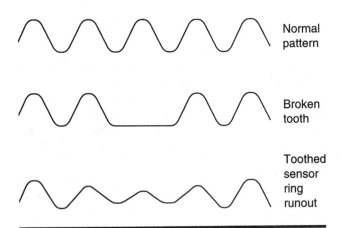

Normal pattern

Broken tooth

Toothed sensor ring runout

Figure 11–22 A wheel speed sensor uses the principle of electromagnetic induction to produce a changing voltage signal (sine wave) as the wheel revolves. A fault such as a broken sensor tooth or a worn bearing can cause sensor runout and changes the output signal. (Courtesy of General Motors)

To induce 1 V, 100,000,000 (100 million) magnetic lines of force must be cut per second. The induced voltage can be increased by increasing the speed with which the magnetic lines of force cut the conductor, or by increasing the number of conductors that are cut. Electromagnetic induction is the principle behind the operation of all ignition systems, starter motors, alternators, and wheel speed sensors. The faster the wheel rotates, the faster the magnetic field changes and the higher the frequency of the wheel speed sensor output (see Figure 11–22).

■ HOW TO READ ELECTRICAL SCHEMATICS

Electrical schematics (wiring diagrams) are like an electrical circuit road map. To "follow" the flow of electricity through a circuit, start at the battery or fuse for the circuit. This is the source of electrical power.

TECH TIP ✔

Relay Terminal Identification

Most automotive relays adhere to common terminal identification. Knowing this terminal information will help in the correct diagnosis and troubleshooting of any circuit containing a relay (see Figure 11–23).

The schematic is often printed or embossed on the side of many relays. The terminals are also labeled to help the technician test and check for proper operation. The identification of relay terminals also helps when wiring accessories, such as auxiliary lighting, into existing wiring.

Despiking diodes or resistors are connected across the coil of most automotive relays (terminals 85 and 86) to reduce high-voltage surges that are generated in the coil windings when the relay is turned off.

The paths or roadways are the electrical wires and connections the electricity has to flow through to get to the electrical "load" or component that is operated by the electrical current (see Figures 11–24 through 11–28 on pages 281–283). Sometimes, such as with a wheel speed sensor (WSS), the "source" of the electrical power (signal) starts with the component.

■ ELECTRICAL FAULTS

Faults in electrical circuits can prevent proper operation of the circuit. There are several types of faults and each has its own characteristics.

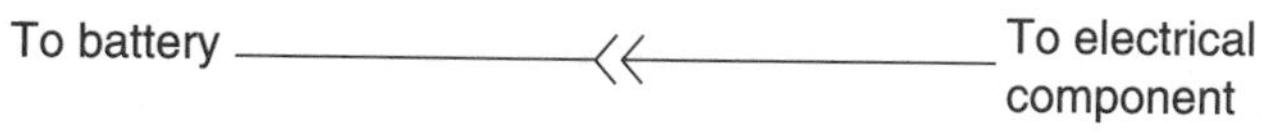

Figure 11–24 Typical electrical wiring connector symbol. Note that the positive (1) terminal is usually a female connector.

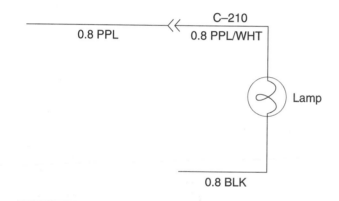

Figure 11–25 Wire color is usually abbreviated on most wiring diagrams. The center wire is a solid-color wire; the two end wires could be labeled BRN/WHT, indicating a brown wire with a white tracer or stripe.

C–210

0.8 PPL   0.8 PPL/WHT

Lamp

0.8 BLK

Figure 11–26 Typical section of a wiring diagram. Notice that the wire color changes at the connector labeled C-210. The label "0.8" represents the metric wire size in square millimeters (18 gauge).

Open Circuits

An open circuit is any circuit that is not complete and lacks continuity (see Figures 11–29 and 11–30 on page 284). No current at all will flow through an incomplete circuit. An open circuit may be created by a break in the circuit or a switch that "opens" (turns off) the circuit and prevents the flow of current. A light switch in a home or the headlight switch in a vehicle are examples of devices that open a circuit to control its operation.

Short to Voltage

If a wire (conductor) or component is shorted to voltage, it is commonly called shorted.

A short to voltage can be summarized as follows:

1. A complete circuit where the current bypasses some or all of the resistance in the circuit
2. Involves the power side of the circuit

TECH TIP ✔

Sometimes It Pays To Look at the Entire Vehicle

There are often strange electrical problems that can occur including false diagnostic trouble codes (DTCs) or intermittent operation of electrical sensors, ABS, accessories, or gauges. Sometimes the root of these problems is due to rust and corrosion after a vehicle was involved in a flood. Here are some telltale signs that a vehicle may have been in a flood or in deep water.

- Mud, silt, or caked dust under the dash and inside the doors
- Corroded electrical connectors at the computer, fuse box, or ABS controller (computer)
- Visible water line in the doors or behind panels
- Rust in abnormal places such as seat springs or brackets behind the dash
- Moisture in lenses
- Musty smell and/or strong air freshener smell
- Powdery corrosion on aluminum parts such as intake manifold and inside the throttle bore
- Rust or moisture inside electrical switches or relays
- Areas that are normally dusty such as an ashtray or glove box are very clean

3. Involves a copper-to-copper connection (therefore, includes the removal of insulation from more than one wire). This usually is caused by heat or movement.
4. Also called a short to voltage
5. May or may not blow a fuse

Short to Ground

A short to ground is a type of short circuit wherein the current bypasses part of the normal circuit and flows directly to ground (the lowest voltage potential in the circuit). Since the ground return circuit is metal (vehicle frame, engine, or body), this type of circuit is identified as having current flowing from "copper to steel." A defective component or circuit that is shorted to ground is commonly called grounded, a concept that can be summarized as follows:

1. Involves the power side of the circuit
2. Called a "short to ground"
3. Involves a "copper-to-steel" connection

NOTE: A short to ground is more common than a short to voltage because this type of electrical problem only requires the loss of insulation on one wire and contact with metal.

Figure 11–27 Typical electrical and electronic symbols used in automotive wiring and circuit diagrams.

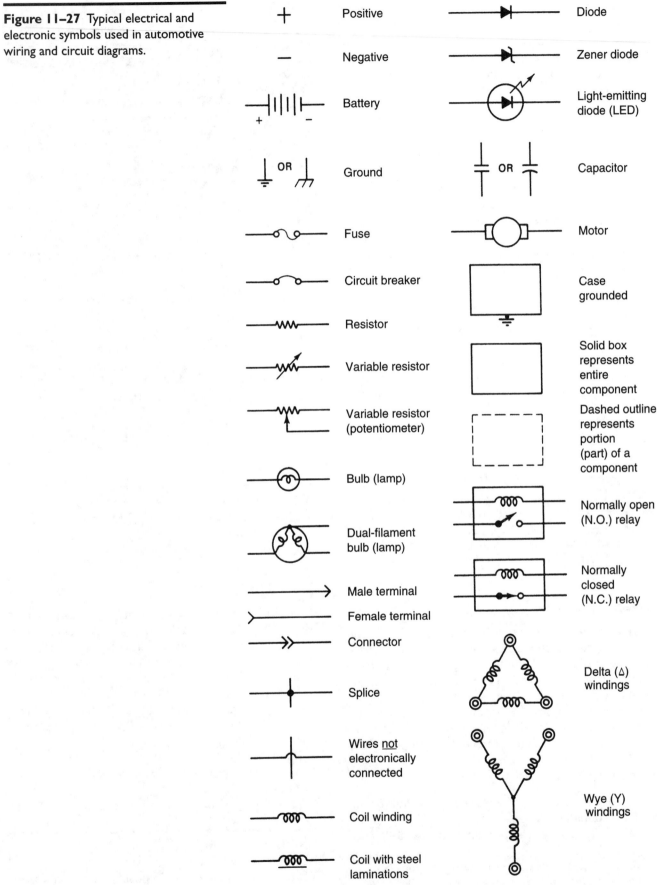

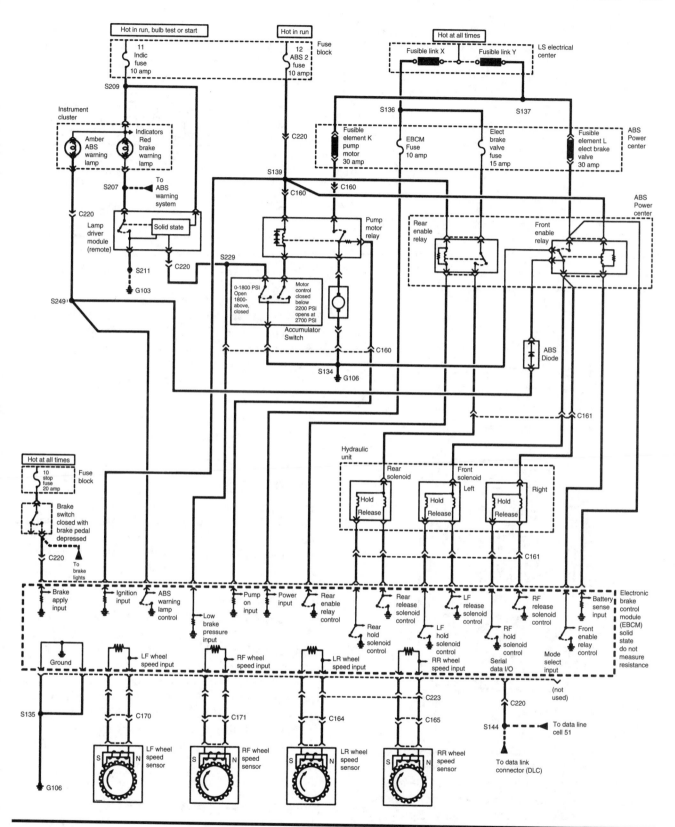

Figure 11–28 Typical ABS wiring diagram. Note how the ABS is powered by a 10-amp fuse and two fusible links all hot at all times. The amber and red brake warning lamps are powered by an ignition-switch-controlled 10-amp fuse. (Courtesy of General Motors)

Open circuits

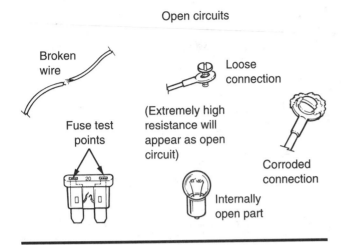

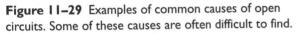

Figure 11–29 Examples of common causes of open circuits. Some of these causes are often difficult to find.

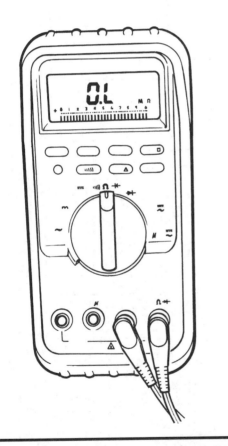

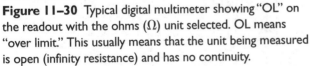

Figure 11–30 Typical digital multimeter showing "OL" on the readout with the ohms (Ω) unit selected. OL means "over limit." This usually means that the unit being measured is open (infinity resistance) and has no continuity.

4. Usually blows a fuse
5. Usually affects only one circuit
6. The current in the circuit bypasses some or all of the resistance in the circuit.

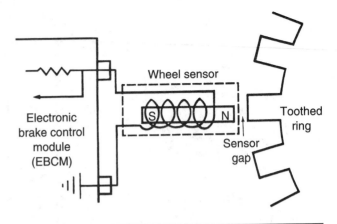

Figure 11–31 Typical wheel speed sensor. When a tooth on the sensor ring is close to the sensor, the strength of the magnetic field is stronger because the metal of the tooth conducts magnetic lines of force better than air. Then when the tooth moves away, the magnetic field strength is reduced. It is this changing magnetic field strength that produces the changing voltage. Frequency of the signal is determined by the speed of the rotating sensor. (Courtesy of General Motors)

Voltage Drops

Any resistance in a circuit causes the voltage to drop in proportion to the amount of the resistance. Since a high resistance will drop the voltage more than a lower resistance, we can use a voltmeter to measure resistance.

■ ELECTRICAL ABS SERVICE

Most ABS electrical components are serviced by replacement only. For example, if an open circuit is detected in one wheel speed sensor wiring harness, the wiring harness section is usually replaced. Other commonly replaced ABS components include relays and wheel speed sensors. Most wheel speed sensors are not adjustable, but some vehicles do provide adjustment (see Figures 11–31, 11–32, and 11–33).

■ HYDRAULIC ABS SERVICE

Before doing any brake work on a vehicle equipped with antilock brakes, always consult the appropriate service information for the exact vehicle being serviced. For example, some manufacturers recommend discharging the hydraulic accumulator by depressing the brake pedal many times before opening

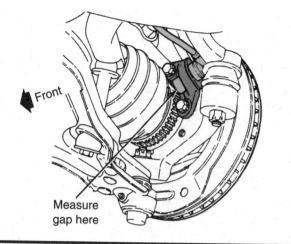

Figure 11–32 The gap between the toothed ring and the wheel speed sensor is important for proper operation. (Courtesy of General Motors)

bleeder valves. Many service checks require that a pressure gauge be installed in the system as shown in Figure 11–34.

■ BLEEDING ABS

After depressing the unit as per manufacturer's recommended procedures, the brakes can be bled using the same procedure as for a vehicle without ABS (see Chapter 3). Air trapped in the ABS hydraulic unit may require that a scan tool be used to cycle the valves.

> **HINT:** To avoid having to bleed the hydraulic unit, use a brake pedal depressor during brake service to avoid losing brake fluid. This simple precaution keeps air from getting into the hard-to-bleed passages of the hydraulic unit.

■ ABS SAFETY PRECAUTIONS

1. Avoid mounting the antenna for transmitting device near the ABS control unit. Transmitting devices include cellular (cell) telephones and citizen-band radios.
2. Avoid mounting tires of different diameter than that of the original tires. Different size tires generate different wheel speed sensor frequencies which may not be usable by the ABS controller.
3. Never open a bleeder valve or loosen a hydraulic line while the ABS is pressurized. The accumulator must be depressurized according to the manufacturer's recommended procedures.

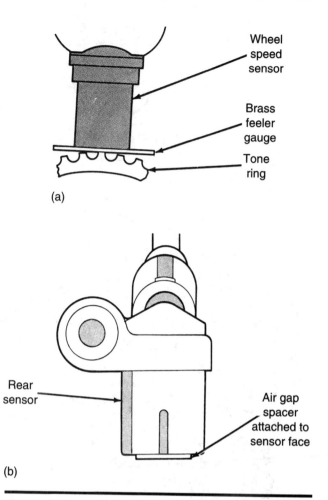

Figure 11–33 (a) Always use a nonferrous (brass or plastic) feeler (thickness) gauge when measuring the gap between the toothed ring and the wheel speed sensor. Since the sensor contains a magnet, a steel feeler gauge would stick to the sensor itself and a true "feel" for the actual gap would be difficult to determine. (b) Sometimes a sensor is equipped with a paper spacer that is the exact thickness of the spacing required between the toothed ring and the sensor. If equipped, the sensor is simply installed with the paper touching the toothed wheel. A typical gap ranges from 0.020″ to 0.050″ (0.5 to 1.3 mm). (Courtesy of Chrysler Corporation)

4. If arc welding on a vehicle, disconnect all computers (electronic control modules) to avoid possible damage due to voltage spikes.
5. Do not pry against or hit the wheel speed sensor ring.

■ DIAGNOSING INTERMITTENT PROBLEMS

Problems or faults that only occur once in a while are called intermittents. Intermittent problems usually involve wiring or wiring connections.

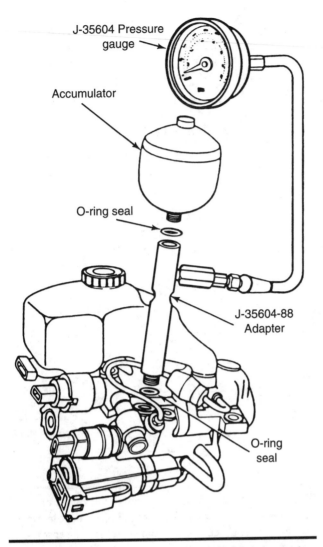

Figure 11–34 Installing a pressure gauge on an integral antilock system. Most service instructions of integral ABS units require that the brake pedal be depressed as many as forty times with the ignition "off" before opening any hydraulic line or valve. (Courtesy of General Motors)

TECH TIP ✔

Don't Forget To Bleed the E-H Unit

Air can easily get trapped in the ABS electronic-hydraulic (E-H) assembly whenever the hydraulic system is opened. Even though the master cylinder and all four wheel cylinders/calipers have been bled, sometimes the brake pedal will still feel spongy. Some E-H units can be bled through the use of a scan tool where the valves are pulsed in sequence by the electronic brake controller (computer). Some units are equipped with bleeder valves; others must be bled by loosening the brake lines. Bleeding the E-H unit also purges out the older brake fluid, which can cause rust and corrosion damage. Only DOT 3 brake fluid is specified for use in an antilock braking system. Always check the label on the brake fluid reservoir and/or service manual or owner's manual.

> *CAUTION:* Some ABS units require that the brake pedal be depressed as many as forty times to discharge brake fluid fully from the accumulator. Failure to discharge the accumulator fully can show that the brake fluid level is too low. If additional brake fluid is added, the fluid could overflow the reservoir during an ABS stop when the accumulator discharges brake fluid back into the reservoir.

> *HINT:* Most electrical faults are caused by heat or movement. Look closely at connectors or wiring near wheel speed sensors or wiring running near components of the exhaust system. Also look closely for aftermarket accessories such as neon lights that could interfere with the wheel speed sensor signals to the ABS computer.

Look carefully at each connector for proper mating or poor terminal-to-wire connection.

PHOTO SEQUENCE   Bleeding a Teves Antilock Braking System

PS11-1 Prepare to bleed the brake hydraulic system by checking the hydraulic system including the master cylinder.

PS11-2 Always use DOT 3 brake fluid in any vehicle equipped with ABS.

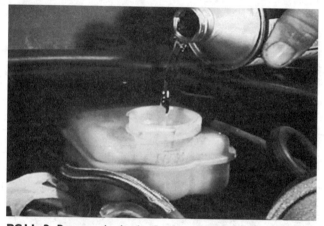

PS11-3 Be sure the brake fluid level in the reservoir is filled to the maximum line. Do not overfill.

PS11-4 Hoist the vehicle safely and raise to a good working level to service the wheel brakes.

PS11-5 Remove the wheels.

PS11-6 The Chrysler service manual specifies that the base brakes be manually bled before using the scan tool to bleed the air in the hydraulic unit. Tapping on the bleeder valve helps break the taper of the bleeder valve.

Bleeding a Teves Antilock Braking System—continued

PS11–7 Use a six-point wrench or socket and loosen the bleeder valve.

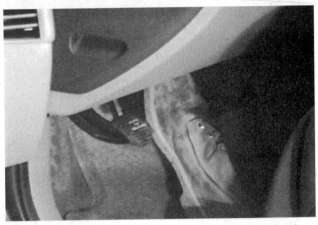

PS11–8 Have an assistant depress the brake pedal slowly to bleed the air from each wheel starting at the right rear, then the left rear, right front, and finally the left front wheel.

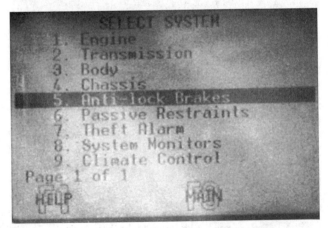

PS11–9 After manually bleeding all four wheels, connect the Chrysler DRB III scan tool to the data link connector (DLC) located under the dash.

PS11–10 Turn the scan tool on and follow the directions on the display.

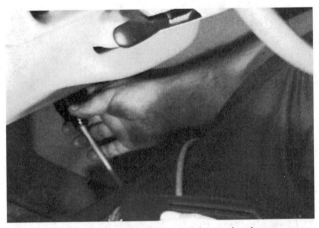

PS11–11 Select "antilock brakes" from the menu.

PS11–12 Select "bleed brakes" from the selection menu.

Bleeding a Teves Antilock Braking System—continued

PS11–13 The scan tool now instructs the service technician to press and hold the brake pedal.

PS11–14 With the brake pedal depressed, the scan tool commands the ABS pump motor to operate.

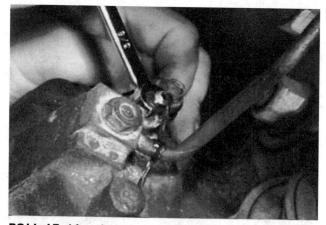

PS11–15 The pump motor will run until the count down on the display reads zero.

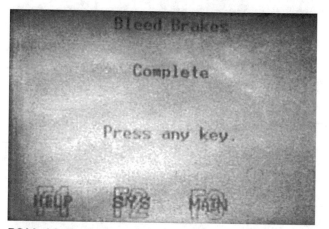

PS11–16 Finally the scan tool display indicates that the brake bleeding process is complete.

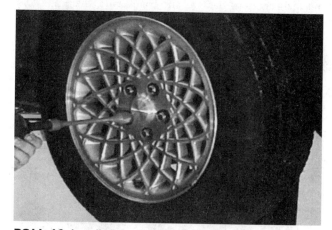

PS11–17 After the scan tool bleeding is complete, fill the master cylinder if necessary and bleed the base brakes again following the same procedure as before. Be sure to refill the master cylinder after bleeding.

PS11–18 Install all four wheels and torque the lug nuts to factory specifications. Test-drive the vehicle to ensure proper braking before returning the vehicle to the customer.

PHOTO SEQUENCE 4WAL ABS Diagnosis

PS11-19 A Chevrolet pickup truck is being driven into the shop with an antilock brake system (ABS) problem.

PS11-20 The amber ABS warning light remains on whenever the ignition is on.

PS11-21 The first step of almost any diagnostic procedure is to perform a thorough visual inspection including checking the level and condition of the brake fluid in the master cylinder reservoir.

PS11-22 A visual inspection should also include an inspection of the wiring and all hydraulic components under the hood.

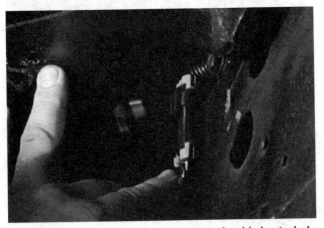

PS11-23 A thorough visual inspection should also include checking all wheel speed sensor wiring and connectors.

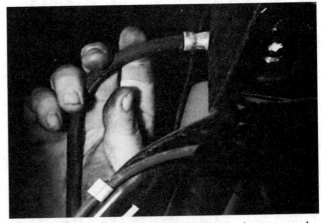

PS11-24 The hydraulic system should also be inspected for obvious faults or damage that could have been caused by road debris such as a cut flexible brake line.

4WAL ABS Diagnosis—continued

PS11–25 After a thorough visual inspection, a scan tool should be used to retrieve any stored diagnostic trouble codes (DTCs). A Tech 2 is being used on this Chevrolet truck.

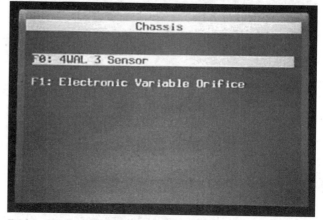

PS11–26 From "chassis" select "4WAL, 3 sensor" ABS on the Tech 2 scan tool.

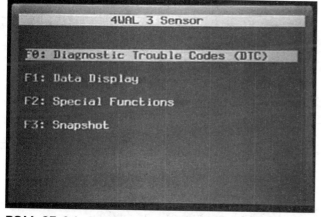

PS11–27 Select "diagnostic trouble codes (DTCs)" from the selection menu.

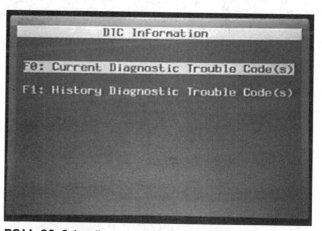

PS11–28 Select "current diagnostic trouble code(s)" from the selection menu.

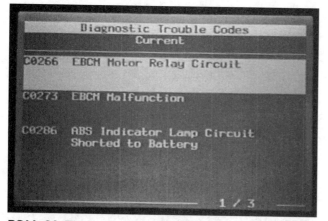

PS11–29 There are three DTCs stored including C0266. The "C" means that it is a chassis code and the "0" indicates that this is an SAE-specified OBD II DTC.

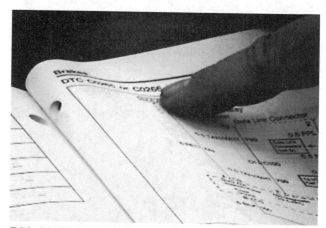

P11–30 The service manual is checked for DTC C0266.

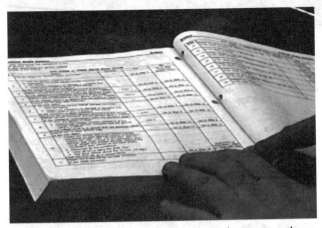

PS11–31 By following the service manual test procedure, the technician is led to the conclusion that the fault is due to a defective ABS controller (computer) which also explains the multiple codes found.

PS11–32 The technician disconnected the battery before replacing the ABS computer. The old computer was returned to the parts store as a core to be rebuilt.

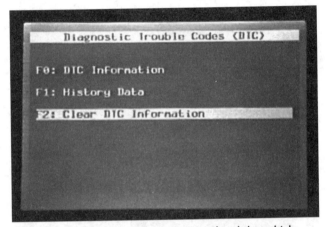

PS11–33 The battery was reconnected and the vehicle driven to check for proper operation of the ABS amber dashboard warning light and for proper ABS brake operation. The Tech 2 was connected again. If another fault had been found, the scan tool should be used to clear the stored DTC and the vehicle driven to confirm that the problem has been corrected.

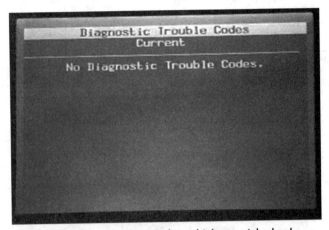

PS11–34 After test-driving the vehicle, a quick check using the Tech 2 indicates no stored DTCs.

PS11–35 If a Tech 2 is not available, a Snap-on Scanner can also be used on this vehicle to retrieve and clear ABS DTCs.

PS11–36 After double-checking that everything is okay with the antilock braking system, the vehicle can be driven out of the stall and returned to the customer.

■ SUMMARY

1. ABS diagnosis starts with checking the status of both the red brake warning lamp and the amber "ABS" warning lamp.

2. The second step in diagnosis of an ABS problem is to perform a thorough visual inspection.

3. The third step in diagnosis of an ABS problem is to test-drive the vehicle and verify the fault.

4. Always consult the factory service information for the specific vehicle being serviced for the proper procedure to use to retrieve diagnostic trouble codes and clear diagnostic trouble codes.

5. A breakout box is used with a digital multimeter to diagnose electrical ABS components.

6. Hydraulic service on most integral ABS units requires that the brake pedal be depressed as many as forty times with the ignition key "off" to depressurize the hydraulic system.

■ REVIEW QUESTIONS

1. Describe proper operation of the red and amber brake warning lamps.

2. List the items that should be checked as part of a thorough visual inspection.

3. Explain how to retrieve a diagnostic trouble code from a General Motors vehicle equipped with Kelsey-Hayes RWAL ABS.

4. Describe how to use a breakout box to check for proper wheel speed sensor operation.

■ ASE CERTIFICATION-TYPE QUESTIONS

1. The red brake warning lamp is on and the amber ABS lamp is off. Technician A says that a fault is possible in the base brake system. Technician B says that the red brake warning lamp can be turned on by a malfunction in an integral ABS with low accumulator pressure. Which technician is correct?
   a. Technician A only
   b. Technician B only
   c. Both Technician A and B
   d. Neither Technician A nor B

2. Technician A says that wheel speed sensors are magnetic. Technician B says that the toothed sensor ring is magnetic. Which technician is correct?
   a. Technician A only
   b. Technician B only
   c. Both Technician A and B
   d. Neither Technician A nor B

3. Technician A says that using the space-saving small spare tire may trigger an ABS amber warning lamp. Technician B says the use of the small spare tire on either front wheel may trigger the red brake warning lamp. Which technician is correct?
   a. Technician A only
   b. Technician B only
   c. Both Technician A and B
   d. Neither Technician A nor B

4. Technician A says that with some antilock braking systems, the diagnostic trouble code may be lost if the ignition is turned off before retrieving the code. Technician B says that some antilock braking systems require that a terminal be grounded to cause the amber ABS warning lamp to flash diagnostic trouble codes. Which technician is correct?
   a. Technician A only
   b. Technician B only
   c. Both Technician A and B
   d. Neither Technician A nor B

5. Technician A says that a scan tool may be required to retrieve data and diagnostic trouble codes from some antilock braking systems. Technician B says that a jumper wire can be used to retrieve diagnostic trouble codes on some antilock braking systems. Which technician is correct?
   a. Technician A only
   b. Technician B only
   c. Both Technician A and B
   d. Neither Technician A nor B

6. Technician A says that a breakout box is often required to diagnose an antilock braking system. Technician B says that a breakout box also requires the use of a digital multimeter. Which technician is correct?
   a. Technician A only
   b. Technician B only
   c. Both Technician A and B
   d. Neither Technician A nor B

7. Technician A says that a dim red brake warning lamp could indicate a fault in the antilock braking system on some vehicles. Technician B says that the ABS fuse may have to be removed to erase some ABS diagnostic codes if a scan tool is not used. Which technician is correct?
   a. Technician A only
   b. Technician B only
   c. Both Technician A and B
   d. Neither Technician A nor B

8. The ABS computer uses the _____ signal from a wheel speed sensor.
   a. Voltage
   b. Frequency
   c. Resistance
   d. Electromagnetic

9. The control terminals for a relay are
   a. 86 and 85
   b. 87 and 30
   c. 87a and 87
   d. 87 and 86

10. Technician A says that the ABS electrohydraulic unit can be bled using bleeder screws and the manual method. Technician B says that a scan tool is often required to bleed the ABS electrohydraulic unit. Which technician is correct?
    a. Technician A only
    b. Technician B only
    c. Both Technician A and B
    d. Neither Technician A nor B

ASE-Style Sample Test

1. A customer complains that the steering lacks power assist all the time. Technician A says that the power steering pump drive belt could be slipping or loose. Technician B says that worn outer tie rod ends could be the cause. Which technician is correct?
   a. Technician A only
   b. Technician B only
   c. Both Technician A and B
   d. Neither Technician A nor B

2. A front-wheel-drive vehicle pulls toward the right during acceleration. The most likely cause is:
   a. Worn or defective tires
   b. Leaking or defective shock absorbers
   c. Normal torque steer
   d. A defective power steering rack and pinion steering assembly

3. When replacing a rubber bonded socket (RBS) tie rod end, the technician should be sure to:
   a. Remove the original using a special tool
   b. Install and tighten the replacement with the front wheels in the straight-ahead position
   c. Grease the joint before installing on the vehicle
   d. Install the replacement using a special clamp vise

4. Whenever installing a tire on a rim, do not exceed:
   a. 25 psi
   b. 30 psi
   c. 35 psi
   d. 40 psi

5. Two technicians are discussing mounting a tire on a wheel. Technician A says that for best balance, the tire should be match mounted. Technician B says that silicone spray should be used to lubricate the tire bend. Which technician is correct?
   a. Technician A only
   b. Technician B only
   c. Both Technician A and B
   d. Neither Technician A nor B

6. Technician A says that radial tires should *only* be rotated front to rear, never side to side. Technician B says that radial tires should be rotated using the modified X method. Which technician is correct?
   a. Technician A only
   b. Technician B only
   c. Both Technician A and B
   d. Neither Technician A nor B

7. For a tire that has excessive radial runout, Technician A says that it should be broken down on a tire-changing machine and the tire rotated 180 degrees on the wheel and retested. Technician B says that the tire should be replaced. Which technician is correct?
   a. Technician A only
   b. Technician B only
   c. Both Technician A and B
   d. Neither Technician A nor B

8. Technician A says that overloading a vehicle can cause damage to the wheel bearings. Technician B says that tapered roller bearings used on a non-drive wheel should be adjusted hand tight only after seating. Which technician is correct?
   a. Technician A only
   b. Technician B only
   c. Both Technician A and B
   d. Neither Technician A nor B

9. Defective wheel bearings usually sound like
   a. A growl
   b. A rumble
   c. Snow tires
   d. All of the above

10. Defective outer CV joints usually make a clicking noise
    a. Only when backing
    b. While turning and moving
    c. While turning only
    d. During braking

11. The proper lubricant usually specified for use in a differential is
    a. SAE 15-40 engine oil
    b. SAE 80W-90 GL-5
    c. STF
    d. SAE 80W-140 GL-1

12. A vehicle owner complained that a severe vibration was felt throughout the entire vehicle only during rapid acceleration from a stop and up to about 20 mph (32 km/h). The most likely cause is
    a. Unequal driveshaft working angles
    b. A bent driveshaft
    c. Defective universal joints
    d. A bent rim or a defective tire

13. To remove a C-clip axle, what step does *not* need to be done?
    a. Remove the differential cover
    b. Remove the axle flange bolts/nuts
    c. Remove the pinion shaft
    d. Remove the pinion shaft lock bolt

14. Drive shaft working angles can be changed by
    a. Replacing the U-joints
    b. Using shims or wedges under the transmission or rear axle
    c. Rotating the position of the driveshaft on the yoke
    d. Tightening the differential pinion nut

15. A driver complains that the vehicle darts or moves first toward one side and then to the other side of the road. Technician A says that bump steer caused by an unlevel steering linkage could be the cause. Technician B says that a worn housing in the spool valve area of the power rack and pinion is the most likely cause. Which technician is correct?
    a. Technician A only
    b. Technician B only
    c. Both Technician A and B
    d. Neither Technician A nor B

16. A vehicle equipped with power rack and pinion steering is hard to steer when cold only. After a couple of miles of driving, the steering power assist returns to normal. The most likely cause of this temporary loss of power assist when cold is
    a. A worn power steering pump
    b. Worn grooves in the spool valve area of the rack and pinion steering unit
    c. A loose or defective power steering pump drive belt
    d. A defective power steering computer sensor

17. A dry park test is performed
    a. On a frame-type lift with the wheels hanging free
    b. By pulling and pushing on the wheels with the vehicle supported by a frame-type lift
    c. On the ground or on a drive-on lift and moving the steering wheel while observing for looseness
    d. Driving in a figure 8 in a parking lot

18. On a parallelogram-type steering linkage, the part that usually needs replacement first is the
    a. Pitman arm
    b. Outer tie rod end(s)
    c. Center link
    d. Idler arm

19. What parts need to be added to a "short" rack to make a "long" rack and pinion steering unit?
    a. Bellows and ball socket assemblies
    b. Bellows and outer tie rod ends
    c. Ball socket assemblies and outer tie rod ends
    d. Outer tie rod ends

20. The adjustment procedure for a typical integral power steering gear is
    a. Overcenter adjustment, then worm thrust bearing preload
    b. Worm thrust bearing preload, then the overcenter adjustment

21. A vehicle is sagging at the rear. Technician A says that standard replacement shock absorbers should restore proper ride (trim) height. Technician B says that replacement springs are needed to properly restore ride height. Which technician is correct?
    a. Technician A only
    b. Technician B only
    c. Both Technician A and B
    d. Neither Technician A nor B

22. Technician A says that indicator ball joints should be loaded with the weight of the vehicle on the ground to observe the wear indicator. Technician B says that the non-indicator ball joints should be inspected *unloaded*. Which technician is correct?
    a. Technician A only
    b. Technician B only
    c. Both Technician A and B
    d. Neither Technician A nor B

23. The maximum allowable axial play in a ball joint is usually:
    a. 0.001″ (0.025 mm)
    b. 0.003″ (0.076 mm)
    c. 0.030″ (0.76 mm)
    d. 0.050″ (1.27 mm)

24. The ball joint used on MacPherson strut suspension is load carrying.
    a. True
    b. False

25. Technician A says that tapered parts, such as tie rod ends, should be tightened to specifications, then loosened 1/4 turn before installing the cotter key. Technician B says that the nut used to retain tapered parts should never be loosened after torquing, but rather tightened further, if necessary, to line up the cotter key hole. Which technician is correct?
    a. Technician A only
    b. Technician B only
    c. Both Technician A and B
    d. Neither Technician A nor B

26. When should the strut rod (retainer) nut be removed?
  a. After compressing the coil spring
  b. Before removing the MacPherson strut from the vehicle
  c. After removing the cartridge gland nut
  d. Before removing the brake hose from the strut housing clip

27. "Dog tracking" is often caused by broken or damaged
  a. Stabilizer bar links
  b. Strut rod bushings
  c. Rear leaf springs
  d. Track (panhard) rod

28. A pull toward one side during braking is one symptom of (a) defective or worn
  a. Stabilizer bar links
  b. Strut rod bushings
  c. Rear leaf springs
  d. Track (panhard) rod

29. Oil is added to the MacPherson strut housing before installing a replacement cartridge to
  a. Lubricate the cartridge
  b. Transfer heat from the cartridge to the outside strut housing
  c. Act as a shock damper
  d. Prevent unwanted vibrations

30. A vehicle will pull toward the side with the
  a. Most camber
  b. Least camber

31. Excessive toe out will wear the edges of both front tires.
  a. Inside
  b. Outside

32. A vehicle will pull toward the side with the
  a. Most caster
  b. Least caster

33. If the turning radius (TOOT) is out of specification, what should be replaced?
  a. The outer tie rod ends
  b. The inner tie rod ends
  c. The idler arm
  d. The steering knuckle

34. SAI and camber together form the
  a. Included angle
  b. Turning radius angle
  c. Scrub radius angle
  d. Setback angle

35. The thrust angle is being corrected. The alignment technician should adjust which angle to reduce thrust angle?
  a. Rear camber
  b. Front SAI or included angle and camber
  c. Rear toe
  d. Rear caster

36. Strut rods adjust if there is a nut on both sides of the frame bushings.
  a. Camber
  b. Caster
  c. SAI or included angle, depending on the exact vehicle
  d. Toe

37–40. Questions 37 through 40 will use the following specifications:
  front camber $0.5° + - 0.3°$
  front caster $3.5°$ to $4.5°$
  toe $0° + - 0.1°$
  rear camber $0° + - 0.5°$
  rear toe $-0.1°$ to $0.1°$
  alignment angles
    front camber left $0.5°$
    front camber right $-0.1°$
    front caster left $3.8°$
    front caster right $4.5°$
    front toe left $-0.2°$
    front toe right $+0.2°$
    total toe $0.0°$
    rear camber left $0.15°$
    rear camber right $-0.11°$
    rear toe left $0.04°$
    rear toe right $0.14°$

37. The first angle corrected should be
  a. Right front camber
  b. Right rear camber
  c. Right rear toe
  d. Left front camber

38. The present alignment will cause excessive tire wear to the inside of both front tires.
  a. True
  b. False

39. The present alignment will cause excessive tire wear to the rear tires.
  a. True
  b. False

40. With the present alignment, the vehicle will
  a. Pull toward the right
  b. Go straight
  c. Pull toward the left

Lug Nut Tightening Torque Chart

To be used as a guide only. Consult the factory service manual or literature for the exact specifications and exceptions for the vehicle being serviced.

Name	Model	Years	Lb. Ft. Torque
Acura	All	86–99	80
American Motors	All	70–87	75
Audi	All	78–99	81
BMW	All except the following	78–99	65–79
	320I	77–83	59–65
	528L	79–81	59–65
Buick	All except the following	76–99	100
	Century	76–81	80
	Regal	78–86	80
	LeSabre	76–85	80
Cadillac	All except	76–99	100
	1976 Seville	1976	80
Chevrolet	Geo Prizm	92–99	100
	Geo Prizm	89–91	76
	Geo Storm	90–99	86.5
	Sprint	85–88	50
	Spectrum	85–88	65
	Chevette	82–87	80
	Chevette	76–81	70
	Nova	85–89	76
	Vega and Monza	76–80	80
	Cavalier	82–99	100
	Celebrity	82–90	100

Name	Model	Years	Lb. Ft. Torque
	Citation	80–86	100
	Camaro	89–99	100
	Camaro	78–88	80
	Malibu and Monte Carlo	76–88	80
	Malibu Wagon	76–86	80
	Impala and Caprice Sedan	77–90	80
	Caprice	91–93	100
	Corvette	84–99	100
	Corvette	76–83	90
	Corsica and Beretta	87–98	100
Chevrolet/ GMC Light Trucks and Vans	Geo Tracker	92–93	60
	Geo Tracker	89–91	37–58
	Lumina APV	90–99	100
	Astro/Safari Van	85–99	100
	S/10 and S/15 Pickup	80–88	80
	T/10 and T/15 Pickup	88–99	100
	C/K Pickup all except:	88–99	120
	C/K Pickup Dual Rear Wheels	88–99	140

Name	Model	Years	Lb. Ft. Torque
	V10 (4WD Full Size) Suburban and Blazer (Aluminum Wheels)	88–89	100
	V10 (4WD Full Size) Suburban and Blazer (Steel Wheels)	88–89	90
	V10 (4WD Full Size) Suburban (All)	90–99	100
	R10 (2WD Full Size) Suburban and Blazer	1989	100
	R/V20 (2WD, 4WD Full Size) Suburban	1989	120
	G10, 20 (Full Size) Van	88–99	100
	G30 (Full Size) Van except:	88–99	120
	G30 (Full Size) Van (Dual Rear Wheels)	88–99	140
	El Camino/ Caballero, Sprint	67–87	90
	Luv Pickup	76–82	90
	C/K10 Blazer and Jimmy	71–87	90
	Chevy and GMC Pickups 10/15, 20/25, 30/35 (Single Rear Wheel with 7/16 and 1/2 Studs)	71–87	90
	Chevy and GMC Pickups 10/15, 20/25, 30/35 (Single Rear Wheel with 9/16 Studs)	71–87	120
Chrysler	Concorde	93–99	95
	Chrysler T/C by Maserati	89–91	95
	Conquest	87–89	65–80
	LeBaron (FWD)	84–93	95
	LeBaron (FWD)	82–83	80
	New Yorker (FWD)	83–99	95
	Town and Country (FWD)	84–88	95
	Town and Country (FWD)	82–83	80
	Fifth Avenue (RWD)	83–90	85
	New Yorker (RWD)	76–82	85
	New Yorker (FWD)	93–99	95
	Laser	84–86	95
	Limousine	85–86	95
	Executive Sedan	84–85	95
	E-Class	83–84	80
	Imperial	90–93	95
	Imperial (RWD)	81–83	85
	Cordoba	76–83	85
	LeBaron (RWD)	78–81	85
	Town and Country (RWD)	78–81	85
	Newport	76–81	85
Daihatsu	Charade	88–91	65–87
Daihatsu Light Trucks and Vans	Rocky (All)	90–91	65–87
Dodge	Intrepid	93–99	95
	Stealth	91–99	87–101
	Spirit	89–93	95
	Shadow	87–93	95
	Colt	76–93	65–80
	Lancer	85–89	95
	Aries	84–89	95
	Aries	81–83	80
	Charger	84–87	95
	Charger	82–83	80
	Daytona	84–93	95
	Omni	84–90	95
	Omni	78–83	80
	Vista	84–93	50–57
	600	84–88	95

Name	Model	Years	Lb. Ft. Torque
	600	1983	80
	Diplomat	78–89	80
	Dynasty	88–93	95
	Monaco	90–91	54–72
	Conquest	1986	65–80
	Conquest	84–85	50–57
	400	82–83	80
	Challenger	78–83	51–58
	Mirada	80–83	85
	St. Regis	79–81	85
	Aspen	76–80	85
Dodge Light Trucks and Vans	Caravan, Ram Van (FWD)	84–99	95
	Rampage (FWD)	82–84	90
	Ramcharge AD, AW100	79–93	105
	Wagons B100/150	72–99	105
	Wagons B200/250	72–99	105
	Wagons B300/350 1/2″ Studs	69–99	105
	Wagons B300/350 5/8″ Studs	79–99	200
	D50 Pickup	78–86	55
	D50 Pickup	87–99	95
	D100/150 Pickup	72–99	105
	D200/250 Pickup	81–99	105
	D300/350 Pickup 1/2″ Studs	79–99	105
	D300/350 Pickup 5/8″ Studs	79–99	200
	W100/150 Pickup	79–99	105
	W200/250 Pickup	79–99	105
	W300/350 Pickup 1/2″ Studs	79–99	105
	W300/350 Pickup 5/8″ Studs	79–99	200
	Dakota	87–99	85
Ford	All except the following	84–99	85–105
	Probe	89–91	65–87

Name	Model	Years	Lb. Ft. Torque
	Festiva	89–93	65–87
	Escort	81–83	80–105
	EXP	82–83	80–105
	Fiesta	78–80	63–85
	Mustang	79–83	80–105
	Pinto	76–80	80–105
	Fairmont	78–83	80–105
	Granada	76–82	80–105
	LTD	79–83	80–105
	LTD	76–78	70–115
	Torino	76–79	80–105
	LTD Crown Victoria	1983	80–105
	Country Sedan and Squire	79–83	80–105
	Thunderbird	80–83	80–105
	Thunderbird	76–79	70–115
Ford Light Trucks and Vans	E150/F150 and Bronco	88–99	100
	E250/E350, F250, F350	88–99	140
	Aerostar	86–99	100
	Bronco	88–93	135
	Bronco	72–87	100
	Explorer	91–99	100
	Club Wagon E100/150	75–87	100
	Club Wagon E200/250	76–87	100
	Club Wagon E300/350 (Single Rear Wheels)	76–87	145
	Club Wagon E300/350 (Dual Rear Wheels)	76–87	220
	Econoline Van E100/150	75–81	100
	Econoline Van E200/250	76–87	100
	Econoline Van E300/350 (Single Rear Wheels)	76–87	145
	Econoline Van E300/350 (Dual Rear Wheels)	76–87	220
	Ranger Pickup	84–87	100

Name	Model	Years	Lb. Ft. Torque
	Courier Pickup	77–83	65
	F100/150 Pickup	75–87	100
	F200/250 Pickup	76–87	100
	F300/350 Pickup (Single Rear Wheels)	76–87	145
	F300/350 Pickup (Dual Rear Wheels)	76–87	220
Honda	All except the following	84–99	80
	Civic All	73–83	58
	Accord All	82–99	80
	Accord All	76–81	58
	Prelude All	79–99	80
Hyundai	All except the following	90–99	65–80
	Excel	86–89	50–57
Infiniti	All	90–99	72–87
Isuzu	Stylus	1991	87
	Impulse	83–91	87
	I Mark	87–89	65
	I Mark	1986	90
	I Mark	1985	50
	I Mark	82–84	50
Isuzu Light Trucks and Vans	Pickup	91–99	72
	Pickup	1990	58–87
	Amigo	1991	72
	Amigo	89–90	58–87
	Rodeo	1991	72
	Trooper	84–91	58–87
Jaguar	All	89–91	65–75
	XJ6 and XJS	1988	75
	All	81–87	80
Eagle	Vision	1993	95
	Premier	89–91	54–72
	Talon	90–99	87–101
	Summit	89–91	65–80
	Medallion	1988	67
Jeep Light Trucks and Vans	Grand Cherokee and Grand Wagoneer	92–99	88
	Wrangler, YJ Cherokee, Comanche	90–99	80
		84–91	75

Name	Model	Years	Lb. Ft. Torque
	Wagoneer and Grand Wagoneer	84–91	75
	Trucks (under 8400 GVW)	84–89	75
	Trucks (over 8400 GVW)	84–89	130
	CJ Series	84–86	80
	CJ Series	81–83	65–80
	Cherokee, Wagoneer	81–83	65–90
	Trucks (under 8400 GVW)	81–83	65–90
	Trucks (over 8400 GVW)	81–83	110–150
Lexus	All	90–99	76
Lincoln	All	84–99	85–105
	Mark IV	80–83	80–105
	Continental	76–83	80–105
	Town Car	81–83	80–105
	Versailles	77–80	80–105
Mazda	All except the following	88–99	65–87
	Navajo	91–99	100
	323	86–87	65–87
	GLC	81–85	65–80
	GLC	77–80	65–80
	GLC Wagon	84–85	65–87
	626	84–87	65–87
	626	1983	65–80
	626	79–82	65–80
	Cosmo	76–78	65–72
	808	76–77	65–72
	RX7	84–87	65–87
	RX7	79–83	65–80
	RX7	76–78	65–72
	RX3	76–78	65–72
Mazda Light Trucks and Vans	B2600	87–99	65–87
	B2200	86–99	65–87
	B2000/ B2200	80–85	72–80
Mercedes	All	76–99	81
Mercury	All	84–99	85–105
	All	76–83	80–105
Mitsubishi	Sigma V6	89–90	65–80
	Mirage	85–91	65–80
	Precis	87–89	51–58
	Cordia/ Tredia	83–88	50–57

Name	Model	Years	Lb. Ft. Torque
	Eclipse	90–99	87–101
	Galant	85–86	50–57
	Galant	1987	65–80
	Galant	88–99	65–80
	Starion	1983	50–57
	Starion	84–89	50–57
Mitsubishi Light Trucks and Vans	Van/Wagons	89–90	87–101
	Montero	89–91	75–87
	Pickups	89–91	72–87
	Pickups	83–87	65
	Montero	83–87	65
Nissan/ Datsun	All	91–99	72–87
	Maxima	89–90	72–87
	Maxima	87–88	72–89
	Maxima	85–86	58–72
	Pulsar SE, SE	87–90	72–87
	Pulsar	83–86	58–72
	Sentra	83–86	58–72
	Stanza All	87–90	72–87
	Stanza	82–86	58–72
	210	79–82	58–72
	310	79–82	58–72
	510	78–81	58–72
	810	1981	58–72
	810	77–80	58–65
	200 SX All	87–88	87–108
	200 SX	80–86	58–72
	200 SX	77–79	58–65
	280 ZX	79–83	58–72
	300 ZX and ZX Turbo	1990	72–87
	300 ZX and ZX Turbo	87–89	87–108
	Axxess	1990	72–87
	240 SX	1989	72–87
Nissan/ Datsun Light Trucks and Vans	All Pickups and Pathfinder	89–99	87–108
	Van	87–88	72–87
	Van	1990	72–87
Oldsmobile	All except the following	76–99	100
	Starfire	76–80	80
	Cutlass (RWD)	76–88	80
	Cutlass Supreme (FWD)	88–93	100
	Delta 88	77–85	80

Name	Model	Years	Lb. Ft. Torque
Oldsmobile Light Trucks and Vans	Silhouette	90–99	100
	Bravado	92–99	95
Plymouth	Colt	83–93	65-80
	Sundance	87–93	95
	Acclaim	89–93	95
	Laser	90–91	87–101
	Caravelle	85–88	95
	Horizon	84–90	95
	Horizon	78–83	80
	Turismo	84–87	95
	Turismo	82–83	80
	Vista	84–91	50–57
	Reliant	84–89	80
	Reliant	81–83	80
	Gran Fury	80–89	85
	Conquest	1986	50–57
	Conquest	84–85	50–57
	Sapporo	78–83	51–58
	Champ	79–82	51–58
Plymouth Light Trucks and Vans	Voyager	84–99	95
Pontiac	All except the following	80–88	100
	T-1000	81–87	80
	Sunbird	76–80	80
	Firebird	76–88	80
	Grand Prix	76–87	80
	Lemans	89–93	65
	Catalina	76–86	80
	Bonneville	76–86	80
	Parisienne	83–86	80
Pontiac Light Trucks and Vans	Trans Sport	90–99	100
Porsche	All	79–99	94
Range Rover	All	91–99	90–95
Saab	All	88–99	80–90
	All	76–87	65–80
Saturn	All	91–99	100
Sterling	All	87–91	53
Subaru	All	76–99	58–72
Toyota	All except the following	84–99	76
	Celica	70–85	66–86
	Supra	79–85	66–86

Name	Model	Years	Lb. Ft. Torque
	Corolla	80–83	66–86
	Corona	75–82	66–86
	Cressida	78–85	66–86
	Corona MK II	1976	65–94
	Tercel	80–85	66–86
	Starlet	81–85	66–86
Toyota Light Trucks and Vans	All except the following	88–99	76
	Land Cruiser	88–91	116
	Pickups	75–87	75
	Land Cruiser	75–84	75
	Van Wagon	84–86	75
Volkswagen	All except		
	Van	88–99	81
	Golf	85–87	81
	Rabbit All	76–84	73–87
	Jetta	81–87	81

Name	Model	Years	Lb. Ft. Torque
	Scirocco	76–84	73–87
	Quantum	82–86	81
	Dasher	76–81	65
	Scirocco	85–87	81
Volkswagen Light Trucks and Vans	Vanagon	80–99	123
	Pickups	79–84	81
	Transporter	77–79	95
Volvo	All	89–99	63
	740 Series	85–88	63
	760 Series	83–88	63
	GLE	76–82	72–94
	260 Series	75–84	72–95
	240 Series	81–88	63
	240 Series	75–80	72–95
Yugo	All with steel wheels	86–90	63
	All with alloy wheels	88–90	81

English–Metric (SI) Conversion*

Inches to Millimeters						Millimeters to Inches		
Inches			Inches				Inches	
Fraction	Decimal	mm	Fraction	Decimal	mm	mm	Decimal	Fraction
1/64	0.016	0.40	17/32	0.531	13.49	0.5	0.020	1/64
1/32	0.031	0.79	9/16	0.563	14.29	1	0.039	3/64
3/64	0.047	1.19	19/32	0.594	15.08	2	0.079	5/64
1/16	0.063	1.59	5/8	0.625	15.88	3	0.118	1/8
5/64	0.078	1.98	21/32	0.656	16.67	4	0.157	5/32
3/32	0.094	2.38	11/16	0.688	17.46	5	0.197	13/64
7/64	0.109	2.78	23/32	0.719	18.26	6	0.236	15/64
1/8	0.125	3.18	3/4	0.750	19.05	7	0.276	9/32
5/32	0.156	3.97	25/32	0.781	19.84	8	0.315	5/16
3/16	0.188	4.76	13/16	0.813	20.64	9	0.354	23/64
7/32	0.219	5.56	27/32	0.844	21.43	10	0.394	25/64
1/4	0.250	6.35	7/8	0.875	22.23	11	0.433	7/16
9/32	0.281	7.14	29/32	0.906	23.02	12	0.472	15/32
5/16	0.313	7.94	15/16	0.938	23.81	13	0.512	33/64
11/32	0.344	8.73	31/32	0.969	24.61	14	0.551	35/64
3/8	0.375	9.53	1	1.000	25.4	15	0.591	19/32
13/32	0.406	10.32				16	0.630	5/8
7/16	0.438	11.11				17	0.669	43/64
15/32	0.469	11.91				18	0.709	45/64
1/2	0.500	12.70				19	0.748	3/4
						20	0.787	25/32
						21	0.827	53/64
						22	0.866	55/64
						23	0.906	29/32
						24	0.945	15/16
						25	0.984	63/64

*Courtesy of FMC.

Decimal Equivalents

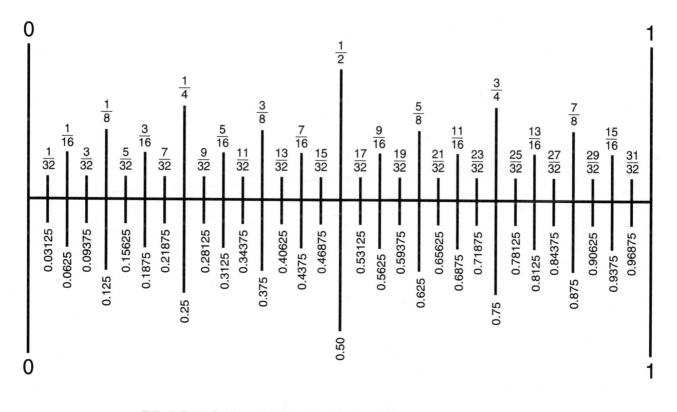

FRACTION/DECIMAL CONVERSION CHART

Shoe and Drum Diameter Chart

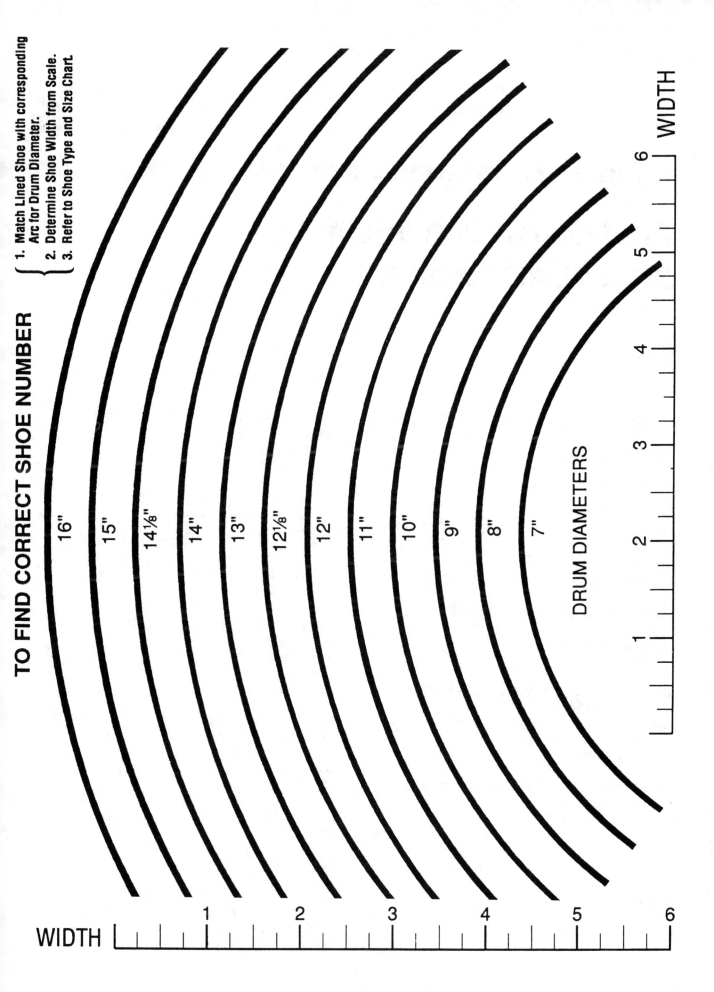

TO FIND CORRECT SHOE NUMBER

{ 1. Match Lined Shoe with corresponding Arc for Drum Diameter.
2. Determine Shoe Width from Scale.
3. Refer to Shoe Type and Size Chart.

WIDTH

16"
15"
14⅛"
14"
13"
12⅛"
12"
11"
10"
9"
8"
7"

DRUM DIAMETERS

1 2 3 4 5 6

WIDTH
1 2 3 4 5 6

Automotive Names and Addresses

A-1/CARDONE
5670 Rising Sun Avenue
Philadelphia, PA 19120
(215) 722-9700
FAX (215) 722-9787

AC-DELCO
3031 West Grand Boulevard
Detroit, MI 48202
(313) 974-0190
FAX (313) 974-1368

ALFRED TEVES TECHNOLOGIES, INC.
(ATE Brakes)
2718 Industrial Row
Troy, MI 48084

ALLIED-SIGNAL INC. AFTERMARKET BRAKES
105 Pawtucket Avenue
East Providence, RI 02916
(401) 431-7000
FAX (401) 431-3253

AMERICAN AUTOMOBILE ASSOCIATION (AAA)
8111 Gatehouse Road
Falls Church, VA 22047
(703) 222-6000

AMERICAN GREASE STICK COMPANY
2651 Hoyt Street P.O. Box 729
Muskegon, MI 49443
(616) 733-2101
FAX (616) 733-1784

AMERICAN PETROLEUM INSTITUTE (API)
1220 L Street, NW
Washington, DC 20005
(202) 682-8000

AMERICAN RACING EQUIPMENT
17600 South Santa Fe Avenue
Rancho Dominguez, CA 90221
(213) 635-7806

AUTO SAFETY HOTLINE
(800) 424-9393

AUTOMOTIVE CALIPER EXCHANGE
7650 Stage Road
Buena Park, CA 90621
(800) 350-2234
FAX (714) 521-3209

AUTOMOTIVE DISMANTLERS AND RECYCLERS
ASSOCIATION (ADRA)
1133 15th Street, NW
Washington, DC 20005
(202) 293-2372

AUTOMOTIVE HALL OF FAME, INC.
P.O. Box 1727
Midland, MI 48641-1727
(517) 631-5760

AUTOMOTIVE PARTS AND ACCESSORIES
ASSOCIATION, INC. (APCS)
5100 Forbes Boulevard
Lanham, MD 20706
(301) 459-9110

AUTOMOTIVE PARTS REBUILDERS ASSOCIATION,
INC. (APRA)
6849 Old Dominion Drive
McLean, VA 22101
(703) 790-1050

AUTOMOTIVE SERVICE ASSOCIATION (ASA)
1901 Airport Freeway
P.O. Box 929
Bedford, TX 76095-0929
(817) 644-6190

AUTOMOTIVE SERVICE COUNCILS, INC. (ASC)
188 Industrial Drive, Suite 112
Elmhurst, IL 60126
(312) 530-2330

AUTOMOTIVE SERVICE INDUSTRY ASSOCIATION
(ASIA)
25 Northwest Point Boulevard
Elk Grove Village, IL 60007-1030
(708) 228-1310

AUTOMOTIVE TECHNICIANS ASSOCIATION
INTERNATIONAL (ATAI)
139 West Maple
Birmingham, MI 48009
(313) 433-0136

AUTOMOTIVE UNDERCAR TRADE ORGANIZATION
(AUTO)
750 Lake Cook Road, Suite 410
Buffalo Grove, IL 60089
(800) 582-1359

AUTOMOTIVE WAREHOUSE DISTRIBUTORS
ASSOCIATION, INC. (AWDA)
9140 Ward Parkway
Kansas City, MO 64114
(816) 444-3500

BECK/ARNLEY WORLDPARTS CORPORATION
1020 Space Park South
Nashville, TN 37211
(615) 834-8080
FAX (615) 834-3628

BENDIX AUTOMOTIVE AFTERMARKET
1904 Bendix Drive
Jackson, TN 38301
(901) 423-1300

BORROUGHS DIVISION, SEALED POWER
CORPORATION
2429 North Burdick Street
Kalamazoo, MI 49007
(616) 345-2700

CALIPER CONNECTION, DIVISION OF
THE BRAKE COMPANIES INC.
80 Bacon Street
Waltham, MA 02154
(617) 647-9500
FAX (617) 647-9603

CAL-VAN TOOLS,
Division of Chemi-Trol Chemicals Company
1500 Walter Avenue
Fremont, OH 43420
(419) 334-2692

CAMPBELL HAUSFELD
100 Production Drive
Harrison, OH 45030
(513) 367-4811

CAR CARE COUNCIL (CCC)
One Grand Lake Drive
Port Clinton, OH 43452
(419) 734-5343

CARQUEST BRAKES
129 Worthington Ridge
Berlin, CT 06037
(203) 828-8290
FAX (203) 828-0613

CHAMPION PARTS REBUILDERS, INC.
2525 22nd Street
Oak Brook, IL 60521
(312) 986-6100

CHICAGO PNEUMATIC TOOL COMPANY
2200 Bleecker Street
Utica, NY 13501
(315 792-2800

CHRYSLER CORPORATION
26001 Lawrence Ave.
Center Line, MI 48015
(800) 422-7975

CORNWELL QUALITY TOOLS
667 Seville Road
Wadsworth, OH 44281
(216) 336-3506

CR SERVICES
735 Tollgate Road
Elgin, IL 60123-9332
(708) 742-7840
FAX (708) 742-5064

DANA CORPORATION
P.O. Box 455
Toledo, OH 43692
(419) 866-7800

DELPHI (DELCO) CHASSIS BRAKE DIVISION
General Motors Corporation
1420 Wisconsin Boulevard
Dayton, OH 45401
(513) 455-5000

EIS BRAKE PARTS, DIVISION STANDARD MOTOR
PRODUCTS
129 Worthington Ridge
Berlin, CT 06037
(203) 828-8290
FAX (203) 828-0613

ENVIRONMENTAL PROTECTION AGENCY (EPA)
401 M Street SW
Washington, DC 20460
(202) 828-3535

EQUIPMENT & TOOL INSTITUTE (ETI)
1545 Waukegan Road
Glenview, IL 60025-2187
(708) 729-8550

FEDERATION OF AUTOMOTIVE QUALIFIED
TECHNICIANS (FAQT)
251 West Franklin Avenue
Reed City, MI 49677
(616) 832-3399
(800) 866-3278

FERODO AUTOMOTIVE PRODUCTS
1 Grizzly Lane
Smithville, TN 37166
(615) 597-6700
FAX (615) 597-5243

FMC CORPORATION
Automotive Service Equipment Division
Exchange Avenue
Conway, AR 72032
(501) 327-4433

FORD PARTS AND SERVICE DIVISION,
FORD MOTOR COMPANY
3000 Schaefer Road
Dearborn, MI 48121
(313) 594-4845

FRICTION MATERIAL COMPANY, INC.
1849 East Sabine Street
Huntington, IN 46750
(800) 348-2399
FAX (219) 356-2410

FRICTION MATERIALS STANDARDS INSTITUTE,
INC. (FMSI)
588 Monroe Turnpike
Monroe, CT 06468
(203) 452-1877
FAX (203) 452-7951

GIBSON PRODUCTS, DIVISION OF ROLERO-
OMEGA, INC.
4933 NEO Parkway
Cleveland, OH 44128
(216) 581-0633
FAX (216) 581-2004

GOODYEAR TIRE AND RUBBER COMPANY
1144 East Market Street
Akron, OH 44316
(216) 796-6827

HAND TOOLS INSTITUTE (HTI)
25 North Broadway
Tarrytown, NY 10591
(914) 322-0040

HOLLANDER PUBLISHING COMPANY, INC.
P.O. Box 9405
Minneapolis, MN 55440
(612) 553-0644

HUNTER ENGINEERING COMPANY
11250 Hunter Drive
Bridgeton, MO 63044
(314) 731-3020

INGERSOLL-RAND COMPANY
Power Tool Division
Allen & Martinsville Roads
P.O. Box 1776
Liberty Corner, NJ 07938
(201) 647-6000

INTER-INDUSTRY CONFERENCE ON AUTO
COLLISION REPAIR (I-CAR)
3701 Algonquin Road, Suite 400
Rolling Meadows, IL 60008-3118
(708) 590-1191

INTERNATIONAL TRUCK PARTS
ASSOCIATION (ITPA)
7127 Braeburn Place
Bethesda, MD 20817
(202) 544-3090

ITT AIMCO
3000 University Drive
Auburn Hills, MI 48321
(313) 340-3500
FAX (313) 340-3542

ITT TEVES AFTERMARKET
606 Beach Drive
Annapolis, MD 21403
(410) 267-6362
FAX (410) 267-8202

KELSEY-HAYES COMPANY, INC.
Kelsey Axle & Brake Division
5800 West Donges Bay Road
Mequon, WI 53092

KENT-MOORE TOOL GROUP
Sealed Power Corporation
28635 Mound Road
Warren, MI 48092
(313) 574-2332

LEE MANUFACTURING, DIVISION
OF ROLERO-OMEGA INC.
4933 NEO Parkway
Cleveland, OH 44128
(216) 581-0633
FAX (216) 581-2004

LISLE CORPORATION
807 East Main Street
Clarinda, IA 51632
(712) 542-5101

LOCTITE CORPORATION
Automotive & Consumer Group
4450 Cranwood Court
Cleveland, OH 44128
(216) 475-3600

LUCAS AFTERMARKET OPERATIONS
5600 Crooks Road
Troy, MI
(313) 828-1000
FAX (313) 828-7653

MAC TOOLS, INC.
P.O. Box 370
Washington Court House, OH 43160
(614) 335-4112

MATCO TOOLS CORPORATION
4403 Allen Road
Stow, OH 44224
(216) 929-4949

MOPAR PARTS DIVISION
26311 Lawrence Avenue
CIMS 423-15-10
Center Line, MI 48015
(800) 422-7975

NATIONAL AUTO AND TRUCK WRECKERS
ASSOCIATION (NATWA)
(*see* Automotive Dismantlers and Recyclers
Association)

NATIONAL AUTOMOBILE DEALERS
ASSOCIATION (NADA)
8400 Westpark Drive
McLean, VA 22102
(703) 821-7000

NATIONAL AUTOMOTIVE TECHNICIANS
EDUCATION FOUNDATION (NATEF)
13505 Dulles Technology Drive
Herndon, VA 22071-3415
(703) 713-0100

NATIONAL HIGHWAY TRAFFIC SAFETY
ADMINISTRATION
U.S. Department of Transportation
400 Seventh Street, SW
Washington, DC 20590
(800) 424-9393
(202) 366-0123

NATIONAL INSTITUTE FOR AUTOMOTIVE
SERVICE EXCELLENCE (ASE)
13505 Dulles Technology Drive
Herndon, VA 22071-3415
(703) 713-3800

NATIONAL LUBRICATION GREASE INSTITUTE
(NLGI)
4635 Wyandotte Street
Kansas City, MO 64112
(816) 931-9480

NATIONAL SAFETY COUNCIL
444 North Michigan Avenue
Chicago, IL 60611
(312) 527-4800

NATIONAL TIRE DEALERS & RETREADERS
ASSOCIATION (NTDRA)
1250 I Street, NW, Suite 400
Washington, DC 20005
(800) 876-8372

NATIONAL WHEEL AND RIM ASSOCIATION (NWRA)
5121 Bowden Road, Suite 303
Jacksonville, FL 32216-5950
(904) 737-2900

NORTH AMERICAN COUNCIL OF AUTOMOTIVE
TEACHERS (NACAT)
P.O. Box 3568
Glen Ellyn, IL 60138-3568
(708) 932-1937

OLDFORGE TOOLS
7750 King Road
Spring Arbor, MI 49283
(517) 750-1840
(800) 338-3360

OCCUPATIONAL SAFETY AND HEALTH
ADMINISTRATION (OSHA)
200 Constitution Avenue, NW, Room N3101
Washington, DC 20210
1-800-582-1708
(202) 219-4667
FAX (202) 219-9266

OTC
Division of Sealed Power Corporation
655 Eisenhower Drive
Owatonna, MN 55060
(507) 455-7102

PERFECT-HOFMANN
P.O. 600
La Verngne, TN 37086
(800) 251-4500

RAYBESTOS/BRAKE PARTS INC.
4400 Prime Parkway
McHenry, IL 60050
(815) 363-9000
FAX (815) 363-9303

ROBERT BOSCH CORPORATION
2800 South 25th Avenue
Broadview, IL 60153
(708) 865-5200
FAX (708) 865-6433

ROCKWELL INTERNATIONAL AUTOMOTIVE
2135 West Maple Road
Troy, MI 48084
(313) 435-1000
FAX (313) 435-1393

ROTARY LIFT
P.O. Box 30205
Airport Station
Memphis, TN 38130
(901) 345-2900

RUBBER MANUFACTURERS ASSOCIATION (RMA)
1400 K Street NW, Suite 900
Washington, DC 20005
(202) 682-4800

SAFETY-KLEEN CORPORATION
777 Big Timber Road
Elgin, IL 60123
(312) 697-8460

SNAP-ON TOOL COMPANY
2801 80th Street
Kenosha, WI 53141
(414) 656-5200

SOCIETY OF AUTOMOTIVE ENGINEERS (SAE)
400 Commonwealth Drive
Warrendale, PA 15096
(412) 776-4841

SOCIETY OF COLLISION REPAIR SPECIALISTS
(SCRS)
P.O. Box 3765
Tustin, CA 92680
(714) 838-3115

SPECIALTY EQUIPMENT MARKET ASSOCIATION
(SEMA)
1575 South Valley Vista Drive
Diamond Bar, CA 92765
(714) 396-0289

STA-LUBE, INC.
3039 Ana Street
Rancho Dominguez, CA 90224
(310) 537-5650
FAX (310) 604-4855

STAINLESS STEEL BRAKES CORPORATION
11470 Main Street
Lancaster, NY 14086
(800) 448-7722
FAX (716) 759-8688

STANLEY TOOLS
Division of the Stanley Works
600 Myrtle Street
New Britain, CT 06050
(203) 225-5111

STEMPF AUTOMOTIVE INDUSTRIES, INC.
6100 Baker Road
Minnetonka, MN 55345
(800) 328-4460
FAX (612) 931-9857

STEWART-WARNER CORPORATION
Alemite and Instrument Division
1826 Diversey Parkway
Chicago, IL 60614
(312) 883-7662

THEXTON MANUFACTURING COMPANY
7685 Parklawn Avenue
P.O. Box 35008
Minneapolis, MN 55435
(612) 831-4171

THE TIRE AND RIM ASSOCIATION, INC.
3200 West Market Street
Akron, OH 44313
(216) 666-8121

TIRE INDUSTRY SAFETY COUNCIL (TISC)
National Press Building, Suite 844
Washington, DC 20045
(202) 783-1022

TRUCK FRAME AND AXLE REPAIR
ASSOCIATION (TFARA)
915 East 99th Street
Brooklyn, NY 11236-4011
(718) 257-6133

TRW, INC.
Replacement Parts Division
8001 Pleasant Valley Road
Cleveland, OH 44131-5582
(216) 447-1879

U.S. DEPARTMENT OF TRANSPORTATION
National Highway Traffic Safety Administration
400 Seventh Street, SW
Washington, DC 20590
(202) 426-1715

WAGNER BRAKE
930 Roosevelt Parkway
Chesterfield, MO 63017
(314) 532-8700
FAX (314) 532-8596

"Machine to" Dimension for Drums and Rotors

Produced by  *for*

CAUTION: If state inspection regulations exceed the O.E. manufacturer's specifications for lining or rotor/drum reserve, the state inspection regulation must be followed.
NOTE: Machining specifications in this catalog pertain to original equipment drums and rotors. Some after market drum and rotor specifications may differ from the O.E.

ABBREVIATIONS

B - Large   **FT.- LBS.-** Foot-Pounds   **T.I.R.-** Total Indicatior Reading   **IN.- LBS.-** Inch-Pound
L- Lower   **S·-** Small   **U-** Upper

Appendix 7 reproduced courtesy of Hunter Engineering Co.

PASSENGER CARS

VEHICLE	BRAKE SHOE	BRAKE DRUM		BRAKE PAD	BRAKE ROTOR	
		DIAMETER			MIN. THICKNESS	
YEAR, MAKE, MODEL	O.E. Minimum Lining Thickness	Standard Size	Machine To	O.E. Minimum Lining Thickness	Machine To	Discard At
ACURA						
94–90 Integra: Front	—	—	—	.060	.750	—
Rear	—	—	—	.060	.310	—
89–86 Integra: Front	—	—	—	.120	.670	—
Rear	—	—	—	.063	.310	—
94–93 Legend: Sedan Front	—	—	—	.060	.830	—
Coupe Front	—	—	—	.060	1.02	—
Rear	—	—	—	.060	.300	—
92–91 Legend: Coupe & Sedan Front	—	—	—	.060	.830	—
Rear	—	—	—	.060	.300	—
90–86 Legend: Coupe & Sedan Front	—	—	—	.120①	.750	—
Rear	—	—	—	.060	.310	—
94–91 NSX: Front	—	—	—	.060	1.020	—
Rear	—	—	—	.060	.750	—
94–92 Vigor: Front	—	—	—	.060	.830	—
Rear	—	—	—	.060	.310	—

① Sedan shown; Coupe .060". ② 1990-89 16 ft/lbs. ③ 1990-89 .006".

AMERICAN MOTORS						
83–82 Concord, Spirit, SX-4:	.030	9.000	9.060	.030③	.815	.810
83–82 Concord Wagon:	.030	10.000	10.060	.030③	.815	.810
81 Concord, Spirit, SX-4:	.030	9.000	9.060	.030③	.815	.810
81 Concord Wagon, Eagle Wagon:	.030	10.000	10.060	.030③	.815	.810
80–78 Concord, Eagle, AMX:	.030	10.000	10.060	.062	.815	.810
88–82 Eagle:	.030	10.000	10.060	.030③	.815	.810
80–78 Gremlin, Spirit: L4 eng.	.030	9.000	9.060	.062	.815	.810
L6 eng.	.030	10.000	10.060	.062	.815	.810
77 Gremlin, Hornet:	.030	10.000	10.060	.062	.815	.810
76–75 Gremlin, Hornet: L6 eng.	.030	9.000	9.060	.062	1.130	1.120
V8 eng.	.030	10.000	10.060	.062	1.130	1.120
74–72 Gremlin, Hornet, Javelin:						
L6 eng. w/drum brakes	.030	9.000	9.060	—	—	—
L6 eng. w/disc brakes	.030	9.000	9.060	.062	—	.940
L6 eng. w/disc brakes (72)	.030	10.000	10.060	.062	—	.940
V8 eng. w/drum brakes	.030	10.000	10.060	—	—	—
V8 eng. w/disc brakes	.030	10.000	10.060	.062	—	.940
78 Matador:	.030	10.000	10.060	.062	—	1.120
77 Matador:	.030	10.000	10.060	.062	—	1.120
76–75 Matador:	.030	10.000	10.060	.062	1.130	1.120
74–72 Matador, Ambassador:	.030	10.000	10.060	.062	—	.940
80–78 Pacer:	.030	10.000	10.060	.062	.815	.810
77 Pacer:	.030	10.000	10.060	.062	.815	.810
76–75 Pacer: Front w/drum brakes	.030	10.000	10.060	—	—	—
Rear w/drum brakes	.030	9.000	9.060	—	—	—
w/disc brakes	.030	9.000	9.060	.062	—	1.120

① Eagle .004". ② 1972 12 in/lbs. ③ .030" over rivet head; if bonded lining use .062".

AUDI

94–92 100, 100 Quattro: Front	—	—	—	.079	—	.906
Rear	—	—	—	.079	—	.315
91–89 100: Front	—	—	—	.078	.807	.787
Rear	—	—	—	.276⑥	.335	.315
91–89 100 Quattro: Front	—	—	—	.078	.945	.905
Rear	—	—	—	.276⑥	.335	.315
91–89 200: Front	—	—	—	.078	.945	.905
Rear	—	—	—	.276⑥	.335	.315
91–89 200 Quattro:						
Front w/single piston	—	—	—	.078	.945	.905
Front w/dual piston	—	—	—	.078	.945	.905
Rear	—	—	—	.276⑥	.335	.315
87–85 4000, Coupe GT:	.097	—	7.894	.079	.728	.709
84–80 4000, Coupe:	.097	—	7.894	.079	.413	.394
87–84 4000 Quattro: Front	—	—	—	.079	.728	.709
Rear	—	—	—	.079	.335	.315
88–81 5000:	.098	9.055	9.075	.079	.807	.787
80–78 5000:	.098	9.055	9.094	.078	.807	.787
88–80 5000 Turbo, 5000 Turbo Quattro, 5000 Quattro:						
Front w/single piston	—	—	—	.079	.807	.787
w/dual piston	—	—	—	.079	.984	.905
Rear w/Girling	—	—	—	.079	.335	.315
w/Teves	—	—	—	.276⑥	.335	.315
94–88 80, 90: Front	—	—	—	.078	.807	.787
Rear	—	—	—	.078	.334	.315
94–88 80 Quattro, 90 Quattro: Front	—	—	—	.078	.807	.787
Rear	—	—	—	.078	.334	.315
79–78 Fox:	.097	7.870	7.900	.078	.413	.393
77–73 Fox:	.097	7.870	7.900	.078	.413	.393
91–90 Quattro Coupe: Front	—	—	—	.078	.945	.905
Rear	—	—	—	.078	.335	.315
85–83 Quattro Turbo Coupe: Front	—	—	—	.079	.807	.787
Rear	—	—	—	.079	.335	.315
94–92 S4: Front	—	—	—	.079	—	.906
Rear	—	—	—	.079	—	.709
94–90 V8 Quattro: Front	—	—	—	.080	.945	.905
Rear	—	—	—	.080	.728	.710

⑥ Measurement of lining & metal.

BMW

76–72 2002:	.120	9.060	9.100	.080	.354	—
74–72 2002tii:	.120	9.060	9.100	.080	.459	—
94–93 318i: Front	—	—	—	.079	.409	.394
Rear	—	—	—	.079	.331	.315
92–91 318i: Front	—	—	—	.079	.437	.421
Rear	—	—	—	.079	.331	.315
91–88 318is, 325i, 325is, 325ix:						
Front	—	—	—	.079	.921	.906
Rear	—	—	—	.079	.331	.315
85–84 318i:	.060	—	9.035	.080	.437	.421
83–82 320i: w/ATE	.118	9.842	9.882	.118	.846	.827
w/Girling Caliper	.118	9.842	9.882	.118	.480	.461
81–77 320i:	.118	9.842	9.882	.118	.846	.827
94–92 325i, 325is: Front	—	—	—	.079	.803	.787
Rear	—	—	—	.079	.331	.315
88–84 325e, 325es: Front	—	—	—	.080	.803	.787
Rear	—	—	—	.080	.331	.315
86–85 524td: Front	—	—	—	.079	.409	.394
Rear	—	—	—	.079	.331	.315
94–83 525i, 528e, 533i, 535i, 535is: Front	—	—	—	.080	.803	.787
Rear	—	—	—	.080	.331	.315
82 528e: Front	—	—	—	.138	.803	—
Rear	—	—	—	.138	.331	—
81–79 528i: Front	—	—	—	.080	.846	.827
Rear	—	—	—	.080	.354	.335
78–77 530i: Front	—	—	—	.080	.480	.461
Rear	—	—	—	.080	.354	.335
79–77 630CSi: Front	—	—	—	.080	.846	.827
Rear	—	—	—	.080	.728	.709
89–83 633CSi, 635CSi: Front	—	—	—	.079	.921	.906
Rear	—	—	—	.079	.331	.315
82–79 633CSi: Front	—	—	—	.080	.846	.827
Rear	—	—	—	.080	.728	.709
92–83 733i, 735i, 735iL, L7: Front	—	—	—	.080	1.039	1.024
Rear	—	—	—	.080	.409	.394
82–78 733i: Front	—	—	—	.080	.846	.827
Rear	—	—	—	.080	.374	.354

(continues)

BMW (Continued)

94–88 740i, 740iL, 750iL, 850i, 850Ci: Front	—	—	—	.079	1.118	1.102
Rear	—	—	—	.079	.724	.709
91–90 M3: Front	—	—	—	.079	.921	.906
Rear	—	—	—	.079	.331	.315
89–88 M3: Front	—	—	—	.079	.921	.906
Rear	—	—	—	.079	.409	.394
87 M3: Front	—	—	—	.079	.921	.906
Rear	—	—	—	.079	.409	.394
93–90 M5: Front	—	—	—	.079	①	1.039
Rear	—	—	—	.079	.724	.709
89–87 M5: Front	—	—	—	.079	1.118	1.102
Rear	—	—	—	.079	.331	.315
89–87 M6: Front	—	—	—	.079	1.118	1.102
Rear	—	—	—	.079	.331	.315

① Do not machine

BUICK

94–88 Century: w/H.D.	③	8.863	8.880	.030	.972	.957
exc. H.D.	③	8.863	8.880	.030	.830	.815
87–86 Century: w/H.D.	③	8.863	8.877	.030	.972	.957
exc. H.D.	③	8.863	8.877	.030	.830	.815
85 Century: w/H.D.	③	8.863	8.920	.030	.972	.957
exc. H.D.	③	8.863	8.920	.030	.830	.815
84 Century: w/H.D.	③	8.863	8.883	.030	.972	.957
exc. H.D.	③	8.863	8.883	.030	.830	.815
83–82 Century:	③	7.879	7.899	.030	.830	.815
81–79 Century, Regal, LeSabre:	③	9.500	9.560	.030	.980	.965
78–77 Century, Regal, LeSabre:	③	9.500	9.560	.030	.980	.965
75 Century, Regal:	③	9.500	9.560	.030	.980	.965
74–73 Century, Regal:	③	9.500	9.560	.030	.980	.965
90–83 Electra, Estate Wagon: (RWD)	③	11.000	11.060	.030	.980	.965
82–79 Electra, Estate Wagon:	③	11.000	11.060	.030	.980	.965
78–77 Electra, Estate Wagon, Riviera:	③	11.000	11.060	.030	.980	.965
76–75 Electra, Custom, LeSabre, Estate Wagon, Riviera:	③	12.000	12.060	.030	1.230	1.215
74–72 Electra, Custom, LeSabre, Centurion, Riviera, Wildcat:	③	11.000	11.060	.030	1.230	1.215
74–73 Estate Wagon:	③	12.000	12.060	.030	1.230	1.215
94–92 LeSabre: (FWD)	.030	8.860	8.880	.030	1.224	1.209
91 LeSabre: (FWD)	③	8.860	8.880	.030	.972	.957
90–83 LeSabre, Electra: (FWD)	③	8.858	8.880	.030	.972	.957
94–92 Park Avenue:	.030	8.860	8.880	.030	1.224	1.209
91 Park Avenue:	③	8.860	8.880	.030	—	1.200
94–88 Regal: (FWD) Front	—	—	—	.030	.984	.972
Rear	—	—	—	.030	.441	.429
87–83 Regal, LeSabre: (RWD)	③	9.500	9.560	.030	.980	.965
82 Regal, LeSabre:	③	9.500	9.560	.030	.980	.965
93–92 Riviera: Front	—	—	—	.030	1.250	1.209
Rear	—	—	—	.030	.423	.374
91–86 Riviera, Reatta: Front	—	—	—	.030	.971	.956
Rear	—	—	—	.030	.444	.429
85–83 Riviera: exc. rear disc brakes	③	9.500	9.560	.030	.980	.965
w/rear disc brakes	—	—	—	.030	.980	.965
82–79 Riviera: exc. rear disc brakes	③	9.500	9.560	.030	.980	.965
w/rear disc brakes	—	—	—	.030	.980	.965
94 Roadmaster:	.030	11.000	11.060	.030	.980	.965
w/rear disc brakes	—	—	—	.030	.735	.728
93–91 Roadmaster:	.030	11.000	11.060	.030	.980	.965
89–82 Skyhawk: vented rotor (89-82)	③	7.880	7.899	.030③	.830	.815
solid rotor (82)	③	7.880	7.899	.030③	.444	.429
80–76 Skyhawk:	③	9.500	9.560	.030	.830	.815
75 Skyhawk:	③	9.000	9.060	.030	.455	.440
94–93 Skylark:	③	7.874	7.899	.030	.751	.736
92–91 Skylark:	③	7.879	7.899	.030	.786	.736
90–80 Skylark, Regal: (FWD)	③	7.880	7.899	.030	.830	.815
79–77 Skylark:	③	9.500	9.560	.030	.980	.965
76–75 Skylark, Apollo:	③	9.500	9.560	.030	.980	.965
72 Skylark, Gran Sport, GS, Sports Wagon:	③	9.500	9.560	.030	.980	.965

③ .030" over rivet head; if bonded lining use .062".

CADILLAC

93	Allante: Front	—	—	—	.030	1.250	1.209
	Rear	—	—	—	.030	.423	.374
92–87	Allante: Front	—	—	—	.030	.971	.956
	Rear	—	—	—	.030	.444	.429
94–93	Fleetwood Brougham: (RWD)	①	11.000	11.060	.030	.980	.965
92–82	Brougham, Fleetwood, Deville: (RWD)	①	11.000	11.060	.030	.972	.957
81–79	Brougham, Fleetwood, Deville, Seville: (RWD)	①	11.000	11.060	.062	.980	.965
	w/rear disc brakes (79)	—	—	—	.062	.980	.965
78–77	Brougham, Seville: Front	—	—	—	.062	.980	.965
	Rear	—	—	—	.062	.910	.905
78–77	DeVille:	①	11.000	11.060	.062	.980	.965
76	Seville:	①	11.000	11.060	.062	.980	.965
76–74	Calais, Deville, Brougham, Fleetwood 75, Commercial Ch.:	①	12.000	12.060	.062	1.220	1.215
73–72	Calais, Deville, Fleetwood 60, Fleetwood 75, Commercial Ch.:	①	12.000	12.060	.062	1.220	1.215
88–82	Cimarron:	①	7.880	7.899	.030	.830	.815
94–91	Commercial Chassis: (FWD)	①	8.860	8.880	.030	1.224	1.209
90–86	Commercial Chassis: (FWD)	①	7.880	7.899	.030⑥	.972	.965
94–92	Eldorado, Seville: Front	—	—	—	.030	1.250	1.209
	Rear	—	—	—	.030	.423	.374
91–86	Eldorado, Seville: Front	—	—	—	.030	.971	.956
	Rear	—	—	—	.030	.444	.429
85–82	Eldorado, Seville: Front	—	—	—	.030	.980	.965
	Rear	—	—	—	.030	.980	.965
81–79	Eldorado, Seville: Front	—	—	—	.062	.980	.965
	Rear	—	—	—	.062	.980	.965
78–77	Eldorado: Front	—	—	—	.062	—	1.170
	Rear	—	—	—	.062	—	1.170
76	Eldorado: Front	—	—	—	.062	1.205	1.190
	Rear	—	—	—	.062	1.205	1.190
75–72	Eldorado:	①	11.000	11.060	.062	1.205	1.190
94–91	Fleetwood, DeVille: (FWD)	①	8.860	8.880	.030	1.224	1.209
90–86	Fleetwood, Deville: (FWD)	①	8.863	8.917	.030	.972	.965
85	Fleetwood, Deville: (FWD)	①	8.858	8.880	.030	.972	.957
85–77	Fleetwood Limo, Comm. Ch.: (RWD)	①	12.000	12.060	.062	1.230	1.215

① .030" over rivet head; if bonded lining use .062".
⑥ Inner Pad shown; outer .062" (thickness over steel)

CHEVROLET

94–93	Beretta, Corsica:	④	7.874	7.899	.030	.751	.736
92	Beretta, Corsica:	④	7.880	7.889	.030	.796	.736
91–87	Beretta, Corsica:	④	7.880	7.899	.030	.830	.815
94–93	Camaro:	.030	9.500	9.560	.030	1.250	1.209
	w/rear disc brakes	—	—	—	.030	.733	.724
92–89	Camaro: exc. H.D.	④	9.500	9.560	.030	.980	.965
	H.D. Front	—	—	—	.030	.980	.965
	H.D. Rear	—	—	—	.030	.744	.724
88–86	Camaro: w/rear drum brakes	④	9.500	9.560	.030	.980	.965
	w/rear disc brakes	—	—	—	.030	.986	.956
85–82	Camaro: w/rear drum brakes	④	9.500	9.560	.030	.980	.965
	w/rear disc brakes	—	—	—	.030	.980	.965
81–79	Camaro, Nova, Malibu, Monte Carlo:	④	9.500	9.560	.030	.980	.965
78–77	Camaro, Nova:	④	9.500	9.560	.030④	.980	.965
76–73	Camaro, Chevelle, Monte Carlo:	④	9.500	9.560	.030④	.980	.965
72	Camaro, Chevelle:	④	9.500	9.560	.030④	.980	.965
94	Caprice, Impala:	④	9.500	9.560	.030	.980	.965
	w/11" rear drum brakes	④	11.000	11.060	.030	.980	.965
	w/rear disc brakes	—	—	—	.030	.735	.728
93–79	Caprice, Impala:	④	9.500	9.560	.030	.980	.965
	w/11" rear drum brakes	④	11.000	11.060	.030	.980	.965
78	Caprice, Impala: exc. wagon	④	9.500	9.560	.030	.980	.965
	wagon	④	11.000	11.060	.030	.980	.965
77	Caprice, Impala: exc. wagon	④	9.500	9.560	.030	.980	.965
	wagon	④	11.000	11.060	.030	.980	.965
76–72	Caprice, Impala, Bel Air:	④	11.000	11.060	.030④	1.230	1.215
94–93	Cavalier:	.030	7.874	7.899	.030	.751	.736
92	Cavalier:	④	7.880	7.889	.030	.751	.736
91–82	Cavalier: vented rotor (91–82)	④	7.880	7.899	.030	.830	.815
	solid rotor (82)	④	7.880	7.899	.030	.444	.429

④ .030" over rivet head; if bonded lining use

CHEVROLET (Continued)

90–87 Celebrity: H.D. Front	—	—	—	.030	.972	.957
exc. H.D. Front	—	—	—	.030	.830	.815
Rear coupe/sedan	④	8.863	8.920	—	—	—
Rear wagon	④	8.863	8.877	—	—	—
w/rear disc brakes	—	—	—	.030	.702	.681
86–85 Celebrity: w/ H.D.	④	8.863	8.920	.030	.972	.957
exc. H.D.	④	8.863	8.920	.030	.830	.815
84–82 Celebrity:	④	7.879	7.899	.030	.830	.815
87–86 Chevette:	④	7.880	7.899	.030	.404	.374
85–84 Chevette:	④	7.874	7.899	.030	.430	.374
83 Chevette:	④	7.874	7.899	.030	.390	.374
82–78 Chevette:	④	7.874	7.899	.030	.390	.374
77 Chevette:	④	7.880	7.899	.030	.456	.441
76 Chevette:	④	7.870	7.899	.030	.448	.433
85–80 Citation:	④	7.880	7.899	.030	.830	.815
94–88 Corvette: Front exc. H.D.	—	—	—	.030	.744	.724
Front H.D.	—	—	—	.030	1.059	1.039
Rear exc. H.D.	—	—	—	.030	.744	.724
Rear H.D.	—	—	—	.030	1.059	1.039
87–84 Corvette: Front	—	—	—	.062	.724	—
Rear	—	—	—	.062	.724	—
82–77 Corvette: Front	—	—	—	.030④	1.230	1.215
Rear	—	—	—	.030④	1.230	1.215
76–72 Corvette: Front	—	—	—	.030④	1.230	1.215
Rear	—	—	—	.030④	1.230	1.215
94–90 Lumina: Front	—	—	—	.030	.984	.972
Rear	—	—	—	.030	.441	.429
88–82 Malibu, Monte Carlo:	④	9.500	9.560	.030	.980	.965
78–77 Malibu, Monte Carlo, Chevelle:	④	11.000	11.060	.030	.980	.965
80–76 Monza:	④	9.500	9.560	.030	.830	.815
75 Monza:	④	9.000	9.060	.030	.455	.440
88–85 Nova:	.039	7.874	7.913	.039	—	.492
w/rear disc brakes	—	—	—	.039	—	.315
76–72 Nova:	④	9.500	9.560	.030④	.980	.965
88–85 Spectrum: exc. Turbo	.031	7.090	7.140	.039	—	.378
w/Turbo	.039	7.090	7.140	.039	—	.650
88–85 Sprint	.110⑩	7.090	7.160	.315	—	.315
77–76 Vega:	④	9.500	9.560	.030	.455	.440
75–72 Vega:	④	9.000	9.060	.030	.455	.440

④ .030″ over rivet head; if bonded lining use .062″   ⑩ Measurement of lining & Metal

CHRYSLER CORP. — Chrysler, Dodge, Eagle, Plymouth

94–90 Acclaim, Spirit	.030	8.661	8.691	.030	.912	.882
w/rear disc brakes				.281	.439	.409
89 Acclaim, Spirit	.030	8.661	8.691	.030	.865	.803
89–83 Aries, Reliant, Lancer, LeBaron, 400, 600:						
w/7 7/8″ rear brakes	.030	7.874	7.904	.030	.912	.882
w/8 21/32″ rear brakes	.030	8.661	8.691	.030	.912	.882
82 Aries, Reliant, LeBaron, 400:	.030	7.870	7.900	.030	.912	.882
81 Aries, Reliant	.030	7.870	7.900	.030	.912	.882
80–76 Arrow: w/rear drum brakes	.040	9.000	9.050	.040	—	.450
w/rear disc brakes	—	—	—	.040	—	.330
81–78 Aspen, Volare:	.030	10.000	10.060	.030	.970	.940
77–76 Aspen, Volare: exc. wagon	.030	10.000	10.060	.030	.970	.940
wagon	.030	11.000	11.060	.030	.970	.940
83–78 Challenger: w/rear drum brakes	.040	9.000	9.050	.040	—	.430
w/rear disc brakes	—	—	—	.040	—	.330
82–79 Champ: (FWD)	.040	7.100	7.150	.040	—	.450
74–73 Charger, Coronet, Challenger, Belvedere, Satellite, Barracuda: w/front disc brakes	.030	10.000	10.060	.030	.970	.940
72 Charger, Coronet, Crestwood, SE, Super Bee, Belvedere, Satelite, GTX, Regent, Road Runner, Sebring, Barracuda, Challenger:						
w/front disc brakes	.030	10.000	10.060	.030	.970	.940
w/10″ drum brakes	.030	10.000	10.060	—	—	—
w/11″ drum brakes	.030	11.000	11.060	—	—	—
94 Colt, Eagle Summit						
Coupe w/1.5L engine	.040	7.100	7.200	.080	—	.450
Coupe w/1.8L engine	.040	7.100	7.200	.080	—	.650
Sedan	.040	8.000	8.100	.080	—	.650
Sedan w/rear disc brakes	—	—	—	.080	—	.330

(continues)

CHRYSLER CORP. — Chrysler, Dodge, Eagle, Plymouth (Continued)

Year	Description						
93	Colt, Eagle Summit Coupe	.040	7.100	7.200	.080	—	.449
	Sedan	.040	8.000	8.100	.080	—	.646
	w/rear disc brakes	—	—	—	.080	—	.331
92–91	Colt, Eagle Summit Hatchback	.040	7.100	7.200	.080	—	.449
	Sedan	.040	7.100	7.200	.080	—	.646
90–89	Colt, Eagle Summit						
	exc. rear disc brakes	.040	7.100	7.200	.080	—	.449
	w/rear disc brakes Front	—	—	—	.080	—	.882
	w/rear disc brakes Rear	—	—	—	.080	—	.331
88	Colt exc. Turbo	.040	7.100	7.200	.080	—	.450
	Turbo	.040	7.100	7.200	.080	—	.645
87–85	Colt exc. Turbo	.040	7.100	7.150	.040	—	.450
87–84	Colt Turbo	.040	7.100	7.150	.040	—	.645
84–79	Colt (FWD) exc. Turbo	.040	7.100	7.150	.040	—	.450
80–78	Colt (RWD)exc. Wagon	.040	9.000	9.050	.080	—	.450
77–73	Colt	.040	9.000	9.050	.080	—	.450
72	Colt	.040	9.000	9.050	.080	—	.374
94–92	Colt Vista, Eagle Summit SW:						
	w/8" drum brakes	.040	8.000	8.071	.080	—	.882
	w/9" drum brakes	.040	9.000	9.079	.080	—	.882
	w/rear disc brakes	—	—	—	.080	—	.331
91–89	Colt Vista, Eagle Vista: (4x2)	.040	8.000	8.100	.080	—	.650
	(4x4)	.040	9.000	9.100	.080	—	.880
88	Colt Vista: (4x2)	.040	8.000	8.100	.080	—	.650
	(4x4)	.040	9.000	9.100	.080	—	.880
87–84	Colt Vista: (4x2)	.040	8.000	8.150	.040	—	.650
	(4x4)	.040	9.000	9.078	.040	—	.880
90–89	Colt Wagon: (4x2)	.040	8.000	8.100	.080	—	.449
	(4x4)	.040	8.000	8.100	.080	—	.646
88	Colt Wagon:	.040	8.000	8.100	.080	—	.450
80–78	Colt Wagon: w/rear drum brakes	.040	9.000	9.050	.040	—	.330
	w/rear disc brakes	—	—	—	.040	—	.330
94–93	Concorde, Intrepid, Vision:	.030	8.661	8.691	.030	—	.882
	w/rear disc brakes	—	—	—	.030	—	.409
89–88	Conquest Front	—	—	—	.080	—	.880
	Rear	—	—	—	.080	—	.650
87–84	Conquest Front	—	—	—	.040	—	.880
	Rear	—	—	—	.040	—	.650
83–82	Cordoba, Mirada:	.030	10.000	10.060	.125	.970	.940
	w/11" rear brakes	.030	11.000	11.060	.125	.970	.940
81–78	Cordoba, Mirada:	.030	10.000	10.060	.030	.970	.940
	w/11" rear brakes	.030	11.000	11.060	.030	.970	.940
77–76	Cordoba, Charger SE:	.030	11.000	11.060	.030	.970	.940
75	Cordoba, Charger:	.030	10.000	10.060	.030	.970	.940
76–75	Dart, Valiant w/disc brakes	.030	10.000	10.060	.030	.970	.940
	w/front drum brakes Front	.030	10.000	10.060	—	—	—
	Rear	.030	9.000	9.060	—	—	—
74–73	Dart, Valiant w/disc brakes	.030	10.000	10.060	.030	.970	.940
	w/front drum brakes Front	.030	10.000	10.060	—	—	—
	Rear	.030	9.000	9.060	—	—	—
72	Dart, Valiant, GT, GTS,						
	Swinger, Demon, Duster,						
	Scamp, Signet w/disc brakes	.030	10.000	10.060	.030	.790	.780
	w/10" drum brakes	.030	10.000	10.060	—	—	—
	w/9" drum brakes	.030	9.000	9.060	—	—	—
93–89	Daytona:	—	—	—	.030	.912	.882
	Rear w/solid rotor	—	—	—	.030	.439	.409
	Rear w/vented rotor.............	—	—	—	.030	.827	.797
88	Daytona:	.030	8.661	8.691	.030	.912	.882
	w/rear disc brakes	—	—	—	.030	.321	.291
87–84	Daytona, Laser: (FWD)						
	exc. rear disc brakes...........	.030	8.661	8.691	.030	.912	.882
	w/rear disc brakes	—	—	—	.030	.321	.291
93–92	Dynasty, New Yorker,						
	Imperial, Fifth Ave.:	.030	8.661	8.691	.030	.912	.882
	w/rear disc brakes	—	—	—	.030	.439	.409
91–89	Dynasty, New Yorker,						
	Imperial, Fifth Ave.:	.030	8.661	8.691	.030	.912	.882
	w/rear disc brakes	—	—	—	.030	.369	.339
88	Dynasty, New Yorker:	.030	8.661	8.691	.030	.912	.882
	w/rear disc brakes	—	—	—	.030	.321	.291
88	Eagle:	.030	10.000	10.060	.030②	.815	.810
78	Fury, Monaco:	.030	10.000	10.060	.030	.970	.940
	w/11" rear brakes	.030	11.000	11.060	.030	.970	.940
77–76	Fury, Monaco, Coronet	.030	11.000	11.060	.030	.970	.940
75	Fury, Monaco, Coronet						
	exc. wagon	.030	10.000	10.060	.030	.970	.940
	wagon	.030	11.000	11.060	.030	.970	.940

② .030" over rivet head; if bonded lining use .062".

(continues)

CHRYSLER CORP. — Chrysler, Dodge, Eagle, Plymouth (Continued)

Description						
74–72 Fury, Monaco, Polara, Newport, New Yorker, Town & Country, V.I.P.:	030	11.000	11.060	.030	1.195	.180
89–82 Gran Fury, Diplomat, Fifth Ave., Newport, New Yorker, Imperial, Caravelle: (RWD)	030	10.000	10.060	.125	.970	.940
w/11" rear brakes	030	11.000	11.060	.125	.970	.940
81–78 Gran Fury, Diplomat, LeBaron, St. Regis, Magnum, Newport, New Yorker, Imperial:	030	10.000	10.060	.030	.970	.940
w/11" rear brakes	030	11.000	11.060	.030	.970	.940
77–75 Gran Fury, Royal Monaco, New Yorker, Newport, Town & Country:	030	11.000	11.060	.030	1.195	.180
75–74 Imperial: Front	—	—	—	.030	1.195	.180
Rear	—	—	—	.030	.970	.940
73–72 Imperial:	030	11.000	11.060	.030	1.195	.180
94–90 Laser, Talon: Front	—	—	—	.080	.912	.882
Rear	—	—	—	.080	.360	.331
94–87 Lebaron:	030	8.661	8.691	.281	.912	.882
Rear w/solid rotor				.281	.439	.409
Rear w/vented rotor				.281	.827	.797
89–88 Medallion:	098	9.000	9.030	.256	⑨	.697
92–91 Monaco, Premier:	132	8.858	8.917	.160	—	.890
w/rear disc brakes	—	—	—	.062	—	.374
90–88 Monaco, Premier:	132	8.858	8.917	.236	⑨	.807
94 New Yorker, LHS: Front	—	—	—	.030	—	.882
Rear	—	—	—	.030	—	.882
88 New Yorker Turbo, Town & Country SW, Caravelle:	030	8.661	8.691	.030	.912	.882
87–83 New Yorker Turbo, Town & Country SW, Caravelle: (FWD) exc. rear disc brakes	030	8.661	8.691	.030	.912	.882
w/rear disc brakes	—	—	—	.030	.321	.291
90–83 Omni, Charger, Horizon, Turismo:	.030	7.874	7.904	.030	.461	.431
82–78 Omni, Horizon:	.030	7.870	7.900	.030	.461	.431
83–78 Sapporo: w/rear drum brakes	.040	9.000	9.050	.040	—	.430
w/rear disc brakes	—	—	—	.040	—	.330
94–89 Shadow, Sundance: w/7 ⁷⁄₈" rear brakes	.030	7.874	7.904	.030	.912	.882
88–86 Shadow, Sundance: w/7 ⁷⁄₈" rear brakes	.030	7.874	7.904	.030	.912	.882
w/8 ²¹⁄₃₂" rear brakes	.030	8.661	8.691	.030	.912	.882
94–91 Stealth: (FWD) Front	—	—	—	.080	—	.880
(FWD) Rear	—	—	—	.080	—	.650
(AWD) Front	—	—	—	.080	—	1.120
(AWD) Rear	—	—	—	.080	—	.720
91–89 TC Maserati:	—	—	—	.030	.912	.882
w/rear disc brakes	—	—	—	.030	.321	.291
94 Viper: Front	—	—	—	.100	1.197	1.167
Rear	—	—	—	.100	.803	.773

⑨ Machining not recommended

DAIHATSU

Description						
92–91 Charade: 1.0 eng.	.039	7.087	7.126	.120	—	.390
1.3 eng.	.039	7.874	7.913	.120	—	.670
89–88 Charade:	.040	7.090	7.126	.120	—	.390

FIAT

Description						
82–75 124, 2000: Front	—	—	—	.080	.368	.354
Rear	—	—	—	.080	.372	.354
74–72 124: Front	—	—	—	.080	.368	.354
Rear	—	—	—	.080	.372	.354
79–73 128:	.060	7.300	7.332	.080	.368	.354
78–75 131:	.181	9.000	9.030	.060	.368	.354
81–79 Brava:	.181	9.000	9.030	.060	—	.386
82–79 Strada:	.060	7.293	7.336	.060	.368	.350
82–74 X 1/9: Front	—	—	—	.080	.368	.354
Rear	—	—	—	.080	.368	.354

FORD MOTOR CO. — Ford, Lincoln, Mercury

94 Aspire:						
w/automatic transmission	.040	7.870	7.930	.080	.817	.780
w/manual transmission	.040	7.870	7.930	.080	.660	.630
94–91 Capri: Front	—	—	—	.120	.660	.630
Rear	—	—	—	.120	.380	.350
77–76 Capri:	.030	9.000	9.050	.100	.460	.450
74–72 Capri:	.030	9.000	9.050	.100	—	⑨
94–93 Continental: Front	—	—	—	.040	—	.974
Rear	—	—	—	.123	—	.500
92 Continental: Front	—	—	—	.125	—	.974
Rear	—	—	—	.123	—	.900
91 Continental: Front	—	—	—	.125	—	.970
Rear	—	—	—	.123	—	.900
90–88 Continental: Front	—	—	—	.125	—	.970
Rear	—	—	—	.125	—	.974
87–84 Continental: Front	—	—	—	.125	—	.972
Rear	—	—	—	.125	—	.895
83–82 Continental: Front	—	—	—	.125	—	.972
Rear	—	—	—	.125	—	.895
81–80 Continental:						
w/10" rear brakes	.030	10.000	10.060	.125	—	.972
w/11" rear brakes	.030	11.030	11.090	.125	—	.972
79–73 Continental:						
w/10" rear brakes	.030	10.000	10.090	.125	—	1.120
w/11" rear brakes	.030	11.030	11.090	.125	—	1.120
72 Continental:	.030	11.030	11.090	.030	1.135	1.120
94–93 Cougar, Thunderbird:	.030	9.800	9.860	.040	—	.974
w/rear disc brakes	—	—	—	.123	—	.657
92 Cougar, Thunderbird:	.030	9.800	9.860	.125	—	.974
w/rear disc brakes	—	—	—	.123	—	.900
91–90 Cougar, Thunderbird:	.030	9.800	9.860	.125	—	.935
w/rear disc brakes	—	—	—	.123	—	.900
89 Cougar, Thunderbird:	.030	9.800	9.860	.125	—	.935
w/rear disc brakes	—	—	—	.123	—	.895
88–87 Cougar, Thunderbird:						
exc. Turbo w/9" rear brakes	.030	9.000	9.060	.125	—	.810
w/10" rear brakes	.030	10.000	10.060	.125	—	.810
w/Turbo	.030	9.000	9.060	.125	—	.972
w/rear disc brakes	—	—	—	.125	—	.895
86–83 Cougar, Thunderbird, XR-7:						
w/9" rear brakes	.030	9.000	9.060	.125	—	.810
w/10" rear brakes	.030	10.000	10.060	.125	—	.810
82–81 Cougar, Thunderbird, XR-7:						
w/9" rear brakes	.030	9.000	9.060	.125	—	.810
w/10" rear brakes	.030	10.000	10.060	.125	—	.810
80 Cougar, Thunderbird:	.030	9.000	9.060	.125	—	.810
79 Cougar, Thunderbird, LTD II:	.030	11.030	11.090	.125	—	1.120
78–77 Cougar, Thunderbird, LTD II:	.030	11.030	11.090	.125	—	1.120
76–74 Cougar: w/10" rear brakes	.030	10.000	10.060	.030	—	1.120
w/11" rear brakes	.030	11.030	11.090	.030	—	1.120
73–72 Cougar, Mustang:	.030	10.000	10.060	.030	.890	.875
94–92 Crown Victoria, Grand Marquis: Front	—	—	—	.125	—	.974
Rear	—	—	—	.125	—	.440
91 Crown Victoria, Grand Marquis:						
w/10" rear brakes	.030②	10.000	10.060	.125	—	.972
w/11" rear brakes	.030②	11.030	11.090	.125	—	.972
90–83 Crown Victoria, Grand Marquis:						
w/11" rear brakes	.030	11.030	11.090	.125	—	.972
w/10" rear brakes	.030	10.000	10.060	.125	—	.972
78–74 Custom, Country Sedan, Country Squire, Galaxie, LTD, Colony Park, Marquis:						
exc. rear disc brakes	.030	11.030	11.090	.125	—	1.120
w/rear disc brakes	—	—	—	.030	—	.895
73 Custom, Country Sedan, Country Squire, Galaxie, LTD, Colony Park, Marquis:	.030	11.030	11.090	.125	—	1.120
72 Custom, Country Sedan, Country Squire, Galaxie, LTD, Colony Park, Marquis:	.030	11.030	11.090	.030	1.135	1.120
94–93 Escort, Tracer:	.040	7.870	7.910	.080	.820	.790
w/rear disc brakes	—	—	—	.040	.310	.280
92–91 Escort, Tracer:	.040	9.000	9.040	.080	.820	.790
w/rear disc brakes	—	—	—	.040	.310	.280
90–89 Escort: w/7" rear brakes	.030②	7.090	7.149	.125	—	.882
w/8" rear brakes	.030②	8.000	8.060	.125	—	.882
88–81 Escort, EXP, Lynx, LN7:						
w/7" rear brakes	.030②	7.090	7.149	.125	—	.882
w/8" rear brakes	.030②	8.000	8.060	.125	—	.882

② .030" over rivet head; if bonded lining use .062".   ⑨ Machining not recommended.

(continues)

FORD MOTOR CO. — Ford, Lincoln, Mercury (Continued)

86–83 Fairmont, Zephyr, LTD,						
Marquis: w/9" rear brakes	.030	9.000	9.060	.125	—	.810
w/10" rear brakes	.030	10.000	10.060	.125	—	.810
82–79 Fairmont, Zephyr:						
w/9" rear brakes	.030	9.000	9.060	.125	—	.810
w/10" rear brakes	.030	10.000	10.060	.125	—	.810
78 Fairmont, Zephyr: exc. Wagon	.030	9.000	9.060	.125	—	.810
Wagon	.030	10.000	10.060	.125	—	.810
93–88 Festiva:	.040	6.690	6.750	.120	.463	.433
80–78 Fiesta:	.060	7.000	—	.060		.340
82–81 Granada: w/9" rear brakes	.030	9.000	9.060	.125	—	.810
w/10" rear brakes	.030	10.000	10.060	.125	—	.810
80–79 Granada, Monarch:	.030	10.000	10.060	.125	—	.810
78–77 Granada, Monarch:	.030	10.000	10.060	.125	—	.810
76–75 Granada, Monarch:						
exc. rear disc brakes	.030	10.000	10.060	.125	—	.810
w/rear disc brakes	—	—	—	.125	—	.895
94–93 Mark VIII: Front	—	—	—	.125	—	.974
Rear	—	—	—	.125	—	.657
92–91 Mark VII: Front	—	—	—	.125	—	.972
Rear	—	—	—	.123	—	.890
90–88 Mark VII: Front	—	—	—	.125	—	.972
Rear	—	—	—	.125	—	.895
87–84 Mark VII: Front	—	—	—	.125	—	.972
Rear	—	—	—	.125	—	.895
83–80 Mark VI: w/10" rear brakes	.030	10.000	10.060	.125	—	.972
w/11" rear brakes	.030	11.030	11.090	.125	—	.972
79–77 Mark V: exc. rear disc brakes	.030	11.030	11.090	.125	—	1.120
w/rear disc brakes	—	—	—	.125	—	.895
77–73 Mark IV: exc. rear disc brakes	.030	11.030	11.090	.125	—	1.120
w/rear disc brakes	—	—	—	.125	—	.895
72 Mark IV:	.030	11.030	11.090	.030	1.135	1.120
78–77 Maverick, Comet	.030	10.000	10.060	.125	—	.810
76–75 Maverick, Comet	.030	10.000	10.060	.125	—	.810
74 Maverick, Comet	.030	10.000	10.060	.125	—	.810
73–72 Maverick, Comet						
w/9" drum brakes	.030	9.000	9.060	—	—	—
w/10" drum brakes	.030	10.000	10.060	—	—	—
94 Mustang: exc. Cobra Front	—	—	—	.040	—	.970
Cobra Front	—	—	—	.040	—	1.040
Rear	—	—	—	.123	—	.500
93–89 Mustang: exc. 5.0L eng.	.030②	9.000	9.060	.125	—	.810
w/5.0L eng.	.030②	9.000	9.060	.125	—	.972
88–87 Mustang: exc. 5.0L eng.						
w/9" rear brakes	.030	9.000	9.060	.125	—	.810
w/10" rear brakes	.030	10.000	10.060	.125	—	.810
w/5.0L eng.						
exc. rear disc brakes...........	.030	10.000	10.060	.125	—	.972
w/rear disc brakes	—	—	—	.125	—	.895
86–83 Mustang, Capri:						
exc. 5.0L eng. or SVO						
w/9" rear brakes	.030	9.000	9.060	.125	—	.810
w/10" rear brakes	.030	10.000	10.060	.125	—	.810
86–83 Mustang: w/5.0L eng. or SVO						
exc. rear disc brakes...........	.030	10.000	10.060	.125	—	.972
w/rear disc brakes	—	—	—	.125	—	.895
82–79 Mustang, Capri:						
w/9" rear brakes	.030	9.000	9.060	.125	—	.810
w/10" rear brakes	.030	10.000	10.060	.125	—	.810
80–77 Pinto, Bobcat, Mustang II:	.030	9.000	9.060	.030	—	.810
76–75 Pinto, Bobcat, Mustang II:	.030	9.000	9.060	.030	—	.810
74 Pinto, Mustang II:	.030	9.000	9.060	.030	—	.875
73–72 Pinto:	.030	9.000	9.060	.030	.700	.685

② .030" over rivet head; if bonded lining use .062".

FORD MOTOR CO. — Ford, Lincoln, Mercury (Continued)

94–93 Probe:	.040	9.000	9.060	.040	.890	.863
w/rear disc brakes	—	—		.040	.345	.315
92–89 Probe:	.040	9.000	9.060	.120	.890	.860
w/rear disc brakes	—	—		.040	.345	.315
94–90 Taurus, Sable: Sedan	.030	8.858	8.918	.040	—	.974
Wagon	.030	9.842	9.902	.040	—	.974
w/rear disc brakes	—	—		.123	—	.900
89–88 Taurus, Sable: Sedan	.030	8.858	8.918	.125	—	.974
Wagon	.030	9.842	9.902	.125	—	.974
87–86 Taurus, Sable: Sedan	.030	8.858	8.918	.125	—	.896
Wagon	.030	9.842	9.902	.125	—	.896
94–91 Tempo, Topaz:	.060	8.060	8.120	.125	—	.882
90–89 Tempo, Topaz:	.030②	8.000	8.060	.125	—	.882
88–84 Tempo, Topaz:	.030②	8.000	8.060	.125	—	.882
76–73 Thunderbird:	.030	11.030	11.090	.125	—	.120
72 Thunderbird:	.030	11.030	11.090	.030	1.135	.120
76–74 Torino, Montego:						
w/10″ rear brakes	.030	10.000	10.060	.030	—	.120
w/11″ rear brakes	.030	11.030	11.090	.030	—	.120
73–72 Torino, Montego:	.030	10.000	10.060	.030	—	.120
94–91 Town Car: Front	—	—	—	.125	—	.974
Rear	—	—	—	.125	—	.440
90–83 Town Car: w/10″ rear brakes	.030	10.000	10.060	.125	—	.972
w/11″ rear brakes	.030	11.030	11.090	.125	—	.972
82–79 Town Car, LTD, Marquis:						
w/10″ rear brakes	.030	10.000	10.060	.125	—	.972
w/11″ rear brakes	.030	11.030	11.090	.125	—	.972
89–88 Tracer: exc. rear disc brakes	.040	7.870	7.910	.120	.660	.630
w/rear disc brakes	—	—	—	.120	.380	.350
80–79 Versailles:						
exc. rear disc brakes	.030	10.000	10.060	.125	—	.810
w/rear disc brakes	—	—	—	.125	—	.895
78–77 Versailles:	.030	10.000	10.060	.125	—	.810

② .030″ over rivet head; if bonded lining use .062″.

GEO

94–92 Metro:	.039	7.090	7.160	.120	—	.315
91 Metro: Hardtop	.110②	7.090	7.160	.315	—	.315
Convertible	.110②	7.090	7.160	.320	—	.630
90–89 Metro:	.110②	7.090	7.160	.315	—	.315
94–93 Prizm:	.039	7.874	7.913	.039	—	.787
92–89 Prizm:	.039	7.874	7.913	.030	—	.669
89 Spectrum: exc. Turbo	.039	7.090	7.140	.039	—	.378
Turbo	.039	7.090	7.140	.039	—	.650
93–90 Storm:	.039	7.870	7.930	.039	—	.811

② Measurement of lining & metal.

HONDA

94–90 Accord: exc.Wagon	.080	8.661	8.701	.063	.827	—
Wagon	.080	8.661	8.701	.063	.910	—
w/rear disc brakes	—	—	—	.063	.315	—
89 Accord: exc. Fuel Inj.	.080	7.870	7.910	.120	.670	—
w/Fuel Inj.	.080	7.870	7.910	.120	.750	—
w/rear disc brakes	—	—	—	.060	.310	—
88 Accord: exc. Fuel Inj.	.080	7.870	7.910	.120	.670	—
w/Fuel Inj.	.080	7.870	7.910	.060	.750	—
87–86 Accord:	.080	7.870	7.910	.120	.670	—
85–84 Accord:	.080	7.870	7.910	.059	.670	—
83–82 Accord:	.079	7.870	7.910	.063	.600	—
81–79 Accord:	.079	7.080	7.130	.063	.413	—
78–76 Accord:	.079	7.080	7.130	.063	.449	.437
91–90 Civic CRX: DX	.080	7.090	7.130	.120	.750	—
HF	.080	7.090	7.130	.120	.590	—
Si	.080	7.090	7.130	.120	.670	—
w/rear disc brakes	—	—	—	.120	.310	—
89 Civic CRX: w/DX, Si	.080	7.090	7.130	.120	.670	—
w/HF	.080	7.090	7.130	.120	.590	—
88 Civic CRX: w/DX, Si	.080	7.090	7.130	.120	.670	—
w/HF	.080	7.090	7.130	.120	.590	—
87–84 Civic CRX: w/1300 HF	.080	7.090	7.130	.120	.350	—
w/1500 exc. HF	.080	7.090	7.130	.120	.590	—
94–93 Civic del Sol:	.080	7.090	7.130	.060	.750	—
94–92 Civic Hatchback, Civic Sedan, Civic Coupe:	.080	7.090	7.130	.060	.750	—
w/H.D. rear drum brakes	.080	7.870	7.910	.060	.750	—
w/rear disc brakes	—	—	—	.060	.310	—
91–90 Civic Hatchback, Civic Sedan:	.080	7.087	7.126	.120	.750	—

(continues)

HONDA (Continued)

89	Civic Hatchback, Civic Sedan:	.080	7.090	7.130	.120	.670	—
88	Civic Hatchback, Civic Sedan:	.080	7.090	7.130	.120	.669	—
87–84	Civic Hatchback: w/1300	.080	7.090	7.130	.120	.390	—
	w/1500	.080	7.090	7.130	.120	.590	—
83	Civic Hatchback: w/1300 4 SPD	.079	7.090	7.130	.063	.350	—
	w/1300 5 SPD	.079	7.090	7.130	.063	.390	—
	w/1500	.079	7.090	7.130	.063	.590	—
82	Civic Hatchback: w/1300 4 SPD	.079	7.090	7.130	.063	.350	—
	exc. 1300 4 SPD	.079	7.090	7.130	.063	.390	—
81–80	Civic Hatchback, Civic CVCC:	.079	7.090	7.130	.063	.350	—
79–75	Civic Hatchback, Civic CVCC:	.079	7.080	7.130	.063	.354	.343
74–73	Civic Hatchback:	.079	7.080	7.130	.063	.354	.343
87–84	Civic Sedan:	.080	7.090	7.130	.120	.590	—
83	Civic Sedan:	.079	7.090	7.130	.063	.590	—
82–81	Civic Sedan:	.079	7.090	7.130	.063	.390	—
91–90	Civic Wagon, Wagovan: (4x2)	.080	7.874	7.913	.120	.750	—
	(4x4)	.080	7.874	7.913	.120	.670	—
89	Civic Wagon, Wagovan: (4x2)	.080	7.870	7.910	.060	.669	—
	(4x4)	.080	7.870	7.910	.120	.669	—
88	Civic Wagon, Wagovan: (4x2)	.080	7.870	7.910	.080	.669	—
	(4x4)	.080	7.870	7.910	.120	.669	—
87–84	Civic Wagon:	.080	7.870	7.910	.120	.590	—
83–80	Civic Wagon:	.079	7.870	7.910	.063	.390	—
79–76	Civic Wagon:	.079	7.870	7.910	.063	.449	.437
94–92	Prelude: Front	—	—	—	.060	.830	—
	Rear	—	—	—	.060	.310	—
91	Prelude: Front	—	—	—	.060	.750	—
	Rear	—	—	—	.060	.310	—
90–88	Prelude: Front exc. Fuel Inj.	—	—	—	.120	.670	—
	w/Fuel Inj.	—	—	—	.120	.750	—
	Rear	—	—	—	.080	.310	—
87–86	Prelude: Front exc. Fuel Inj.	—	—	—	.118	.670	—
	Rear	—	—	—	.063	.310	—
	Front w/Fuel Inj.	—	—	—	.120	.670	—
	Rear	—	—	—	.063	.310	—
85–84	Prelude: Front	—	—	—	.120	.670	—
	Rear	—	—	—	.060	.310	—
83	Prelude:	.080	7.870	7.910	.120	.670	—
82–79	Prelude:	.079	7.080	7.130	.063	.413	—

HYUNDAI

94–92	Elantra:	.059	8.000	8.079	.079	—	.787
94–91	Excel:	.039	7.087	7.165	.039	—	.669
90	Excel:	.039	7.100	7.165	.039	—	.670
89	Excel:	.040	7.100	7.200	.040	—	.450
88	Excel: w/solid rotor	.040	7.100	7.200	.040	—	.450
	w/vented rotor	.040	7.100	7.200	.040	—	.670
87–85	Excel:	.040	7.086	7.165	.040	—	.450
87–86	Pony Sedan:	.039	7.992	④	.079	—	.449
85–83	Pony Sedan:	.039	7.992	④	.079	—	.449
94–91	Scoupe:	.039	7.100	7.165	.039	—	.669
93–91	Sonata:	.031	8.858	8.936	.079	—	.797
	w/rear disc brakes	—	—	—	.031	—	.413
90	Sonata:	.039	9.000	9.079	.079	—	.787
	w/rear disc brakes	—	—	—	.031	—	.413
89	Sonata:	.059	9.000	9.079	.079	—	.787
87	Stellar:	.040	9.000	9.079	.040	—	.669
86–85	Stellar:	.060	9.000	—	.060	—	.450

④ Machining specification is not available; discard at 8.071".

INFINITI

94–91	G20: Front	—	—	—	.079	—	.787
	Rear	—	—	—	.079	—	.310
94–93	J30: Front	—	—	—	.079	—	1.024
	Rear	—	—	—	.079	—	.551
92–90	M30: Front	—	—	—	.079	—	.787
	Rear	—	—	—	.079	—	.354
94–90	Q45: Front	—	—	—	.079	—	1.024
	Rear	—	—	—	.079	—	.315

ISUZU

89-88 I-Mark:						
exc. Turbo or DOHC eng.	.040	7.090	7.140	.040	—	.378
w/Turbo or DOHC eng.	.040	7.090	7.140	.040	—	.650
87-85 I-Mark:	.039	7.090	7.140	.039	—	.378
84-81 I-Mark:	.039	9.000	9.040	.067	.354	.338
92-90 Impulse: Front	—	—	—	.039	—	.810
Rear	—	—	—	.039	—	.299
89-85 Impulse: Front	—	—	—	.040	.668	.654
Rear	—	—	—	.040	.668	.654
84-83 Impulse: Front	—	—	—	.125	.706	.654
Rear	—	—	—	.125	.706	.654
93-91 Stylus: w/rear drum brakes	.039	7.870	7.929	.039	—	.653
w/rear disc brakes	—	—	—	.039	—	.810

JAGUAR

94-88 XJ6, XJ12: Front	—	—	—	.125	—	②
Rear	—	—	—	.125	—	②
87-75 XJ6, Vanden Plas: Front	—	—	—	.125	—	②
Rear	—	—	—	.125	—	.450
74-72 XJ6: Front	—	—	—	.125	—	.450
Rear	—	—	—	.125	—	.450
94-76 XJS, Saloons: Front	—	—	—	.125	—	②
Rear w/overdrive	—	—	—	.125	—	②
Rear exc. Overdrive	—	—	—	.125	—	.450
79-78 XJ12: Front	—	—	—	.125	—	②
Rear	—	—	—	.125	—	.450
77-72 XJ12, V12: Front	—	—	—	.125	—	②
Rear	—	—	—	.125	—	.450

② Minimum thickness is stamped on rotor.

LEXUS

91-90 ES250: Front	—	—	—	.039	—	.945
Rear	—	—	—	.039	—	.354
94-92 ES300: Front	—	—	—	.039	—	1.063
Rear	—	—	—	.039	—	.354
94 GS300: Front	—	—	—	.039	—	1.181
Rear	—	—	—	.039	—	.591
94-93 LS400: Front	—	—	—	.039	—	1.181
Rear	—	—	—	.039	—	.591
92-91 LS400: Front	—	—	—	.039	—	1.024
Rear	—	—	—	.039	—	.591
90 LS400: Front	—	—	—	.039	—	.906
Rear	—	—	—	.039	—	.591
94-92 SC300: Front	—	—	—	.039	—	1.024
Rear	—	—	—	.039	—	.591
94-92 SC400: Front	—	—	—	.039	—	1.181
Rear	—	—	—	.039	—	.591

MAZDA

94-92 323, Protege:	.040	7.870	7.910	.080	—	.790
w/rear disc brakes	—	—	—	.040	—	.310
91-90 323, Protege:	.040	9.000	9.040	.080	—	.790
w/rear disc brakes	—	—	—	.040	—	.280
89-88 323 Hatchback, 323 Sedan:	.040	7.870	7.910	.080	—	.630
w/rear disc brakes	—	—	—	.040	—	.310
87-86 323 Hatchback, 323 Sedan:	.040	7.870	7.910	.118	—	.630
w/rear disc brakes	—	—	—	.040	—	.350
88-87 323 Wagon:	.040	9.000	9.040	.118②	—	.630
94-93 626, MX-6:	.040	9.000	9.059	.080	—	.870
w/rear disc brakes	—	—	—	.040	—	.310
92-88 626, MX-6:	.040	9.000	9.060	.080	—	.870
w/rear disc brakes	—	—	—	.040	—	.310
87-86 626:	.040	7.870	7.910	.118	—	.710
w/rear disc brakes	—	—	—	.040	—	.350
85 626: w/gas eng.	.040	7.870	7.910	.118	—	.470
w/diesel eng.	.040	7.870	7.910	.118	—	.710
84-83 626:	.040	7.874	7.913	.040	—	.490
82-79 626:	.040	9.000	9.040	.040	—	.472
77-74 808:	.040	7.874	7.914	.256④	—	.394
73-72 808:	.040	7.874	7.914	.256④	—	.394
94-92 929: Front	—	—	—	.040	—	.870
Rear	—	—	—	.040	—	.630
91-90 929: Front	—	—	—	.080	—	.790
Rear	—	—	—	.080	—	.630
89-88 929: Front	—	—	—	.080	—	.790
Rear	—	—	—	.080	—	.310
78-76 Cosmo: Front	—	—	—	.276④	—	.669
Rear	—	—	—	.276④	—	.354
85 GLC Hatchback, GLC Sedan:	.040	7.090	7.130	.118	—	.390

(continues)

MAZDA   (Continued)

84–81 GLC Hatchback, GLC Sedan: …	.040	7.090	7.130	.040	—	.393
80–77 GLC Hatchback, GLC SEdan: …	.040	7.874	7.914	.040	—	.472
83–81 GLC Wagon: …	.040	7.874	7.913	.040	—	.472
94 Miata MX-5: Front …	—	—	—	.040	—	.710
Rear …	—	—	—	.040	—	.310
93–91 Miata MX-5: Front …	—	—	—	.040	—	.630
Rear …	—	—	—	.040	—	.280
90 Miata MX-5: Front …	—	—	—	.040	—	.630
Rear …	—	—	—	.080	—	.280
93–92 MX-3: …	.040	7.870	7.910	.080	—	.790
w/rear disc brakes …	—	—	—	.040	—	.310
73–72 RX-2: …	.040	7.874	7.914	.276④	—	.433
77–75 RX-3: …	.040	7.874	7.914	.276④	—	.394
73–72 RX-3: …	.040	7.874	7.914	.256④	—	.394
78–74 RX-4: …	.040	9.000	9.040	.276④	—	.433
94–93 RX-7: Front …	—	—	—	.040	—	.790
Rear …	—	—	—	.040	—	.710
91–89 RX-7: Front Std. …	—	—	—	.080	—	.790
Front H.D. …	—	—	—	.080	—	.790
Rear Std. …	—	—	—	.040	—	.310
Rear H.D. …	—	—	—	.040	—	.710
88–86 RX-7: Front w/14" Wheels …	—	—	—	.040	—	.790
Front w/15" Wheels …	—	—	—	.118	—	.790
Rear w/14" Wheels …	—	—	—	.040	—	.310
Rear w/15" Wheels …	—	—	—	.040	—	.710
85–80 RX-7: …	.040	7.874	7.914	.040	—	.670
w/rear solid rotor …	—	—	—	.040	—	.354
w/rear vented rotor …	—	—	—	.040	—	.787
79 RX-7: …	.040	7.874	7.914	.040	—	.670

④ Measurement of lining & metal.

MERCEDES BENZ

93–86 190E: 2.3, 2.3-16, 2.6 Front	—	—	—	.138	.787	.764
2.3, 2.3-16, 2.6 Rear	—	—	—	.138	.300	.287
90–84 190D,E: Front	—	—	—	.138	.374	.354
Rear	—	—	—	.079	.300	.287
94 220C, 280C, 300E Diesel:						
Front	—	—	—	.078	.787	.764
Rear	—	—	—	.078	.300	.287
93–86 260E, 300CE,TE,DT,E,TDT,D:						
Front	—	—	—	.079	.787	.764
Rear	—	—	—	.079	.300	.287
91–81 300 SD,SE,SEL,						
300 SDL Turbo Diesel,						
350 SD,SDL, 380 SE,SEC,SEL,						
420 SEL, 500 SEC,SEL,						
560 SEC,SEL:						
Front Fixed Caliper 60mm	—	—	—	.079	.787	.764
Fixed Caliper 57mm	—	—	—	.079	1.024	1.000
Floating Caliper	—	—	—	.138	.787	.764
Rear	—	—	—	.079	.339	.327
94 320E: Front	—	—	—	.078	.787	.764
Rear	—	—	—	.078	.866	.843
94 320E Cabriolet Front	—	—	—	.078	.906	.882
Rear	—	—	—	.078	.300	.287
94 320E Wagon: Rear	—	—	—	.078	.697	.685
Front	—	—	—	.078	.906	.882
94 320S, 350S Turbo Diesel:						
Front 2 Piston Caliper	—	—	—	.078	1.023	1.000
Front 4 Piston Caliper	—	—	—	.078	1.102	1.079
Rear	—	—	—	.078	.413	.385
94 320SL, 500SL: Front	—	—	—	.078	1.026	1.000
Rear	—	—	—	.078	.300	.287
93–90 300SL, 500SL: Front	—	—	—	.079	1.024	1.000
Rear	—	—	—	.079	.300	.287
94 420S, 500S, 600S, 600SL:						
Front 2 Piston Caliper	—	—	—	.078	1.023	1.000
Front 4 Piston Caliper	—	—	—	.078	1.102	1.079
Rear	—	—	—	.078	.787	.764
94 500E: Front	—	—	—	.078	1.023	1.000
Rear	—	—	—	.078	.866	.843
93–92 400E, 500E: Front	—	—	—	.079	1.024	1.000
Rear	—	—	—	.079	.866	.842

(continues)

MERCEDES BENZ (Continued)

94	600SL: Front	—	—	—	.078	1.122	1.102
	Rear	—	—	—	.078	.787	.764
89–86	560SL: Front	—	—	—	.079	.787	.764
	Rear	—	—	—	.079	.338	.327
85–73	380SL,SLC, 450SL,SLC: Front	—	—	—	.079	—	.811①
	Rear	—	—	—	.079	—	.327
85–77	230, 240D, 300D,CD,TD, 280E,CE: Front	—	—	—	.079	—	.417
	Rear	—	—	—	.079	—	.327
80	280SE, 300SD, 450SEL: Front	—	—	—	.079	—	.764
	Rear	—	—	—	.079	—	.327
79–73	280S,SE, 300SD, 450SE,SEL, 6.9: Front	—	—	—	.079	—	.787
	Rear	—	—	—	.079	—	.327
76–72	220,D, 220/8, 230, 240D, 250,C, 280,C, 300D: Front	—	—	—	.079	—	.432②
	Rear	—	—	—	.079	—	.327
73–72	280,SE,SEL, 300SEL: Front	—	—	—	.079	—	.431③
	Rear	—	—	—	.079	—	.327
72	600: Front	—	—	—	.354	—	.725
	Rear	—	—	—	.079	—	.570

① w/57mm caliper piston shown; w/60mm caliper piston up to 3/80 .787″ from 3/80 .763″.
② w/57mm caliper piston shown; w/60mm caliper piston .417
③ 1st version shown; 2nd version .700″.

MERKUR

90–88	Scorpio: Front	—	—	—	.140	—	.900
	Rear	—	—	—	.150	—	.350
89–85	XR4Ti:	.040	10.000	10.060	.060	.927	.897

① 1987 .0004″.   ② 1990 .002″.

MITSUBISHI

94–91	3000GT: (FWD) Front	—	—	—	.080	—	.880
	(FWD) Rear	—	—	—	.080	—	.650
	(AWD) Front	—	—	—	.080	—	1.120
	(AWD) Rear	—	—	—	.080	—	.720
88	Cordia, Tredia: exc. Turbo	.040	8.000	8.100	.080	—	.650
	w/Turbo	.040	8.000	8.100	.080	—	.880
87–84	Cordia, Tredia:	.040	8.000	8.050	.040	—	.650
83	Cordia, Tredia:	.040	8.000	8.050	.040	—	.450
94–92	Diamante: Front	—	—	—	.080	—	.880
	exc. Wagon Rear	—	—	—	.080	—	.650
	Wagon Rear	—	—	—	.080	—	.720
94–90	Eclipse: Front	—	—	—	.080	—	.882
	Rear	—	—	—	.080	—	.331
94	Galant	.040	8.976	9.078	.080	—	.882
	w/rear disc brakes Rear	—	—	—	.080	—	.331
93–89	Galant w/rear drum brakes	.040	8.000	8.100	.080	—	.882
	w/rear disc brakes	—	—	—	.080	—	.331
90–88	Galant Sigma: Front	—	—	—	.079	—	.882
	Rear	—	—	—	.079	—	.646
87	Galant w/rear drum brakes	.040	8.000	8.050	.040	—	.880
	w/rear disc brakes	—	—	—	.040	—	.330
86–85	Galant w/rear drum brakes	.040	8.000	8.050	.040	—	.650
	w/rear disc brakes	—	—	—	.040	—	.330
94–93	Mirage: w/solid rotor	.040	7.100	7.200	.080	—	.449
	w/vented rotor	.040	8.000	8.100	.080	—	.646
	w/rear disc brakes	—	—	—	.080	—	.331
92–91	Mirage: w/solid rotor	.040	7.100	7.200	.080	—	.449
	w/vented rotor	.040	7.100	7.200	.080	—	.646
	w/rear disc brakes Front	—	—	—	.080	—	.882
	Rear	—	—	—	.080	—	.331
90	Mirage: exc. disc brakes	.040	7.100	7.200	.080	—	.449
	Front w/rear disc brakes	—	—	—	.080	—	.882
	Rear	—	—	—	.080	—	.331
89	Mirage: exc. rear disc brakes	.040	7.100	7.200	.080	—	.449
	Front w/rear disc brakes	—	—	—	.080	—	.882
	Rear	—	—	—	.080	—	.331
88–85	Mirage: exc. Turbo	.040	7.100	7.150	.040④	—	.450
	w/Turbo	.040	7.100	7.150	.040	—	.650
94–90	Precis:	.040	7.087	7.165	.040	—	.670
89–88	Precis: w/solid rotor	.040	7.100	7.200	.040	—	.450
	w/vented rotor	.040	7.100	7.200	.040	—	.670
89–83	Starion: Front	—	—	—	.040④	—	.880
	Rear	—	—	—	.040④	—	.650

④ 1989-88 .080″.

NISSAN (DATSUN)

Model						
88–87 200SX: Front w/4 cyl. eng.	—	—	—	.079	—	.630
Front w/6 cyl. eng.	—	—	—	.079	—	.787
Rear	—	—	—	.079	—	.354
86–84 200SX: w/rear drum brakes	.059	9.000	9.055	.079	—	.630
w/rear disc brakes	—	—	—	.079	—	.354
83 200SX: Front	—	—	—	.079	—	.354
Rear	—	—	—	.079	—	.413
82 200SX: Front	—	—	—	.079	—	.354
Rear	—	—	—	.079	—	.413
81 200SX: Front	—	—	—	.079	—	.339
Rear	—	—	—	.063	—	.413
80 200SX: Front	—	—	—	.079	—	.339
Rear	—	—	—	.079	—	.413
79 200SX:	.059	9.000	9.055	.060	—	.331
78–77 200SX:	.059	9.000	9.055	.063	—	.331
82–79 210:	.059	8.000	8.050	.063	—	.331
94–89 240SX: exc. ABS Front	—	—	—	.079	—	.709
w/ABS Front	—	—	—	.079	—	.787
Rear	—	—	—	.079	—	.315
83–82 280ZX: Front	—	—	—	.080	—	.709
Rear	—	—	—	.080	—	.339
81–79 280ZX: Front	—	—	—	.080	—	.709
Rear	—	—	—	.080	—	.339
78–72 280Z, 260Z, 240Z:	.059	9.000	9.055	.080	.423	.413
94–91 300ZX: Front	—	—	—	.079	—	1.102
Rear	—	—	—	.079	—	.630
90 300ZX: Front	—	—	—	.079	—	.945
Rear	—	—	—	.079	—	.630
89–87 300ZX: Front w/Turbo	—	—	—	.079	—	.945
Front exc. Turbo	—	—	—	.079	—	.787
Rear	—	—	—	.079	—	.709
86–84 300ZX: Front	—	—	—	.080	—	.787
Rear	—	—	—	.080	—	.354
82–79 310:	.059	8.000	8.050	.079	—	.339
81–78 510:	.059	9.000	9.055	.080	—	.331
73–72 510:	.059	9.000	9.055	.040	—	.331
76–75 610:	.059	9.000	9.055	.063	—	.331
74–73 610:	.059	9.000	9.055	.040	—	.331
77–76 710:	.059	9.000	9.055	.063	—	.331
75–73 710:	.059	9.000	9.055	.063	.341	.331
88–85 810 Maxima: Front	—	—	—	.079	—	.787
Rear	—	—	—	.079	—	.354
84–83 810 Maxima:	.059	9.000	9.055	.079	—	.630
w/rear disc brakes	—	—	—	.079	—	.354
82 810 Maxima:	.059	9.000	9.055	.079	—	.630
w/rear disc brakes	—	—	—	.079	—	.339
81 810:	.059	9.000	9.055	.079	—	.630
w/rear disc brakes	—	—	—	.079	—	.339
80–77 810:	.059	9.000	9.055	.080	—	.413
73–72 1200:	.059	8.000	8.051	.063	—	.331
94–93 Altima:	.059	9.000	9.060	.079	—	.787
w/rear disc brakes	—	—	—	.059	—	.315
78–74 B210:	.059	8.000	8.050	.063	—	.331
78–76 F10:	.039	8.000	8.051	.063	—	.339
94–92 Maxima:	.059	9.000	9.060	.079	—	.787
w/rear disc brakes	—	—	—	.079	—	.315
91–90 Maxima:	.059	9.000	9.060	.079	—	.787
w/rear disc brakes	—	—	—	.079	—	.354
89 Maxima:	.059	9.000	9.060	.079	—	.787
w/rear disc brakes	—	—	—	.079	—	.315
90–87 Pulsar NX: exc. SE	.059	8.000	8.050	.079	—	.394
SE	.059	8.000	8.050	.079	—	.630
86 Pulsar NX:	.059	8.000	8.050	.079	—	.433
85 Pulsar NX:	.059	8.000	8.050	.079	—	.394
84–83 Pulsar NX:	.059	7.090	7.130	.080	—	.394
94–91 Sentra, NX Coupe:						
Front exc. SE	—	—	—	.079	—	.630
Front SE	—	—	—	.079	—	.945
w/rear drum brakes	.059	7.090	7.130	—	—	—
w/rear disc brakes	—	—	—	.079	—	.236
90–88 Sentra: (4x2) exc. Wagon	.059	8.000	8.050	.079	—	.394
Wagon	.059	8.000	8.050	.079	—	.630
(4x4)	.059	9.000	9.050	.079	—	.630
87 Sentra: w/gas eng.	.059	8.000	8.050	.079	—	.394
w/diesel eng.	.059	8.000	8.050	.079	—	.630
86–85 Sentra: w/gas eng. (1986)	.059	8.000	8.050	.079	—	.433
w/gas eng. (1985)	.059	8.000	8.050	.079	—	.394
w/diesel eng.	.059	8.000	8.050	.079	—	.630
84–83 Sentra: w/gas eng.	.059	7.090	7.130	.080	—	.394
w/diesel eng.	.059	8.000	8.050	.080	—	.630

(continues)

NISSAN (DATSUN) (Continued)

92–91 Stanza:	.059	9.000	9.060	.079	—	.787
w/rear disc brakes	—	—	—	.079		.354
90 Stanza:	.059	9.000	9.060	.079	—	.787
w/rear disc brakes	—	—	—	.079		.354
89–88 Stanza:	.059	9.000	9.060	.079		.787
87 Stanza: exc. Wagon	.059	10.240	10.300	.079		.787
86–84 Stanza: exc. Wagon	.059	8.000	8.050	.080		.630
83–82 Stanza:	.059	8.000	8.050	.080		.630
88–86 Stanza Wagon: (4x2)	.059	9.000	9.060	.079		.787
(4x4)	.059	10.240	10.300	.079		.787

OLDSMOBILE

94–93 98:	.030	8.863	8.880	.030	1.224	1.209
92–91 98:	②	8.860	8.880	.030	1.224	1.209
94–93 Achieva:	.030	7.874	7.899	.030	.751	.736
92 Achieva:	.030	7.879	7.899	.030	.796	.736
91 Calais:	②	7.879	7.899	.030	.786	.736
90–80 Calais, Omega:	②	7.880	7.899	.030	.830	.815
94–88 Ciera, Cruiser: Front H.D.	—	—	—	.030	.972	.957
Front exc. H.D.	—	—	—	.030	.830	.815
Rear	②	8.863	8.877	—	—	—
87–86 Ciera: H.D.	②	8.863	8.877	.030	.972	.957
exc. H.D.	②	8.863	8.877	.030	.830	.815
85 Ciera: H.D.	②	8.863	8.920	.030	.972	.957
exc. H.D.	②	8.863	8.920	.030	.830	.815
84 Ciera: H.D.	②	8.863	8.883	.030	.972	.957
exc. H.D.	②	8.863	8.883	.030	.830	.815
83–82 Ciera:	②	7.879	7.899	.030	.830	.815
91–78 Custom Cruiser, Delta 88, 98: (Delta 88 w/403) (RWD)	②	11.000	11.060	.030	.980	.965
77 Custom Cruiser, Delta 88, 98: (Delta 88 w/403) (RWD)	②	11.000	11.060	.030	.980	.965
94–88 Cutlass: (FWD) Front	—	—	—	.030	.987	.972
Rear	—	—	—	.030	.444	.429
77–76 Cutlass:	②	11.000	11.060	.030	.980	.965
75–72 Cutlass, Omega: exc. Vista Cruiser	②	9.500	9.560	.062	.980	.965
94–93 Delta 88:	.030	8.863	8.880	.030	1.224	1.209
92 Delta 88:	②	8.860	8.880	.030	1.224	1.209
91 Delta 88:	②	8.860	8.880	.030	.972	.957
90–83 Delta 88, 98: (FWD)	②	8.858	8.880	.030	.972	.957
88–82 Delta 88, Cutlass: (RWD)	②	9.500	9.560	.030	.980	.965
81–78 Delta 88, Cutlass: (RWD) (Delta 88 w/o 403 eng.)	②	9.500	9.560	.030	.980	.965
77 Delta 88: (RWD) (w/o 403 eng.)	②	9.500	9.560	.030	.980	.965
76–72 Delta 88, 98: exc. Wagon & H.D. Pkg.	②	11.000	11.060	.062	1.230	1.215
76–72 Delta 88: Wagon & H.D. Pkg.	②	12.000	12.060	.062	1.230	1.215
88–82 Firenza: vented rotor (88-82)	②	7.880	7.899	.030	.830	.815
solid rotor (82)	②	7.880	7.899	.030	.444	.429
79–78 Omega: w/5 Speed	②	11.000	11.060	.030	.980	.965
w/o 5 Speed	②	9.500	9.560	.030	.980	.965
77–76 Omega: w/5 Speed	②	11.000	11.060	.030	.980	.965
w/o 5 Speed	②	9.500	9.560	.030	.980	.965
80–76 Starfire:	②	9.500	9.560	.062	.830	.815
75 Starfire:	②	9.000	9.060	.062	.455	.440
92 Toronado, Trofeo: Front	—	—	—	.030	1.250	1.209
Rear	—	—	—	.030	.423	.374
91–86 Toronado, Trofeo: Front	—	—	—	.030	.971	.956
Rear	—	—	—	.030	.444	.429
85–79 Toronado:	②	9.500	9.560	.030	.980	.965
w/rear disc brakes	—	—	—	.030	.980	.965
78–72 Toronado:	②	11.000	11.060	.062	1.185	1.170
75–72 Vista Cruiser:	②	11.000	11.060	.062	.980	.965

② .030″ over rivet head; if bonded lining use .062″.

OPEL

79–76 Coupe, Sedan:	.040	9.000	9.040	.067	—	.339
75 Manta, 1900 Wagon:	.040	9.000	9.040	.067	—	.465
74–72 1900 Coupe, 1900 Sedan, 1900 Wagon, Manta, GT:	.030	9.060	9.090	.067	.404	.394

PEUGEOT

92–89 405: Front	—	—	—	—	—	.728
Rear	—	—	—	—	—	.315
83–80 504: Front	—	—	—	—	.443	.423
w/10 in. drum Rear	—	10.039	10.079	—	—	—
w/11 in. drum Rear	—	11.023	11.063	—	—	—
w/10 mm caliper Rear	—	—	—	—	.354	.335
w/12 mm caliper Rear	—	—	—	—	.433	.413
91–80 505: w/solid rotors	—	—	10.098	—	—	.443
91–85 505: w/vented rotors	—	—	—	—	—	.709
91–80 505: w/rear disc brakes	—	—	—	—	—	.315
84–82 604: Front	—	—	—	—	—	.709
Rear	—	—	—	—	—	.394

PONTIAC

91–89 6000: Front w/H.D.	—	—	—	.030	.972	.957
exc. H.D.	—	—	—	.030	.830	.815
Rear coupe/sedan	④	8.863	8.920	—	—	—
wagon	④	8.863	8.877	—	—	—
w/rear disc brakes	—	—	—	.030	.702	.681
88–87 6000: Front w/H.D.	—	—	—	.030	.972	.957
exc. H.D.	—	—	—	.030	.830	.815
Rear coupe/sedan	④	8.863	8.920	—	—	—
wagon	④	8.863	8.877	—	—	—
w/rear disc brakes	—	—	—	.030	.444	.429
86–85 6000: exc. H.D.	④	8.863	8.920	.030	.830	.815
86 6000: w/H.D.	④	8.863	8.920	.030	.978	.931
85 6000: w/H.D.	④	8.863	8.920	.030	.972	.957
84 6000: w/H.D.	④	8.863	8.883	.030	.972	.957
exc. H.D.	④	8.863	8.883	.030	.830	.815
83–82 6000:	④	7.879	7.899	.030	.830	.815
94–92 Bonneville:	.030	8.860	8.880	.030	1.224	1.209
91–87 Bonneville:	④	8.860	8.880	.030	.972	.957
89–77 Bonneville, Catalina, LeMans, Grand Prix, Grand Am, Parisienne, Safari:						
(RWD) w/9.5″ rear brakes	④	9.500	9.560	.030	.980	.965
(RWD) w/11″ rear brakes	④	11.000	11.060	.030	.980	.965
76–72 Bonneville, Catalina, Gran Ville: exc. Wagon	.125	11.000	11.060	.125	1.230	1.215
Wagon, Grand Safari	.125	12.000	12.060	.125	1.230	1.215
88 Fiero: Front	—	—	—	.030	.702	.681
Rear	—	—	—	.030	.702	.681
87–84 Fiero: Front	—	—	—	.062	.386	.374
Rear	—	—	—	.062	.440	.430
94–93 Firebird:	.030	9.500	9.560	.030	1.250	1.209
w/rear disc brakes	—	—	—	.030	.733	.724
92–89 Firebird: exc. H.D.	④	9.500	9.560	.030	.980	.965
H.D. Front	—	—	—	.030	.980	.965
H.D. Rear	—	—	—	.030	.744	.724
88–86 Firebird: w/rear drum brakes	④	9.500	9.560	.030	.980	.965
w/rear disc brakes	—	—	—	.030	.986	.956
85–82 Firebird: w/rear drum brakes	④	9.500	9.560	.030	.980	.965
w/rear disc brakes	—	—	—	.030	.980	.965
81–77 Firebird, Ventura, Phoenix:	④	9.500	9.560	.030	.980	.965
w/rear disc (81-79)	—	—	—	.030	.921	.905
88–85 Firefly:	.110	7.090	7.160	.315	—	.315
94–93 Grand Am: (FWD)	④	7.874	7.899	.030	.751	.736
92–91 Grand Am: (FWD)	④	7.879	7.899	.030	.751	.736
90–80 Grand Am, Phoenix: (FWD)	④	7.880	7.899	.030	.830	.815
94–89 Grand Prix: (FWD) Front	—	—	—	.030	.984	.972
Rear	—	—	—	.030	.441	.429
88 Grand Prix: (FWD) Front	—	—	—	.030	1.019	.972
Rear	—	—	—	.030	.441	.429
93–88 LeMans: w/9″ solid rotor	.030	7.870	7.900	.030	.420	.380
w/9″ vented rotor	.030	7.870	7.900	.030	.669	.646
w/10″ vented rotor	.030	7.870	7.900	.030	.870	.830
76–74 LeMans, Firebird, Grand Prix, Ventura: exc. Wagon	.125	9.500	9.560	.125	.980	.965
Wagon	.125	11.000	11.060	.125	.980	.965
73–72 LeMans, Firebird, Grand Prix:	.125	9.500	9.560	.125	.980	.965
94–93 Sunbird:	.030	7.874	7.899	.030	.751	.736
92 Sunbird, J2000:	.030	7.880	7.900	.030	.751	.736

④ .030″ over rivet head; if bonded lining use .062″.

(continues)

PONTIAC (Continued)

91–82 Sunbird, J2000:						
vented rotor (91-82)	④	7.880	7.899	.030	.830	.815
solid rotor (82)	④	7.880	7.899	.030	.444	.429
80–76 Sunbird, Astre:	④	9.500	9.560	.030	.830	.815
89–85 Sunburst, Storm: exc. Turbo	.039	7.090	7.140	.039	—	.378
Turbo	.039	7.090	7.140	.039	—	.650
87–86 T1000:	④	7.880	7.899	.030	.404	.374
85–83 T1000:	④	7.874	7.899	.030	.390	.374
82–81 T1000:	④	7.874	7.899	.030	.390	.374
73–72 Ventura:	.125	9.500	9.560	.125	—	.980

④ .030" over rivet head; if bonded lining use .062".

PORSCHE

94–90 911 Carrera 2,4: Front	—	—	—	.079	1.047	1.024
Rear	—	—	—	.079	.890	.866
94 911 Turbo 3.6: Front	—	—	—	.079	1.200	1.180
Rear	—	—	—	.079	1.050	1.020
89–84 911: exc. Turbo & Turbo Look						
Front	—	—	—	.079	.890	.866
Rear	—	—	—	.079	.890	.866
Turbo & Turbo Look Front	—	—	—	.079	1.200	1.180
Rear	—	—	—	.079	1.050	1.020
83–78 911: Front	—	—	—	.079	.750	.728
Rear	—	—	—	.079	.732	.709
77–72 911: Front	—	—	—	.079	.732	.709
Rear	—	—	—	.079	.732	.709
76–72 914: Front	—	—	—	.080	.394	.375
Rear	—	—	—	.080	.351	.335
76–72 914, 916: Front	—	—	—	.080	.732	.709
Rear	—	—	—	.080	.374	.354
88–86 924S: Front	—	—	—	.079	.751	.728
Rear	—	—	—	.079	.751	.728
82–80 924: Turbo Front	—	—	—	.079	.751	.728
Turbo Rear	—	—	—	.079	.755	.732
82–77 924: exc. Turbo	.098	9.055	9.094	.079	.472	.453
94–86 928S, 928S-4, 928GT: Front	—	—	—	.079	1.205	1.181
Rear	—	—	—	.079	.890	.866
85–82 928, 928S: Front	—	—	—	.079	1.228	1.205
Rear	—	—	—	.079	.756	.732
81–78 928: Front	—	—	—	.079	.756	.732
Rear	—	—	—	.079	.756	.732
90 944: Turbo S Front	—	—	—	.079	1.205	1.180
Turbo S Rear	—	—	—	.079	.890	.866
91–90 944 S2: Front	—	—	—	.079	1.047	1.024
Rear	—	—	—	.079	.890	.866
90–83 944: exc. Turbo Front	—	—	—	.079	.752	.728
exc. Turbo Rear	—	—	—	.079	.756	.732
90–86 944: Turbo Front	—	—	—	.079	1.047	1.024
Turbo Rear	—	—	—	.079	.890	.866
94 968: Front	—	—	—	.079	1.050	1.020
wsport suspension Front	—	—	—	.079	1.200	1.180
Rear	—	—	—	.079	.890	.866

RENAULT

86–84 18i Sportwagon:	.188②	9.000	9.040	.359②	—	.709
83–80 18i:	.020	8.996	9.035	.276②	—	.433
87–83 Alliance, Encore:	.020	8.000	8.060	.276②	—	.433
85–80 Fuego: exc. Turbo	.020	8.996	9.035	.276②	—	.433
84–82 Fuego: Turbo	.020	8.996	9.035	.276②	—	.709
80–74 Gordini:	.203②	9.000	9.035	.276②	—	.354
87 GTA:	.020	8.000	8.060	.276②	—	.750
84–76 LeCar: (5 Series)	.203②	7.096	7.136	.275②	—	.354
89–88 Medallion:	.098	9.000	9.030	.256	①	.697

① Machining not recommended.   ② Measurement of lining & metal.   ③ .001"-.002" end play.

SAAB

Year/Model						
94 900, 900 S, 900 Turbo: Front	—	—	—	.200	.890	.870
Rear	—	—	—	.200	.330	.310
93–88 900, 900 S, 900 Turbo: Front	—	—	—	.040	.870	.850
Rear	—	—	—	.040	.320	.300
87–86 900: Turbo 16 Valve Front	—	—	—	.040	.744	.709
Rear	—	—	—	.040	.374	—
87–79 900: exc. Turbo 16 Valve						
Front	—	—	—	.040	.461	—
Rear	—	—	—	.040	.374	—
94–88 9000 Turbo: Front	—	—	—	.040	.950	.910
Rear	—	—	—	.040	.325	.300
87 9000 Turbo: Front	—	—	—	.040	.890	.850
Rear	—	—	—	.040	.325	.300
94–90 9000 S, 9000 CS, 9000 CD:						
Front	—	—	—	.040	.950	.910
Rear	—	—	—	.040	.325	.300
89–87 9000 S: Front	—	—	—	.040	.890	.850
Rear	—	—	—	.040	.325	.300
87–86 9000: Front	—	—	—	.039	.787	.768
Rear	—	—	—	.039	.295	.276
78–75 99: Front	—	—	—	.080	.461	—
Rear	—	—	—	.080	.374	—
74–70 99: Front	—	—	—	.080	.374	—
Rear	—	—	—	.080	.374	—

SATURN

Year/Model						
94–91 SC, SC1, SC2, SL, SL1, SL2, SW1, SW2: w/rear drum brakes	—	7.870	7.900	—	.633	.625
w/rear disc brakes	—	—	—	—	.370	.350

STERLING

Year/Model						
91–87 825: Front	—	—	—	.322[1]	—	.748
Rear	—	—	—	.283[1]	—	.314

[1] Measurement of lining & metal.

SUBARU

Year/Model						
86–85 DL, GL:	.060	7.090	7.170	.295[2]	—	.630
w/rear disc brakes	—	—	—	.256[2]	—	.335
84–83 DL, GL: w/solid rotor	.060	7.090	7.120	.295[2]	—	.394
w/vented rotor	.060	7.090	7.120	.295[2]	—	.610
82–80 DL, GL:	.060	7.090	7.120	.295[2]	—	.394
79–75 DL, GL:	.060	7.090	7.120	.060	—	.330
74–72 DL, GL Coupe:	.060	7.090	7.120	.060	—	.330
74–72 DL, GL Sedan, Wagon: Front	.060	9.000	9.040	—	—	—
Rear	.060	7.090	7.120	—	—	—
94–93 Impreza: w/13" rotor Front	—	—	—	.295	—	.630
w/14" rotor Front	—	—	—	.259	—	.870
wrear drum brakes Rear	.059	9.000	9.079	—	—	—
wrear disc brakes Rear	—	—	—	.256	—	.335
94–89 Justy: w/12" Wheels	.067	7.090	7.170	.295[2]	—	.610
w/13" Wheels	.067	7.090	7.170	.315[2]	—	.610
88–87 Justy:	.067	7.090	7.170	.295[2]	—	.610
94–90 Legacy: Front	—	—	—	.295[2]	—	.870
Rear	—	—	—	.256[2]	—	.335
94–87 Loyale:	.060	7.090	7.170	.295[2]	—	.630
w/rear disc brakes	—	—	—	.256[2]	—	.335
94–92 SVX: Front	—	—	—	.295[2]	—	1.020
Rear	—	—	—	.256[2]	—	.335
91–85 XT:	.060	7.090	7.170	.295[2]	—	.630
w/rear disc brakes	—	—	—	.256[2]	—	.335
91–88 XT6: Front	—	—	—	.295[2]	—	.787
Rear	—	—	—	.315[2]	—	.335

[2] Measurement of lining & metal.

SUZUKI

Year/Model						
94–93 Swift GA, Swift GS: Hatchback	.110[1]	7.090	7.160	.315[1]	—	.590
Sedan	.110[1]	7.870	7.950	.315[1]	—	.590
92–89 Swift GLX:	.110[1]	7.090	7.160	.315[1]	—	.590
94–89 Swift GT, Swift GTI: Front	—	—	—	.315[1]	—	.650
Rear	—	—	—	.236[1]	—	.315

[1] Measurement of lining & metal.

TOYOTA

94–92 Camry: w/rear drum brakes	.039	9.000	9.079	.039	—	1.024
w/rear disc brakes				.039	—	.354
91–88 Camry: w/rear drum brakes	.040	9.000	9.079	.040	—	.945
w/rear disc brakes	—	—	—	.040	—	.354
87 Camry:	.040	9.000	9.079	.040	—	.827
86–83 Camry:	.040	7.874	7.913	.040	—	.827
93–92 Celica: w/rear drum brakes	.039	7.874	7.913	.039	—	.906
w/rear disc brakes	—	—	—	.039	—	.354
91–90 Celica: w/rear drum brakes	.040	7.874	7.913	.040	—	.787
w/rear disc brakes	—	—	—	.040	—	.354
89–88 Celica: (4x2) exc. ABS	.040	7.874	7.913	.040	—	.827
(4x2)w/ABS Front	—	—	—	.040	—	.945
(4x2)w/ABS Rear	—	—	—	.040	—	.354
(4x4) Front	—	—	—	.040	—	.945
(4x4) Rear	—	—	—	.040	—	.354
87–86 Celica: w/rear drum brakes	.040	7.874	7.913	.040	—	.827
w/rear disc brakes	—	—	—	.040	—	.354
85–82 Celica: w/rear drum brakes	.040	9.000	9.040	.118	—	.750
w/rear disc brakes	—	—	—	.118	—	.670
81 Celica:	.040	9.000	9.040	.118	—	.450
80–77 Celica:	.040	9.000	9.040	.040	—	.450
76 Celica:	.040	9.000	9.040	.040	—	.350
75–72 Celica:	.040	9.000	9.040	.040	—	.350
94–93 Corolla:	.039	7.874	7.913	.039	—	.787
92 Corolla:	.039	7.874	7.913	.039	—	.669
91–90 Corolla: Front SOHC eng.	.040	7.874	7.913	.040	—	.669
Front DOHC eng.	.040	7.874	7.913	.040	—	.827
Rear	—	—	—	.040	—	.315
89–88 Corolla FX, Corolla FX16:						
w/rear drum brakes	.040	7.874	7.913	.040	—	.665⑤
w/rear disc brakes	—	—	—	.040	—	.315
87 Corolla FX16: Front	—	—	—	.040	—	.669
Rear	—	—	—	.040	—	.315
87–84 Corolla: exc. Coupe, FX16	.040	7.874	7.913	.040	—	.492
Coupe w/front disc brakes	.040	9.000	9.079	.040	—	.669
Coupe w/rear disc brakes	—	—	—	.040	—	.354
83–80 Corolla:	.040	9.000	9.040	.040	—	.453
79–75 Corolla 1200:	.040	7.874	7.914	.040	—	.350
74–72 Corolla 1200:	.040	7.874	7.914	.040	.360	.350
79–75 Corolla 1600:	.040	9.000	9.040	.040	—	.350
74–72 Corolla 1600:	.040	9.000	9.040	.040	—	.350
82–75 Corona:	.040	9.000	9.040	.040	—	.450
74 Corona: Deluxe	.040	9.000	9.040	.040	—	.450
Standard	.040	9.000	9.040	.040	—	.350
73–72 Corona:	.040	9.010	9.050	.040	—	.350
76–73 Corona Mark II:	.040	9.000	9.040	.040	—	.450
73–72 Corona Mark II:	.040	9.000	9.040	.040	—	.450
92–89 Cressida: Front	—	—	—	.040	—	.827
Rear	—	—	—	.040	—	.669
88–85 Cressida: w/rear drum brakes	.040	9.000	9.040	.040	—	.830
w/rear disc brakes	—	—	—	.040	—	.670
84–83 Cressida: w/rear drum brakes	.040	9.000	9.040	.040	—	.830
w/rear disc brakes	—	—	—	.040	—	.670
82–81 Cressida:	.040	9.000	9.040	.040	—	.669
80–78 Cressida:	.040	9.000	9.040	.040	—	.450
93–91 MR2: Front	—	—	—	.040	—	.945
Rear	—	—	—	.040	—	.591
89–87 MR2: Front	—	—	—	.118	—	.827
Rear	—	—	—	.040	—	.354
86–85 MR2: Front	—	—	—	.040	—	.670
Rear	—	—	—	.040	—	.354
94–92 Paseo:	.039	7.087	7.126	.039	—	.669
84–81 Starlet:	.040	7.870	7.910	.040	—	.354
94–93 Supra: Front Non-turbo	—	—	—	.040	—	1.102
Front Turbo	—	—	—	.040	—	1.181
Rear	—	—	—	.040	—	.591
92–86 Supra: Front	—	—	—	.040	—	.827
Rear	—	—	—	.040	—	.669
86–82 Supra: Front	—	—	—	.118	—	.750
Rear	—	—	—	.118	—	.669
81–79 Supra: Front	—	—	—	.118	—	.450
Rear	—	—	—	.040	—	.354
94–91 Tercel:	.040	7.087	7.126	.040	—	.669
90–85 Tercel: Sedan	.040	7.087	7.126	.040	—	.394
Wagon	.040	7.874	7.913	.040	—	.394
84–83 Tercel: (4x2)	.040	7.087	7.126	.040	—	.394
(4x4)	.040	7.874	7.913	.040	—	.394
82–80 Tercel:	.040	7.087	—	.040	—	.354

⑤ FX, FX16 DOHC eng. shown; SOHC eng. .439".

VOLKSWAGEN

74–72 411, 412: Sedan	.100	9.768	9.803	.080	—	.393
78–72 Beetle: Front	.100	9.059	9.068	—	—	—
Rear	.100	9.055	9.094	—	—	—
92–87 Cabriolet	.098	7.087	7.106	.276④	—	.709
92–90 Corrado: Front	—	—	—	.276④	—	.787
Rear	—	—	—	.276④	—	.315
81–78 Dasher:	②	7.850	7.900	.080	.413	.393
77 Dasher:	②	7.850	7.900	.080	.413	.393
76–74 Dasher:	②	7.850	7.900	.080	.433	.413
91–87 Fox: exc. Wagon	.098	7.087	7.106	.276④	—	.393
Wagon	.098	7.874	7.894	.276④	—	.393
92–85 Golf, GTI, Jetta: exc. ABS						
w/solid front rotor . . . . exc. ABS	.098	7.087	7.106	.276④	—	.393
w/vented front rotor	.098	7.087	7.106	.276④	—	.709
w/rear disc brakes	—	—	—	.276④	—	.315
92–89 Jetta: w/ABS Front	—	—	—	.276④	—	.709
w/ABS Rear	—	—	—	.276④	—	.315
74–73 Karman Ghia:	.100	9.055	9.094	.080	—	.335
72 Karman Ghia:	.100	9.055	9.094	.080	—	.335
94–90 Passat: Front	—	—	—	.276④	—	.709
Rear	—	—	—	.276④	—	.315
88–82 Quantum: w/4 cyl. eng.	.098	7.874	7.894	.276④	.413	.393
w/5 cyl. eng.	.098	7.874	7.894	.276④	—	.709
88–85 Quantum Syncro: Front	—	—	—	.276④	—	.709
Rear	—	—	—	.276④	—	.315
86–85 Rabbit: Conv.	.098	7.086	7.150	.250④	.413	.393
84–83 Rabbit GTI:	.098	7.086	7.150	.375④	.728	.709
84–82 Rabbit, Jetta, Scirocco:	.098	7.086	7.105	.250④	.413	.393
81–80 Rabbit, Jetta, Scirocco:						
w/Girling Caliper	②	7.086	7.105	.080	.413	.393
w/Kelsey-Hayes Caliper	②	7.086	7.105	.080	.413	.393
79–77 Rabbit: w/drum brakes Front	.040	9.059	9.079	—	—	—
w/drum brakes Rear	②	7.086	7.105	—	—	—
79–75 Rabbit, Scirocco:						
w/Girling Caliper	②	7.086	7.105	.080	.452	.413
w/ATE Caliper	②	7.086	7.105	.080	.452	.413
89–86 Scirocco: Front exc. 16 V eng.	.098	7.087	7.106	.276④	—	.709
Front w/16 V eng.	—	—	—	.276④	—	.709
Rear	—	—	—	.276④	—	.315
85 Scirocco:	.098	7.086	7.150	.250④	.413	.393
73–72 Squareback, Fastback:	.100	9.768	9.803	.080	—	.393
79–72 Super Beetle: Front	.100	9.768	9.803	—	—	—
Rear	.100	9.055	9.094	—	—	—

② .098″ riveted; .059″ bonded.   ④ Measurement of lining & metal.

VOLVO

74–72 140: Front	—	—	—	—	—	—
Rear w/Girling	—	—	—	.062	.457	—
Rear w/ATE	—	—	—	.062	.331	—
75–72 160: Front	—	—	—	.062	.331	—
Rear w/Girling	—	—	—	.062	.900	—
Rear w/ATE	—	—	—	.062	.331	—
73–72 1800: Sport Coupe Front	—	—	—	.062	.331	—
Rear	—	—	—	.062	—	.520
93–88 240: Front Solid Disc	—	—	—	.062	—	.331
Front Vented: ATE	—	—	—	.120	.500	—
Front Girling	—	—	—	.120	.898	—
Rear	—	—	—	.120	.803	—
87–75 240: Front w/ATE: vented disc . . .	—	—	—	.120	.330	—
Front w/Girling: vented disc	—	—	—	.062	.897	—
Front Solid disc	—	—	—	.062	.818	—
Rear w/ATE	—	—	—	.062	.519	—
Rear w/Girling	—	—	—	.062	.331	—
82–76 260:	—	—	—	.062	.331	—
Front w/vented disc brakes	—	—	—	—	—	—
Front w/solid disc brakes	—	—	—	.062	.818	—
Rear w/ATE	—	—	—	.062	.519	—
Rear w/Girling	—	—	—	.062	.331	—
92–88 740: Front Solid disc	—	—	—	.062	.331	—
Front Vented disc	—	—	—	.120	—	.433
Front Vented H.D.	—	—	—	.120	—	.788
Rear Standard	—	—	—	.120	—	.910
Rear w/Multi-Link	—	—	—	.078	—	.393
	—	—	—	.078	—	.314

(continues)

VOLVO (Continued)

87–82 740, 760, 780:						
Front w/solid disc brakes	—	—	—	.118	—	.433
Front w/vented disc brakes	—	—	—	.118	—	.788
Rear	—	—	—	.078	—	.330
91–88 760, 780: Front	—	—	—	.120	—	.788
Rear	—	—	—	.078	—	.314
94–93 850: Front	—	—	—	.120	.937	.905
Rear	—	—	—	.120	.350	.330
94–91 940, 960:						
Front w/solid disc brakes	—	—	—	.120	—	.433
Front w/vented disc brakes	—	—	—	.120	—	.788
Front w/H.D. vented disc	—	—	—	.120	—	.910
Rear w/Multi-Link	—	—	—	.078	—	.314
Rear Standard	—	—	—	.078	—	.330

YUGO

92–86 Cabrio, GV, GVL, GVX:	.059	7.293	7.336	.059	.368	.354

LIGHT TRUCKS

CHRYSLER CORP. TRUCK — Chrysler, Dodge, Plymouth

82–79 Arrow Pickup:	.040	9.500	9.550	.040	—	.720
85–76 B100, B150, PB100, PB150:						
w/10″ rear brakes	.030	10.000	10.060	.030	1.210	1.180
w/11″ rear brakes	.030	11.000	11.060	.030	1.210	1.180
75–73 B100, PB100:						
w/10″ rear brakes	.030	10.000	10.060	.030	1.210	1.180
w/11″ rear brakes	.030	11.000	11.060	.030	1.210	1.180
72 B100: w/10″ rear brakes	.030	10.000	10.060	.030	1.210	1.180
w/11″ rear brakes	.030	11.000	11.060	.030	1.210	1.180
94–86 B150, B250:	.030	11.000	11.060	.125⑨	1.210	1.180
83–78 B200, B250, PB200, PB250:	.030	10.000	10.060	.030	1.210	1.180
77–76 B200, PB200:	.030	11.000	11.060	.030	1.210	1.180
75–73 B200, PB200:	.030	11.000	11.060	.030	1.210	1.180
72 B200: w/10″ rear brakes	.030	10.000	10.060	.030	1.210	1.180
w/11″ rear brakes	.030	11.000	11.060	.030	1.210	1.180
85–84 B250, PB250:	.030	11.000	11.060	.030	1.210	1.180
85–79 B300, B350, CB300, CB350, PB300, PB350: w/3,600lb. F.A.	.030	12.000	12.060	.030	1.210	1.180
w/4,000lb. F.A.	.030	12.000	12.060	.030	1.160	1.130
78–76 B300, CB300, PB300:	.030	12.000	12.060	.030	1.160	1.130
75–73 B300, CB300, PB300:	.030	12.000	12.060	.030	1.160	1.130
72 B300, CB300:	.030	12.000	12.060	.030	1.160	1.130
94–87 B350: w/3,600lb. F.A.	.030	12.000	12.060	.125⑨	1.210	1.180
w/4,000lb. F.A.	.030	12.000	12.060	.125⑨	1.155	1.125
86 B350: w/3,600lb. F.A.	.030	12.000	12.060	.125⑨	1.210	1.180
w/4,000lb. F.A.	.030	12.000	12.060	.125⑨	1.155	1.125
94–93 Caravan, Voyager: (FWD)	.030	9.000	9.060	.030	.912	.882
: (AWD)	.030	11.000	11.060	.030	.912	.882
92–91 Caravan, Voyager: (FWD)	.090	9.000	9.060	.090	.833	.803
(AWD)	.090	11.000	11.060	.090	.833	.803
90–84 Caravan, Mini Ram Van, Voyager:	.030	9.000	9.060	.030⑦	.833	.803
83–75 D100, D150: exc. w/9¼″ rear axle	.030	10.000	10.060	.030	1.220	1.190
76–75 D100: w/9¼″ rear axle	.030	11.000	11.060	.030	1.220	1.190
74–73 D100: exc. w/11″ front brakes	.030	10.000	10.060	.030	1.220	1.190
73–72 D100: w/11″ front brakes	.030	11.000	11.060	—	—	—
72 D100:	.030	10.000	10.060	.030	—	1.180
94–90 D150:	.030	11.000	11.060	.030	1.220	1.190
89–84 D150:	.030	11.000	11.060	.030	1.220	1.190
94–90 D200, D250: w/3,300lb. F.A.	.030	12.000	12.060	.030	1.220	1.190
94–90 D200, D250, D300, D350: W/4,000lb. F.A.	.030	12.000	12.060	.030	1.220	1.190
89–81 D200, D250: w/3,300lb. F.A.	.030	12.000	12.060	.030	1.220	1.190
89–79 D200, D250, D300, D350: w/4,000lb. F.A.	.030	12.000	12.060	.030	1.160	1.130
80–79 D200:						
w/3,300lb.F.A.over 6,200lbs.GVW	.030	12.000	12.060	.030	1.220	1.190
w/3,300lb. F.A. 6,200lbs. GVW	.030	12.120	12.180	.030	1.220	1.190
78–75 D200: w/6600lbs. GVW	.030	12.120	12.180	.030	1.160	1.130
78–75 D200, D300: over 6,000lbs. GVW	.030	12.000	12.060	.030	1.160	1.130
74 D200: w/6,000lbs. GVW	.030	12.120	12.180	.030	1.160	1.130
74 D200, D300: over 6,000lbs. GVW	.030	12.000	12.060	.030	1.160	1.130
73 D200: w/6,000lbs. GVW	.030	12.120	12.180	.030	—	1.125
w/12.57″ rotor diameter	.030	12.000	12.060	.030	—	1.180
w/12.82″ rotor diameter	.030	12.000	12.060	.030	—	1.125

⑦ .030″ over rivet head; if bonded lining use .062″.

⑨ Combined shoe & lining thickness .3125″.

(continues)

CHRYSLER CORP. TRUCK — Chrysler, Dodge, Plymouth (Continued)

72	D200: w/6,000lbs. GVW	.030	12.120	12.180	.030	—	1.125
	w/12.57″ rotor diameter	.030	12.000	12.060	.030	—	1.180
	w/12.82″ rotor diameter	.030	12.000	12.060	.030	—	1.125
73–72	D300:	.030	12.000	12.060	—	—	—
94–87	Dakota:						
	(4x2) w/9″ rear brakes	.030	9.000	9.060	.250	.841	.811
	(4x2) w/10″ rear brakes	.030	10.000	10.060	.250	.841	.811
	(4x4) w/9″ rear brakes	.030	9.000	9.060	.250	.841	.811
	(4x4) w/10″ rear brakes	.030	10.000	10.060	.250	.841	.811
89–88	Raider:	.040	10.000	10.079	.079	—	.803
87	Raider:	.040	10.000	10.079	.040	—	.724
93–87	Ram 50: (4x2)	.040	10.000	10.079	.080	—	.803
	(4X4)	.040	10.000	10.079	.080	—	.803
86–83	Ram 50: w/9½″ rear brakes	.040	9.500	9.570	.040	—	.720
	W/10″ rear brakes	.040	10.000	10.070	.040	—	.720
82–79	D 50, Ram 50:	.040	9.500	9.550	.040	—	.720
93–90	Ramcharger: (4x2)	.030	11.000	11.060	.030	1.220	1.190
	(4x4)	.030	11.000	11.060	.030	1.220	1.190
89–84	Ramcharger: (4x2)	.030	11.000	11.060	.030	1.220	1.190
	(4x4)	.030	11.000	11.060	.030	1.220	1.190
83–79	Ramcharger: (4x2)	.030	10.000	10.060	.030	1.220	1.190
	(4x4)	.030	10.000	10.060	.030	1.220	1.190
78–74	Ramcharger: (4x2)	.030	11.000	11.060	.030	1.220	1.190
	(4x4)	.030	11.000	11.060	.030	1.220	1.190
84–83	Rampage, Scamp:	.030	7.874	7.904	.030	.461	.431
82	Rampage:	.030	7.780	7.900	.030	.461	.431
94–93	Town & Country Van: (FWD) ...	.030	9.000	9.060	.030	—	.882
	(AWD) ...	.030	11.000	11.060	.030	—	.882
92–90	Town & Country Van:	.030	9.000	9.060	.030⑦	.833	.803
83–79	W100, W150:	.030	10.000	10.060	.030	1.220	1.190
78–77	W100:	.030	11.000	11.060	.030	1.220	1.190
76–75	W100:	.030	11.000	11.060	.030	1.220	1.190
74–72	W100:	.030	11.000	11.060	—	—	—
94–90	W150:	.030	11.000	11.060	.030	1.220	1.190
89–84	W150:	.030	11.000	11.060	.030	1.220	1.190
94–90	W200, W250: exc. w/Spicer 60	.030	12.000	12.060	.030	1.220	1.190
94–79	W200, W250, W300, W350:						
	w/Spicer 60	.030	12.000	12.060	.030	1.160	1.130
89–79	W200, W250: exc. w/Spicer 60	.030	12.000	12.060	.030	1.160	1.130
78–75	W200: exc. w/Spicer 60	.030	12.000	12.060	.030	1.160	1.130
78–75	W200, W300: w/Spicer 60	.030	12.000	12.060	.030	1.160	1.130
74–72	W200: Front	.030	12.120	12.180	—	—	—
	Rear	.030	12.000	12.060	—	—	—
74–72	W200, W300: w/4,500lb. F.A.	.030	12.000	12.060	—	—	—

⑦ .030″ over rivet head; if bonded lining use .062″.

DAIHATSU TRUCK

92–90	Rocky:	.039	10.000	10.060	.060	—	.450

FORD MOTOR CO. TRUCK

94–86	Aerostar: w/9″ rear brakes	.030	9.000	9.060	.030	—	.810
	w/10″ rear brakes	.030	10.000	10.060	.030	—	.810
94	Bronco: exc. integral rotor	.030	11.031	11.091	.030	—	.960
	w/integral rotor	.030	11.031	11.091	.030	—	.960
93–90	Bronco: w/integral rotor	.030	11.031	11.091	.030	—	1.120
	exc. integral rotor	.030	11.031	11.091	.030	—	1.120
89–86	Bronco: w/integral rotor	.030	11.031	11.091	.030	—	1.120
	exc. integral rotor	.030	11.031	11.091	.030	—	1.120
85–81	Bronco:	.030	11.031	11.091	.030	—	1.120
80–76	Bronco:	.030	11.031	11.091	.030	—	1.120
75–72	Bronco: w/10″ brakes	.030	10.000	10.060	—	—	—
	w/11″ brakes	.030	11.000	11.060	—	—	—
82–79	Courier:	.039	10.236	10.244	.276⑭	.433	—
78–77	Courier:	.039	10.236	10.244	.314⑭	.433	—
76–74	Courier:	.039	10.236	10.244	—	—	—
73–72	Courier:	.039	10.236	10.244	—	—	—
94–90	E150: (4x2)	.030	11.031	11.091	.030	—	1.120
89–86	E150, F150: (4x2)	.030	11.031	11.091	.030	—	1.120
85–77	E100, E150, F100, F150:						
	w/4,600-4,900lbs. GVW	.030	10.000	10.060	.030	—	.810
	....	.030	11.031	11.091	.030	—	1.120
76–75	E100, E150, F100, F150:	.030	11.031	11.091	.030	—	1.120
74–72	E100, F100: w/10″ brakes	.030	10.000	10.060	—	—	—
	w/11″ brakes	.030	11.031	11.091	.030	—	1.120
94–90	E250, F250, F350:						
	(4x2) w/single rear wheels	.030	12.000	12.060	.030	—	1.180
	(4x2) w/dual rear wheels	.030	12.000	12.060	.030	—	1.180
89–86	E250, F250, F350:						
	(4x2) w/single rear wheels	.030	12.000	12.060	.030	—	1.180
	(4x2) w/dual rear wheels	.030	12.000	12.060	.030	—	1.180

⑭ Measurement of lining & metal.

FORD MOTOR CO. TRUCK (Continued)

85–78 E250, E350, F250, F350:						
6,900lbs. GVW H.D.	.030	12.000	12.060	.030	—	1.180
77 E250, E350, F250, F350:						
6,900lbs. GVW H.D.	.030	12.000	12.060	.030	—	1.214
76 E250, E350, F250, F350:						
w/12″ rear brakes	.030	12.000	12.060	.030	—	1.180
w/12 ⅛″ rear brakes	.030	12.125	12.185	.030	—	1.180
75 E250, E350:	.030	12.000	12.060	.030	—	940
74–72 E250:	.030	11.031	11.091	—	—	—
74–72 E350:	.030	12.000	12.060	—	—	—
94–90 F-Super Duty: Front	—	—	—	.030	—	1.430
Rear	—	—	—	.030	—	1.430
89–88 F-Super Duty: Front	—	—	—	.030	—	1.430
Rear	—	—	—	.030	—	1.430
94 F150: (4X2)	.030	11.031	11.091	.030	—	.960
(4x4) exc. integral rotor	.030	11.031	11.091	.030	—	.960
(4x4) w/integral rotor	.030	11.031	11.091	.030	—	.960
93–90 F150: (4x4) w/integral rotor	.030	11.031	11.091	.030	—	1.120
(4x4) exc. integral rotor	.030	11.031	11.091	.030	—	1.120
89–86 F150: (4x4) w/integral rotor	.030	11.031	11.091	.030	—	1.120
(4x4) exc. integral rotor	.030	11.031	11.091	.030	—	1.120
85–81 F100, F150, F200:						
(4x4) w/Dana 44IFS F.A.	.030	11.031	11.091	.030	—	1.120
80–76 F100, F150: (4x4)	.030	11.031	11.091	.030	—	1.120
75–72 F100: (4x4) Front	.030	11.000	11.060	—	—	—
(4x4) Rear	.030	11.031	11.091	—	—	—
94–86 F250, F350:						
(4X4) w/Dana 44IFS axle	.030	12.000	12.060	.030	—	1.180
(4x4) exc. Dana 44IFS axle	.030	12.000	12.060	.030	—	1.180
85–83 F250, F350:						
(4X4) exc.Dana 44IFS F.A.	.030	12.000	12.060	.030	—	1.180
85–77 F250: 6,900lbs. GVW std.	.030	12.000	12.060	.030	—	1.120
82–81 F250, F350: (4X4)	.030	12.000	12.060	.030	—	1.180
(4x4)	.030	12.000	12.060	.030	—	1.180
80–76 F250, F350: (4x4)	.030	12.000	12.060	.030	—	1.180
76–75 F250: 6,900lbs. GVW						
Std. w/12″ rear brakes	.030	12.000	12.060	.030	—	1.120
w/12 ⅛″ rear brakes	.030	12.125	12.185	.030	—	1.120
75–72 F250, F350: w/12″ rear brakes	.030	12.000	12.060	.030	—	.940
w/12 ⅛″ rear brakes	.030	12.125	12.185	.030	—	.940
75–72 F250: (4x4) Front	.030	12.125	12.185	—	—	—
(4x4) Rear	.030	12.000	12.060	—	—	—
74–73 F250: 6,900lbs. GVW						
Std. w/12″ rear brakes	.030	12.000	12.060	.030	—	1.120
w/12 ⅛″ rear brakes	.030	12.125	12.185	.030	—	1.120
72 F250: std. w/12″ brakes	.030	12.000	12.060	—	—	—
w/12 ⅛″ brakes	.030	12.125	12.185	—	—	—
75–72 F350: (4X4)	.030	12.000	12.060	.030	—	.940
94–91 Ranger, Explorer:						
(4x2) w/9″ rear brakes	.030	9.000	9.060	.030	—	.810
(4x2) w/10″ rear brakes	.030	10.000	10.060	.030	—	.810
(4x4) w/9″ rear brakes	.030	9.000	9.060	.030	—	.810
(4x4) w/10″ rear brakes	.030	10.000	10.060	.030	—	.810
90–83 Ranger, Bronco II:						
(4x2) w/9″ rear brakes	.030	9.000	9.060	.030	—	.810
(4x2) w/10″ rear brakes	.030	10.000	10.060	.030	—	.810
(4x4) w/9″ rear brakes	.030	9.000	9.060	.030	—	.810
(4x4) w/10″ rear brakes	.030	10.000	10.060	.030	—	.810

GENERAL MOTORS TRUCK — Chevrolet, GMC

94–85 Astro, Safari Van:						
W/1.04″ rotor..................	.030	9.500	9.560	.030	.980	.965″
w/1.25″ rotor	.030	9.500	9.560	.030	1.230	1.215
94–92 Blazer, Jimmy, Pickup,						
Sonoma: S/T Series	.030	9.500	9.560	.030	.980	.965
91–88 Blazer, Jimmy, Pickup:						
(S/T Series)	.062	9.500	9.560	.030	.980	.965
87–83 Blazer, Jimmy, Pickup:						
(S/T Series)	.062	9.500	9.560	.030	.980	.965
94–92 Blazer, Yukon: C/K Series	.030	10.000	10.051	.030	1.230	1.215
91–88 Blazer, Jimmy: (Full Size)	.030	11.150	11.210	.030	1.230	1.215
87–83 Blazer, Jimmy: (Full Size)	.062	11.150	11.210	.030	1.230	1.215
82–76 Blazer, Jimmy: (4x2)	.062	11.150	11.210	.030	1.230	1.215
(4x4)	.062	11.150	11.210	.030	1.230	1.215
75–74 Blazer, Jimmy: (4x2)	.030	11.000	11.060	.030	1.230	1.215
(4x4) w/11″ rear brakes	.030	11.000	11.060	.030	1.230	1.215
(4x4) w/11 ⅛″ rear brakes	.030	11.150	11.210	.030	1.230	1.215
73–72 Blazer, Jimmy: (4x2)	.030	11.000	11.060	.030	1.230	1.215
(4x4)	.030	11.000	11.060	.030	1.230	1.215

(continues)

GENERAL MOTORS TRUCK — Chevrolet, GMC (Continued)

91–88 C10, C15, K10, K15:						
w/1.0″ rotor	.142	10.000	10.051	.030	.980	.965
w/1.25″ rotor	.142	10.000	10.051	.030	1.230	1.215
87–76 C10, C15, R10, R15,						
Suburban R10, Suburban R15:						
w/1.0″ rotor						
w/11″ rear brakes	.062	11.000	11.060	.030	.980	.965
w/11 1/8″ rear brakes	.062	11.150	11.210	.030	.980	.965
w/1.25″ rotor						
w/11″ rear brakes	.062	11.000	11.060	.030	1.230	1.215
w/11 1/8″ rear brakes	.062	11.150	11.210	.030	1.230	1.215
75–74 C10, C15, Suburban C10,						
Suburban C15:						
w/11″ rear brakes	.030	11.000	11.060	.030	1.230	1.215
w/11 1/8″ rear brakes	.030	11.050	11.210	.030	1.230	1.215
73–72 C10, C15, Suburban C10,						
Suburban C15:	.030	11.000	11.060	.030	1.230	1.215
94–92 1500 C/K Pickup: w/1.0″ rotor	.030	10.000	10.051	.030	.980	.965
w/1.25″ rotor	.030	10.000	10.051	.030	1.230	1.215
94–92 2500 C/K Pickup:	.030	11.150	11.210	.030	1.23	1.215
94–92 3500 C/K Pickup:						
w/1.54″ rotor	.030	13.000	13.060	.030	1.480	1.465
w/1.26″ rotor	.030	13.000	13.060	.030	1.230	1.215
Chassis Cab F	—	—	—	.030	1.480	1.465
Chassis Cab R	—	—	—	.030	1.480	1.465
94–92 1500 Suburban,						
2500 Suburban: w/1.25″ rotor	.030	11.150	11.210	.030	1.230	1.215
w/1.26″ rotor	.030	13.000	13.060	.030	1.230	1.215
91–88 C20, C25, C30, C35, K20, K25,						
K30, K35:						
w/11 1/8″ rear brakes	.142	11.150	11.210	.030	1.230	1.215
w/13″ rear brakes	.142	13.000	13.060	.030	1.230	1.215
87–76 C20, C25, C30, C35, R20, R25,						
R30, R35, Suburban R20,						
Suburban R25:						
under 8,600 lbs. GVW						
w/11 1/8″ rear brakes	.062	11.150	11.210	.030	1.230	1.215
under 8,600 lbs. GVW						
w/13″ rear brakes	.062	13.000	13.060	.030	1.230	1.215
75–74 C20, C25, C30, C35,						
Suburban C20, Suburban C25:						
w/11 1/8″ rear brakes	.030	11.150	11.210	.030	1.230	1.215
w/13″ rear brakes	.030	13.000	13.060	.030	1.230	1.215
73–72 C20, C25:						
w/11 1/8″ rear brakes	.030	11.150	11.210	.030	1.230	1.215
W/12″ rear brakes	.030	12.000	12.060	.030	1.230	1.215
w/13″ rear brakes	.030	13.000	13.060	.030	1.230	1.215
87–76 C30, C35, G30, G35, R30,						
R35: over 8,600lbs. GVW	.062	13.000	13.060	.030	1.480	1.465
75–74 C30, C35, G30, G35:						
over 8,600lbs. GVW	.030	13.000	13.060	.030	1.480	1.465
73–72 C30, C35, G30, G35:						
w/13″ rear brakes	.030	13.000	13.060	.030	1.230	1.215
w/15″ rear brakes	.030	15.000	15.060	.030	1.230	1.215
88–82 El Camino:	①	9.500	9.560	.030	.980	.965
81–79 El Camino:	①	9.500	9.560	.030	.980	.965
78 El Camino:	①	11.000	11.060	.030	.980	.965
77 El Camino:	①	11.000	11.060	.030	.980	.965
76–73 El Camino:	①	9.500	9.560	.030①	.980	.965
72 El Camino:	①	9.500	9.560	.030①	.980	.965
94–92 G10, G15, G20, G25:	.030	11.150	11.210	.030	1.230	1.215
94–92 G30, G35: exc. Chassis Cab	.030	13.000	13.060	.030	1.230	1.215
91–88 G10, G15: w/11″ rear brakes	.030	11.000	11.060	.030	1.230	1.215
w/11 1/8″ rear brakes	.030	11.150	11.210	.030	1.230	1.215
87–76 G10, G15: w/1.0″ rotor						
w/11″ rear brakes	.062	11.000	11.060	.030	.980	.965
w/11 1/8″ rear brakes	.062	11.150	11.210	.030	.980	.965
w/1.25″ rotor						
w/11″ rear brakes	.062	11.000	11.060	.030	1.230	1.215
w/11 1/8″ rear brakes	.062	11.150	11.210	.030	1.230	1.215
75–74 G10, G15: w/11″ rear brakes	.030	11.000	11.060	.030	1.230	1.215
w/11 1/8″ rear brakes	.030	11.050	11.210	.030	1.230	1.215
73–72 G10, G15:	.030	11.000	11.060	.030	1.230	1.215
91–88 G20, G25:	.030	11.150	11.210	.030	1.230	1.215
87–76 G20, G25, G30, G35:						
under 8,600 lbs. GVW						
w/11 1/8″ rear brakes	.062	11.150	11.210	.030	1.230	1.215
under 8,600 lbs. GVW						
w/13″ rear brakes	.062	13.000	13.060	.030	1.230	1.215
75–74 G20, G25, G30, G35:						
w/11 1/8″ rear brakes	.030	11.150	11.210	.030	1.230	1.215
w/13″ rear brakes	.030	13.000	13.060	.030	1.230	1.215

① .030″ over rivet head; if bonded lining use .062″

(continues)

GENERAL MOTORS TRUCK — Chevrolet, GMC (Continued)

73–72 G20, G25:	.030	11.000	11.060	.030	1.230	1.215
94–92 G30, G35: Chassis Cab	.030	13.000	13.060	.030	1.480	1.465
91–88 G30, G35: w/1.28″ rotor	.030	13.000	13.060	.030	1.230	1.215
w/1.54″ rotor	.030	13.000	13.060	.030	1.480	1.465
87–76 K10, K15, K20, K25, V10, V15, V20, V25, Suburban:						
w/11 1/8″ rear brakes	.062	11.150	11.210	.030	1.230	1.215
w/13″ rear brakes	.062	13.000	13.060	.030	1.230	1.215
75–74 K10, K15, K20, K25:						
w/11″ rear brakes	.030	11.000	11.060	.030	1.230	1.215
w/11 1/8″ rear brakes	.030	11.150	11.210	.030	1.230	1.215
W/13″ rear brakes	.030	13.000	13.060	.030	1.230	1.215
73–72 K10, K15, K20, K25:						
w/11″ rear brakes	.030	11.000	11.060	.030	1.230	1.215
w/11 1/8″ rear brakes	.030	11.150	11.210	.030	1.230	1.215
w/13″ rear brakes	.030	13.000	13.060	.030	1.230	1.215
87–77 K30, K35, V30, V35:	.062	13.000	13.060	.030	1.480	1.465
94–93 Lumina APV:	.030	8.863	8.877	.030	1.224	1.209
92–90 Lumina APV:	①	8.863	8.877	.030	.972	.957
82–81 LUV Pickup:	.059	10.000	10.059	.236	.668	.653
80–76 LUV Pickup:	.059	10.000	10.059	.236	.668	.653
75–72 LUV Pickup:	.059	10.000	10.059	—	—	—
91–88 R10, R15, Suburban R10, Suburban R15:	.030	11.150	11.210	.030	1.230	1.215
91–88 R20, R25, R30, R35, Suburban R20, Suburban R25:						
w/1.28″ rotor	.030	13.000	13.060	.030	1.230	1.215
w/1.54″ rotor	.030	13.000	13.060	.030	1.480	1.465
91–88 V10, V15, Suburban V10, Subruban V15:	.030	11.150	11.210	.030	1.230	1.215
91–88 V20, V25, V30, V35, Suburban V20, Suburban V25:						
w/1.28″ rotor	.030	13.000	13.060	.030	1.230	1.215
w/1.54″ rotor	.030	13.000	13.060	.030	1.480	1.465

① .030″ over rivet head; if bonded lining use .062″.

GEO TRUCK

94–91 GEO Tracker:	.039	8.660	8.740	.030	.345	.315
90–89 GEO Tracker:	.039	8.660	8.740	.030	.345	.315

HONDA TRUCK

94 Passport: w/2.6L eng. Front	—	—	—	.039	.826	.811
w/3.2L eng. Front	—	—	—	.039	.983	.969
Rear	—	—	—	.039	.668	.654

HYUNDAI TRUCK

87–86 Pony Pickup:	.039	7.992	①	.060	—	.449
85–83 Pony Pickup:	.098	7.992	①	.060	—	.314

① Machining specification is not available; discard at 8.071″.

ISUZU TRUCK

94 Amigo: w/rear drum brakes	.039	10.000	10.059	.039	.985	.970
w/rear disc brakes	—	—	—	.039	.669	.654
93–90 Amigo: w/rear drum brakes	.039	10.000	10.059	.039	.826	.811
w/rear disc brakes	—	—	—	.039	.432	.417
94–88 Pickup: w/rear drum brakes ...	.039	10.000	10.059	.039	.826	.811
w/rear disc brakes	—	—	—	.039	.432	.417
87–84 Pickup:	.039	10.000	10.039	.039	.658	.654
83–81 Pickup:	.039	10.000	10.039	.039	.453	.437
94–93 Rodeo: w/2.6L eng.	.039	10.000	10.059	.039	.826	.811
w/3.2L eng. Front	—	—	—	.039	.983	.969
Rear	—	—	—	.039	.668	.654
92–91 Rodeo:	.039	10.000	10.059	.039	.826	.811
94–92 Trooper: Front	—	—	—	.039	.983	.969
Rear	—	—	—	.039	.668	.654
91–88 Trooper II: Front	—	—	—	.039	.826	.811
Rear	—	—	—	.039	.432	.417
87 Trooper II:	.039	10.000	10.039	.039	.826	.811
86–84 Trooper II:	.039	10.000	10.039	.039	.668	.654

JEEP TRUCK

94	Cherokee: Front				.030	—	.890
	Rear w/9″ drum	.030	9.000	9.060			
	Rear w/10″ drum	.030	10.000	10.060			
93–91	Cherokee: (4x2)	①	9.000	9.050	.030	—	.866
	(4X4)	①	9.000	9.050	.030	—	.890
90	Cherokee: (4x2)	①	9.000	9.050	.030	—	.860
	(4x4)	①	9.000	9.050	.030	—	.940
89–84	Cherokee, Wagoneer: (Sportwagons)	.030	10.000	10.060	.030	—	.815
89–82	Cherokee, Wagoneer: (Full Size)	①	11.000	11.060	.062	—	1.215
81–78	Cherokee, Wagoneer:	①	11.000	11.060	.062	—	1.215
77–76	Cherokee, Wagoneer:	①	11.000	11.060	.062	—	1.215
75–74	Cherokee, Wagoneer:	.030	11.000	11.060	.062	1.230	1.215
86–82	CJ, Scrambler:	①	10.000	10.060	.062	—	.815
81–79	CJ:	①	10.000	10.060	.062	—	.815
78–77	CJ:	①	11.000	11.060	.062	—	1.120
76–72	CJ:	.030	11.000	11.060	—	—	—
92–90	Comanche:						
	(4x2) w/9″ rear brakes	①	9.000	9.050	.030	—	.860
	(4x2) w/10″ rear brakes	①	10.000	10.060	.030	—	.860
92–91	Comanche:						
	(4x4) w/9″ rear brakes	①	9.000	9.050	.030	—	.890
	(4x4) w/10″ rear brakes	①	10.000	10.060	.030	—	.890
90	Comanche:						
	(4x4) w/9″ rear brakes	①	9.000	9.050	.030	—	.940
	(4x4) w/10″ rear brakes	①	10.000	10.060	.030	—	.940
89–84	Comanche:	.030	10.000	10.060	.030	—	.815
94	Grand Cherokee:	.030	10.000	10.060	.030	—	.890
	w/rear disc brakes	—	—	—	.030	—	—
93	Grand Cherokee, Grand Wagoneer:	.030	10.000	10.060	.030	—	.890
91–90	Grand Wagoneer:	①	11.000	11.060	.030	—	1.215
89–82	J10 Pickup:	①	11.000	11.060	.062	—	1.215
81–78	J10 Pickup:	①	11.000	11.060	.062	—	1.215
77–76	J10 Pickup:	①	11.000	11.060	.062	—	1.215
75–74	J10 Pickup:	.030	11.000	11.060	.062	1.230	1.215
87–82	J20 Pickup:	①	12.000	12.060	.062	—	1.215
81–78	J20 Pickup:	①	12.000	12.060	.062	—	1.215
77–76	J20 Pickup:	①	12.000	12.060	.062	—	1.215
75–74	J20 Pickup:	.030	12.000	12.060	.062	1.230	1.215
94–92	Wrangler:	.030	9.000	9.060	.030	—	.890
91	Wrangler:	①	9.000	9.050	.030	—	.890
90	Wrangler:	①	9.000	9.050	.030	—	.940
89–87	Wrangler:	.030	10.000	10.060	.030	—	.815
73–72	Wagoneer, Pickup:						
	w/11″ brakes	.030	11.000	11.060	—	—	—
	w/12″ brakes	.030	12.000	12.060	—	—	—
73–72	Camper: 8,000lbs. GVW	.030	12.125	12.185	—	—	—

① .030″ over rivet head; if bonded lining use .062″.

MAZDA TRUCK

94	B2300 Pickup, B3000 Pickup, B4000 Pickup: (4x2)	.030	9.010	9.040	.118	—	.810
	(4x4)	.030	10.000	10.030	.118	—	.810
93–87	B2200 Pickup, B2600 Pickup:						
	(4x2)	.040	10.240	10.300	.118	—	.710
	(4x4)	.040	10.240	10.300	.118	—	.790
87–86	B2000 Pickup:	.040	10.240	10.310	.118	—	.710
84	B2200 Pickup:	.040	10.236	10.275	.040	—	.748
84	B2000 Pickup:	.040	10.236	10.275	.040	—	.433
83–82	B2200 Pickup:	.040	10.236	10.275	.276①	—	.748
83–77	B1800 Pickup, B2000 Pickup:	.040	10.236	10.275	.276①	—	.433
76–72	B1600 Pickup:	.040	10.236	10.275	—	—	—
77–74	Pickup: Rotary eng.	.040	10.236	10.275	.276①	—	.433
94	MPV: 2WD Front	—	—	—	.080	—	1.100
	4WD Front	—	—	—	.080	—	1.020
	w/rear disc brakes	—	—	—	.080	—	.630
93–92	MPV: 2WD	.040	10.240	10.300	.080	—	1.100
	4WD	.040	10.240	10.300	.080	—	1.020
91–89	MPV:	.040	10.240	10.300	.080	—	.870
94–91	Navajo: w/9″ rear brakes	.030	9.000	9.060	.062	—	.810
	w/10″ rear brakes	.030	10.000	10.060	.062	—	.810

① Measurement of lining & metal.

MERCURY TRUCK

94–93	Villager:	.059	9.840	9.900	.080	.974	.945

MITSUBISHI TRUCK

94–92 Expo, Expo LVR:						
w/8" drum brakes	.040	8.071	8.100	.080	—	.880
w/9" drum brakes	.040	9.079	9.100	.080	—	.880
w/rear disc brakes	—	—	—	.080	—	.330
94–92 Montero: Front	—	—	—	.079	—	.882
Rear	—	—	—	.079	—	.646
91–88 Montero:	.040	10.000	10.079	.079	—	.803
87 Montero:	.040	10.000	10.040	.040	—	.724
86–83 Montero:	.040	10.000	10.040	.040	—	.720
94–87 Pickup: (4x2)	.040	10.000	10.079	.080	—	.803
(4x4)	.040	10.000	10.079	.080	—	.803
86–83 Pickup: w/9½" rear brakes	.040	9.500	9.550	.040	—	.720
w/10" rear brakes	.040	10.000	10.070	.040	—	.720
90–87 Van:	.040	10.000	10.080	.079	—	.803

NAVISTAR — INTERNATIONAL TRUCK

80–72 Scout II:	.030	11.000	11.060	.125	—	1.120
75–74 Travel All 100/150: (½ Ton)	.030	11.000	11.060	.125	—	1.120
75–74 Travel All 200: (¾ Ton)	.030	12.000	12.060	.125	—	1.120

NISSAN (DATSUN) TRUCK

79–78 620 Pickup:	.059	10.000	10.055	.080	—	.413
77–72 620 Pickup:	.059	10.000	10.055	—	—	—
86–84 720 Pickup: w/single wheel	.059	10.000	10.060	.080	—	.787
w/dual wheels	.059	8.660	8.720	.080	—	.787
83–82 720 Pickup:	.059	10.000	10.055	.080	—	.413
81 720 Pickup:	.059	10.000	10.055	.080	—	.413
80 720 Pickup:	.059	10.000	10.055	.080	—	.413
90 Axxess: w/9" rear brakes	.059	9.000	9.060	.079	—	.787
w/10" rear brakes	.059	10.240	10.300	.079	—	.787
94–86 D21 Pickup:						
(4x2) w/4 cyl. gas eng...........	.059	10.240	10.300	.079	—	.787
(4x2) exc. 4 cyl. gas eng.						
w/8.66" rear brakes	.059	8.660	8.720	.079	—	.945
w/10" rear brakes	.059	10.000	10.060	.079	—	.945
w/10.24" rear brakes	.059	10.240	10.300	.079	—	.945
(4x4) w/10.24" rear brakes	.059	10.240	10.300	.079	—	.945
(4x4) w/11.61" rear brakes	.059	11.610	11.670	.079	—	.945
94–90 Pathfinder: Front	—	—	—	.079	—	.945
Rear w/10.24" rear brakes	.059	10.240	10.300	—	—	—
Rear w/11.61" rear brakes	.059	11.610	11.670	—	—	—
Rear w/rear disc brakes	—	—	—	.079	—	.630
89–87 Pathfinder: w/rear drum brakes	.059	10.000	10.060	.079	—	.945
w/rear disc brakes	—	—	—	.079	—	.630
94–93 Quest:	.079	9.840	9.900	.079	—	.945
88–87 Vanette:	.059	10.240	10.300	.079	—	.945

OLDSMOBILE TRUCK

94–91 Bravada:	①	9.500	9.560	.030	.980	.965
94–93 Silhouette APV:	.030	8.863	8.877	.030	1.224	1.209
92–90 Silhouette APV:	①	8.863	8.877	.030	.972	.957

① .030" over rivet head; if bonded lining use .062".

PONTIAC TRUCK

94–93 Trans Sport APV:	.030	8.863	8.877	.030	1.224	1.209
92–90 Trans Sport APV:	①	8.863	8.877	.030	.972	.957

① .030" over rivet head; if bonded lining use .062".

SUBARU TRUCK

86–85 Brat:	.060	7.090	7.170	.295②	—	.630
w/rear disc brakes	—	—	—	.256②	—	.335
84–83 Brat: w/solid rotor	.060	7.090	7.120	.295②	—	.394
w/vented rotor	.060	7.090	7.120	295②	—	.610
82–80 Brat:	.060	7.090	7.120	.295②	—	.394
79–77 Brat:	.060	7.090	7.120	.060	—	.330

② Measurement of lining & metal.

SUZUKI TRUCK

94–86 Samurai:	.120①	8.660	8.740	.236①	—	.334
94–89 Sidekick: 2 Door	.120①	8.660	8.740	.315①	—	.315
94–92 Sidekick: 4 Door	.120①	10.000	10.070	.315①	—	.591

① Measurement of lining & metal.

TOYOTA TRUCK

94–92 4 Runner:	.039	11.614	11.693	.039	—	.906
91–89 4 Runner:	.040	11.614	11.693	.040	—	.709
88–87 4 Runner:	.040	11.614	11.693	.040	—	.748
86 4 Runner:	.060	11.614	11.654	.040	—	.748
85–84 4 Runner:	.040	10.000	10.060	.040	—	.453
94–93 Land Cruiser:	.060	11.614	11.693	.157	—	1.181
wrear disc brakes	—	—	—	.039	—	.709
92–91 Land Cruiser:	.060	11.614	11.693	.157	—	.984
w/rear disc brakes	—	—	—	.039	—	.709
90–89 Land Cruiser:	.060	11.614	11.693	.157	—	.748
88–85 Land Cruiser:	.060	11.614	11.693	.040	—	.748
84–75 Land Cruiser:	.060	11.610	11.650	.040	—	.748
74–72 Land Cruiser:	.060	11.400	11.440	—	—	—
94–89 Pickup: (4x2) ½ Ton	.039	10.000	10.079	.039	—	.787
1 Ton exc. H.D. brakes	.039	10.000	10.079	.039	—	.906
1 Ton w/H.D. brakes	.039	10.000	10.079	.039	—	1.102
88–85 Pickup: (4x2) ½ Ton	.040	10.000	10.060	.040	—	.827
1 Ton H.D.	.040	10.000	10.060	.040	—	.945
84 Pickup: (4x2)	.040	10.000	10.060	.040	—	.827
83–75 Pickup: (4x2)	.040	10.000	10.060	.040	—	.453
83–79 Cab & Chassis: (4x2)	.040	10.000	10.060	.040	—	.748
74–72 Pickup: (4x2) w/10" brakes	.040	10.000	10.060	—	—	—
72 Pickup: (4x2) w/9" brakes	.040	9.000	9.060	—	—	—
94–89 Pickup: (4x4) ½ Ton	.039	11.614	11.693	.039	—	.709
88–87 Pickup: (4x4)	.040	11.614	11.693	.040	—	.748
86 Pickup: (4x4)	.060	11.614	11.654	.040	—	.748
85–84 Pickup: (4x4)	.040	10.000	10.060	.040	—	.453
83–79 Pickup: (4x4)	.040	10.000	10.060	.040	—	.453
94–92 Previa: w/rear drum brakes	.039	10.000	10.079	.039	—	.906
w/rear disc brakes Front	—	—	—	.039	—	.787
Rear	—	—	—	.039	—	.669
91 Previa: w/rear drum brakes	.040	10.000	10.080	.040	—	.827
w/rear disc brakes	—	—	—	.040	—	.669
94–93 T100 Pickup: (4x2) ½ Ton	.039	11.610	11.690	.039	—	.906
(4x2) 1 Ton	.039	11.610	11.690	.039	—	.906
(4x4)	.039	11.610	11.690	.039	—	.906
88–87 Van: (4x2)	.040	10.000	10.079	.040	—	.748
(4x4)	.040	10.000	10.079	.118	—	.945
86–84 Van:	.040	10.000	10.060	.040	—	.748

VOLKSWAGEN TRUCK

91–86 Vanagon:	.098	9.921	9.960	.079	—	.512
85–80 Vanagon:	.098	9.921	9.960	.078	.452	.433
79–77 Van, Bus, Wagon, Transporter, Kombi:	.098	9.921	9.960	.080	.492	.453
76–73 Van, Bus, Wagon, Transporter, Kombi:	.100	9.921	9.960	.080	—	.472
72 Van, Bus, Wagon, Transporter, Kombi:	.100	9.921	9.960	.080	.482	.472
84–82 Rabbit Pickup:	.098	7.874	7.894	.250④	.413	.393
81–80 Rabbit Pickup: w/Kelsey-Hayes Caliper	②	7.086	7.105	.080	.413	.393

② .098" riveted; .059" bonded.   ④ Measurement of lining & metal.

Answers to Even-Numbered ASE Certification-Type Questions

Glossary

ABS   Antilock braking system.

Align   To bring the parts of a unit into the correct position with respect to each other.

Anchor pin   Steel stud firmly attached to the backing plate. One end of the brake shoes is either attached to or rests against it.

Aramid   Generic name for aromatic polyamide fibers developed in 1972. Kevlar is the Dupont brand name for aramid.

Asbestosis   Health condition where asbestos causes scar tissue to form in the lungs, causing shortness of breath.

ASR   Acceleration slip regulation.

ATe   Alfred Teves Engineering, a manufacturer of brake system components and systems.

Atmospheric pressure   Pressure exerted by the atmosphere on all things (14.7 pounds per square inch).

Backing plate   Steel plate upon which the brake shoes are attached. The backing plate is attached to the steering knuckle or axle housing.

Ball joint   Flexible joint having a ball-and-socket type of construction, used in suspension systems.

Barrel shaped   Brake drum having a frictional surface that is larger in the center than at the open end or at the rear of the drum.

Base brakes   *See* Service brakes.

Bell mouthed   Brake drum with a frictional surface larger at the open end of the drum than at any other point toward the rear of the drum.

Belt   Fabric or woven steel material over the body plies of a tire, and just under the tread area, to help keep tread from squirming.

Bleeder screw   Valve in wheel cylinders (and other locations) for bleeding air from the hydraulic system.

Boots   Rubber dust protectors on the ends of wheel or caliper cylinders.

BPMV   Brake pressure modulator valve.

Brake fade   Result of heat buildup. The reduction in braking force due to loss of friction between the brake shoes and the drum.

Brake lining   Friction material fastened to the brake shoes. It is pressed against the rotating brake drum to accomplish braking.

Brake shoe   Part of the brake system to which the brake lining is attached.

Btu (British thermal unit)   Unit of heat measurement.

Caliper   U-shaped housing that contains the hydraulic cylinders and holds the pads on disc brake applications.

Chatter   Sudden grabbing and releasing of the drum when brakes are applied.

CFRC   Carbon fiber-reinforced carbon.

Coefficient of friction   Method of expressing friction between two bodies in mathematical terms.

Compensating port   Port located in the master cylinder that allows excess fluid to return to the reservoir. *See also* Vent port.

Concentric   Perfectly round—the relationship of two round parts on the same center.

Cylinder   Tool that uses an abrasive to smooth out and bring to exact measurement such things as wheel cylinders.

Deflection   Bending or distorting motion. Usually applied to a brake drum when it is forced out-of-round during brake application.

Diaphragm   Flexible cloth-rubber sheet that is stretched across an area, separating two compartments.

DOT   Department of Transportation.

Double flare   Tubing end made such that the flare area has two wall thicknesses.

Dual master cylinder   Two-compartment master cylinder.

Duo-Servo   Brand name of a Bendix dual-servo drum brake.

Dynamic balance   When the weight mass centerline of a tire is in the same plane as the centerline of the object.

EBCM   Electronic brake control module.

Eccentric   Relationship of two round parts having different centers. A part that contains two round surfaces, not on the same center.

EHCU   Electrohydraulic control unit.

Elastomer   Another term for rubber.

Emergency brake   *See* Parking brake.

Energized shoe   Brake shoe that receives greater applied force from wheel rotation.

Energy   Capacity for performing work.

EPA   Environmental Protection Agency.

EPR   Ethylene propylene rubber.

Fade   To grow weak; brakes becoming less effective.

Filler vent   Breather hole in the filler cap on the master cylinder.

Floating caliper   Type of caliper used with disc brakes which moves slightly to ensure equal pad pressure on both sides of the rotor.

FMSI   Friction Materials Standards Institute.

Foundatin brakes   *See* Service brakes.

4WAL   Four-wheel antilock.

Glazed drum   Drum surface hardened excessively by intense heat.

Grab   Seizure of the drum on linings when brakes are applied.

Hand brake   *See* Parking brake.

Heat checked   Cracks in the braking surface of a drum caused by excessive heat.

HEPA   High-efficiency particulate air filter.

Inlet port   *See* Replenishing port.

Kevlar   Dupont brand name of aramid fibers.

Kinetic energy   The energy in any moving object. The amount of energy depends on the weight (mass) of the object and the speed of the object.

LMA   Low-moisture-absorption type of brake fluid (DOT 4).

Master cylinder   Part of the brake hydraulic system where the pressure is generated.

Mechanical brakes   Brakes that are operated by a mechanical linkage or cable connecting the brakes to the brake pedal.

Mesothelioma   Fatal type of cancer of the lining of the chest or abdominal cavity.

Metering valve (hold-off valve)   Valve installed between the master cylinder and front disc brakes which prevents operation of front disc brakes until 75 to 125 psi is applied to overcome rear drum brake return spring pressure.

Mu (μ)   Greek letter representing the coefficient of friction.

NAO   Nonasbestos organic.

NAS   Nonasbestos synthetic.

Nitrile   Type of rubber that is okay for use with petroleum.

OSHA   Occupational Safety and Health Administration.

Parking brake   Components used to hold a vehicle on a 30 degrees incline. Called the *emergency brake* before 1967, when dual master cylinders and split braking systems became law. Also called the *hand brake*.

Pawl   Lever for engaging in a notch. Used to rotate the notched star wheel on self-adjusting brakes.

Phenolic brake pistons   Hard type of plastic disc brake caliper pistons which do not rust or corrode.

Pressure bleeder   Device that forces pressure into the master cylinder so that when the bleeder screws are opened at the wheel cylinder, air will be forced from the system.

Pressure-differential switch   Switch installed between the two separate braking circuits of a dual master to light the dash brake light in the event of a brake system failure, causing a *difference* in brake pressure.

Primary shoe   Brake shoe installed facing the front of the vehicle.

Proportioning valve   Valve installed between the master cylinder and rear brakes that limits the amount of pressure to the rear wheels to prevent rear wheel lockup.

Push rod   Link rod connecting the brake pedal to the master cylinder piston.

RABS   Rear antilock braking system.

Race   Inner and outer machined surfaces of a ball or roller bearing.

RBWL   Red brake warning lamp.

Reaction disc   Feature built into a power brake unit to provide the driver with a "feel" of the pedal.

Recirculating ball-steering gear   Steering gear that uses a series of ball bearings that feed through and around the grooves in the worm and nut.

Replenishing port   Society of Automotive Engineers (SAE) term for the rearward low-pressure master cylinder port. Also called *inlet port, bypass port, filler port,* or *breather port.*

Residual check valve   Valve in the outlet end of the master cylinder to keep the hydraulic system under a light pressure on drum brakes only.

RWAL   Rear-wheel antilock.

SAE   Society of Automotive Engineers.

SBR   Styrene-butadiene rubber.

Scoring   Grooves worn into the drum or disc braking surface.

Secondary shoe   Brake shoe installed facing the rear of the vehicle.

Self-adjusting brakes   Brakes that maintain the proper lining-to-drum clearance by automatic adjusting mechanism.

Self-energizing   Brake shoe that, when applied, develops a wedging action that assists the braking force applied by the wheel cylinder.

Semi-mets   Semimetallic brake linings.

Service brakes   Main driver-operated vehicle brakes.

Servo action   Brake construction having the end of the primary shoe bear against the secondary shoe. When the brakes are applied, the primary shoe applies force to the secondary shoe.

Shimmy   Type of tire vibration usually noticed as a rapid back-and-forth motion in the steering wheel. Usually caused by dynamic out-of-balance or a bent wheel.

Shock absorber Device used to control spring movement in the suspension system.

Shoe pad Raised support on the backing plate against which the shoe edge rests; also called *shoe ledge*.

Sintered metal *See* Sintering.

Sintering Process where metal particles are fused together without melting.

Split mu Term used to describe two different friction (μ) surfaces under the wheels of a vehicle. μ is the Greek letter for coefficient of friction.

Split system Divided hydraulic brake system.

Spongy pedal When there is air in the brake lines, the pedal will have a springy or spongy feeling when applied.

Squeal High-pitched noise caused by high-frequency vibrations when brakes are applied.

Star wheel Notched wheel with a left- or right-hand threaded member for adjusting brake shoes.

Static balance When a tire has an even distribution of weight about its axis, it is in static balance.

Step-bore cylinder Wheel cylinder having a different diameter at each end.

Table The portion of the shoe to which the lining is attached.

Tandem cylinder Master cylinder with two pistons arranged one ahead of the other. One cylinder operates rear brakes and the other front brakes.

TC Traction control.

Torque Twisting force.

Torque wrench Wrench that registers the amount of applied torque.

Tramp Up-and-down vibration of a tire/wheel assembly, usually due to out-of-round tire or out-of-balance condition.

Vacuum Any pressure less than atmospheric pressure.

Vacuum booster Vacuum power brake unit.

Vacuum power unit Device utilizing engine manifold vacuum to assist application of the brakes—reducing pedal effort.

Vent port Society of Automotive Engineers (SAE) term for the front port of a master cylinder; also called the *compensating port* or *bypass*.

VSS Vehicle speed sensor.

Warning light Light on the instrument panel to alert the driver when one-half of a split hydraulic system fails, as determined by the pressure-differential switch.

Web Stiffening member of the shoe to which the shoe table is attached.

Wheel cylinder Part of the hydraulic system that receives pressure from the master cylinder and applies the brake shoes to the drums.

WSS Wheel speed sensor.

Zerk fitting Name for a chassis grease fitting, also known as an Alamite fitting (named for Oscar U. Zerk).

Index